Loving the Poor,
Saving the Rich

Loving the Poor, Saving the Rich

Wealth, Poverty, and Early Christian Formation

▶•◀ HELEN RHEE ▶•◀

Baker Academic

a division of Baker Publishing Group
Grand Rapids, Michigan

© 2012 by Helen Rhee

Published by Baker Academic
a division of Baker Publishing Group
P.O. Box 6287, Grand Rapids, MI 49516-6287
www.bakeracademic.com

Printed and bound by CPI Group (UK) Ltd, Croydon, CR0 4YY

Library of Congress Cataloging-in-Publication Data

Rhee, Helen.
    Loving the poor, saving the rich : wealth, poverty, and early Christian formation / Helen
Rhee.
      p. cm.
    Includes bibliographical references (p.   ) and index.
    ISBN 978-0-8010-4824-1 (pbk.)
    1. Wealth—Religious aspects—Christianity—History. 2. Poverty—Religious aspects—
Christianity—History. 3. Church history—Primitive and early church, ca. 30–600. I. Title.
BR115.W4R44 2012
261.8′509015—dc23   2012018187

Contents

Abbreviations

Primary Sources

Acts Andr.	Acts of Andrew	Cod. theod.	Codex theodosianus
Acts John	Acts of John	Comm. Matt.	Commentarium in evange-
Acts Just.	Acts of Justin and		lium Matthaei
	Companions	Comm. Rom.	Commentarii in Romanos
Acts Paul	Acts of Paul	Cultu fem.	De cultu feminarum
Acts Paul Thec.	Acts of Paul and Thecla	De dom.	De domo suo
Acts Pet.	Acts of Peter	Demetr.	Ad Demetrianum
Acts Scill.	Acts of Scillitan Martyrs	De off.	De officiis
Acts Thom.	Acts of Thomas	De vit. beat.	De vita beata
Adv. Christianos	Adversus Christianos	Dial.	Dialogue with Trypho
AGIBM	Ancient Greek Inscriptions	Did.	Didache
	in the British Museum	Didasc.	Didascalia apostolorum
Ann.	Annales	Diog. Laert.	Diogenes Laertius, Lives
Ant.	Jewish Antiquities		of Eminent Philosophers
Ap. Const.	Apostolic Constitution	Diogn.	Epistle to Diognetus
Ap. Trad.	Apostolic Tradition	Dom. or.	De dominica oration
Apoc. Paul	Apocalypse of Paul	Don.	Ad Donatum
Apoc. Peter	Apocalypse of Peter	DSS	Dead Sea Scrolls
Apol.	Apologeticum	Eleem.	De opera et eleemosynis
Autol.	Ad Autolycum	Ench.	Enchiridion
Barn.	Epistle of Barnabas	Ep., Epp.	Epistulae
Bell.	Wars of the Jews	Eph.	Ignatius, To the Ephesians
Ben.	De beneficiis	Exh. cast.	De exhortation castitatis
Cat.	Bellum catalinae	Fort.	Ad Fortunatum
CD	Cairo Damascus	Fr. Luc.	Fragmenta in Lucam
	Document	Fug.	De fuga in persecutione
Cels.	Contra Celsum	Hab. virg.	De habitu virginum
CIL	Corpus inscriptionum	Haer.	Adversus haereses
	latinarum	HE	Historia ecclesiastica
1–2 Clem.	1–2 Clement	Hist.	Historiae
Clem.	Seneca, De clementia		

Hom. Jer.	*Homilae in Jeremiam*	*Mart. Ptol.*	*Martyrdom of Ptolemaeus*
Hom. Jos.	*Homiliae in Josuem*		*and Lucius*
Hom. Lev.	*Homilae in Leviticum*	*Mor.*	*Moralia*
Idol.	*De idololatria*	*Mort.*	Lactantius, *De mortibus*
Comm. Tit.	*Commentariorum in*		*persecutorum*
	Epistulam ad Titum liber	*Mort.*	Cyprian, *De mortalitate*
IGRRP	*Inscriptiones Graecae ad*	*Nat. Hist.*	*Naturalis historia*
	Res Romanas Pertinentes	*Nic. Eth.*	*Nichomachean Ethics*
Inst.	*Divinarum institutionum*	NT	New Testament
	libri VII	*Oct.*	*Octavius*
Instr.	*The Instructions*	*Or.*	*Oratio ad Graecos*
Laps.	*De lapsis*	OT	Old Testament
Leg.	*Legatio*	*Paed.*	*Paedagogus*
Magn.	Ignatius, *To the*	*Paen.*	*De paenitentia*
	Magnesians	*Pan.*	*Panegyricus*
Mand.	*Shepherd of Hermas,*	*Pat.*	*De patientia*
	Mandate(s)	*Phil.*	*To the Philippians*
Marc.	*Adversus Marcionem*	P. Oxy.	The Oxyrhynchus Papyri
Mart.	Tertullian, *Ad martyras*	*Ps.-Crates*	*Pseudo Crates*
Mart. Agapê	*Martyrdom of Apapê,*	*Quis div.*	*Quis dives salvatur*
	Irenê, Chionê, and	*Ref.*	Hippolytus, *Refutation of*
	Companions		*All Heresies*
Mart. Apol.	*Martyrdom of Apollonius*	*Rom.*	Ignatius, *To the Romans*
Mart. Carp.	*Martyrdom of Carpus,*	*Rom. Hist.*	*Roman History*
	Papylus, and Agathonicê	*Sat.*	*Satirae*
Mart. Dasius	*Martyrdom of Dasius*	*Scap.*	*Ad Scapulam*
Mart. Felix.	*Martyrdom of Felix the*	*Sim.*	*Shepherd of Hermas,*
	Bisho		*Similitude(s)*
Mart. Julius	*Martyrdom of Julius the*	*Smyrn.*	Ignatius, *To the*
	Veteran		*Smyrnaeans*
Mart. Lyons	*Letter of the Churches of*	*Spec.*	*De specialibus legibus*
	Lyons and Vienne	*Strom.*	*Stromata*
Mart. Mon.	*Martyrdom of Montanus*	*Trall.*	Ignatius, *To the Trallians*
and Luc.	*and Lucius*	*Unit. eccl.*	*De catholicae ecclesiae*
Mart. Pal.	*De martyribus Palaestinae*		*unitate*
Mart. Perp.	*Martyrdom of Perpetua*	*Ux.*	*Ad uxorem*
	and Felicitas	*Vir. ill.*	*De viris illustribus*
Mart. Pion.	*Martyrdom of Pionius*	*Vis.*	*Shepherd of Hermas,*
Mart. Pol.	*Martyrdom of Polycarp*		*Vision(s)*
Mart. Potam.	*Martyrdom of Pota-*	*Vita Olymp.*	*Vita Olympiadis*
	miaena and Basilides	*Vit. Const.*	*Vita Constantini*

Secondary Sources and Modern Editions

ABD	*Anchor Bible Dictionary*	*ANF*	*Ante-Nicene Fathers*
ACW	Ancient Christian Writers	*ANRW*	*Aufstieg und Niedergang der*
AJP	*American Journal of Philology*		*römischen Welt*

ATR	*Anglican Theological Review*	JSNTSup	Journal for the Study of the New Testament: Supplement Series
BJRL	*Bulletin of the John Rylands Library*	JSOT	*Journal for the Study of the Old Testament*
BJS	*British Journal of Sociology*		
BTB	*Biblical Theology Bulletin*	JSOTSup	Journal for the Study of the Old Testament: Supplement Series
CBQ	*Catholic Biblical Quarterly*		
CBQMS	*Catholic Biblical Quarterly Monograph Series*	JTS	*Journal of Theological Studies*
		LCL	Loeb Classical Library
CCSL	Corpus Christianorum Series Latina	Mid-AJT	*Mid-American Journal of Theology*
CSEL	Corpus scriptorium ecclesiasticorum latinorum	NIDNTT	*New International Dictionary of New Testament Theology*
EHR	*Economic History Review*	NTA	*New Testament Apocrypha*
ETL	*Ephemerides theologicae lovanienses*	NTS	*New Testament Studies*
		OECT	Oxford Early Christian Texts
FC	Fathers of the Church	PBSR	*Papers of the British School at Rome*
GP	Gospel Perspectives		
HPT	*History of Political Thought*	PG	Patrologia graeca
HSCP	*Harvard Studies in Classical Philology*	PL	Patrologia latina
		PTS	Patristische Texte und Studien
HTR	*Harvard Theological Review*	QR	*Quarterly Review*
JAAR	*Journal of the American Academy of Religion*	SBL	Society of Biblical Literature
		SecCent	*The Second Century*
JAC	*Jahrbuch für Antike und Christentum*	StPatr	*Studia Patristica*
		StTheol	*Studia Theologica*
JBL	*Journal of Biblical Literature*	TAPA	*Transactions of the American Philological Association*
JECS	*Journal of Early Christian Studies*		
		TDNT	*Theological Dictionary of the New Testament*
JEH	*Journal of Ecclesiastical History*		
JESHO	*Journal of the Economic and Social History of the Orient*	TS	*Theological Studies*
		VC	*Vigiliae Christianae*
JFSR	*Journal of Feminist Studies in Religion*	VCSup	Vigiliae Christianiae: Supplement Series
JHI	*Journal of the History of Ideas*	WUNT	Wissenschaftliche Untersuchungen zum Neuen Testament
JMM	*Journal of Markets & Morality*		
JNES	*Journal of Near Eastern Studies*	ZNW	*Zeitschrift für die neutestamentliche Wissenschaft und die Kunde de älteren Kirche*
JRE	*Journal of Religious Ethics*		
JRH	*Journal of Religious History*		
JRA	*Journal of Roman Archaeology*	ZPE	*Zeitschrift für Papyrologie und Epigraphik*
JRS	*Journal of Roman Studies*		
JSNT	*Journal for the Study of the New Testament*	ZTK	*Zeitschrift für Theologie und Kirche*

Preface

Writing on a topic of wealth and poverty has not been easy. For one thing, it is deeply personal even if you treat this as an academic subject; it naturally leads you to reflect on, wrestle with, and evaluate your own beliefs and practices. This is a good thing. At the same time, it has not been easy because it could so easily slip into a mere theoretical, scholarly project. I had to remind myself that it was about not just theological ideas, rhetoric, or societal/institutional values and systems but actual people—of the past and the present—enjoying, using, and working for their wealth, struggling with their wealth and poverty, and suffering from poverty.

Writing this book has also been a laborious and challenging journey. Since the inception of this project and initial research in the summer of 2005, exigencies of life prevented me from progressing and moving toward the finish line for a while: my father's heart attack and ensuing heart reconstruction surgery in the same summer; a loss of my backpack, which, among other things, contained my thirty-six-page-plus handwritten research notes and outlines during a conference in Australia in January 2008; the Tea Fire that gravely damaged the Westmont College campus and faculty housing community (in which I live) in November 2008; my serious car accident in February 2009, which has severely aggravated a preexisting condition and acutely compromised my health ever since; the death of my beloved grandmother, whom I still miss, in 2010, just to name a few major ones. It has been a journey of faith, hope, and perseverance against hope, and I have written a major portion of the book in significant pain and groaning aches. I am exceedingly grateful for the support, encouragement, and assistance of many who enabled me to see the completion of this book.

My gratitude first goes to my family of God in the Westmont community (especially the faculty housing community) and my local and home churches. Their consistent prayers, love, care, and tangible and intangible support throughout this journey, especially since my car accident, have been truly re-markable; they have been the embodiment of the early Christian *koinonia* and hospitality to me even as I strived to return their love (not quite successfully) and pass it on to others. The administration of Westmont—Richard Pointer, the former acting provost, and Bill Wright, associate provost and director of off-campus programs, in particular—offered me generous institutional support for coping with my physical challenge and granted me medical and sabbatical leaves. My colleagues at Westmont, both within and outside the Religious Studies Department, embraced my condition and walked with me along this journey. I also remember many of my current and former students who cared to understand my condition and encouraged me along the way. One of them, Mariah Kimbriel, proofread this manuscript with care and diligence. I would like to acknowledge consistently timely and professional assistance of all the staffmembers of Voskuyle Library at Westmont College (particularly the interlibrary loan department).

I want to acknowledge my professional colleagues outside Westmont for their works in this field that I could draw on and for exchanges of stimulat-ing ideas, correspondences, feedback, and comments, including Bronwen Neil, Wendy Mayer, David Downs, and others, as well as the COMCAR organizers—Steven Friesen, Christine Thomas, Dan Schowalter, and James Walters—for helping me appreciate archaeology and material culture bet-ter. I am grateful to the excellent editorial team at Baker Academic—Robert Hosack, Robert Hand, and Hillary Danz—for their meticulous and efficient work. Last but not least, I owe an enormous debt of love and prayers to my family, my parents in particular—ever so sacrificial, ever so understanding, and ever so accommodating to my needs and challenges.

Helen Rhee
Santa Barbara, California

Introduction

The issue of wealth and poverty and their relation to Christian faith is as ancient as the New Testament and reaches farther back to the Hebrew Scriptures. As frequently noted, Jesus's teachings in the Synoptics demanded a kind of discipleship that barred any competing commitment to peoples or things other than himself, including money and possessions. From the very beginning of the Christian movement, how to deal with riches and how to care for the poor were important aspects of Christian discipleship and were thought to express "an essential articulation of our faith in God and of our love for our fellow humans."[1] This study examines the ways that early Christians interpreted, applied, communicated, and struggled with what they understood as the Christian mandate regarding wealth and poverty while they were still "strangers" in Greco-Roman society. I aim to show how early Christians adopted, appropriated, and transformed the Jewish and Greco-Roman moral teachings and practices of giving and patronage, as well as how they developed their distinctive theology and social understanding of wealth/the wealthy and poverty/the poor. By doing so, I hope to demonstrate their critical link to early Christian identity formation.

It is my thesis that Christian reformulation and practice of wealth and poverty were indispensable for shaping Christian self-definitions vis-à-vis the Greco-Roman and Jewish worlds. The concept of identity is a twentieth-century notion typically associated with modern individualism, and scholars tend to qualify its usage when speaking of the "emergence of Christian identity" in the first two centuries.[2] Nevertheless, it is still possible to speak of "Christian identity" in order to construct a sense of Christian continuity and com-

1. L. T. Johnson, *Sharing Possessions: Mandate and Symbol of Faith* (Philadelphia: Fortress, 1981), 16.
2. For example, J. M. Lieu, *Christian Identity in the Jewish and Graeco-Roman World* (Oxford: Oxford University Press, 2004).

mon boundaries in relation to (or in terms of) otherness and differentiation; boundaries of Christian identity "involve selection out of both similarity and difference, and promote interchange as well as distancing."[3] This (collective) identity is constructed in constant social interactions with the surrounding societies and cultures, and it defines and redefines those "others," such as Jews, pagans, heretics, etc. The distinctiveness of a Christian way of life is formed not just by the boundary but also *at* the boundary according to Kathryn Tanner, who states, "Christian distinctiveness is something that emerges in the very cultural processes occurring *at* the boundary, processes that construct a distinctive identity for Christian social practices through the distinctive use of cultural materials *shared with others*."[4] Therefore, as with any other identities, Christian identity is "essentially relational"[5] and "contextualized and contingent"[6] upon time and space; yet it also presents and projects Christian ideals and universal claims through the selective process of self-definition.[7] Since the second and third centuries are critical for the formation and development of distinct (gentile) Christian self-definitions, my main focus is the social and theological development in that era, leading up to the "Constantinian revolution" of the early fourth century. In that regard, I will explore the vital role and intricate relationship of wealth and poverty to the construction of eschatology, soteriology, and ecclesiology in the social and cultural context of the time. I will also trace the development of the institutionalization of (alms-)giving and its theological and social rationale, on the one hand, and the limits of institutionalization and social and ecclesiastical conservatism, on the other. Regardless of how they theologized wealth and poverty, early Christians had to grapple with and respond to the clear call of the social responsibilities of the gospel.

I will pursue this thesis with some fundamental assumptions. First of all, early Christians were part of a larger Greco-Roman world, which means that they lived and operated within the existing social, economic, political, religious, and cultural framework of the Mediterranean world dominated by the Roman Empire. Therefore, understanding the Greco-Roman economy, social structure and values, and attitude toward wealth and poverty is not only illuminating but also critical to understanding early Christian social thoughts and engagement. Christian social practices were formed by creative processes of incorporating, engaging, and negotiating with "institutional forms from

3. J. M. Lieu, "'Impregnable Ramparts and Wall of Iron': Boundary and Identity in Early 'Judaism' and 'Christianity,'" *NTS* 48 (2002): 311.

4. K. Tanner, *Theories of Culture: A New Agenda for Theology* (Minneapolis: Fortress, 1997), 115 (italics added).

5. Ibid., 112.

6. Lieu, *Christian Identity*, 18.

7. H. Rhee, *Early Christian Literature: Christ and Culture in the Second and Third Centuries* (London: Routledge, 2005), 7.

elsewhere" in dominant culture.[8] Second, most of the literary texts of the time come from the elite—the rich and powerful—and therefore inherently carry a perspective of the upper order, even when the authors write about the poor and poverty. Consequently, we must use caution in assessing the reliability of these literary texts and recognize their rhetorical constructions and effect. They need to be juxtaposed with other "hard" evidences such as archaeological artifacts, inscriptions, papyri, etc., when appropriate and possible.

The primary sources for this study include a variety of Christian literary and nonliterary sources of the pre-Constantinian era: the respective literary categories known as the Apostolic Fathers, the Apologies, the Martyr Acts, the New Testament Apocrypha, the gnostic writings (Nag Hammadi), and the heresiologist writings such as those of Irenaeus, Tertullian, and "Hippolytus" provide scattered and incomplete, but still substantial, records and information; the literary works (treatises, letters, apologies, etc.) of the "old catholic" Greek Fathers such as Clement of Alexandria and Origen, and the Latin Fathers, Tertullian and Cyprian, offer critical witnesses to the changing theological and social dynamics of wealth and poverty from the late second to the mid-third centuries. Eusebius's *Church History* illuminates (and sometimes complicates) a larger context and helps connect the dots between individuals and events. Furthermore, the church manuals, such as the *Didache* (Antioch), *Didascalia* (Antioch?), and *Apostolic Tradition* (Rome), allow us to observe the developing institutionalization of hospitality, liturgy, and "social ministries" of the clergy and church as a whole in the first three centuries. Finally, the often neglected but invaluable nonliterary sources, such as inscriptions, material objects, art, and architecture, shed light on and complement the literary ones when used judiciously.

The first group of sources can be further specified within each literary category; I mention here only the substantial works upon which I will consistently draw: The Apostolic Fathers include *The Didache: The Teachings of the Twelve Apostles*, *The Shepherd of Hermas*, *1 Clement*, the seven letters of Ignatius of Antioch, Polycarp's *To the Philippians*, and the *Epistle of Diognetus*. Among the Apologies, Aristides's apology (fragment), Justin Martyr's apologies, Tertullian's *Apologeticum*, Origen's *Contra Celsum*, Minucius Felix's *Octavius*, and the works of the early fourth-century apologist Lactantius are significant for this study. For the Martyr Acts, I select the most relevant ones (e.g., *The Martyrdom of Polycarp* and *The Martyrdom of Apollonius*) from Herbert Musurillo's (somewhat dated) edition as the most historically reliable, important, and instructive martyr accounts from the mid-second to the early fourth centuries.[9] From the New Testament Apocrypha, I will mainly deal with the *Acts of Peter* and *Acts of Thomas* along with the *Gospel of Thomas*, and for

8. Tanner, *Theories of Culture*, 112; cf. Rhee, *Early Christian Literature*, 194.
9. See *The Acts of the Christian Martyrs* (1972; repr., Oxford: Oxford University Press, 2000).

the gnostic writings, I will focus on the *Acts of Peter and the Twelve Apostles*. Lastly, the main heresiologist writings include Irenaeus's *Against All Heresies*, Tertullian's *Against Marcion*, and the *Refutation of All Heresies* attributed to a certain Hippolytus (along with *The Apostolic Tradition*).

A few words may be appropriate concerning these sources. First, many do not directly take up our topic but rather provide various and composite social situations and theological assumptions for our topic, so we must exercise caution when using them. I recognize their different genres, natures, and intentions and try to situate them both socially and historically. Yet, I also attempt to engage with them in their distinctive symbolic and theological worlds, which are equally significant in constructing the complex Christian realities and ideals of dealing with wealth and poverty in the second and third centuries that were decisive for subsequent Christian history.

One might notice a general absence of the voice of the poor themselves in these (literary) sources. This, unfortunately, is not a unique problem when studying any underrepresented group, particularly in antiquity. It raises formidable challenges to studying poverty and the poor at first hand and almost inevitably makes studies related to wealth and poverty more like studies on wealth rather than on poverty.[10] While I recognize the unilateral dimension of extant ancient texts, this apparent silence should not undermine the relevance and value of the sources available; given this reality, a selection of comprehensive and wide-ranging sources seems justified and necessary, and it can rather underscore the constructive and interpretive nature of early Christian social consciousness. Lastly, these sources represent a broad spectrum of Christian contextualization of Greco-Roman culture and Jewish practices in light of their respective interpretations of the gospel. In this study, I will examine these Christian sources in relation to the relevant contemporary Greco-Roman and Jewish texts when appropriate: for example, Cicero's *On Duty*, Seneca's *On Benefits*, Plutarch's *On Love of Wealth*, as well as various texts of the Second Temple literature, rabbinic Judaism, and the Dead Sea Scrolls.

These diverse sources moreover testify to the vibrant and multifaceted nature and forms of second- and third-century Christianity. Christians of this time period created various communities and even competing claims among themselves and at the same time increasingly developed core doctrines, structure, and practices that defined a certain common Christian identity (or identities) in relation to the Greco-Roman and Jewish worlds. These apparently paradoxical developments were in fact indicative of the significant growth of Christianity over various regions of the empire (especially in urban centers) and of its active interaction with the existing culture and milieu of those areas. Christian expansion was not limited to geography and numbers, however; converts to

---

10. This is also acknowledged in S. Holman, *The Hungry Are Dying: Beggars and Bishops in Roman Cappadocia* (Oxford: Oxford University Press, 2001), 12.

Christianity came from various social strata, especially in the third century, including the elite in the upper order and the people with financial means and relative security (though they did not belong to the official upper order)—as well as the poor and the marginalized. This social advance created as many challenges and conflicts as opportunities for Christian communities. In an ever-widening gap between the rich and the poor within Christian communities, securing one's salvation and heavenly abode directly entailed sharing one's possessions, sometimes giving them away altogether, and the miracle of the rich entering heaven was becoming more and more humanly possible. Theology thus was to accommodate and address this changing social reality and practicality.

This book is a work of social *and* theological (and to an extent, cultural) history. Utilizing and drawing from the insights of social historians, social scientists, and even Christian ethicists, I seek to show how theology and social phenomena intersect and mutually inform and influence, and how they together shape certain ethical norms. I approach this topic not from the perspective of a history of ideas[11] or ethics per se but from that of a sociocultural *and* theological historian using diverse interdisciplinary tools and sources. I have arranged the chapters by topic with reasonable chronological developments in each given topic.

This study proceeds in chapter 1 with the socioeconomic, cultural, and theological context of early Christian teachings and behaviors with regard to wealth and poverty. I will present, on the one hand, the basic structure of the Roman economy and of Greco-Roman perceptions and practices of benefaction and patronage based on the principle of reciprocity and embedded in social hierarchy. I will also introduce, on the other hand, the Jewish understanding of almsgiving mandated in the Hebrew Bible and developed in the Second Temple literature. In this context, I will bring in Greco-Roman and Jewish moral teachings on wealth and avarice and their respective understandings of the rich and the poor in their social, economic, and theological worlds; the notion of "the pious poor and the wicked rich" in some Jewish apocryphal writings will prove to be particularly significant for early Christians. Then I will provide general observations on the New Testament teachings concerning the rich and the poor, wealth and poverty, in light of their larger context, noting the reality of social stratification and differences within the growing Christian communities that began to produce *Christian* material culture in the early third century. This social composition and stratification would only intensify as Christianity made great inroads into Greco-Roman society in the second and third centuries.

From chapter 2 forward, I will explore how the specific social realities and issues facing Christian communities shaped theological concerns and

---

11. This approach is taken by Justo González, *Faith and Wealth: A History of Early Christian Ideas on the Origin, Significance, and Use of Money* (San Francisco: Harper & Row, 1990).

were in turn reflected and affected by these concerns. In chapter 2, I will discuss the relationship of wealth, poverty, and eschatology. Because eschatological concerns were still alive within Christian communities, discussions of wealth and poverty were colored by eschatological expectations of Christ's return and the judgment. The visions of the future kingdom of Christ and God's reign, and of the accompanying judgment (projected in material and physical terms), shaped Christian understandings of earthly conduct involving wealth and poverty. In this context, I will discuss how our sources interpreted and reformulated definitions of wealth and poverty and the inherited notion of "the pious poor and the wicked rich." The notion of eschatological prosperity and justice, aided by a biblical theme of the eschatological "great reversal," encouraged the rich to leave their enslavement to earthly wealth and to invest in heavenly riches through almsgiving. Therefore, the dualism of heavenly and earthly riches corresponds to eschatological dualism as almsgiving becomes a means of relativizing earthly riches and heightening a symbiosis between the rich and the poor in this world and the world to come.

Chapter 3 deals with the related and pointed issue of wealth, poverty, and salvation. Salvation, which is an eschatological reality, starts with baptism in the name of the Trinity in the present and involves a continuing journey toward spiritual and moral maturity and perfection. In light of the apparent delay of Christ's coming and the thorny problem of postbaptismal sin, how are the rich to be saved, if it is at all possible? What about the salvation of the poor? I will examine the theology and practice of "redemptive almsgiving" in the context of developing soteriology in the Alexandrian/Egyptian and the North African milieu. I will focus on how Clement of Alexandria's *Who Is a Rich Man That Is Saved?* and Origen's writings spiritualize wealth and poverty, and the rich and the poor, and how they relate almsgiving to the care of self in the soteriological continuum. One also notices seemingly contrasting movements of the radical interiorization and renunciation of wealth and poverty appearing in the similar theological milieu of several Nag Hammadi texts. Then moving to North Africa, I will engage with how Tertullian interprets the salvation of the rich against Marcion's asceticism and Cyprian's understanding of almsgiving as merit and penance that sustains the salvation of the rich in his challenging historical situation. By the time of Lactantius in the early fourth century, this notion of almsgiving would be firmly established. Redemptive almsgiving not only opens the way of salvation for the rich by deconstructing "the pious poor and the wicked rich" but also makes the poor visible and indispensible for the salvation of the rich (though in a restricted way) by confirming the spiritual imbalance between them. In this context, some pointed issues will also receive attention, such as the relation between the sufficiency of Christ's atoning sacrifice and redemptive almsgiving, repeated appeals to the self-interest of almsgivers, the "utility of the poor,"[12] and the proper recipients of almsgiving (the Christian poor or all poor in general).

In chapter 4, I move on to the role of wealth and poverty in Christian koinonia. In light of the eschatological and soteriological significance of almsgiving in the previous chapters, this chapter deals with the practical workings of these theological developments in concrete Christian communities. I will remind readers of the reality of diverse social composition and stratification within Christian communities as the by-product of Christian growth and the challenges it poses to inner and outer workings of Christian self-definition. As is often observed, what bound Christian communities together was the great commandment of loving God and one's neighbors. Based on the love of God, the primary obligations of Christian love and fellowship were for fellow Christians and were demonstrated in acts of mercy and justice: common chest, common meals, and hospitality. Hospitality took further shape in entertaining missionaries and strangers, burying the dead, caring for confessors, ransoming captives, and caring for the sick. I will highlight the role of women in these concrete forms of Christian koinonia as well as how these acts of mercy constituted acts of justice: merit and obligation were not to be separated in Christian ways of life.

Chapter 5 traces the development of the institutionalization of almsgiving and the Christianization of patronage. I will first revisit Greco-Roman philanthropy and patronage and then chart how the church as a formidable institution (by the mid-third century) fused Christian charity and Greco-Roman benefaction for the care of the poor and the vulnerable. At the center of this significant development were the clergy, particularly the bishop, who, acting as patron, centralized almsgiving as a means of social cohesion and social control. This is most clearly exemplified in the theology and activities of Cyprian, bishop of Carthage. In this context, I will further chart the development of church treasury (common chest), which allowed the church to collect, own, and distribute alms and services on behalf of the poor and others in need and therefore made the church the rightful recipient of alms and their sole dispenser. This transition into church ownership also accompanied ecclesiastical business and commercial dealings and will be treated in relation to the process of the larger institutionalization of the church.

In chapter 6, I turn to the theme of wealth, poverty, and Christian identity; this theme has been an undercurrent of the entire book but receives explicit and focused attention in this chapter. Christians considered their understanding and treatment of wealth and poverty (particularly the use of wealth) "to communicate a distinctive self-image of the community"[13] that set them apart

12. This phrase comes from C. Lindberg, *Beyond Charity: Reformation Initiatives for the Poor* (Minneapolis: Fortress, 1993), 30.

13. P. Brown, *Poverty and Leadership in the Later Roman Empire* (Hanover, NH: University Press of New England, 2002), 3.

from their surroundings. The negative association of wealth and Christian identity is clearly seen, for example, in the concerns of *Hermas* and Tertullian about wealth leading to a blurring of Christian identity and possibly even apostasy by the rich; and in Cyprian's interpretation of the cause of the Decian persecution as the attachment to earthly wealth. In this sense, Christian self-definition includes unequivocal denunciation of avarice and luxury as irrational desires and displays of wealth. The positive association of wealth and Christian identity is through almsgiving as a Christian boundary marker; it is what distinguishes Christians from pagans and "orthodox" believers from "heretics," for it is ultimately an imitation of Christ. I will conclude this chapter by exploring how the Constantinian revolution reinforced and changed this Christian self-definition in relation to wealth and poverty, which paved a way for the recapitulation of the earlier Christian teachings in a new, altered context. With overwhelming imperial favors, the church was given new privilege and new responsibility to care for (all) the poor on behalf of the emperor, and the bishop emerged as the lover of the poor par excellence. With the rise of the elitist monastic asceticism, is the church calling for a radical democratization of almsgiving or default two-tier Christianity?

Finally, chapter 7 will present my reflection on wealth, poverty, and Christian formation in the contemporary postmodern world as a way of concluding this study on early Christianity. How can our study of early Christian understandings of and practices on wealth and poverty shed light on the contemporary scene? I will engage with this question partly by relating to the works of prominent contemporary authors—sociologists, economists, ethicists, and theologians—on this theme. I will also bring in the Catholic Social Teaching and the phenomenon of "prosperity Pentecostalism" in the global South, in which poverty defines the existence of an overwhelming majority of people. Given that the majority of world Christians live in the "non-Western" Southern Hemisphere, and that many of those Christians live under the poverty line, the issue of riches and Christian faith not only is all the more poignant, complex, and pressing, but calls Christians to act—in one way or another—especially if we take the early Christian witness seriously. The coexistence of the rich and the poor always presented to early Christians an "inconvenient truth" of Christian material responsibility regardless of the "worthiness" of the poor in *collective* social consciousness and practices. Even with growing social conservatism in the subsequent centuries, the church never ceased to define its mission and identity in terms of serving the poor and caring for the needy (along with salvation), a task that the contemporary church needs to recover, reform, and reinforce. The blessed rich are the obligated rich.

1

༆◁༆◁༆◁༆◁༆◁༆◁༆◁༆◁༆◁༆◁༆◁༆◁༆◁༆◁༆◁༆◁༆◁༆◁

The Social, Economic, and Theological World of Early Christianity

The social, economic, and theological world of early Christianity belongs to that of the Greco-Roman world, and in this chapter we will broadly chart the relevant issues of wealth and poverty in that context. I will first present a fundamental analysis of the Roman economy in light of recent studies and archaeological data, and in relation to Rome's sociopolitical structure and systems, which governed and controlled the basic social values and ways of life in the vast empire. This will lead to a discussion of the Greco-Roman understanding of and attitude toward wealth and poverty, mainly reflected in elite literary sources. Then I will switch gears to traditional Israelite and Jewish understandings of and teachings on wealth and poverty within a general historical framework. In the collection of the earliest Christian literatures, the New Testament, early Christians inherited and shared the Jewish teachings on the rich and the poor while selectively incorporating and responding to Greco-Roman social values and practices. I will lastly describe the Christian growth and expansion in the second and third centuries, giving particular attention to its social aspects, composition, and challenges vis-à-vis the dominant culture.

1.1. Economy and Social Structure in the Greco-Roman World

1.1.1. Roman Economy and Social Structure

Since Moses Finley's monumental and influential study, *The Ancient Economy*, it has become a truism that the ancient economy (including the Roman economy as part of all premodern economies) was a preindustrial and under-developed economy, and that it was primarily based on subsistence agriculture, with the role of cities as loci of consumption rather than production.[1] According to Finley and his protégés (the so-called primitivists[2]), ancient, preindustrial economies were qualitatively different from modern industrial economies because they did not take the notions of market economy and economic growth for granted, nor were they aided by major technological advancement. In the Roman world, agriculture, the backbone of an agrarian economy, was mostly for subsistence, not for the market, and the vast majority of the population lived by agriculture in the country. Business and trade were neither market-driven nor market-oriented, but rather were based on scarcity and were mainly used for consumption and self-sufficiency. Landed aristocracy and craftsmen did not aim for maximizing profits in interregional markets nor for surplus-oriented agricultural or industrial specialization through investing capital (land) in trade or manufacturing. Technologically, neither mass production of goods nor their mass transportation was possible, with the exception of some high-value or specialized commodities such as grain, wine, oil, pottery, bricks, and textiles. Both small-scale production and the high costs of land transportation of goods limited large-scale manufacturing and transregional trade in general and therefore created a mainly local exchange economy. Cities usually functioned as centers not of production but of consumption, and urban artisans provided for the needs of the urban settlers. While most inhabitants of the Roman imperial society lived in the country and worked the land for subsistence, the elite lived in the cities as owners of landed properties and controlled both city and country with judicial underpinnings. Since the wealth of the elite was concentrated on land, the organization and management of resources tended to be acquisitive and conservative rather than productive. Though fractional in terms of actual numbers, these landed elites governed local, regional, and empire-wide politics and policies that allowed them to profit from taxation and other imperial policies.[3] In this context (to borrow Polanyi's term) Roman economy was "embedded" in social institutions such as

1. M. I. Finley, *The Ancient Economy* (Berkeley: University of California Press, 1973; updated ed., with a forward by I. Morris, 1999).
2. There have been prolonged debates among the scholars, the classicists and archaeologists, and some economists, in particular, about how to understand and assess Roman economy (and ancient economy in general). The so-called primitivists or minimalists like Finley laid out fundamental characteristics of the Roman (ancient) economy in contrast to the "modernists" or "maximalists," such as Michael Rostovtzeff, who approached Roman economy as an early form of capitalism with the early twentieth-century sociological interpretations. The former in general emphasize the qualitative difference while the latter stress only the quantitative difference between Roman (ancient), preindustrial economy and modern market economy.
3. See S. Friesen, "Injustice or God's Will? Early Christian Explanations of Poverty," in *Wealth and Poverty in Early Church and Society* (ed. S. R. Holman; Grand Rapids: Baker Academic, 2008), 19.

kinship, marriage, and age groups, and was particularly tied to the hierarchical social and political power structure.[4] Hence, in Roman society, "economic behaviour was governed more by the value systems of social groups than by economic rationality (thus precluding the use of modern economic theory for the analysis of the ancient economy)."[5]

This does not mean, however, that the Roman economy did not experience any growth or development. Recent studies, especially aided by archaeology and quantitative studies, have provided important correctives to Finley's argument without necessarily trumping his overall thesis. They underscore a more advanced and complex nature of Roman economy ("advanced agrarian economy"), highlighting a boom in production and trade, technological development, and their combined positive impact on Roman economy.[6] For example, there was "intensive" growth and large-scale investment as well as technological advance in provincial agriculture (e.g., improved olive production through advanced olive presses, water mills, manuring, terracing, and iron tools), especially in North Africa, facilitated by rising urban demand and documented by archaeological record.[7] A wealth of papyrological and archaeological evidence in Roman Egypt reveals the sizable growth of viticulture and agriculture due to investments and technical improvements (e.g., greater use of animals in irrigation, cultivation, and transport) and a lively market-oriented economy with increased urban production and consumption not only in agriculture (wheat in particular) but also in textiles and glass.[8] Egypt also had a heyday in trade with "the development of Alexandria as the commercial center of the eastern Mediterranean, mediating the east-west flows of goods and wealth" to and from Italy, Asia Minor, Arabia, and India with an efficient transport system.[9] Roman mining (e.g., in Britain and Las Medulas

---

4. K. Polanyi, *Primitive, Archaic, and Modern Economies: Essays of Karl Polanyi* (Garden City, NY: Anchor Books, 1968), 84.

5. W. Jongman, "The Roman Economy: From Cities to Empire," in *The Transformation of Economic Life under the Roman Empire: Proceedings of the Second Workshop of the International Network, Impact of Empire (Roman Empire, c. 200 BC–AD 476)* (ed. L. de Blois and J. Rich; Amsterdam: Gieben, 2002), 33.

6. For a helpful overview of Roman imperial economy, see parts 6, "The Early Roman Empire," and 7, "Regional Development in the Roman Empire," in *The Cambridge Economic History of the Greco-Roman World* (ed. W. Scheidel, I. Morris, and R. P. Saller; Cambridge: Cambridge University Press, 2007), 543–740.

7. See Hitchner, "'The Advantage of Wealth and Luxury': The Case for Economic Growth in the Roman Empire," in *The Ancient Economy: Evidence and Models* (ed. J. G. Manning and I. Morris; Stanford: Stanford University Press, 2005), 207–22; Hitchner, "Olive Production and the Roman Economy: The Case for Intensive Growth in the Roman Empire," in *The Ancient Economy* (ed. W. Scheidel and S. von Reden; New York: Routledge, 2002), 71–83; D. J. Mattingly, "Oil for Export: A Comparison of Spanish, African and Tripolitanian Olive Oil Production," *JRA* 1 (1988): 33–56.

8. D. W. Rathbone, "Roman Egypt," in *Cambridge Economic History* (ed. Scheidel, Morris, and Saller), 700–709.

9. Ibid., 710–11.

in Spain) underwent great technological developments too (such as the use of hydraulic techniques), and its imperial enterprise operated "on a scale and at a level of sophistication unequalled until the industrial age"—as was also the case of stone extraction and transportation in the eastern Egyptian desert.[10] Furthermore, ample evidence of Roman coinage (throughout the empire) that was used in commercial transactions and interest-bearing loans, and of prices equilibrating grain markets in the early empire, points to extensive market exchanges typical of the market economy seen in other advanced agrarian economies.[11] This increased monetization of the economy could be witnessed in taxation and rents as well, and though it was imposed by coercive imperial policies, it increased the volume of trade in the empire in the first few centuries because producers—farmers, cultivators, artisans, etc.—were forced to produce and sell more food and products beyond subsistence and local consumption in order to pay taxes and rents in money.[12] Its cumulative impact over time suggests "a significant increase in agricultural production, an increase in the division of labour, growth in the number of artisans, . . . development of local markets and of long-distance commerce, . . . the commercialization of exchange, an elongation of the links between producers and consumers, the growth of specialist intermediaries (traders, shippers, bankers), and an unprecedented level of urbanization."[13] This rise in interregional trade (especially in the period 200 BCE–200 CE) is confirmed by archaeological findings from the numerous shipwrecks mostly in the western Mediterranean during this time (545 dated).[14] Moreover, careful studies on the distributions of amphorae (thick ceramic containers used extensively for transporting wine, oil, and fish products) along the Mediterranean and Adriatic coasts (e.g., Gaul, Italy, Spain, North Africa, and even Britain) identify a number of regions as loci of (surplus) production (rather than consumption) for distant consumption.[15]

10. D. J. Mattingly and J. Salmon, "The Productive Past: Economics beyond Agriculture," in *Economics beyond Agriculture in the Classical World* (ed. D. J. Mattingly and J. Salmon; London: Routledge, 2001), 6; G. D. B. Jones and D. Mattingly, *An Atlas of Roman Britain* (Oxford: Oxford University Press, 1990), 179–96; V. A. Maxfield, "Stone Quarrying in the Eastern Desert with Particular Reference to Mon Claudianus and Mons Porphyrites," in *Economics beyond Agriculture* (ed. Mattingly and Salmon), 143–70; C. E. P. Adams, "Who Bore the Burden? The Organization of Stone Transport in Roman Egypt," in *Economics beyond Agriculture* (ed. Mattingly and Salmon), 171–92.

11. See P. Temin, "A Market Economy in the Early Roman Empire," *JRS* 91 (2001): 169–81; on the rise of money supply, cf. K. Hopkins, "Taxes and Trade in the Roman Empire [200 BC–AD 400]," *JRS* 70 (1980): 106–7.

12. Hopkins, "Taxes and Trade," 101–25.

13. Ibid., 102.

14. Ibid., 105–6; A. J. Parker, "Classical Antiquity: The Maritime Dimension," *Antiquity* 64 (1990): 335–46.

15. For example, G. Woolf, "Imperialism, Empire and the Integration of the Roman Economy," *World Archaeology* 23 (1992): 283–93; J. Paterson, "Salvation from the Sea: Amphorae and Trade in the Roman West," *JRS* 72 (1982): 146–57.

This in turn confirms the different scales of exchange—local, regional, and empire-wide trades—though the last category was indeed rare.[16]

Nonetheless, one should be careful not to overreach by seeing the Roman economy as "proto-capitalism" as a result of these findings (the so-called modernists). Given the overwhelming importance and dominance of agriculture (75–80 percent) in Roman economy, other economic activities beyond agriculture would have had a limited scope and impact overall.[17] In Kevin Greene's words, Finley's "overall framework has remained intact: gross disparities in wealth, the importance of political power and social status, and the limitations of financial systems, are not in dispute."[18] But "most commentators are more positive about the level and nature of economic activity that took place within this framework. A lack of 'capitalist spirit' is not a sign of aversion to growth, but one of caution."[19] In other words, the Roman economy, with local and regional variations, experienced "significant" growth and was market-oriented from the perspective of that historical period and place; from the perspective of modern economies, however, the growth was "imperceptible" and unsustainable[20] since "under ancient social and political conditions the interests of the elite were well served without it."[21] After all, the Roman economy was "predominantly a subsistence economy" even with contextualized economic rationalism and "economics beyond agriculture" in trade and industry,[22] which meant that the bulk of self-sufficient production "always stood outside the money economy" and that "on average levels of consumption were not dramatically above the minimum level of subsistence."[23] Indeed, markets and economic behaviors were still embedded in and determined by society.[24]

In light of this understanding of the Roman economy, what were the dominant social values and systems in the Roman empire that influenced economic behaviors and social conditions, and how were they constructed? Roman society was formally and informally divided into hierarchical distinctions and categories, and our sources (which mainly contain the perspectives of elite men) present more or less a unified vision of a conservative and stable social order. As Richard Saller notes, this aristocratic ideology of social

16. Woolf, "Imperialism," 287.
17. Temin, "Market Economy," 180; cf. Mattingly and Salmon, "Productive Past," 11.
18. K. Greene, "Technological Innovation and Economic Progress in the Ancient World: M. I. Finley Re-considered," *EHR* 53 (2000): 52.
19. Ibid., 52.
20. See R. P. Saller, "Framing the Debate over Growth in the Ancient Economy," in *The Ancient Economy* (ed. Manning and Morris), 223–38, esp. 237.
21. Mattingly and Salmon, "Productive Past," 11.
22. Hopkins, "Taxes and Trade," 102; "Economics beyond Agriculture" is the subtitle of Mattingly and Salmon's volume.
23. Hopkins, "Taxes and Trade," 104.
24. Temin, "Market Economy," 180.

hierarchy and order was taken for granted and strongly justified by the elite: "if these distinctions [of *ordines* and *dignitas*] are confused," writes Pliny the Younger, "nothing is more unequal than equality itself."[25] Then, enormous and structural inequalities constituted the very fabric of sociopolitical stratification and the values that governed the economic behaviors of various social groups. Ekkehard and Wolfgang Stegemann single out the three criteria for stratification:

1. power through position (political office or role) and power through acquisition and transmission of property and wealth (influence);
2. privilege in legal, socioeconomic, and political realms—for example, there were two tracks in criminal law and double standards at court (differential evaluation of legal testimony) according to rank,[26] as well as reserved seats in theaters and banquets;
3. prestige, i.e., social esteem as a function and result of that power and privilege.[27]

Indeed, Roman society was obsessed with maintaining social distinctions and hierarchy.

The formal orders (*ordines*) consisted of senators, equestrians (knights), regional and municipal decurions, and undifferentiated plebs (freeborn citizens). These orders formed a steep social pyramid in terms of power, privilege, and prestige, and they were based upon and reinforced the traditional aristocratic criteria of birth, wealth, esteem, and (moral) excellence.[28] Augustus introduced properly defined social orders between senators and equestrians not only by

25. Pliny the Younger, *Ep.* 9.5; R. P. Saller, "Status and Patronage," in *The High Empire, AD 70–192* (vol. 11 of *The Cambridge Ancient History*; 2nd ed.; ed. A. K. Bowman, P. Garnsey, and D. Rathbone; Cambridge: Cambridge University Press, 2000), 818.

26. See G. Hamel, *Poverty and Charity in Roman Palestine, First Three Centuries CE* (Berkeley, CA: University of California Press, 1990), 195, no. 175: "in the matter of punishments, their severity had less to do with the crime itself than with the dignity of the person involved. This becomes particularly true in the Severan period." Hamel also includes a quote from the late *Historia Augusta, Alexander Severus*: "Moreover, if any man turned aside from the road into someone's private property, he was punished in the Emperor's presence according to the character of his rank." A. Giardina, in "The Transition to Late Antiquity," in *Cambridge Economic History* (ed. Scheidel, Morris, and Saller), 761, notes that this judicial double standard is first attested in the Hadrian era. Finally, consider this statement by M. Peachin, "Introduction," in *Specvlvm Ivris: Roman Law as a Reflection of Social and Economic Life in Antiquity* (ed. J.-J. Aubert and B. Sirks; Ann Arbor, MI: University of Michigan Press, 2002), 13: "In short, a highly conservative legal tradition of the rich, by the rich, and essentially for the rich should not be a surprise in the Roman context."

27. E. Stegemann and W. Stegemann, *The Jesus Movement: A Social History of Its First Century* (trans. O. C. Dean Jr.; Minneapolis: Fortress, 1999), 60–65. Cf. Saller, "Status and Patronage," 852.

28. Cf. Saller, "Status and Patronage," 817; Cassius Dio, *Roman History* 52.19.1–4.

prescribing minimum census requirements of one million and 400,000 sesterces respectively[29] but also by mapping out their respective careers, ranks, honors, and privileges as well as judicial boundaries of marriage and inheritance. Senators, the highest office holders, numbering in the hundreds, wore a toga with a broad purple stripe, and their sons were allowed to enter the senate as observers; they were given special seats in the theater and arena and were prohibited to marry persons of freed status (this applied to their children and grandchildren as well). The "second order," equestrians, numbering in the thousands, were the nonsenatorial, landed aristocracy of Italy but evolved to fill important positions in the army and governmental offices in Rome and the provinces (such as prefects and procurators); they wore a toga with a thin purple stripe and a gold ring and were given separate seats at the spectacles as well. Both orders, though not legally prescribed, practically functioned hereditarily due to these aristocratic criteria. Their provincial and municipal counterparts were the decurions, civic elites who filled the important political and religious positions in the cities (especially of the East) with attendant privileges. They had a minimum census requirement of 100,000 sesterces (this requirement varied city to city). In the second and third centuries, the decurion-ate increasingly became a channel to the equestrian and even senatorial orders. Then, though not part of these three orders, a rather amorphous group of the rich, who lacked adequate pedigree but possessed considerable wealth, such as the vassal kings and their families of Rome, retainers, and wealthy (impe-rial) freedmen with prominent cultic, military, and administrative positions (see below on social mobility) rounded up the upper strata. Finally, "plebs" referred to the common people, the ordinary freeborn citizens, but later came to mean masses in general; they were the ones who lacked power, privilege, and prestige. These formal orders excluded citizen women and children, not to mention ordinary noncitizens, the freed, and slaves, since the *ordines* point to the essentially legal (not economic) nature of these orders—as illustrated by the fourth group of the elite, which does not nicely fit the status distinctions within the upper stratum.

These orders were further reflected in a conceptual distinction (by the elite) between *honestiores* (the honorable) and *humiliores* (the humble) that came to be *legally* formalized in the second century.[30] To the former belonged the imperial family, senatorial and equestrian aristocracies, provincial decurions, and the "other rich" (later it would include army veterans, certain judges, and officials as well); they were typically the landed aristocrats who lived off

29. See R. Alston, *Aspects of Roman History, AD 14–117* (London: Routledge, 1998), 216. Cf. *The Letters of St. Cyprian of Carthage* (vol. 3; trans. and anno. G. W. Clarke; ACW 46; Mahwah, NJ; Newman, 1986), 284n11: "a day-labourer's basic wage at this period [mid-third century] could be put somewhere (very approximately) in the vicinity of 30 HS [sesterces] per month."

30. See Saller, "Status and Patronage," 851–52.

of the rent and labors of others, and it was they, comprising approximately 1–3 percent of the population of the empire,[31] who constructed the prevailing value system. The *humiliores* served as a sort of "catch-all" term for the nonelite, encompassing "everybody else," the mass (97–99 percent)[32] of the population. In the eyes of the *honestiores*, they were the ones who had to earn a living for themselves and their families through their own work and labor.[33] Among them, fundamental distinctions were between free and slave, and between citizen and noncitizen. Both distinctions indicated again a legal status, not necessarily economic or social status, however; free citizens could be rich or poor, just as slaves could be rich or poor.

We should note here that in Roman society, while "a sizeable heterogeneous group of men of free birth can be distinguished from both the elite orders and the humble masses, . . . there was no 'middle class' in the sense of an intermediate group with independent economic resources or social standing."[34] In principle, Roman society (ancient societies in general) had a dichotomous model of social stratification (cf. Stegemann, Brunt, etc.). The ancient writers consistently envisioned and divided a society in binary terms (early Christian writers were not exceptions to this conceptualization), as exemplified by the second-century orator Aelius Aristides's social division in the opposites of the rich and the poor, the great and the humble, the esteemed and the unknown, and the noble and the ordinary.[35] This does not mean, however, that the elite and nonelite consisted of respective homogeneous groups. There were gradations and differentiations within the elite (the upper strata) and the nonelite (the lower strata). We have already discussed the three distinct *ordines* and the vague fourth group within the *honestiores*—the elite, which as a whole controlled 15 to 25 percent of total income (see table 1 for heuristic mapping of Roman economic scales; PS 1–3;

31. These percentages tend to shift among scholars, though not significantly. See W. Scheidel, "Stratification, Deprivation and Quality of Life," in *Poverty in the Roman World* (ed. M. Atkins and R. Osborne; Cambridge: Cambridge University Press, 2006), 42, no. 6, for 1 percent; but in his latest collaborative work with S. Friesen, "The Size of the Economy and Distribution of Income in the Roman Empire," *JRS* 99 (2009): 83, the percentage is expanded to 1.5 percent out of seventy million. Steven Friesen's earlier poverty scale estimates the elite 1 percent of the total population and 2.8 percent of the urban population: see "Poverty in Pauline Studies: Beyond the So-Called New Consensus," *JSNT* 26 (2004): 323–61; Friesen, "Injustice or God's Will?" 17–36. Stegemann and Stegemann, *Jesus Movement*, 77, estimate the upper stratum (elite) to be between 1 and 5 percent of the overall population. In any case, one can clearly see a very thin upper stratum, a tip of the vast iceberg of the Roman world.

32. Scheidel and Friesen, "Size of the Economy," 85, distinguish military families (1.5 percent) "who were maintained by the public sector share" from both the elite (1.5 percent) and nonelite people (97 percent).

33. Cf. Cicero, *De off.* 1.150–51; cf. Stegemann and Stegemann, *Jesus Movement*, 70–71.

34. P. Garnsey and R. Saller, *The Roman Empire: Economy, Society and Culture* (London: Duckworth, 1987), 116.

35. *Ad Romans* 39.

ES 1–3).[36] Within the *humiliores*, differentiations were a lot more fluid and even extreme, ranging from the moderately prosperous, to the relatively poor, to the absolutely poor, as their occupations varied from propertied merchants, middle-lower level civic or imperial administrators, veterans, ordinary centurions, (large or small) shop owners, artisans, traders, builders, clothing manufacturers, to tenant farmers, unskilled day laborers, and beggars. With the help of heuristic outlines of Roman economy, we may call about the top 7–12 percent of the *humiliores*, the relatively prosperous, a socioeconomic "middling" group with moderate surplus resources above subsistence (PS 4; ES 4),[37] which took in another 15–25 percent of the total income (see table 1).[38]

Table 1:
Comparison of Population Percentage
in Poverty Scale (PS) of Friesen (2004)
and Economic Scale (ES) of Longenecker (2010)
in Urban Context of the Roman Empire

Scale: Friesen (Longenecker)	Categories	Include	Friesen %	Longenecker %
PS 1 (ES 1)	Imperial elites	Imperial dynasty, Roman senatorial families, a few retainers, local royalty, a few freedpersons	0.04%	ES 1–3: 3% (the same percentage for the total elite groups; no further break-down given)
PS 2 (ES 2)	Regional or provincial elites	Equestrian families, provincial officials, some retainers, some decurial families, some freed persons, some retired military officers	1%	(See above)
PS 3 (ES 3)	Municipal elites	Most decurial families, wealthy men and women who do not hold office, some freed-persons, some retainers, some veterans, some merchants	1.76%	(See above)
PS 4 (ES 4)	Moderate surplus resources	Some merchants, some traders, some freedpersons, some artisans (especially those who employ others), and military veterans	7% (estimated)	15% (adding two particular groups: *apparitores*[a] and *Augustales*[b])

36. Scheidel and Friesen, "Size of the Economy," 85.
37. Ibid., 84, estimate a middling income as "2.4 times 'bare-bones' gross subsistence."
38. Ibid., 84–85.

Scale: Friesen (Longenecker)	Categories	Include	Friesen %	Longenecker %
PS 5 (ES 5)	Stable near subsistence level (with reasonable hope of remaining above the minimum level to sustain life)	Many merchants and traders, regular wage earners, artisans, large shop owners, freedpersons, some farm families	22% (estimated)	27%
PS 6 (ES 6)	At subsistence level (and often below minimum level to sustain life)	Small farm families, laborers (skilled and unskilled), artisans (especially those employed by others), wage earners, most merchants and traders, small shop/tavern owners	40%	30%
PS 7 (ES 7)	Below subsistence level	Some farm families, unattached widows, orphans, beggars, disabled, unskilled day laborers, prisoners	28%	25%

a. Those "working for civic magistrates as scribes, messengers, lectors, and heralds": see Bruce W. Longenecker, *Remember the Poor: Paul, Poverty, and the Greco-Roman World* (Grand Rapids: Eerdmans, 2010), 329, for his sources.

b. Mostly freedmen who constituted the priesthood of the cult of Augustus: see Longenecker, *Remember the Poor*, 330–32, for his sources and discussion.

This leaves 85–90 percent of the population, which took in about the remaining 50 percent of all income, close to subsistence level—near, at, or below.[39] These relatively poor (*penētes*) are the ones who can afford to provide "at least an adequate subsistence" for themselves and their families, i.e., "an appropriate dwelling and sufficient food and clothing."[40] They could be subdivided into those who are relatively stable near subsistence level (PS 5), comprising about 22 percent of urban population (8–19 percent in total population), and those right at subsistence level (PS 6), comprising about 40 percent of urban population (55–60 percent in total population), according to Steven Friesen's seven-point poverty scale,[41] which attempts to do justice to the complexities of the composition of the often undifferentiated mass population. The absolute

39. Ibid., 84–85; see also Friesen, "Injustice or God's Will?" 20.

40. Stegemann and Stegemann, *Jesus Movement*, 71. Cf. the similar working definition of the poor in P. Garnsey and G. Woolf, "Patronage of the Rural Poor in the Roman World," in *Patronage in Ancient Society* (ed. A. Wallace-Hadrill; New York: Routledge, 1989), 153: "The poor are those living at or near subsistence level, whose prime concern is to obtain the minimum food, shelter and clothing necessary to sustain life, whose lives are dominated by the struggle for physical survival."

41. See Friesen, "Injustice or God's Will?" 20, for percentage in urban population; and Scheidel and Friesen, "Size of the Economy," 82–84, for percentage in total population.

poor (*ptōchoi*) are those who live "at or under the level of minimum existence," lacking necessary subsistence for food, shelter, and clothing (PS 7),[42] and constituted about 28 percent of urban population (10–22 percent in total population).[43] Recently, Bruce Longenecker's more optimistic economic scale (modified from Friesen's) significantly expands the "middling group" (ES 4) to 15 percent of urban population and the "stable near subsistence" level (ES 5) to 27 percent of urban population while reducing the last two groups of living at and below subsistence level (ES 6 and ES 7) to 30 percent and 25 percent of urban population, respectively.[44] Given the recent modifications to Finley's thesis (which suggest economic growth and active trading based on technological improvement), this "elongated" middling group is reasonable and plausible. Nonetheless, while Longenecker's upward adjustment should caution us not to overgeneralize "poverty as a way of life" for "nearly everyone in the Roman empire" as Friesen did,[45] still, a vast majority in the Roman world (75–90 percent in range, both urban and rural contexts combined)[46] lived near or on subsistence level, struggling for survival and sustenance. A stark inequality in income distribution, which was built in a social system and hierarchy, was a fact of life.

In spite of this rigid social structure with its overwhelming consciousness of hierarchy, social mobility was still possible depending on one's social network (see the next section on patronage), talents, and fortune. Within the upper *ordines*, the equestrian order, whose political and military career was invented by Augustus and expanded by the subsequent emperors, a (very) limited potential for mobility opened up for the freeborn citizens based on imperial favor and promotion (often) in tension with the old senatorial aristocracy.[47] In fictitious advice to Augustus by Maecenas, Cassius Dio, a senator during the Severan Age, approved reception of distinguished equestrians into

---

42. Stegemann and Stegemann, *Jesus Movement*, 71.

43. P. Garnsey, arguing for the poverty of most Romans, categorizes the poor in slightly different ways: the "temporary poor" who were liable to slip into poverty at any given moment in times of shortage or difficulty; the "permanent poor" who lived at the very edge of subsistence; and the destitute, struggling for physical survival: *Cities, Peasants and Food in Classical Antiquity: Essays in Social and Economic History* (ed. P. Garnsey and W. Scheidel; Cambridge: Cambridge University Press, 1998), 226–27.

44. Given his interest in the socioeconomic context of early "Jesus movement" (especially Pauline communities), Longenecker is mainly concerned about percentages in urban settings in which early Christian movements arose (as Friesen's 2004 figures); see Longenecker, *Remember the Poor*, 44–59, for his rationale and qualification.

45. Friesen, "Poverty in Pauline Studies," 358; cf. J. J. Meggitt, *Paul, Poverty and Survival* (Edinburgh: T&T Clark, 1998), 50.

46. Typically, the ratio of urban to rural population is 20 to 80 percent in the Greco-Roman world; cf. Saller, "Framing the Debate," 236.

47. For a sociological and structural analysis of significant aspects of elite mobility, see K. Hopkins, "Élite Mobility in the Roman Empire," in *Studies in Ancient Society* (ed. M. I. Finley; London: Routledge and Kegan Paul, 1974), 103–20.

the senate,[48] which reflected a changing reality, though still uncommon, of the early third century. Indeed, in the second and third centuries, an increasing number of the provincial aristocrats (for example, from North Africa) moved into Roman nobility as the imperial throne came to be occupied increasingly by the provincials themselves, such as the Severans from North Africa.

The one social group that was particularly well suited for and navigated through upward social mobility even to the elite was that of freedmen, who constituted a numerous and significant group in the imperial society.[49] Those slaves with profitable skills and business or managerial experience who found favor with their masters and thus obtained manumission during the masters' lifetime or in their wills entered into various occupations and commercial life, were active in voluntary associations, and could accumulate considerable property and fortunes. Moreover, the freedmen of Roman citizens also participated in the Roman citizen body, occupying many of the (lower) clerical and military posts in the imperial and municipal administrations, including the office of *Augustalis* (priesthood of the cult of Augustus), which was virtually reserved for the freedmen as the apex of their career.[50] Their startling social advance even prompted Emperor Claudius to order property confiscation and reversal of their freed status against freedmen who posed as equestrians.[51] At the same time, however, according to Pliny the Elder, it was also the freedmen of Claudius, such as Callistus, Narcissus, and Pallas,[52] who wielded considerable political influence, with wealth greater than senators[53]; each of their wealth ranged from 200 million to 400 million sesterces, and Plutarch in the second century reported that an amount just shy of 288 million sesterces was supposed to constitute the largest private assets.[54] On a less spectacular but just as impressive scale, a certain Caecilius Isidorus bequeathed more than 60 million sesterces in cash in addition to 3,600 yoke of oxen, 257,000 cattle, and 4,116 slaves.[55] Achievements of other illustrious freedmen (especially under Claudius) include certain physicians and grammarians whose fortunes ranged

48. *Roman History* 52.25.6.

49. See P. R. C. Weaver, "Social Mobility in the Early Roman Empire: The Evidence of the Imperial Freedmen and Slaves," in *Studies in Ancient Society* (ed. Finley), 121–40.

50. N. Lewis and M. Reinhold, eds., *The Empire* (vol. 2 of *Roman Civilization: Selected Readings*; 3rd ed.; New York: Columbia University Press, 1990), 167–68.

51. Suetonius, *Claudius* 25.

52. His fortune, when he was executed by Nero, amounted to 300 million sesterces; his brother was Felix, prefect of Judea who conducted a hearing of Paul in Caesarea (Acts 23–24).

53. *Nat. Hist.* 33.10.134; Callistus had more than 200 million sesterces in fortune. Cf. Dio Cassius, *Rom. Hist.* 6.34.4 on Narcissus, who had a 400-million-sesterces estate upon his death. Note that Seneca, one of the wealthiest senators in mid-first century, had personal fortune of 300 million sesterces according to Tacitus, *Ann.* 13.42 and Dio Cassius, *Rom. Hist.* 61.10.3.

54. Plutarch, *Life of Publicola* 15.3 (equivalent of 12,000 talents).

55. Pliny, *Nat. Hist.* 33.10.135.

from 20 to 30 million sesterces.[56] Finally, Claudius Classicus, an imperial freedman of Claudius or Nero, even rose to the equestrian rank of procuratorship of Alexandria under Nerva and Trajan.[57]

As in the case of many freedmen, often the most significant factor in social mobility was acquisition (or loss) of wealth; "indeed, the 'wealth of freedmen' became proverbial" in many literary sources.[58] And with wealth came privileges, but not necessarily prestige. Some wealthy freedmen gained prestige through taking a role of civic benefactor (see below) such as one Publis Decimius Eros Merula, a surgeon, who contributed nearly 70,000 sesterces to his community for his membership of *Augustalis*, for the erection of statues in the temple of Hercules, and for paving streets.[59] In contrast, in Petronius's famous *Satyricon*, a comically boorish, vulgar, and ostentatious freedman, Trimalchio, who boasts of his rise to riches through his ship-building business in his sumptuous but coarse dinner party, represents the "typical" *nouveaux riches* that clearly lack cultural refinement and appropriate social etiquette and thus become objects of scorn rather than esteem, particularly from the proper elite perspective. As a matter of fact, freedmen were subject to both legal regulation and social discrimination. They were legally barred from equestrian or senatorial rank and from the highest municipal and imperial magistracies and priesthoods. In addition, a freedman was also legally bound to provide his former master (patron) "obedience and services" of various kinds, including support in the case of his patron's need, and was not allowed to take his patron to court.[60] Those who failed to follow these obligations were liable to harsh punishment, to the extent of exile and reversal of their status. Freedwomen still remained under the authority of their patrons and could not enact any business without the latter's authority.[61] Once again, however, there was some discrepancy between principle and reality, and legal and economic status. As mentioned, wealthy freedmen could join the elite, though not as members of the *ordines*. Sons and grandsons of freedmen were treated as other freeborn Romans—for instance, the poet Horace and the emperor Pertinax were sons of freedmen. Also, numerous funerary inscriptions testify to a generally close and mutually amicable relationship between patrons and freedmen/freedwomen[62] as patrons often provided burial places for their freedmen's family in their own family tomb and left legacies to their freedmen. The case of social mobility,

---

56. See, for example, Petronius, *Satyricon* 45, 71, 76, 88, 117.

57. *L'Année Epigraphique*, no. 574, in Lewis and Reinhold, *The Empire*, 168. For more examples of the socially mobile imperial freedmen, including the imperial creation of freedmen bureaucracy to counterbalance the senate, see Weaver, "Social Mobility," 123–39.

58. Lewis and Reinhold, *The Empire*, 167.

59. *CIL*, vol. XI, no. 5,400, in Lewis and Reinhold, *The Empire*, 170.

60. Lewis and Reinhold, *The Empire*, 167.

61. R. Alston, *Aspects of Roman History*, 213.

62. See Lewis and Reinhold, *The Empire*, 171–73, for examples.

particularly of freedmen, illustrates both the legal control and boundary of social hierarchy, and the status dissonance and limited fluidity experienced within that social system.

1.1.2. Greco-Roman Patronage

The embedded nature of the Roman economy within a structural hierarchy that presupposed and dealt with pervasive inequalities can be best illustrated by patronage. Patronage, "defined as a voluntary, continuing exchange relationship [of goods and services] between men of unequal power or status, remained fundamental in Roman society . . . as the glue that held human society together."[63] In this relationship, the patron, the social superior, provided his client, the dependent, with protection and economic and political benefits (*beneficia/officia*), such as food, land, house, cash, loans, dinner invitations, recommendations and appointments to office, and even inheritance and bequests. The client in turn was obliged to return the favor with loyalty, votes, services, formal visits, and most of all public display of support, gratitude, and praise, which enhanced the patron's honor and status. This gave the patron a legitimate basis for displaying further benefits for the client. Seneca speaks of this "most honorable contest [*honestissimam contentionem*] in outdoing benefits by benefits";[64] the beneficiary "who has a debt of gratitude to pay never catches up with the favour unless he outstrips it."[65] Thus, patron-client relations were grounded in and formed a part of the Greco-Roman ethic of reciprocity, which was basic, informal, and ubiquitous in various social relations. At the same time, though, it was built into a system of social hierarchy as an unspoken medium of accessing and exercising power and influence. This "system" of patronage linked different social orders vertically and penetrated all social levels, resulting in a less than clear distinction between patrons and clients at times, since one man's patron was another man's client not just between the orders but also within the same orders. Some scholars differentiate the patron-client system of asymmetrical relationship from reciprocal friendship between the social equals (*amicitia*) because Roman etiquette distinguished friends (*amici*) from clients (*clientes*). At the same time, however, Romans also "applied the same language of friendship, trust and obligation to both indifferently."[66] According to Andrew Wallace-Hadrill, both qualify as patronage since it "involves exchanges between those closer to the centre

---

63. R. P. Saller, "Status and Patronage," in *The High Empire, AD 70–192* (vol. 11 of *The Cambridge Ancient History*, 2nd ed., ed. A. K. Bowman, P. Garnsey, and D. Rathbone; Cambridge: Cambridge University Press, 2000), 838; cf. Seneca, *Ben.* 1.4.2.

64. *Ben.* 1.4.4.

65. *Ben.* 1.4.3.

66. A. Wallace-Hadrill, "Patronage in Roman Society: From Republic to Empire," in *Patronage in Ancient Society* (ed. A. Wallace-Hadrill; New York: Routledge, 1989), 77.

of power and those more distant from it, and has the effect of mediating state resources through personal relationships."[67] Whether it was between near equals or between unequals, the point is that access to the center of power was mediated through relationships.[68] "It was this inaccessibility of the centre except through personal links that generated the power of patronage,"[69] and patronage presupposed and thrived on competition for scarce power resources, on the one hand, and desire for enhancement of status and honor, on the other. Hence, while this "crisscrossing web of personal links" underpinned social inequality and functioned as a means of social control, it also, within limits, served as an instrument of social integration and offered the dependent (the social inferior) some opportunities and means to influence their patrons.[70] In this sense, patronage was "an obligation laid on the powerful, a means by which they competed with one another and a legitimation of their supremacy as a group."[71]

Patronage worked in various scales and ways: private/individual patronage, patronage of a private group/association, and public patronage, or euergetism. Both imperial patronage and aristocratic patronage illustrate its varying scales and manifold dimensions. Imperial ideology portrayed the emperor as the patron par excellence who benefited and protected his friends, clients, and subjects.[72] Augustus set an example for future emperors by legitimizing his unprecedented power with the account of his exceptional benefactions to the Roman people (*plebs*) in his *Res Gestae* (15–18). He occasionally handed each male citizen a sizable sum of cash as he progressively assumed tribunal power and consulship in the years between 36 BCE and 5 BCE (15–16); the sums mentioned in *Res Gestae* amounted to the equivalent of at least several months' rent for the poor.[73] Augustus gave particular attention to providing the plebs with basic urban commodities and amenities such as food (grain, corn, oil), water, housing, baths, and entertainment. He utilized an extensive repertoire of games and festivals to distribute his largesse in a generous and public manner.[74] Indeed, Augustus "surpassed all his predecessors in the frequency, variety, and

---

67. Ibid., 77.

68. Garnsey and Woolf, "Patronage of the Rural Poor," 154, consider patronage (only) between those of unequal social and economic status.

69. Wallace-Hadrill, "Patronage in Roman Society," 74.

70. Ibid., 77. On patronage as a system as well as relation, see T. Johnson and C. Dandeker, "Patronage: Relation and System," in *Patronage in Ancient Society* (ed. A. Wallace-Hadrill; New York: Routledge, 1989), 219–41.

71. G. Woolf, "Food, Poverty, and Patronage: The Significance of the Epigraphy of the Roman Alimentary Schemes in Early Imperial Italy," *Papers of the British School at Rome* 58 (1990): 217.

72. Saller, "Status and Patronage," 840.

73. Garnsey and Saller, *Roman Empire*, 150.

74. M. Le Glay, J.-L. Voisin, and Y. Le Bohec, *A History of Rome* (3rd ed.; Oxford: Blackwell, 2004), 220; cf. Pliny's praise of Trajan's generosity in public *beneficia*, *alimenta*, and *spectacula* in *Pan.* 25.3–5; 27.3–4.

magnificence of his public shows" and benefactions.[75] He also made sure to reward soldiers along with the plebs by giving them separate cash handouts and special privileges upon retirement (the army and plebs were two potential sources of trouble).[76] Those who had access to the emperor, especially members of the imperial household (*familia Caesaris*) and aristocratic "friends" of the emperor (*amici Caesaris*), could engage in private patronage with and receive personal benefits from the emperor, such as senatorial and equestrian offices and honors, priesthoods,[77] money, and especially authority (*dignitas*) to secure imperial *beneficia* on behalf of their own friends or protégés (clients). For instance, a significant number of extant letters of the senatorial notable, such as Pliny (fifteen to emperor Trajan alone) and Fronto (nearly twenty), is devoted to patronal recommendations of their friends, relatives, and clients for office, promotion, and other personal privileges.[78] Pliny requested Trajan to grant his masseur Harporas, an Egyptian freedman, Roman citizenship.[79] Since imperial clients like Pliny (other aristocrats, plebs, soldiers, etc.) could not return the favors in kind, they repaid with loyalty, deference, and honor. Therefore, the image of the emperor as a great patron through his generous benefactions became a crucial aspect of the image of the good emperor who could be "protected by his benefits," i.e., by the good will and loyalty of his grateful subjects.[80] Increasingly, extraordinary expressions of reciprocal gratitude, praise, and loyalty to the emperor took religious forms, since "the highest honor was worship."[81] The imperial cult, which served to unite the vast empire, was a special form of honoring the divine benefactor, the emperor.[82]

75. Suetonius, *Augustus* 43.1.

76. *Res Gestae* 16.

77. On the relationship between priesthood and euergetism—especially how emperors used the posts of Roman sacerdotal college as a means of their patronage to create their "symbolic capital" for further dependency and loyalty of the elite clients—see R. Gordon, "The Veil of Power: Emperors, Sacrificers and Benefactors," in *Pagan Priests: Religion and Power in the Ancient World* (ed. M. Beard and J. North; Ithaca, NY: Cornell University Press, 1990), 199–231, esp. 219–31.

78. G. E. M. de Ste. Croix, "*Suffragium*: From Vote to Patronage," *British Journal of Sociology* 5 (1954): 41.

79. Pliny, *Ep*. 10.5–7, 10.

80. Garnsey and Saller, *Roman Empire*, 149; cf. Seneca, *Clem*. 1.13.5.

81. G. W. Bowersock, *Augustus and the Greek World* (Oxford: Clarendon, 1965), 112; cf. Pliny, *Ep*.

82. On the imperial cult, see, for example: J. R. Fears, "Rome: The Ideology of Imperial Power," *Thought* 55 (1980): 98–109; S. J. Friesen, *Twice Neokoros: Ephesus, Asia, and the Cult of the Flavian Imperial Family* (Leiden: Brill, 1993); R. A. Horsley, ed., *Paul and Empire: Religion and Power in Roman Imperial Society* (Harrisburg, PA: Trinity Press International, 1997), 10–86; S. R. F. Price, "From Noble Funerals to Divine Cult," in *Rituals of Royalty* (ed. D. Cannadine and S. R. F. Price; Cambridge: Cambridge University Press, 1987), 56–105; S. R. F. Price, *Rituals and Power: The Roman Imperial Cult in Asia Minor* (Cambridge: Cambridge University Press, 1984); P. Zanker, *The Power of Images in the Age of Augustus* (Ann Arbor: University of Michigan Press, 1988).

In this way, imperial patronage served as a coherent and effective means of social integration and control.[83]

Aristocratic patronage imitated the imperial patronage on a smaller scale, but not in a less serious or compelling way. Members of the *ordines* and other imperial officials, particularly provincial governors, acted both as mediators of imperial *beneficia* and as patrons themselves, with a complex web of clients and friends to whom they distributed their largesse and resources and from whom they expected to receive honors and gratitude in return. For example, Pliny the Younger, for his hometown Comum, established a public library, gave a half-million sesterces for support of citizen children, and bequeathed a sumptuous amount for the construction and upkeep of baths for his one hundred freedmen, and for an annual banquet for the people. In return, the town dedicated an inscription reciting Pliny's career and benefactions on the baths built with his bequest.[84] One of the most famous benefactor-patrons was Athenian Herodes Atticus, who held the consulship twice in the early second century CE. He directed Hadrian's patronage to supply water for the town of Troy, bequeathed to each Athenian citizen one hundred drachma for annual distribution, and provided lavish sacrificial feasts and religious and athletic festivals for the city. He "also dedicated the stadium at Delphi to the Pythian god, and the aqueduct at Olympia to Zeus, and for the Thessalians and Greeks around the Maliac Gulf, the swimming pools at Thermopylae that heal the sick."[85] In other cases, provincial governors' *beneficia* included securing citizenship and offices from Rome and granting favorable legal decisions on behalf of their provincial clients—as many North African inscriptions by provincials testify, which are themselves public symbols of honors.[86] Provincial elites (those on the periphery) in turn considered a patronage network to be an instrument of political negotiation with the dominant imperial power. Plutarch advised his local protégé "always to have some friends in the circles of the most powerful as a firm support for the city. For the Romans themselves are best disposed to the civic exertions of friends. And it is good that those who enjoy benefits from friendship with the powerful use it for the prosperity of the people."[87] This kind of notion is confirmed by surviving inscriptions: for instance, the decurions and citizens of the colony Julia Augusta Tupusuctu contracted a patronage with a certain Quintus Julius II, imperial legate with rank of praetor, and placed themselves under his protection and *beneficia*.[88]

83. For examples of the imperial patronage during the third century, see Giardina, "Transition to Late Antiquity," 760–61.

84. *CIL* 5.5262 and Pliny, *Ep.* 11.1, 13, in Lewis and Reinhold, *The Empire*, 269–71.

85. Philostratus, *Lives of the Sophists* 2.1.

86. Garnsey and Saller, *Roman Empire*, 151–52.

87. *Mor.* 814C, quoted in Saller, "Status and Patronage," 843.

88. *CIL* 8.8837, in Lewis and Reinhold, *The Empire*, 263.

As the ethics of reciprocity dictated the nature and function of patronage and benefaction in the cities and countryside across the vast empire, the motivation of love of honor (*philotimos* or *philodoxia*) and the tradition of love of city (*philopatris*) came together in the public euergetism or *liberalitas* of the elite. Public recognitions of honor and gratitude in various forms (commemorative dedications, inscriptions, civic decrees, etc.) sustained enough "cheerful givers" among the rich and powerful for the "love of their cities." Just as the emperors showed their liberality to the people of "their cities" (Roman plebs) by choice *and* by necessity for legitimation of their rule, the elite of the cities and country "cheerfully" displayed their public euergetism for the same reason. The bottom line was that "cheerful giving," which would garner gratitude and honor in return, meant maintenance of power for the elite.[89] This partly explains why municipal patronage was so prevalent under the early empire.[90] In municipal benefactions of many parts of the East, particularly of gifts of cash and food in public feasts (*sportulae/epula*), distributions showed "a marked bias in favour of high-status individuals . . . getting two or three times as much as the commons."[91] A series of inscriptions that record gifts given by a certain Menodora, daughter of Megacles of Sillyon, on numerous occasions shows varying amounts of cash for different social levels: eighty-five *denarii* for city councilors, eighty for elders, seventy-seven for assemblymen, nine for citizens, three for freedmen and *paroikoi* (noncitizen residents who worked on land), and three denarii each for the wives of the first three groups.[92] And an Ephesian inscription commemorating a Roman equestrian who endowed an annual civic handout similarly displays different rates to councilors, elders, citizens, ephebes, and temple ministers.[93] These cases illustrate that "just as clients were treated differently according to how close they were to the patron, so entitlement to public distributions was governed by factors such as civic rank, citizenship and free birth."[94] Indeed, as noted by Richard Gordon, part of the function of euergetistic gestures was "to register and naturalize the inequalities of the social system in each community, just as the emperors' patronage and generosity marshals and orchestrates the overall hierarchy of the system as a whole."[95]

Then what can these examples tell us about the recipients of benefactions in addition to the point that patronage reflected and strengthened the existing

89. Gordon, "Veil of Power," 224n68.

90. See Woolf, "Food, Poverty, and Patronage," 216.

91. Ibid. For a rabbinic parallel in the community charity distribution, see Hamel, *Poverty and Charity*, 218.

92. *IGRRP* 3:800–803, cited in Woolf, "Food, Poverty, and Patronage," 214.

93. *AGIBM*, cited in ibid.

94. Woolf, "Food, Poverty, and Patronage," 215. See also the examples in A. R. Hands, *Charities and Social Aid in Greece and Rome* (London: Thames & Hudson, 1968), 91.

95. Gordon, "Veil of Power," 229.

hierarchy? The recipients of public benefactions—which evidently were not designed to relieve poverty—were identified as the members of particular civic communities, including the privileged elite, and the recipients' needs were not considered favorable factors in distribution. The poor received gifts only indirectly. When they were included in the distribution, it was not because they were poor but because they were simply part of and participated in the civic community; the poor were never singled out for any special treatment, let alone for any public distributions (e.g., alimentary).[96] In this sense, the poor were "ubiquitous but more or less invisible."[97] Rather, the exact opposite was true. It was the rich, prestigious, and powerful who received favorable treatment in public benefactions, because in a hierarchical society "justice means that each should receive *proportionally to his status*, not his need."[98]

1.1.3. Greco-Roman Understandings of Wealth and Poverty—Image and Reality

We are now ready to focus our attention on Greco-Roman perception of and teachings on poverty/the poor and wealth/the wealthy. Greco-Roman authors, who themselves were wealthy and privileged, approached wealth and, for that matter, poverty in a moralizing and ambiguous way. Although the poor did not constitute a single distinct socioeconomic "class" or group, the elite authors closely associated poverty with social status and order. Therefore they linked the poor with those who did not belong to the upper-stratum elite: i.e., the poor were the *humiliores*, the ones who had to work for their living whether in the fields or in shops, who lacked the leisure of the rich.[99] C. R. Whittaker notes that Romans used terms like *inopes* (resourceless), *egentes* (needy), *pauperes* (poor), *humiles* (lowly), and *abiecti* (outcast) rather indiscriminately and imprecisely and also combined them with terms for the "mob" such as *vulgus, turba, multitudo*, or simply *plebs*, therefore underscoring their political or social significance.[100] The variety of terms used by the elite did not reflect a social reality of different degrees of poverty; rather, poverty was a relative

96. Cf. Hands, *Charities and Social Aid*, 89, 115; Hamel, *Poverty and Charity*, 219–21.
97. P. Garnsey and G. Woolf, "Patronage of the Rural Poor in the Roman World," in *Patronage in Ancient Society* (ed. A. Wallace-Hadrill; New York: Routledge, 1989), 153.
98. Woolf, "Food, Poverty, and Patronage," 215, mentioning Dumont's study.
99. See C. R. Whittaker, "The Poor," in *The Romans* (ed. A. Giardina; trans. L. G. Cochrane; Chicago: University of Chicago Press, 1993), 280.
100. Whittaker, "The Poor," 278. A recent study, K. Ayer's "Measuring Worth: Articulations of Poverty and Identity in the Late Roman Republic" (PhD diss., Macquarie University, 2006), notes two types of poverty in late Roman republican discourse: first, poverty associated with virtues in the terms such as *paupertas, simplicitas*, and *frugalitas*, and related to Stoic ideas of simplicity and self-sufficiency; second, poverty linked to vices with not only moral but also sociopolitical implications in words like *enopia, egestas*, and *mendicitas*, describing neediness, want, and destitution as a threat to social order.

term covering a very broad spectrum of *humiliores* and open to contextual meanings and interpretations. We may recall that there were various gradations within the *humiliores*, ranging from the relatively prosperous to the relatively poor to the absolutely poor.

Traditionally Greeks used the term "the poor" to describe the working poor (*penētes*) as opposed to the rich (*ploūsioi*), but distinguished them from the destitute beggars (*ptōchoi*). According to Aristophanes's play *Ploutos*, "it is the beggar's life to live possessed of nothing, but the poor man's life to live frugally and by applying himself to work, with nothing to spare indeed, but not really in want."[101] The key to understanding the poor is to see that they *had to* work for their living, and work represented subservience and dependence and was therefore contemptible. Again, they "were all those people who needed to work in shops or in the fields and were consequently *without the leisure*" and self-sufficiency, "characteristic of the rich gentry, who were free to give their time to politics, education, and war."[102] The poor man's lot was measured in a relative, ever-sliding scale depending on his occupation, income, property, family situation, etc., whereas a wandering beggar was the one on the margins of a society, "who makes [one's] livelihood by endless entreaties," having "lost many or all of one's family and social ties."[103] This distinction was maintained during Roman times as well. The Roman poet Martial echoes the relative understanding of poverty: "It is not poverty to have nothing."[104] Indeed, for the satirist Juvenal, a man who possessed an annual income of twenty thousand sesterces and four slaves was still a poor man in Rome,[105] when in reality a minimum wealth of the same amount was sufficient for membership in the *decurion* order in the smaller North African cities![106] Thus, the Latin *pauperes* (and its synonyms) referred to the relatively prosperous artisans, craftsmen, and shopkeepers, who were surely poor compared to the elite "in the sense of being on the edge of conjunctural poverty," *as well as* to the destitute and beggars.[107]

Defining and understanding poverty in this way, the elite both normalized it as part of the natural order of things and perpetuated the binary category

101. Aristophanes, *Ploutos* 551–54, quoted in Hands, *Charities and Social Aid*, 62.

102. Hamel, *Poverty and Charity*, 168–69 (italics added).

103. Ibid., 170. Note Origen's own Christianized yet traditional understanding on this distinction: "reportedly, a beggar (*ptōchos*) is he who has fallen from wealth, whereas a poor man (*penēs*) is he who earns his subsistence by toil. For Scripture says: *Rich people have become poor* (Ps. 33:11 in LXX), and also: *For we have been brought very low* (Ps. 78:8 in LXX)" (Fragments in Ps. 111:6 = PG 12.1201B).

104. *Epigram* 11.328.

105. *Sat.* 9.140-45. See further V. Rimell, "The Poor Man's Feast: Juvenal," in *The Cambridge Companion to Roman Satire* (ed. K. Freudenburg; Cambridge: Cambridge University Press, 2005), 81–94.

106. Stegemann and Stegemann, *Jesus Movement*, 85.

107. Whittaker, "The Poor," 279.

of the rich and the poor by collapsing the various grades of socioeconomic structure into just two. This blurred a vast social hierarchy and inequality and concealed substantial social distance not only between the rich and the poor but also between the relatively prosperous ("the middling group"), the less poor, the poorer mass, and the extreme poor.[108] The elite's conceptual tie between social status and poverty, which was a product of the old aristocratic contempt for manual labor and trade, naturally led them to ascribe negative and servile characteristics to "the poor," befitting their social status, such as "*leves, inquinati, improbi, scelerati*, etc. terms implying dishonesty."[109] It was particularly "the urban poor and the conditions of urban living that always attract[ed] the attention of writers and the fears of the rich,"[110] as Cicero's notorious description of them as *sordem urbis et faecem* ("the poverty-stricken scum of the city") illustrates.[111] Roman authors typically presented the urban poor as the idle mob whose grievances and moral defect (such as laziness) led them to crimes, riots, and sedition. They were seen as a threat to social harmony and stability, and could only be controlled by satisfying their insatiable cravings for "bread and circuses."[112] These characterizations of the poor were certainly behind the reasons why the rich elite had no expressed concern, sympathy, or aid for the needs of the poor per se, as opposed to those of the *populus*.[113]

While the Roman elite pathologized urban poverty with vices, violence, and disease in their political discourses, they idealized the rural poverty of a peasant farmer as that of "the virtuous hard-working citizen, who had no time for anything except earning his living on his farm and doing his civic duty."[114] It was a kind of poverty characterized by an idyllic simple life and "unwealth," but not deprivation or destitution.[115] This poverty was praised as the paradigm of good and honest living with the virtues of frugality and self-sufficiency,[116] far removed from the corruption, vulgarity, and ills of urban poverty, on the one hand, and opposed to avarice and abuse of wealth, on the other. Thus, poverty in the elite writings often features as a heuristic device in the context of proper use of wealth, having nothing to do with the actual experiences of the actual poor.[117] Construction of this kind of romantic image served to

108. For a more quantitative analysis of poverty range and "middling" income sector, see Scheidel and Friesen, "Size of the Economy," 26–30, 33.

109. Hands, *Charities and Social Aid*, 64.

110. Whittaker, "The Poor," 281.

111. *De dom.* 89, mentioned in Hands, *Charities and Social Aid*, 64.

112. E.g., Juvenal, *Sat.* 10.78–81; Sallust, *Cat.* 37; Tacitus, *Hist.* 1.4.

113. Cf. N. Morley, "The Poor in the City of Rome," in *Poverty in the Roman World* (ed. Atkins and Osborne), 39.

114. Morley, "Poor in the City of Rome," 27, 35; cf. Cicero, *Tusculanae disputationes* 3.23.57.

115. Cf. G. Woolf, "Writing Poverty in Rome," in *Poverty in the Roman World* (ed. Atkins and Osborne), 94.

116. Cf. Hands, *Charity and Social Aid*, 63; cf. Seneca, *Ep.* 18.7, 87.

117. Woolf, "Writing Poverty in Rome," 92.

alleviate the elite's disgust and fear about the (urban) poor and helped them to separate the good (deserving) from the bad (undeserving) poor in their civic benefaction and euergetism, such as food distributions.

There was no question that poverty was widespread and ubiquitous in the Roman Empire and that the social reality of the poor, whether in cities or countryside, was harsh without any public safety net.[118] The rural poor suffered not only by frequent crop failures and debt but also by the influx of slave labor purchased by the landed rich; many poor farmers became day laborers and tenant farmers.[119] For the urban poor, crime, illness, violence, miserable sanitation, and crowded living conditions became part of their experiences as well as debt. In general, the poor, a vast majority of the Roman population, were most vulnerable to food shortages and crises, and infectious diseases, and were subject to the shame, alienation, and the bias and indifference of the rich.[120]

Since the elite did not generally associate moral excellence or virtue (*dignitas*) with poverty or the poor, and since patronal benefaction was a means of enhancing social control and submission among those who could reciprocate service, they carefully separated the deserving and worthy (i.e., respectable citizens) from the undeserving and unworthy poor in their euergetism. Aristotle had emphasized "giving rightly," that is, a generous person "will give to the right people" (i.e., men of virtue);[121] this spirit was captured by Cato's maxim of *bono benefacito* ("do good to the good"). Cicero urged giving to those who are "worthy" (*idonei*).[122] One should give to the "most deserving" (*dignissimi*), to "the good" or those "capable of being made good," writes Seneca.[123] If anyone deserved the pity (*eleēmosynē; misericordia*) of the rich elite, it was to be "appropriately given on an exchange basis to men of like character, and not to those who are not going to show pity in return."[124] In this sense, "to give to a beggar is to do him an ill service."[125] Indeed, "the true object of pity," taught Plato, "is not the man who is hungry or in some similar needy case, but the man who has sobriety of soul or some other virtue, or share in such virtue, and misfortune to boot."[126] Hence, it was the "fallen" rich who experienced a sudden "reversal of fortune" and loss of status that deserved the pity and "good deeds" (euergetism) of their peers, not the poor,

118. Cf. Garnsey and Woolf, "Patronage of the Rural Poor," 153.

119. Whittaker, "The Poor," 283.

120. See further Morley, "Poor in the City of Rome," 33–36; Hamel, *Poverty and Charity*, 193–97, 201.

121. *Nic. Eth.* 4.1.12.

122. *De off.* 1.14.45. According to Cicero, the donors should "take into consideration [the recipient's] moral character, his attitude toward us, the intimacy of his relations to us, and our common social ties, as well as the services he has hitherto rendered in our interest" (1.14.45).

123. *De vit. beat.* 23–24; cf. Hands, *Charities and Social Aid*, 74.

124. Thucydides, 3.40.3, quoted in Hands, *Charities and Social Aid*, 80.

125. Hands, *Charities and Social Aid*, 80.

126. *Laws* 11.936b.

whether the working poor or the destitute.[127] The interests of the rich "lay not in general poverty, which they regarded with indifference, but in marginalizing extreme poverty as a form of moral degeneration."[128]

While the Greco-Roman rich and moralists disregarded the poor and poverty in general, they were concerned with wealth and the ethics of wealth. Both Plato and Aristotle conceived of a good man (a sage) as an aristocratic man who had wealth but also took wealth as a functional means—that is, not as an end in itself but as having a value and significance relative to achieving virtue. The value of wealth depends upon one's attitude toward it and its proper use toward achieving virtue. Wealth liberates one's life from manual labor, should lead to the pursuit of justice, and makes possible a life dedicated to virtue, not to further accumulation of wealth.[129] However, wealth comes with its attendant "faults" and "temptations," such as avarice, miserliness, prodigality, and ambition.[130] While Aristotle regarded wealth always as a material means, Plato, distinguishing two kinds of riches, considered it as both material and spiritual assets, such as wisdom, virtue, and culture.[131]

The Cynics radicalized this received thought by positing wealth not as a vehicle but as an impediment to virtue, which is necessary to the life of self-sufficiency (*autarkeia*) and freedom in all things; wealth and virtue are mutually exclusive. Hence, they despised wealth and luxury along with other social conventions (e.g., marriage) and extolled poverty by urging the complete renunciation of material possessions and *voluntary* adoption of the lifestyle of a beggar (*ptōchos*). This is exemplified by Diogenes of Sinope.[132] According to Pseudo-Crates, true wealth is to be found only in poverty, which is necessary to virtue as such (*Ps.-Crates* 7). Nonetheless, we should remember that the "anti-wealth and pro-poverty" stance of Cynics was an *affordable choice* purely for their philosophical pursuit; it was certainly unconventional and "antisocial" but did not entail any special concern or care for the plight of the involuntary poor.[133]

While sharing the Cynic view of self-sufficiency and independence from externals, the Stoics placed wealth in the realm of *adiaphora*, "things morally indifferent," along with health, honor, fame, etc., but did not regard or avoid wealth as an obstruction to virtue. No external things, neither poverty nor wealth as such, determine human essence, moral worth, and destiny, and

127. Cf. Aristotle, *Rhetoric* 2.8; Hands, *Charities and Social Aid*, 80; Hamel, *Poverty and Charity*, 196.

128. Whittaker, "The Poor," 294.

129. F. Hauck and W. Kasch, "*ploutos*," *TDNT* 6:321.

130. Cf. E. N. O'Neil, "*De Cupiditate Divitiarum (Moralia* 523c–528b)," in *Plutarch's Ethical Writings and Early Christian Literature* (ed. H. D. Betz; Studia ad corpus Hellenisticum Novi Testamenti 4; Leiden: Brill, 1978), 295.

131. Hauck and Kasch, *TDNT* 6:322.

132. See *Diog. Laert.* 6.20–81.

133. Cf. Hands, *Charities and Social Aid*, 76.

therefore none should affect the rational person's goal of life, passionlessness (*apatheia*). However, certain *adiaphora*, such as wealth and health, can be advantageous or preferred to poverty and sickness. While "wealth has no value relative to virtue," the "value of wealth is relative to poverty" in a sense that "a rational being is naturally predisposed to prefer wealth to poverty if it is open to him to select either of these."[134] Virtue depends on what one makes of external (material) things such as wealth or poverty (their lack thereof) but can accommodate enjoyment of the very things the Stoics regarded as indifferent to virtue.[135] As long as wealth does not interfere with reason and thus virtue, the sage could opt for wealth over poverty and health over illness.[136] Therefore, Stoics could have two sides to living out their understanding of and attitude to wealth. Whereas Musonius Rufus and Epictetus presumably preached and practiced an ascetic life with bare necessities in terms of food, clothing, and shelter against the burdens of wealth,[137] Seneca, while claiming his indifference to a lavish palace or a bridge with beggars, still preferred the palace, a nice toga, and a comfortable mattress and fully capitalized the lifestyle of the rich and famous.[138]

In this (aristocratic) ethic of wealth, the philosophers/moralists paid particular attention to giving and obtaining wealth. According to Aristotle, generosity (*eleutheriotēs*; *liberalitas*, a Latin equivalent) is a virtue worthy of and necessary to the good man and should be motivated not by a selfish cause but by the "nobility of giving."[139] The donor is to give "cheerfully" and "gladly" without pain,[140] and "the motive of the magnificent man in such giving will be the nobility of action."[141] For Cicero, *liberalitas*, a disposition where the act of *beneficium* is derived, is a duty of the wealthy and a category within the virtue of justice (*iustitia*).[142] He lays out its three rules: first, it

134. A. A. Long, *Hellenistic Philosophy: Stoics, Epicureans, Sceptics* (2nd ed.; Berkeley: University of California Press, 1986), 192–93.

135. Cf. Plutarch's critique of this apparent hypocrisy in *Mor.* 1063c–1064f.

136. Cf. R. M. Royalty Jr., *The Streets of Heaven: The Ideology of Wealth in the Apocalypse of John* (Macon, GA: Mercer University Press, 1998), 91–92.

137. For example, Musonius XVIIIA–XX, in *Musonius Rufus: The Roman Socrates* (ed. C. E. Lutz; Yale Classical Studies 10; New Haven: Yale University Press, 1947); Epictetus, *Ench.* 33.7.

138. *De vita beata* 25.1–3; also discussed in Royalty, *Streets of Heaven*, 90. Cf. Tacitus *Annals* 13.42, on Seneca: "By what wisdom, by what principles of philosophy had he acquired 300,000,000 sesterces within four years of [Nero's] royal favor? At Rome the childless and their wills are snared in his nets, as it were; Italy and the provinces are drained by his enormous usury." An apparent contradiction or discrepancy in the Stoic attitude toward wealth (along with the Cynic attitude toward poverty) is also caricatured in Lucian's *Lives for Sale* (20–25).

139. *Nic. Eth.* 4.1.14; cf. E. F. Bruck, "Ethic vs. Law: St. Paul, the Fathers of the Church, and the 'Cheerful Giver' in Roman Law," *Traditio* 2 (1944): 101.

140. *Nic. Eth.* 4.1.13, 14.

141. *Nic. Eth.* 4.2.7.

142. *De off.* 1.20.68; cf. C. E. Manning, "*Liberalitas*—The Decline and Rehabilitation of a Virtue," *Greece & Rome* 32, no. 1 (1985): 73.

must not be hurtful to the recipients (i.e., "friends"); second, it should not be beyond one's means; finally, it should be proportionate to the worthiness of the recipient.[143] Stoics also emphasized "cheerful giving"; Seneca exhorted the donors to "give willingly, promptly, and without any hesitation" only for the recipients' enrichment.[144] Common to Aristotle, Cicero, and Seneca are emphases on right motive in giving—apparent absence of self-interest—and a general expectation of giving on the part of the aristocratic men. In this sense, giving is a characteristic of the Greco-Roman elite ideal, "the essence of the noble man's virtues" (*kalokagathia*), and it augments the donor's honor and virtue.[145] However, the same Seneca who disparages self-motives in giving also points out that "the benefits that stir most gratitude are those which are readily and easily obtainable and rush to our hands."[146] Therefore, *liberalitas*, despite philosophers' claims to the contrary, was ultimately self-regarding, befitting and reinforcing the structure of patronal reciprocity. By the imperial period, these philosophical/moral perspectives have become the operating principle of the ruling *ordines*, particularly of the *princeps*, hence the frequent occurrence of *liberalitas* in imperial descriptions and panegyrics.[147] Ironically, the ideology of *liberalitas* of the rich became pervasive to such an extent that Plutarch in the early second century complained that "the masses hate a rich man who does not share his prosperity more than a poor man who steals public property."[148]

If generosity was the quintessential virtue of a good man, love of wealth (*philargyria, philoploutia; avaritia*, a Latin equivalent) was the classic vice of Greco-Roman moral philosophy across the spectrum.[149] Not surprisingly, the Cynic Diogenes condemned it as a primary source of all evils.[150] Cicero warns his readers to watch out for "ambition for wealth" and states that the characteristic of the most petty and notorious person is love of riches, *amare divitias*.[151] A host of classical poets, writers, and philosophers have recognized the attendant faults of wealth, prominent among which were greed (*avaritia*), ambition (*ambitio*), miserliness (*avaritia*), and prodigality or showiness (*luxuria*). In *On Love of Wealth* (*De cupiditate divitiarum*) the Middle Platonist

143. *De off.* 1.14.42–45.

144. *Ben.* 2.1.2 and *De vita beata* 24, respectively. For Stoics, however, giving should not be motivated by pity (*misericordia*), i.e., irrational and self-regarding emotion (*pathos*), which disturbs a life of virtue, i.e., passionlessness (*apatheia*); but it should be motivated by reason, which governs a life of virtue.

145. Bruck, "Ethic vs. Law," 102; cf. *Nic. Eth.* 4.1.12.

146. *Ben.* 2.1.3.

147. Cf. Manning, "*Liberalitas*," 74, 78; e.g., Tacitus, *Hist.* 1.1; Suetonius, *Augustus* 41.

148. Plutarch, *Mor.* 821–22; cf. Hands, *Charities and Social Aid*, 41.

149. Cf. L. T. Johnson, *Sharing Possessions: Mandate and Symbol of Faith* (Philadelphia: Fortress, 1986), 119.

150. *Diog. Laert.* 6.40, 50.

151. *De off.* 1.20.68.

with Cynic-Stoic influence Plutarch distinguishes natural (necessary) wealth and nonnatural (superfluous and useless) wealth and focuses on the irrational desire to possess great (nonnatural) wealth (*philargyria, philoploutia, pleonexia*). Building on the very classical theme of the inherent danger and limit of wealth,[152] Plutarch sees the love of wealth as a disease manifesting in conventional ways: greed, miserliness (illiberality), prodigality, and ambition; particularly, miserliness results from the nonuse of wealth and prodigality from misuse of wealth, but all of them are signs of suffering from the insatiable desire for wealth, which is "mental poverty." For Plutarch, the ideal, which corresponds to his philosophical ideal, is self-control and self-sufficiency (*autarkeia*) of simple essentials (natural wealth) as opposed to ostentatious extravagance infected by love of wealth.[153]

Luxury (prodigality), one of the chief manifestations of love of wealth, brought about particular concerns and anxieties over its social and moral effects among the Roman moralists and the ruling elite, including the emperors. Livy, Cicero, and Pliny the Elder lamented over greed (*avaritia*) and luxury (*luxuria*) as foreign imports and destructive plagues that had been introduced to Romans through their conquests of Asia. Greed and luxury affected the upper *ordines* first but spread downward even to the plebs and slaves with depraving effect.[154] Therefore, throughout the late republic and early imperial period, the senate and the emperors repeatedly passed legislation against aristocratic *luxuria*. Since sumptuous banquet was one of the main ways of displaying aristocratic riches and status in Roman society, the "anti-luxury" laws primarily targeted luxuries of their dinner table by limiting the number of nonfamily invitees to the dinner by the elite (e.g., *lex Orchia* of 182 BCE), restricting the amount of nonbasic foodstuffs served at dinners on feast days, or prohibiting specific foodstuffs, such as certain types of fish and pig offal (e.g., *senatus decretum* and *lex Fannia* of 161 BCE; *lex Iulia sumptuaria* of 18 BCE).[155] However, while almost all of these laws received passionate support by the elite themselves, they were hardly enforced and effective at all. Then what made the elite keep preaching and legislating simplicity while practicing extravagance?[156] The elite moralists were aware of the apparent power of

152. See O'Neil, "*De Cupiditate Divitiarum*," 295.

153. Here we need to remember that although Greco-Roman moralists strongly condemned love of wealth and pointed out potential problems of wealth, they rarely condemned wealth in itself; the radical attitude of Cynics constituted the only notable exception.

154. Livy, 34.3; 39.6.7–9; Cicero, *De Legibus* 3.30–31; Pliny, *Nat. Hist.* 33.148. See A. Wallace-Hadrill, "The Social Spread of Roman Luxury: Sampling Pompeii and Herculanum," *Papers of the British School at Rome* 58 (1990): 145–48.

155. A. Wallace-Hadrill, *Rome's Cultural Revolution* (Cambridge: Cambridge University Press, 2008), 329–30.

156. De Ligt, "Restraining the Rich, Protecting the Poor: Symbolic Aspects of Roman Legislation," in *After the Past: Essays in Ancient History in Honour of H. W. Pleket* (ed. W. Jongman and M. Kleijwegt; Leiden: Brill, 2002), 5.

luxury as a status marker and symbol and used it "to articulate important concerns about social order."[157] That is, these laws were not meant to change the actual behavior (of basically their own) but to symbolically define and broadcast Roman values that they themselves set (especially for the rest of the Roman society): i.e., to affirm simplicity and restraint as central Roman values, while defining *luxuria* as a "foreign" intrusion particularly for those *nouveaux riches* (e.g., wealthy freedmen) who were contesting the established social hierarchy and wished to display their new status through imitating the behaviors of the ruling *ordines*.[158] Therefore, as "luxury mapped effectively onto the traditional structures of social power (clientele),"[159] these sumptuous laws on table in fact aimed to strengthen the status quo by intentionally leaving doors open for the elite to continue their conspicuous consumption on other items—such as houses, clothing, weddings, and funerals as marks of social distinction—and thus after all to protect their own elite interests and traditional social order while gesturing to preserve ideal Roman values with their symbolic effect.[160]

1.2. The Israelite and Jewish Setting for the Rich and the Poor and Teachings on Wealth and Poverty

The Israelite and Jewish understanding of wealth and poverty has a different starting point from that of the Greco-Roman tradition. It is rooted in Yahweh's deep concern for the poor in the Torah and developed over the whole history of Israel—particularly during the monarchy and the exilic and postexilic periods in the prophetic, wisdom, and apocalyptic traditions. The Torah reveals Yahweh's special care and protection for the poor by establishing social obligation toward the poor.[161] Since Israel's land belongs to God (Lev. 25:23),[162] the Torah declares as Yahweh's will that there should be no poor in the covenant community (Deut. 15:4). The book of the covenant (Exod. 20:22–23:19) institutes the sabbatical year for debt servitude (21:2), grants the poor the produce of the land in the fallow year (23:10–11), and forbids the exploitation of the poor (22:22–27) and perversion of justice against them

157. Wallace-Hadrill, *Rome's Cultural Revolution*, 329, 333.

158. Cf. De Ligt, "Restraining the Rich," 10–12; see also Wallace-Hadrill, *Rome's Cultural Revolution*, 348–53, particularly for Pliny's anxiety over the upward mobility of freedmen who imitate the luxury of the upper stratum.

159. Wallace-Hadrill, *Rome's Cultural Revolution*, 333.

160. See ibid., 345–55; De Ligt, "Restraining the Rich," 38–42.

161. For a thorough study of wealth and poverty in the Torah in a larger ancient Near Eastern context, see D. Baker, *Tight Fists or Open Hands? Wealth and Poverty in Old Testament Law* (Grand Rapids: Eerdmans, 2009).

162. This claim of Yahweh is repeated throughout the Hebrew Bible: e.g., Josh. 22:19; 2 Chron. 7:20; Ps. 85:1; Isa. 14:2, 25; Jer. 2:7; Ezek. 36:5; Joel 1:6.

(23:6).[163] The community is obliged to open their hands to the poor and needy (Deut. 15:7, 11) and not to oppress them, especially the Levites (e.g., Deut. 14:27), resident aliens (e.g., Exod. 23:9), and widows and orphans (e.g., Deut. 24:17–18; cf. Ps. 68:5), for they are the landless or socially helpless (cf. Exod. 22:21–24; Deut. 10:17–19; 26:12; 27:19).

At the same time, the Israelite attitude is also tied to God's covenantal blessings and curses in the Deuteronomic tradition, which entail material prosperity and poverty respectively. Riches are God's gift to the righteous for their faithfulness to God and his covenant, and poverty is a consequence of disobedience (Deut. 11:26–32; 28:1–14; 30:11–20; Lev. 26:3–5, 9–10). This notion continues in the wisdom tradition, which affirms wealth as God's blessings to the righteous and poverty as a natural result of laziness and foolish behaviors (e.g., Prov. 3:9–10, 15–16; 10:4, 22; 13:4; 22:4; 26:13, 15).[164] Nonetheless, the Wisdom literature recognizes the limited and relative value of riches to wisdom and the danger of riches (e.g., Prov. 11:4; 13:8; 15:16–17; 16:8, 16; 17:1; 21:4; 23:4–5; 28:6); moreover, it enjoins the rich to do justice and be generous to the poor and the weak and to care for them (e.g., Prov. 11:24; 19:17; 22:9; 28:27; 29:7, 14; 31:9; cf. Job 29:12–16; 31:16–28; Ps. 10:1–3, 9, 12; 82:3–4) and warns them of dishonesty involving wealth (e.g., Prov. 10:2; 13:23; 16:8; 21:6).

Under the monarchy, the economic and urban development incurred the emergence of a small group of aristocratic and plutocratic landowners and the impoverishment of the majority of the population with ever-growing social distinctions between them.[165] The prophets saw this process not only socially but also theologically, because it ran contrary to Yahweh's will for Israel (Amos 2:10; Mic. 6:3–4; Jer. 2:6–7; cf. Deut. 15:4); and they denounced the wealthy and powerful (the same people) not only for idolatry but also for their social and economic injustice and oppression of the poor in particular. The powerful rich oppress the poor and crush the needy (Amos 4:1; cf. Ezek. 45:9) with their avarice, their covetousness for amassing more wealth, and their ruthless acquisition of the land at the expense of the poor (Mic. 2:2; 3:2–3). They defraud the laborers of their wages, rob the fatherless, wrong the widows and orphans, extort the resident aliens, and pervert justice for the poor by taking bribes (Isa. 10:1–2; Mal. 3:5; Ezek. 22:6–7, 12; Mic. 7:3). The wealthy are equivalent to the wicked who are "full of violence," dishonesty, and falsehood (Mic. 6:9–12; cf. Isa. 53:9). The "transgressions of Israel" consist of the rich trampling "the head of the poor into the dust of the earth" and

163. Cf. Esser and Brown, NIDNTT 2:822.

164. A major contrast to this Deuteronomic principle is Job, a paradigmatic godly rich man (besides the patriarchs) who suffers and experiences poverty despite his righteousness. Nevertheless, the ending of the book of Job (God's blessing of Job with a double portion after his repentance) does ultimately confirm the Deuteronomic ideal at work.

165. P. U. Maynard-Reid, Poverty and Wealth in James (Maryknoll, NY: Orbis Books, 1987), 26–27; Hauck and Kasch, TDNT 6:324.

pushing "the afflicted out of the way" (Amos 2:7); the "iniquities" of Judah are precisely robbing the poor of their rights (Isa. 10:2; Jer. 5:25, 28) and ruining the poor through treachery and deceit (Isa. 32:7). In the "Day of the Lord," God would surely bring his judgment upon the rich who violated the core of God's law and the whole people of Israel (Isa. 3:13–15; 5:8–9; Amos 5:11–13; Mic. 6:13–16; cf. Mal. 3:5); and the destruction of the kingdoms of Israel and Judah was God's punishment for their oppression of the poor and needy (Ezek. 22:29; Zech. 7:9–14; cf. Isa. 5:13).

The prophetic oracles against the oppressive rich can be juxtaposed with psalmists' self-identification with the poor and needy, most frequently in psalms of lament (e.g., 40:17; 69:29, 32–33; 70:5; 86:1; 109:22; cf. 22:24, 26; 34:6; 69:29; 74:19). In these Psalms, the poor are the victims of the "wicked" (*rash'im*) and suffer from the latter's injustice and oppression, which often cause or result in material poverty (10:3–11; 31:15; 35:10; 37:14; 94:3–7; 109:16).[166] Being helpless and lowly, the poor cry out and turn to God for help in times of distress and appeal to God's righteousness and salvation (9:12; 22:24; 34:18). God is portrayed as the just defender and protector of the poor from their enemies (10:17–18; 12:5; 34:6–7; 64:1, 10; 70:5; 140:12; cf. 68:5–6; 69:32–33), provider for the needy (68:10; 107:9), deliverer of the oppressed and the righteous (34:17; 72:12–14; 82:1–4), and lifter of the poor and lowly for his glory (113:7–9; 145:14). The notion of poverty, then, is extended to the religious and spiritual level, and the poor are identified as the humble, the afflicted, the oppressed, and the righteous who turn to God, depend on his help, and enjoy his special favor.[167] Thus, "poor" and "pious" form a parallel concept (86:1–2; 132:15–16; cf. 74:21) as friends of God (55:13), and the enemy of the poor is also the enemy of God (107:39–41; 109:31; cf. 74:18–23).[168] This development echoes in the exilic and postexilic prophetic oracles of the eschatological restoration of Israel when they identify the poor with the nation of Israel as a whole against the "wicked" nations (Isa. 41:16–17; 49:13; 51:21–23; 61:1–4).[169]

In the Second Temple period, there was a more explicit development of the notion of "the pious poor and the wicked rich" in two aspects. First of all, the Septuagint, a product of the Hellenistic Judaism of this period, set a precedent and tone for Jewish (and Christian) understanding of the poor in the Greco-Roman context. The most common words for poor in the Hebrew Bible are *'any* and *'evyon*; both terms, especially *'any*, were prominent in the prophetic literature and the Psalms and acquired religious significance in

166. Cf. E. Bammel, "*ptōchos*," *TDNT* 6:892.
167. Some psalms describe the righteous rich who fear the Lord and have given to the poor (e.g., 112; 128).
168. M. Dibelius, *James: A Commentary on the Epistle of James* (Hermeia; rev. H. Greeven; trans. M. A. Williams; Philadelphia: Fortress, 1976), 39.
169. Cf. J. D. Pleins, "Poor, Poverty," in *ABD* (ed. D. N. Freedman; vol. 5; New York: Doubleday, 1992), 408–9.

addition to their social and economic meaning.[170] According to Hamel, the Greek translators, while aware of the difference between *'any* and *'evyon*, and of that between *penēs* (the working poor) and *ptōchos* (the destitute), usually translated *'any* as *ptōchos* rather than *penēs* probably because "both *'any* and *'evyon* acquired a strong religious value early enough to obfuscate the difference in social meaning by the time Greek versions were made."[171] The afflicted and oppressed *'any* placed in God all hope for salvation and vindication, and despite its negative connotations in Greek culture, *ptōchos* was thought to be fitting in describing that kind of destitution and absolute dependence on God.[172] It was

> the most important transformation . . . that the religious or moral meaning of *'any* (and *'anaw*) accrued to the word *ptōchos* in a new, Hellenized and [later] Christianized, environment. With the Greek translation, the Bible brought into the open a view of the beggar rarely found in Greco-Roman society, or at least not publically acceptable.[173]

Second, with this significant linguistic adaptation, the emerging genre and perspective of apocalypse—especially in the apocryphal and pseudepigraphical literature—contributed to and developed further the "righteous poor/ oppressive rich" theme in dealing with a bleak reality. In its sociopolitical and historical context, the Second Temple period was the time of continuous foreign domination from the Persians, Greeks, and Romans, with a brief hiatus of the Hasmonean rule. It was thus a time of harsh social reality and living conditions for the masses. The generosity and virtues of the righteous rich (e.g., Abraham, Job, Judith, and Susanna) are highlighted in these literatures (*Jub.* 16.22–25; *T. Ab.* 1.5; *T. Job* 9–13; Jdt. 8–16; Sus.), and the traditional piety of caring for the poor as an essential religious duty is continued in the wisdom tradition (Sir. 3.30–31; 4.1–10; Tob. 1.8; Wis. 19.14–15). However, the issue of the poor and the rich increasingly became that of theodicy and was linked with and subsumed under the prevailing apocalyptic and eschatological framework,[174] which envisioned the struggle between the righteous and the wicked as well as God's final vindication of the righteous and judgment of the wicked. In this struggle, the righteous were presented as the victimized poor and the wicked were identified as the powerful rich. This eschatological conflict between the righteous poor and the wicked rich (cf. *Jub.* 23.19)

---

170. Cf. ibid., 5:403, 408, 409: Out of eighty occurrences *'any* appears twenty-five times in the prophetic literature and thirty-one times in the Psalms, often in the psalms of lament; out of sixty-one occurrences *'evyon* appears seventeen times in the prophetic literature and twenty-three times in the Psalms, most often in the psalms of lament.

171. See Hamel, *Poverty and Charity*, 171–72.

172. Ibid., 172.

173. Ibid., 172–73.

174. Cf. Hauck and Kasch, *TDNT* 6:325.

involved the "great reversal" of their earthly fortunes in the last day. The close association of the rich with the wicked and of the poor with the righteous, and their eschatological reckoning by God, are most conspicuously depicted in *1 Enoch* and *Psalms of Solomon*.

Written in the first century BCE, *1 Enoch* (Ethiopic), which significantly influenced early Christian literature, portrays a bitter struggle between the "righteous" (*dikaioi, eusebeis*) and the "sinners" (*hamartōloi*).[175] In one of the five main sections, the *Epistle of Enoch* (*1 Enoch*, 91–105), where this dual theme is unequivocally expounded, the righteous are the ones who are persecuted, oppressed, hated, abused, robbed, and devoured (95.7; 103.9–15) by the rich and mighty (e.g., the Maccabees and the Sadducees), who are deceitful, unrighteous, and ungodly (94.6–8; 96.7), and trust their own wealth for future security. The self-indulgent and godless wealthy gain their wealth unjustly, and these foolish sinners will perish with their possessions (98.1–10). They are doomed to destruction on the day of judgment because of their wicked deeds (99.1; 100.4, 9; 102.5).[176] The writer juxtaposes a series of woes and indictments to the rich (e.g., 94.6–8; 95.4–7; 96.4–8; 97.7–8; 98.9–16; 99.1–16), accounting their sins and divine judgment with a series of exhortations to the righteous calling them to courage and hope because of divine vindication and the promise of eternal life in the coming judgment (e.g., 94.6–11; 96.4–8; 97.3–10; 99.1–16; 100.7; 102.4–5; 104.2).[177] Despite the absence of the term "poor," the identification of the righteous with the poor appears clearly, since the sinners are singled out as the rich; the righteous are the helpless and precarious victims of socioeconomic exploitation and injustice by the rich and powerful sinners who prosper in this life. Death is a great equalizer of earthly fortunes, and it is God's just judgment that brings about the reversal of their twisted fortunes. While the poor are not named as such in *1 Enoch*, in the *Psalms of Solomon* (first century BCE), the rich remain unnamed but the poor (*ptōchoi*) are identified as the righteous (i.e., the Pharisees) who have experienced God's deliverance (5.2, 11; 10.6–7; 15.1; 18.2). God stands on the side of the poor, and this signifies again the religious quality of poverty.

In this light, the Qumran community seemed to use the term "poor" for self-designation of the sect.[178] The community *apparently* renounced private property as its rule (1QS 3.2; 5.1) and practiced communalism (1QS 1.12; 5.2;

175. Nickelsburg, "Riches, the Rich, and God's Judgment in I Enoch 92–105 and the Gospel according to Luke," *NTS* 25 (1979): 26–32, provides a succinct study of the wicked rich in *1 Enoch* 92–105.

176. Cf. C. Osiek, *Rich and Poor in the Shepherd of Hermas: An Exegetical-Social Investigation* (CBQMS 15; Washington, DC: Catholic Biblical Association of America, 1983), 20.

177. Cf. Nickelsburg, "Riches, the Rich," 327.

178. Bammel, *TDNT* 6:897; Esser, *NIDNTT* 2:824. L. Keck, "The Poor among the Saints in Jewish Christianity and Qumran," *ZNW* 57 (1966): 54–78, argues that although the Qumran community used this term as a self-description, it was not a technical name for the community.

6.17; 7.6; cf. Josephus, *War* 2.8.3) as a way of erasing distinctions between the rich and poor in expectation of eschatological salvation and in attempt to mirror the form of life God would bring about with the coming age.[179] Earthly wealth and possession is the most obvious sign of imprisonment to this world and thus something "wicked" and unclean from which the members of the community should abstain (CD 6.15; 1QS 5.20; 8.23; cf. Josephus, *Bell.* 2.122). While the members are exhorted to strengthen the poor and needy in the community (CD 6.16, 21; 14.14), they themselves constitute the "congregation of the poor" who endured and survived the persecution and violence of the Wicked Priest and the Jerusalem priests (1QpHab 12.3–10; 4QpPs 2.10). Whereas the poor will inherit the land as the "congregation of his [Yahweh's] elect," the wicked will no longer exist (4QpPs 2.4–5, 9). Therefore, God is praised as the one who delivers the life of the poor (1QH 2.32–35; cf. 3.25) and rescues the soul of the needy from the powerful wicked (1QH 5.12–18). He does wonders for the poor with his mighty hand (1QH 5.16; cf. 1QM 13.14), strikes down the hordes of Belial by the hand of the poor, and will deliver the enemies of all the countries into their hands (1QM 11.9, 13). As the archaeological finds show, however, the Qumran community does not seem to have been economically destitute compared to the majority of the population of Palestine.[180] Thus, the Qumran writers use the term "poor" more to denote their sectarian identity and as a title of honor as the object of God's mercy and eschatological dealings.[181]

1.3. Early Christian Teachings and Practices

In first-century Palestine, the social scene betrayed the concentration of wealth in the hands of a small elite group (the landed aristocracy) and the general impoverishment of the majority of the population (the landless peasants). The tension between the wealthy landed minority and the peasant landless majority goes back to the late monarchical period, but throughout the Second Temple period and especially during Herod's rule, the situation grew increasingly worse through the continuing economic oppression and confiscation of the land by the rich and powerful.[182] Creation of huge estates through the exploita-

---

179. Cf. Bammel, *TDNT* 6:898.

180. See Hamel, *Poverty and Charity*, 181; also R. de Vaux, *Archaeology and the Dead Sea Scrolls* (London: Oxford University Press, 1973), 84–87.

181. Cf. Hamel, *Poverty and Charity*, 184–85: "For a good part, the 'poverty' of the Essenes signified their total dependence on God. . . . Poverty at Qumran was primarily a mystical notion, and an essential one for people wishing to gain access to the divine mystery." Also cf. L. W. Countryman, *The Rich Christian in the Church of the Early Empire: Contradictions and Accommodations* (New York: Edwin Mellen, 1980), 30–31.

182. On socioeconomic tensions and "class struggles" in Palestine, see M. Hengel, *Property and Riches in the Early Church* (Philadelphia: Fortress, 1974), 15–16; Maynard-Reid, *Poverty*

tion of the land and through mortgage interest produced a growing number of landless tenants or hired laborers in the very land they had once owned.[183] And the coalition between the great landowners and the mercantile groups over the monopoly of the agricultural goods made the peasant workers' lot more difficult to endure.[184] These avaricious landlords were basically the pro-Roman priestly aristocrats, the Sadducees, who also dominated the Sanhedrin, controlled the Temple treasury, and exploited the lower priests.[185] Furthermore, besides this "firm imprint of feudalism,"[186] other changes that aggravated the socioeconomic conditions in Palestine—overpopulation and overcultivation of the land, natural disasters such as famines[187] and earthquakes,[188] and increase in taxes, tributes, and tithes—forced the already poor majority into the arduous struggle for unfortunate survival in a highly stratified society.[189] This kind of socioeconomic "determinism" became the cradle for social upheaval and rebellion throughout the period, including the revolt of Judas the Galilean (6 CE), the Jewish War (66–70 CE), and even the Bar Kochba rebellion (132–35 CE).[190] It accompanied and became the fitting environ for the fermenting apocalyptic hope deeply rooted in the tradition of "piety of the poor" with the theme of "great reversal" at the judgment, as evidenced by the prolific Second Temple apocalyptic literature.

In this political and socioeconomic climate, the early followers of Jesus believed that, with the coming of Jesus, the eschatological new age had indeed dawned. They also inherited the tradition of poverty-piety in that Jewish eschatological context along with a new vocabulary for the poor (*ptōchoi*) from the Septuagint.[191] Jesus's attitude toward poverty and wealth is frequently

---

and Wealth, 13–23, 87–90; J. B. Adamson, *James: The Man and His Message* (Grand Rapids: Eerdmans, 1989), 230–58; in general, see K. C. Hanson and D. E. Oakman, *Palestine in the Time of Jesus: Social Structures and Social Conflicts* (Minneapolis: Fortress, 1998), 63–159; R. A. Horsley, *Jesus and the Spiral of Violence* (San Francisco: Harper & Row, 1987; Minneapolis: Fortress, 1993); G. E. M. De Ste. Croix, *The Class Struggle in the Ancient Greek World* (Ithaca, NY: Cornell University Press, 1981).

183. Hengel, *Property and Riches*, 15.

184. Wall, "James, Letter of," 550.

185. Cf. R. P. Martin, "The Life-Setting of the Epistle of James in the Light of Jewish History," in *Biblical and Near Eastern Studies: Essays in Honor of William Sanford LaSor* (ed. G. A. Tuttle; Grand Rapids: Eerdmans, 1978), 97–103; J. Jeremias, *Jerusalem in the Time of Jesus* (Philadelphia: Fortress, 1969), 95, 228; Countryman, *Rich Christian*, 26–32, 82.

186. Hengel, *Property and Riches*, 16.

187. Josephus, *Ant.* 20.2.5; Acts 11:28.

188. Cf. Mark 13:8.

189. See G. Theissen, *Sociology of Early Palestinian Christianity* (trans. J. Bowden; Philadelphia: Fortress, 1978), 39–45.

190. Wall, "James, Letter of," 550.

191. Note that in the New Testament, unlike the classic Greco-Roman tradition but following the Septuagint, the most common term for the poor is *ptōchoi*, the (beggarly) destitute (thirty-four times), and it is they who are juxtaposed with the rich, *plousioi*, not the working poor (*penētes*), which appears only once in 2 Cor. 8:9.

depicted in the Synoptic Gospels, and the Epistle of James often alludes to this Jesus tradition.[192] While Jesus does associate with the wealthy and powerful (cf. Matt. 27:57; Luke 19:1–9; John 3:1) and is often a recipient of people's hospitality and financial support for his itinerant ministry (e.g., Mark 14:3, 13–16; Luke 7:36; 8:2–3; 10:38; 14:1), he tells the rich man (ruler) to sell his possessions and give to the poor in order to inherit eternal life (Mark 10:21; Luke 18:22, "all"; cf. Matt. 19:21, "if you wish to be perfect"), regards the "lure of wealth" (*agapē tou ploutou*) coupled with cares and desires of life as something that chokes God's Word (Mark 4:19; Luke 8:14, *merimnōn, ploutou, hēdonōn*; cf. Matt. 13:22), and values the offering of the poor widow who gave all she had more than that of the rich out of their wealth (Mark 12:41–44; Luke 21:1–4). Whereas it is to the poor (*ptōchoi*) that the good news is preached (Matt. 11:5; Luke 7:22–23), it *appears* virtually impossible for the rich to enter the kingdom of God (Matt. 19:24; Mark 10:25; Luke 18:25).[193] Serving wealth (*mamōnas*) is antithetical to serving God (Matt. 6:24; Luke 16:13), and discipleship entails forsaking all (possessions and family ties) for Jesus and following him (Matt. 4:18–22; Mark 1:16–20; 2:13–14; Luke 5:1–11; cf. John 1:35–51; also Matt. 10:37–39; Mark 8:34-35; Luke 9:57–60; 14:25–33). In the Sermon on the Mount in Matthew, Jesus, while taking the traditional practices of piety (almsgiving along with prayer and fasting) for granted, focuses on inner disposition and motive for those practices (Matt. 6:1–4; cf. works of mercy in 23:23; 25:31–46). He speaks of "the poor in spirit"[194] as the heirs of God's kingdom (5:3, "kingdom of heaven"), contrasts the eternal and incorruptible treasures with the transient and corruptible treasures (6:19–21), and commands the audience not to worry about wealth but to seek first God's kingdom and righteousness (6:25–32)—God's kingdom being the eschatological reality. The poor in spirit (*hoi ptōchoi tō pneumati*) inheriting the kingdom of heaven stands in close relation to the meek (*hoi praeis*) inheriting the earth in 5:5[195] and reflects the theological (as well as

---

192. For Jesus's attitude to wealth in the Synoptics, see Hauck and Kasch, *TDNT* 6:327–28; F. Selter, "*ptōchos*," *NIDNTT* 2:840–45. Cf. P. H. Davids, "James and Jesus," in *Jesus Tradition outside the Gospels* (ed. D. Wenham; Sheffield: JSOT Press, 1985), 63–84. For the treatment of wealth in the Synoptics see T. E. Schmidt, *Hostility to Wealth in the Synoptic Gospels* (Sheffield: JSOT Press, 1987), esp. 101–62.

193. "It is easier for a camel to go through the eye of a needle than for someone who is rich to enter the kingdom of God" (Mark 10:25). In S. C. Barton's words, "The disciples' shocked response, 'Then who can be saved?' [Mark 10:26] may be heard as a response representative of that deeply rooted biblical and sapiential tradition according to which wealth is a sign of divine blessing," in "Money Matters: Economic Relations and the Transformation of Value in Early Christianity," in *Engaging Economics: New Testament Scenarios and Early Christian Reception* (ed. B. W. Longenecker and K. D. Liebengood; Grand Rapids: Eerdmans, 2009), 47.

194. "Poor in spirit" has both spiritual and physical meaning: see Hamel, *Poverty and Charity*, 174.

195. Cf. Bammel, *TDNT* 6:904.

socioeconomic) understanding of poverty-piety developed from the (later) Psalms on—the poor are the afflicted and humble ones whose confidence rests only in God.

As recognized by most scholars, it is the Lukan Gospel that places a particular concern and favor on the poor, on the one hand, and a strong disapproval on the rich and their wealth, on the other.[196] The theme of the "great reversal" in judgment and salvation is carefully woven together throughout the Gospel, especially in the uniquely Lukan materials. While Mary rejoices in the Magnificat that God has exalted the lowly and hungry but sent the rich away empty, quoting Isaiah 61:1, Jesus at the beginning of his ministry proclaims preaching good news to the poor (*euangelisasthai ptōchois*)as his specific mission (4:18a), as part of the fulfillment of eschatological Jubilee with his coming (4:18–19; cf. Lev. 25; Isa. 61:1–2a). He commands the host of the feast to invite not the relatives or rich neighbors but the poor and disabled, pointing to the latter's place at the great eschatological banquet (14:13, 21), and thus turns traditional Greco-Roman reciprocity and patronage upside down. In the Sermon on the Plain, eschatological blessings pronounced to the poor are coupled with woes to the rich who have already received their reward (6:20–26). The parable of the rich fool (12:16–21) shows the folly of the rich man's avarice and luxury and of trusting wealth as a means of future security, which is a sign of his spiritual "poverty" toward God and thus a basis of God's condemnation. This theme is dramatized in the parable of Dives and Lazarus (16:19–31), where eternal torment is the destiny of the rich man (*plousios*), who enjoyed good things in life, whereas consolation of Abraham is the destiny of Lazarus as a poor man (*ptōchos*), who suffered bad things on earth (v. 25).[197] Whereas both the rich fool and Dives fail to care for the poor and consider God while on earth, Zacchaeus, a "sinful rich publican," receives salvation through almsgiving to the poor and making restitution for ill-gotten wealth (19:1–10); and Jesus himself exhorts the disciples to "make friends for [themselves] with dishonest wealth" for their eternal abode (16:9). Without idealizing poverty, the Lukan Gospel portrays the poor as the object of God's eschatological salvation and the rich as the ungodly ones who are alienated from God because of their present comfort and reliance on wealth; and without vilifying wealth per se, it provides both warnings against the dangers of wealth and paradigms for the right use of wealth.

Although the early Christian groups did not formally identify themselves as the "poor," they, in general—whether Jesus and his disciples (Matt. 8:20), the Jerusalem church (Rom. 15:26; Gal. 2:10), or Pauline communities (1 Cor. 1:26–27; 2 Cor. 8:1)—belonged to the socioeconomic category of the lower stratum and

196. On this see Bammel, *TDNT* 6:906–7; Osiek, *Rich and Poor*, 24–32; Nickelsburg, "Riches, the Rich," 332–40.
197. Bammel, *TDNT* 6:906.

"the poor" in varying degrees;[198] and they experienced oppression and maltreatment by the rich and powerful in one way or another (cf. Luke 12:11–12; Acts 4:1–3; 8:1–3; 12:1–4; 2 Cor. 11:23–27; Heb. 10:32–34). Particularly, the Jewish Christians in Jerusalem were not exempt from the socioeconomic plight in Palestine and suffered from financial pressure, famine, and impoverishment (cf. Acts 11:28–30), as attested by the Pauline collection (1 Cor. 16:3; 2 Cor. 8:14; Rom. 15:26, 31; cf. Gal. 2:10.)[199] In this context, the early Jerusalem assemblies in Acts had special concerns for meeting the needs of the community members: they held all things in common and redistributed possessions to all according to one's need, to the effect that "there were no needy persons among them" (Acts 2:42–47; 4:32–37, quote at 4:34 NIV),[200] and they appointed the seven to correct inequality (or injustice?) in the community's ministry (charity) to Hellenistic widows (6:1–7), all of which indicates the presence of those with substantial means and property among them (e.g., Barnabas in 4:36–37; Ananias and Sapphira in 5:1–2). As the gospel moves beyond Jerusalem, the exemplary acts of charity of Dorcas (9:36–43) and Cornelius, a Roman centurion (10:2, 4, 31), and those of the first gentile church in Antioch are highlighted as part of their individual and collective devotion to God and his mission. The emphasis in these descriptions is not poverty itself or the poor but voluntary sharing and charity[201] in addressing the needs of the various emerging Christian communities as the fundamental mark of unity in the Holy Spirit, as God is leading the

198. Cf. L. E. Keck, "The Poor among the Saints in the New Testament," *ZNW* 56 (1965): 100–129. "The poor" or poverty was not "a technical designation" but "an actual description" of the early church (110); Stegemann and Stegemann, *Jesus Movement*, 251–316. See also Steven J. Friesen, "Injustice or God's Will?" 17–36; Steven J. Friesen, "Poverty in Pauline Studies," 323–61, as well as Longenecker, *Remember the Poor*, 220–78, particularly for economic profiles of Paul's communities. Note that although both place no elites (PS 1–3; ES 1–3, respectively) within Pauline communities, Longenecker's profiles tend to be higher (more in a middling group, ES 4) than those by Friesen (mostly in PS 5–7).

199. In his recent book, *Remember the Poor*, especially 157–206, Longenecker argues that Gal. 2:10 ("remember the poor") does not refer to the poor saints in Jerusalem but to local indigenous poor in Pauline mission areas, and therefore this text is to be distinguished from other Pauline Jerusalem collection texts. Note on p. 188: "it is important to differentiate between remembrance of the poor and the collection effort, with remembrance of the poor being the general marker of identity within communities of Jesus-followers . . . and the collection for the Jerusalem poor being a specific application of that principle."

200. For detailed discussions on these passages and their so-called primitive communalism, see, for example, S. S. Bartchy, "Community of Goods in Acts: Idealization or Social Reality?" in *The Future of Early Christianity: Essays in Honor of Helmut Koester* (ed. B. A. Pearson; Minneapolis: Fortress, 1991), 309–18; B. J. Capper, "Community of Goods in the Early Jerusalem Church," in *ANRW* 2.26.2 (ed. H. Temporini and W. Haase; Berlin: De Gruyter, 1995), 1730–74; G. Lüdemann, *Early Christianity according to the Traditions in Acts* (Minneapolis: Fortress, 1989), 60–63; Hengel, *Property and Riches*, 31–34; J. L. González, *Faith and Wealth: A History of Early Christian Ideas on the Origin, Significance, and Use of Money* (San Francisco: Harper & Row, 1990), 79–86.

201. Cf. Keck, "The Poor," 105.

unstoppable movement of Jesus followers beyond Judea and Samaria through the Spirit. In the narrative of Paul's missionary journeys in the latter half of Acts, however, there is an eclipse of a parallel movement between "church growth" and "community or individual charity for the needy." Paul's collection, which was theologically, socially, and symbolically important for Paul (as indicated in his letters), hardly receives any attention in Acts; instead, there is a parallel movement between (1) "church growth" through Paul's missions (horizontal spread of the gospel) and (2) an upward political and socioeconomic profile of Paul's audiences and community members (vertical spread of the gospel).[202] The collective concern for the poor members in the earlier chapters is transformed to individual hospitality for missionaries (e.g., Lydia in 16:15; Jason in 17:7–8; Priscilla and Aquila in 18:1–3).

Judging from the evidence in the Pauline letters (both undisputed and disputed), however, in the Pauline communities of the Greco-Roman urban setting, members were drawn predominantly from free laborers and artisans, slaves, and recent immigrants, "groups that constituted the *plebs urbana, misera ac ieiunia*"[203]—unlike Acts' portrayal. As a group, the Pauline Christians would have shared the typical anxieties and insecurities of urban plebs over their severe socioeconomic realities.[204] And Paul, whose Roman citizenship is apologetically highlighted in Acts (16:37–39; 22:25–29), mentions not his Roman citizenship but his own poverty and afflictions to defend his apostolic ministry and to highlight the spiritual riches it offers (1 Cor. 4:9–13; 2 Cor. 4:8–10; 6:10; 11:21–33).[205] At the same time, however, despite such harsh realities, a degree of (at least) moderate wealth was to be expected in the house churches founded by Paul,[206] i.e., the "middling" group of the relatively prosperous—those who could offer their places for assemblies and hospitalities for Paul and his associates and therefore act as "patrons" for the communities (e.g., Phoebe in Rom. 16:1–2; Gaius in 1 Cor. 1:14; Rom. 16:23; Philemon in Philem. 1–2).[207] The Pauline communities were not exempt from the tension between the rich and

202. For example, Proconsul Sergius Paulus in Acts 13:6–12; Dionysios the Areopagite in 17:34; not a few of the Greek men and women of high standing in 13:50; 17:4, 12. On this profile see S. Friesen, "Injustice or God's Will?," 31.

203. Meggitt, *Paul, Poverty and Survival*, 97.

204. Ibid., 99; cf. 2 Cor. 8:2.

205. The fact that Paul never mentions his Roman citizenship in his extant letters does not necessarily disprove his possession of it. On historical plausibility of his Roman citizenship, see, for example, M. Hengel, *The Pre-Christian Paul* (London: SCM, 1991), 1–17; Longenecker, *Remember the Poor*, 302–4. On Paul's downward economic mobility from the relative security prior to his Christophany, see, for example, E. A. Judge, "The Social Identity of the First Christians," *JRH* 11 (1980): 201–17; Longenecker, *Remember the Poor*, 307–10.

206. T. Hanks, "Poor, Poverty," in *ABD* (ed. D. N. Freedman; vol. 5; New York: Doubleday, 1992), 418.

207. On economic profiles in Paul's communities, including a close prosopographic survey of individuals mentioned in Pauline letters, see Longenecker, *Remember the Poor*, 220–58.

the poor, particularly surrounding the dining table, including social pretensions and prejudices (1 Cor. 1:11–12; 6:12–20; 11:17–34). Again in this context, the standard Pauline teachings are charity (good works) and hospitality for fellow believers, which are shared by the rest of the New Testament (Heb. 13:2, 16; 1 Pet. 4:9; 3 John 5–8). These teachings follow traditional Jewish piety based on the concern and activity of God and Christ: caring for the poor (Gal. 2:10); working with one's own hands as to avoid idleness and dependence (Eph. 4:28; 1 Thess. 4:11–12; 2 Thess. 3:6–12); warnings against greed (*pleonexia*) (1 Cor. 5:11; 1 Tim. 3:8; Titus 1:7); and generosity and hospitality toward others, particularly fellow believers (Rom. 12:8, 13; 1 Cor. 16:2; 2 Cor. 8:2; Eph. 4:28), rooted in Christ's own generosity (2 Cor. 8:9). Especially important for Paul was his collection for the needy saints in Jerusalem (Rom. 15:26, 31; 1 Cor. 16:3; 2 Cor. 8:14; cf. Gal. 2:10) as a demonstration of unity between Jewish and gentile congregations and therefore of the legitimacy of his apostolic ministry (to the gentiles), among other reasons.[208] In the (later) Pastoral Letters, Christians are exhorted to do "good works" (i.e., almsgiving/charity for those in need) (Titus 2:14; 3:8, *kalōn ergōn*; cf. Gal. 6:9–10, "to work the good," *ergazōmetha to agathon*), and the rich believers are especially commanded to be humble, put their hope in God rather than in the uncertainty of riches, and practice generosity (1 Tim. 6:17–18), which will result in spiritual blessing in the age to come (1 Tim. 6:19).[209] Warnings against "love of money" (*philargyria*) and "pursuing dishonest gain" (1 Pet. 5:2 NIV) are prominent for qualifications for church leadership (1 Tim. 3:3, 8; cf. 6:10; cf. Heb. 13:5a) in direct contrast to descriptions of false teachers and the people in the last days as "lovers of money" (2 Tim. 3:2, 4 NIV) and those seeking "dishonest gain" (Titus 1:11 NIV; cf. 2 Pet. 2:3, 14). In a Pauline corpus, there are further adaptations from Greco-Roman moral teachings of the time: the importance of cheerful giving (2 Cor. 9:7),[210] contentment (1 Tim. 6:6–8; cf. Heb. 13:5a), and self-sufficiency (*autarkēs*) in all circumstances (Phil. 4:11; cf. 1 Tim. 6:7–8).

In James, the theme of the rich and the poor is interwoven with James's communal concerns and eschatological outlook[211] and is strategically placed throughout the epistle (1:9–12; 2:1–7; and 5:1–6). First, in 1:9–12, James exhorts the lowly brother (*ho adelphos ho tapeinos*) to boast in his exaltation but

208. On Paul's collection for Jerusalem saints see for example: D. J. Downs, *The Offering of the Gentiles: Paul's Collection for Jerusalem in Its Chronological, Cultural, and Cultic Contexts* (*WUNT* II/248; Tübingen: Mohr Siebeck, 2008); D. Georgi, *Remembering the Poor: The History of Paul's Collection for Jerusalem* (Nashville: Abingdon, 1992).

209. For spiritual blessings in this life, see 2 Cor. 9:10–15; Phil. 4:14–20.

210. Cf. E. F. Bruck, "Ethic vs. Law: St. Paul, the Fathers of the Church and the 'Cheerful Giver' in Roman Law," *Traditio* 2 (1944): 97–114.

211. Thus R. W. Wall sees James as "Apocalyptic Paraenesis": R. W. Wall, "James as Apocalyptic Paraenesis," *Restoration Quarterly* 32 (1990): 11–22.

the rich person (*plousios*)[212] in his humiliation, for the rich will suddenly pass away like the wildflower (cf. Isa. 40:7). The contrast with the rich makes clear that the "believer who is lowly" is poor in the socioeconomic sense. With the poverty-piety tradition, the eschatological overtone is clear in the reversal of fortunes in connection with the transient nature and worthlessness of riches in the face of death and judgment (as reinforced by resemblance to Jer. 9:23–24 and allusion to Isa. 40:7). The polarity between the pious poor and the wicked rich is dramatized concretely in the community in 2:1–7. The community's partiality toward the ones "with gold rings and in fine clothes" over against the "poor" (2:1–4) prompts James to remind them that it is the poor that God has chosen to be pious and heirs of his kingdom; but the rich oppress with legal assault and persecute the very poor (the community members) God has chosen. Hence, by favoring the rich, they dishonor the poor (2:6); and the community's action of dishonoring the poor not only betrays their core faith and hope in the God of "the pious poor" but also places themselves in the ironic position of the wicked rich who will be judged by God (the identity of the rich as the outsiders becomes obvious in their blaspheming of Christ, 2:7). The most biting attack on the rich is reserved for 5:1–6. James's adaptation of the prophetic imageries and rhetorical diatribe heightens the literary vividness of the sure fall of the rich: they are hoarding their wealth whose remain will only destroy them (5:2–3b); they are laying up their treasure in the last days (5:3c) and feasting on the day of slaughter (5:5b); the cries of the defrauded poor have already reached the ears of the Lord of hosts (5:4b). Therefore, the readers need to be patient and endure the present suffering until the coming of the Lord, who will come soon as the Judge, says James (5:7–11). The pronouncement of the imminent destruction of the rich merges with the practical exhortation to the community again with God's vindication and the eschatological reversal of the members' present predicament.

In the Apocalypse of John, the "unrighteous rich" *topos* takes the form of the cosmic powers of evil, manifested chiefly in the socioeconomic and religiopolitical systems of the Roman Empire (Babylon).[213] The mighty and oppressive Babylon with her self-indulgent luxury, commerce, and earthly riches comes under the

212. The term *ho (hoi) plousios (oi)* appears three times in James (1:10; 2:6; 5:1); in the latter two occurrences it is reasonably clear that *hoi plousioi* are non-Christian outsiders of the believing community. However, there is an ongoing debate among scholars whether *ho plousios* at 1:10 is Christian ("a rich brother") or not. The interpretation of the identity of a rich person subsequently determines the tone and meaning of the "humiliation" in v. 10. I am inclined to take the view that sees *ho plousios* as a non-Christian outsider in light of James's consistency in use of the term and of ironic indictment in all three passages, and the letter's theological, social, and literary context. For a detailed discussion, including the history of scholarship on this topic, see G. M. Stulac, "Who Are 'The Rich' in James," *Presbyterion* 16, no. 2 (1990): 89–102.

213. For ideological analysis of wealth imagery in John's Apocalypse, see Royalty, *Streets of Heaven*. For a detailed study of the Revelation's economic critique of Rome, see R. Bauckham, "The Economic Critique of Rome in Revelation 18," in *Images of Empire* (ed. L. Alexander;

divine woe and cataclysmic judgment (chaps. 17–18) whereas the new Jerusalem, "the focus of eschatological hope,"[214] adorned with magnificent wealth (jasper, crystal, pure gold, pearls, etc.), is reserved for those who are afflicted, persecuted, and yet persevere through the tribulation and injustice of evil powers of Rome/ Babylon, the group that corresponds to the "righteous poor" (21:1–26; cf. 2:9). At the judgment, these "righteous poor" will live in the new heaven and new earth as the place of abundance (22:2), and they will worship the Lord God Almighty, the righteous judge, in the heavenly throne room characterized by the same kind of stunning material opulence as the new Jerusalem (4:3–6).

1.4. The Geographic Spread and Social Situations of Christian Communities in the Second and Third Centuries

Before we delve into the developing understanding of and attitude toward wealth and poverty and their impact on Christian identity formation in subsequent chapters, we should survey the basic social composition and development of Christian communities in the second and third centuries. Despite relatively meager evidence that hardly warrants any certainty, we can observe and measure the spread of Christianity to a reasonable extent. In terms of its geographic spread, this time period marks a watershed in the history of Christianity.[215] No longer an insignificant religious movement from Palestine, the Christian church in this period witnessed significant external and internal growth. With the end of the second Jewish War (135 CE), the church experienced a critical stage of separation from Judaism,[216] and outside observers became increasingly aware of its discrete identity and claims. This ushered in the era of a more distinctively "gentile Christianity," and it made a substantial (though uneven) growth especially in the urban centers of the Greek-speaking world.

Building on the foundations laid in the first century, the provinces of Asia Minor took the lead in this advance as Christianity continued to gain a significant foothold throughout the inland and west coast even up to the Black Sea, as attested in Pliny's letters and Lucian's satires[217] as well as the critics of

---

JSOTSup 12; Sheffield, UK: Sheffield Academic Press, 1991), 47–90; see also J. S. Perry, "Critiquing the Excess of Empire: A Synkrisis of John of Patmos and Dio of Prusa," *JSNT* 29 (2007): 473–96.

214. Royalty, *Streets of Heaven*, 71.

215. I can only briefly chart the Christian spread here; for fuller treatments see, for example, R. Mullen, *The Expansion of Christianity: A Gazetteer of Its First Three Centuries* (VCSup 69; Leiden: Brill, 2004); M. Edwards, "Christianity, AD 70–192," in *The Crisis of the Empire AD 193–337* (vol. 12 of *The Cambridge Ancient History*; 2nd ed.; Cambridge: Cambridge University Press, 2005), 573–88; G. Clarke, "Christianity in the First Three Centuries: Third-Century Christianity," in *Crisis of the Empire*, 589–616.

216. This does not imply no interaction between Jews and Christians; they continued to interact with each other well into the fourth century, though not necessarily in cordial terms.

217. Pliny, *Ep.* 10.96; Lucian, *Alexander* 25; *Peregrinus*.

the New Prophecy that spread from Phrygia.[218] Both literary and epigraphic sources report Christian presence in Galatia, Lydia, Cappadocia, and Pontus.[219] In Bithynia, at the time of the Great Persecution in the early fourth century, both Eusebius and Lactantius testified to a significant presence of Christians in the imperial service (civil servants, soldiers, eunuchs, and slaves) as a formidable target of pagan polemics.[220] In Greece, Athens, as well as Corinth, under Bishop Dionysius saw solid ecclesiastical development.[221] In Alexandria, while Walter Bauer presumed the earliest Christian community as a gnostic mission (of Basilides and Valentinus) rather than that of "orthodox" Christianity, it seems more likely that Alexandrian Christianity came from a mission from Palestinian Jewish Christianity.[222] Around 190 CE Bishop Demetrius was leading an already sizable "orthodox" congregation, and the catechetical school led first by Pantaenus and then Clement attracted a substantial number of educated Greeks. Throughout the third century, Alexandria boasted an impressive chain of Christian teachers such as Origen, Dionysius, and Peter of Alexandria, who addressed the relatively well-educated and prosperous audience. By the late third century, Christianity penetrated into smaller towns in middle and upper Egypt—as evidenced by the production of Coptic Christian texts and the Oxyrhynchus papyri. In Palestine, while Jerusalem still enjoyed its status as the site of Christian origins, Caesarea became a prominent locus of Christian scholarship with Origen's sojourn and Pamphilus's library and school.[223] In Syria, while promising mission work among the upper-stratum pagans continued in Antioch under Serapion, Christianity spread to and became well established in Nisibis and Edessa, which became centers of Syriac Christianity, and then further to Persia and east of the Euphrates.[224]

In the West, Christianity advanced further in Italy, Gaul, Spain, and North Africa. The greatest growth took place in Rome with the rise of the hierarchical development and with the flowering of divergent Christian teachings. The church in Rome attracted prominent Christian teachers of every camp, especially from the East, including Cerdo, Marcion, and Valentinus, on the

218. Eusebius, *HE* 5.16.
219. See Mullen, *Expansion of Christianity*, 83–132.
220. Eusebius, *HE* 8.6; 9.9; Lactantius, *Mort.* 14.3–4; 15.1–2.
221. See Eusebius, *HE* 4.23; cf. Origen, *Contra Celsum* 3.30, a "meek and quiet" community in Athens ca. 250.
222. D. Brakke, "The East (2): Egypt and Palestine," in *The Oxford Handbook of Early Christian Studies* (ed. S. A. Harvey and D. G. Hunter; Oxford: Oxford University Press, 2008), 347. Contra K. Baus, *History of the Church* (ed. H. Jedin and H. Dolan; vol. 1 of *From the Apostolic Community to Constantine*; New York: Seabury, 1980), 208; see also W. Bauer, *Orthodoxy and Heresy in Earliest Christianity* (London: SCM, 1972).
223. Clarke, "Christianity in the First Three Centuries," 603; cf. Mullen, *Expansion of Christianity*, 22–33.
224. On Syrian Christianity, see H. J. W. Drijvers, *East of Antioch: Studies in Early Syriac Christianity* (London: Variorum, 1984).

one hand, and Polycarp, Justin, Tatian, and Hegesippus, on the other. Further-more, Eusebius records that as early as in the reign of Commodus (late second century), "many of those who at Rome were famous for wealth and family turned to their own salvation with all their house and with all their kin."[225] At least by the mid-third century, if not the early third century, the Roman church apparently maintained separate "Christian" burial grounds (see below), and around the same time Bishop Cornelius provided a much-quoted "statistics" for the church, suggesting a well-organized and broad-based community with substantial resources at its disposal: "there are forty-six presbyters, seven deacons, seven sub-deacons, forty-two acolytes, fifty-two exorcists, readers and doorkeepers, above fifteen hundred widows and persons in distress, all of whom are supported by the grace and loving-kindness of the Master."[226] Cornelius also reported on a council of sixty Italian bishops in Rome in 251.[227] Around 270 the Neoplatonist critic Porphyry lamented the rampant spread of the "disease" of Christianity in the imperial city, claiming that it had dissipated Aesculapius's healing powers.[228] In Gaul a well-established Christian commu-nity in Lyons and Vienne is attested to in the famous account of martyrdom (177 CE)[229] and by the work of Bishop Irenaeus, who also reports churches in Germany and Iberia.[230] By the mid-third century, according to Cyprian, bishoprics were established beyond Lyons, such as at Arles and other towns;[231] and by the time of the Great Persecution in 303, there were church buildings (*conventicula*) that Constantius pulled down under Diocletian's first edict.[232] As for Christian communities in Spain, Cyprian mentions establishment of several bishoprics;[233] and around the wake of the Great Persecution, repre-sentatives from thirty-seven Spanish Christian communities held a regional council at Elvira (Iliberris).[234] In North Africa, Carthage was a main center for Christianity, where a substantial number of Christians was also evidenced by the extensive catechetical and literary work of Tertullian (ca. 200 CE) and equally impressive leadership and works of Cyprian (ca. 250 CE), with elabo-rate social organization and ecclesiastical hierarchy for charitable support. Christianity was also growing in Numidia and Tunisia, and around 220 CE Bishop Agrippinus could already summon seventy bishops to a local synod.[235] In the West, North Africa and Rome were the only areas in this period that

225. Eusebius, *HE* 5.21.1.
226. Eusebius, *HE* 6.43.2.
227. Eusebius, *HE* 6.43.2.
228. Theodoret of Cyrrhus, *De curatione Graec. affect.* 12 (PG 83.1151).
229. Eusebius, *HE* 5.1; *Mart. Lyons.*
230. *Haer.* 1.10.2.
231. Cyprian, *Ep.* 68.1.1; 2.1.
232. Clarke, "Christianity in the First Three Centuries," 591.
233. Cyprian, *Ep.* 67.
234. Clarke, "Christianity in the First Three Centuries," 592–93.
235. Cyprian, *Ep.* 71.4.

could be compared with the mission and vitality of Asia Minor, Egypt, and Syria in the East.[236]

In terms of the numbers, recent studies provided a rough framework estimating the number of Christians to be about 40,000 in 150 CE (0.07 percent), about 760,000 by 225 CE (1.27 percent), and about 6,300,000 in the empire by 300 CE—10.5 percent of the total population of the empire.[237] While scholars vary somewhat in estimating Christian population up to the time of Constantine, and although the absolute number of Christians still might be relatively insignificant,[238] this period marked the first leap of significant growth in Christianity, particularly in Rome, Carthage, and the urban centers of the eastern Mediterranean,[239] confirmed by its literary and nonliterary sources.

In terms of the social advancement of Christianity, as already mentioned, some major missionary activities were directed to the members of the upper strata during this time, especially in Alexandria, Syria, Rome, and North Africa; and converts to Christianity came from several social spectra. Despite pagan critic Celsus's scorn that Christianity attracted only the uneducated, slaves, outcasts, and women,[240] the Christian social makeup resembled in fact the typical social pyramid of the Roman Empire (i.e., a vast majority in the lower strata), with a growing minority from elite and subelite "middling" groups, especially in the third century. Both literary and epigraphic sources mention community membership of artisans,[241] workers,[242] businesspeople

236. Cf. Baus, *History of the Church*, 1:210.

237. These figures are based on the imperial population of sixty million and on a projected growth rate of 40 percent per decade until 350 CE in R. Stark, *The Rise of Christianity* (Princeton, NJ: Princeton University Press, 1996), 5–13; K. Hopkins, "Christian Number and Its Implications," *JECS* 6, no. 2 (1998): 192–95.

238. It usually ranges from 7 percent to 12 percent around 300 CE, 10 percent being a sort of hinge point. For various estimates and analyses of Christian numbers, see R. MacMullen, *The Second Church: Popular Christianity AD 200–400* (Atlanta: SBL, 2009), 102–4, 173n8; J. Bodel, "From *Columbaria* to Catacombs: Collective Burial in Pagan and Christian Rome," in *Commemorating the Dead: Texts and Artifacts in Context: Studies of Roman, Jewish, and Christian Burials* (ed. L. Brink and D. Green; Berlin: Walter de Gruyter, 2008), 183–84; T. M. Finn, "Mission and Expansion," in *The Early Christian World* (ed. P. Esler; vol. 1; London: Routledge, 2000), 295–96.

239. Cf. J. Bodel, "From *Columbaria* to Catacombs," 184, with Christians amounting to 20–27 percent of the urban population by the Diocletian Persecution in the early fourth century.

240. Origen, *Cels.* 3.44, 55.

241. *Did.* 12.3; Justin, *2 Apol.* 10; W. Tabbernee, *Montanist Inscriptions and Testamonia: Epigraphic Sources Illustrating the History of Montanism* (Patristic Monograph Series 16; Macon, GA: Mercer University Press, 1997), 223–25, fig. 33 (cobbler); G. J. Johnson, *Early-Christian Epitaphs from Anatolia* (SBL Texts and Translations 35; Early Christian Literature Series 8; Atlanta, GA: Scholars Press, 1995), 72–73, no. 2.19 (shoemaker); 106–7, no. 3.14 (wood carver); 108–9, no. 3.16 (goldsmith).

242. *1 Clem.* 34.1; Johnson, *Early-Christian Epitaphs from Anatolia*, 108–9, no. 3.17 (orchard keeper).

and traders,[243] soldiers,[244] lawyers,[245] and even city councilors (of small cities);[246] many of those mentioned might be freedmen.[247] The emergence of the refined Christian apologists in the late second century points to not only development of Christian literary culture but (at least a beginning of) Christian penetration into the educated rank of the society, which disturbed and threatened the conservative pagan elites; philosophers such as Celsus and Porphyry took up Christianity as a worthy target for both their philosophical and social polemic. Furthermore, Christians emerge quickly in official ranks in available sources. In the mid-third century, Emperor Valerian's rescript against Christian communities first targeted the high clergy and Christian assembly (257 CE); then he ordered (258 CE) their execution and the execution of all the *honestiores* (*senatores vero et egregii viri et equites Romani*) who would insist on remaining Christians even after the loss of their status and property. Furthermore, matrons (*matronae*) and members of the imperial household (*Caesariani*) would be dispossessed of their property; and the former would be exiled and the latter would be reduced to slavery.[248] During this period, particularly prominent were the conversions of high-status women,[249] Christians' remarkable orientation to literary texts and activities, and their increasing financial and organizational capacity, which could indicate some fair number of Christians from the top 10 percent of Roman society.[250] Although overall Christian writings during this time, still written predominantly in Greek, were not high literature, they "do reflect access to literacy, familiarity with rhetorical convention and hermeneutical practice, and general affinities with contemporary cultures of performance and spectacle."[251] In addition, by the

243. *Mand.* 3.5; 10.1.4–5; *Sim.* 4.5, 7; 8.8.1–2; 9.20.1; Johnson, *Early-Christian Epitaphs from Anatolia*, 105, no. 3.13 ("a dealer in general merchandise").

244. E.g., *Acts Maximillian*; *Acts Marcellus*; *Mart. Julius*; *Mart. Dasius.*

245. Johnson, *Early-Christian Epitaphs from Anatolia*, 135, no. 4.12.

246. Tabbernee, *Montanist Inscriptions and Testamonia*, 229–31, fig. 34; Johnson, *Early-Christian Epitaphs from Anatolia*, 82–83, no. 3.2; 84–85, no. 3.3; 86–87, no. 3.4; 88–89, no. 3.6; 90–91, no. 3.7.

247. E.g., Tabbernee, *Montanist Inscriptions and Testamonia*, 124–26, fig. 16; cf. Stegemann and Stegemann, *Jesus Movement*, 315.

248. Cyprian, *Ep.* 80.1.

249. On the topic of prominence of upper-stratum women, see further J. Bremmer, "Why Did Early Christianity Attract Upper Class Women?" in *Fructus Centesimus: Mélanges G. J. M. Bartelink* (ed. A. Bastiaensen, A. Hilhorst, and C. H. Kneepkens; Instrumenta Patristica 19; Dordrecht: Kluwer, 1989), 37–48; and Stegemann and Stegemann, *Jesus Movement*, 389–95. Cf. A. Harnack, *The Mission and Expansion of Christianity in the First Three Centuries* (trans. J. Moffatt; 2 vols; New York: G. P. Putnam's Sons, 1908; repr., Gloucester, MA: Peter Smith, 1972), 217–39; Stark, *Rise of Christianity*, 95–128.

250. Cf. Hopkins, "Christian Number and Its Implications," 207–9; H. Y. Gamble, *Books and Readers in the Early Church: A History of Early Christian Texts* (New Haven: Yale University Press, 1995), 1–41, esp. 4, 10.

251. V. Burrus and R. Lyman, "Introduction: Shifting Focus of History," in *Late Ancient Christianity* (ed. V. Burrus; vol. 2 of *A People's History of Christianity*; Minneapolis: Fortress, 2005), 8.

end of the third century, Christian presence in the army was significant enough to prompt Dicoletian's purging of Christians in the military.[252] His first edict at the wake of the Great Persecution ordered that, in addition to confiscation of sacred books and church valuables, Christians with social status and judicial privileges (*honestiores*) be reduced to the status of *humiliores* and that Christian freedmen be reenslaved.[253] Furthermore, a growing number of Christian martyrs were noted for their high rank and positions especially during the Great Persecution.[254] It is also telling that around the same time the canons of the regional council of Elvira, Spain, prescribed behaviors of landowners (*can.* 40, 49), slave owners (*can.* 5, 41), civic magistrates (*duumvir*; *can.* 56), and even provincial high priests of the imperial cult (*flamen*; *can.* 2, 4), which indicates that those most likely belonged to the local Christian communities. While we should be careful not to exaggerate Christian penetration into the conservative *honestiores* during this period, it is important to recognize Christianity's appeal to a socially mobile group of people and the rank and file of Roman society, and also the upward social mobility of Christians and consequently increasing social gaps and tensions among individuals within Christian communities (see chapter 4).

The corresponding emergence of Christian material culture and "corporate property" in the third century also attests to changing Christian social situations. According to a document ascribed to Hippolytus, Bishop Zephyrinus of Rome (ca. 199–217) handed over to a deacon Callistus (Hippolytus's episcopal nemesis, whom he scorned for being a former slave) the administration of the subterranean cemetery with underground galleries on the Via Appia that especially served to bury the poorest members of the Roman Christian communities (known as the Catacomb of S. Callisto).[255] Considering the long-standing legal restriction on corporate ownership of property, particularly in reference to burial sites, and also the common Roman custom of appointing overseers to manage private tomb properties, this site, at least initially, seems

252. See for example, *Acts Maximilian*; *Acts Marcellus*; *Mart. Julius*.

253. Lactantius, *Mort.* 13.1; Eusebius, *HE* 8.2.4; *Mart. Pal.* 1.1.

254. E.g., Marinus, "honoured by high rank in the army and distinguished besides by birth and wealth" (Eusebius, *HE* 7.15.1); Philoromus in the imperial administration at Alexandria and Phileas, bishop of the church of the Thmuites (Eusebius, *HE* 8.9.6–8); Adauctus, "a man of illustrious Italian birth" who held the imperial magistracy and ministry of finance (Eusebius, *HE* 8.11.2); Domnina, an Antiochene woman well-known for "wealth, birth and sound judgment" and other Antiochene maidens "famous by birth" and "distinguished for their manner of life" (Eusebius, *HE* 8.12.3; 8.12.5); a Nichomedian man (probably Euethius), "highly honoured as the world counts pre-eminence" (Eusebius, *HE* 8.5.1); Agapê, Irenê, Chionê, Thessalonian virgins who "abandoned their native city, their family, property, and possessions because of their love of God" (*Mart. Agapê* 1); cf. in the late second and early third centuries: Vivia Perpetua, a North African matron of noble family (*Mart. Perp.* 2.1); Apollonius, famous "for his education and philosophy" (Eusebius, *HE* 5.21.2).

255. *Ref.* 9.12.14.

to refer to individual private property utilized by the Christian community in Rome for the poor, rather than corporate property of the church.[256] This may be the case of other literary evidence of "corporate ownership" of real estate by the church elsewhere in the third century. Around 203 CE, Tertullian in Carthage reports existence of "Christian cemeteries" (*areae Christianorum*) that are known to the pagans as Christian property.[257] In Alexandria Origen also mentions the existence of collective cemeteries (ca. 200–230 CE).[258] For the Catacomb of S. Callisto, Peter Lampe conjectures its practical (but not legal) transition to "community property" with the burial of bishops here around 235 CE.[259] Fabian here buried his two predecessors Anteros (235) and Pontianus (230–35), and in the site popularly known as the "Crypt of the Popes," six more bishops were buried in this catacomb throughout the third century: Fabian (235–50), Cornelius (251–55), Lucius (253–54), Eutychian (275–83), Caius (283–96), and Eusebius (310).[260] While Valerian's rescript against Christians specifically prohibits Christian assembly in their cemeteries,[261] Gallienus in his edict of toleration (260 CE) expressly orders restoration of both their worship places and cemeteries, thus affirming the property rights of Christian communities.[262] In the early fourth century, the Edict of Toleration (313 CE) by Constantine and Licinius distinguishes the corporate property belonging to the community from the private one (*ad ius corporis eorum id est ecclesiarum, non hominum singulorum, pertinenta*) and proclaims restoration of ecclesiastical property, assembly places, and cemeteries that had existed before Diocletian's persecutions.[263] On the walls of these cemeteries we also have the

256. P. Lampe, *From Paul to Valentinus: Christians at Rome in the First Two Centuries* (trans. M. Steinhauser; ed. M. D. Johnson; Minneapolis: Fortress, 2003), 370–71; Bodel, "From *Columbaria* to Catacombs," 203–5, 230–31; *contra* G. F. Snyder, *Ante Pacem: Archaeological Evidence of Church Life before Constantine* (Macon, GA: Mercer University Press, 1985, 1991), 85–87; and V. F. Nicolai, F. Bisconti, and D. Mazzoleni, *The Christian Catacombs of Rome: History, Decoration, Inscriptions* (2nd ed.; Regensburg: Schnell & Steiner, 2002), 13–17. For a possibility of Zephyrinus as the owner of the cemetery, see Lampe, *From Paul to Valentinus*, 26–27; *Liber Pontificalis* 1.139.

257. *Scap.* 3.1; cf. *Apol.* 39.5–6.

258. *Hom. Jer.* 4.3.16.

259. Lampe, *From Paul to Valentinus*, 371.

260. Snyder, *Ante Pacem*, 86. Callistus himself was buried in the Catacomb of Calepodio on the Via Aurelia.

261. *Acta Cypriani* 1.1; cf. Dionysius's blame of Macarianus, Valerian's "minister over the imperial accounts," in Eusebius, *HE* 7.10.6.

262. Eusebius, *HE* 7.13.

263. Eusebius, *HE* 10.5.11: "And inasmuch as these same Christians had not only those places at which it was their wont to assemble, but also are known to have had others, belonging not to individuals among them, but to the lawful property of their corporation, that is, of the Christians, all these, under the provisions of the law set forth above, thou wilt give orders to be restored without any question whatsoever to these same Christians, that is, to their corporation and assembly"; also Lactantius, *Mort.* 48.8.9: "Churches received by gift and any other places formerly belonging to Christians to be restored. Owners may apply for compensation."

first substantial appearance of Christian art and funerary symbols that began to define their cultural identity.[264]

Speaking of assembly places, Christians in the second century continued to meet in localized household settings, in the homes of Christian owners and/or patrons where communal meals (*agapē*) were shared. The earliest and unchallenged archaeological example of the *domus ecclesiae*, i.e., a kind of church building resulting from a partial architectural adaptation of certain space for worship within private domestic structures,[265] is that of Dura-Europos in Syria.[266] Dated about 240 CE, this two-story structure had a large rectangular assembly room made out of two smaller ones and a baptistery, connected through a room for catechumens, all linked to a courtyard. It ceased to be a private home but became a church building practically belonging to a local Christian community; with the emergence of separate church buildings and the practical difficulties of sharing meals in those settings, there was also a gradual separation of the stylized eucharistic liturgy from the earlier casual form of communal dining.[267] Moreover, starting in the 260s, the Greek word *ekklēsiai* began to be used to refer to both Christian communities and their physical structures[268] as attested by a pagan critic Porphyry in criticizing Christians building a splendid structure in Syria[269] and also by Eusebius, in describing showy, beautiful, and imposing church buildings in "every city," such as in Caesarea and Nicomedia in the late third and early fourth centuries.[270] As mentioned earlier, one of the first acts against Christians by Diocletian was destroying church buildings throughout the empire, including the one facing the imperial palace in Nicomedia.[271]

This brief survey of the social makeup and situations of pre-Constantinian Christianity, along with an overview of Greco-Roman and Jewish notions of and approaches to wealth and poverty, provides an important backdrop for the early Christian treatment of wealth and poverty in relation to their developing theology, practices, and institutionalization in subsequent chapters. Numerical

264. Snyder, *Ante Pacem*, 163–65. On the origin of Christian art see, for example, L. V. Rutgers, *Subterranean Rome: In Search of the Roots of Christianity in the Catacombs of the Eternal City* (Leuven: Peteers, 2000), 82–117; J. Elsner, *Imperial Rome and Christian Triumph: The Art of the Roman Empire AD 100–450* (Oxford History of Art; Oxford: Oxford University Press, 1998), 251–59.

265. On *domus ecclesiae*, see L. M. White, *Building God's Houses in the Roman World: Architectural Adaptation among Pagans, Jews, and Christians* (vol. 1 of *The Social Origins of Christian Architecture*; Valley Forge, PA: Trinity Press International, 1990), 111–23.

266. On the "house church" in Dura-Europos, see White, *Building God's Houses*, 111–20; MacMullen, *Second Church*, 9; Snyder, *Ante Pacem*, 68–71.

267. White, *Building God's Houses*, 120.

268. MacMullen, *Second Church*, 9.

269. *Adv. Christianos* fr. 76 in Macarius Magnes 4.21, quoted in Lactantius, *Mort.* 12.3–4; Eusebius, *HE* 7.30.8–9.

270. E.g., Eusebius, *HE* 8.1.2–5; 8.2.1–4; *Mart. Pal.* 11.28.

271. Lactantius, *Mort.* 12; see also Eusebius, *Mart. Pal.* 1.5.2; *Vit. Const.* 2.2.

growth, increasing penetration into the upper echelon of Roman society, and the emergence of a distinct material culture and collective property by Christians during this time period meant that Christians began to settle in as permanent citizens of the empire, not just to pass through the alien world as temporary sojourners. They correspondingly dealt with growing social gaps within their local communities as they struggled to keep the eschatological hope alive and relevant to the changing reality. On the one hand, the eschatological language and framework still provided a dominant worldview for early Christians; on the other hand, Christians of this period made practical moves and began to establish their place in economic and social arenas as though they expected to stay for a while. In the next chapter, we will consider how this seemingly paradoxical balancing act between being in the world yet not of the world in terms of socioeconomic teachings and practices would develop and play out, i.e., how understanding and practices of wealth and poverty would be affected by eschatological vision and expectations.

2

‍>‍<‍>‍<‍>‍<‍>‍<‍>‍<‍>‍<‍>‍<‍>‍<‍>‍<‍>‍<‍>‍<‍>‍<‍>‍<‍>‍<‍>‍<‍>‍<‍>‍<‍>‍<

Wealth, Poverty, and Eschatology

This chapter examines the extent to and ways in which eschatology permeated and penetrated the specific issue of wealth and poverty and the tension between the rich and the poor, one of the major social challenges in the early Christian communities. As the patristic writers responded to the issues surrounding attitudes toward wealth, they consistently resorted to eschatological language and paradigm to paint "a comprehensive picture of what is wrong and why, and of how life ought to be organized"[1] toward the ultimate salvation and judgment of individuals and communities. First I will address terminologies and a functional relationship between eschatology and its social and ethical dimensions in early Christianity; then I will deal with a few major related areas of eschatological concern with regard to wealth and poverty: (1) how the future visions of the new age and its attendant judgment and woes enhanced the material understanding of divine blessings and curses; (2) how the idea of the divine judgment on the rich and the poor functioned as the basis for the right conduct of the rich; and, finally, (3) how the eschatological dualism of this world and the other world shaped moral paraenesis in the dualism of earthly and heavenly riches.

2.1. Patristic Eschatology and Ethics

Eschatology, broadly understood as the study or doctrine of last things, refers to the entire range of beliefs and notions concerning the end of history and final destiny of humanity and the world. Apocalypticism, a specific kind of

1. W. A. Meeks, *The First Urban Christians: The Social World of the Apostle Paul* (New Haven: Yale University Press, 1983), 173.

eschatological belief, holds that the end (eschaton), which characteristically includes some sort of crisis/conflict, judgment, and vindication, is imminent.[2] The life in this present age, imperfect and impermanent, will be brought to an end in which the sovereign God will triumph over evil, judge the righteous and the wicked, and make all things new.[3] Ancient Jews in the exile and under the Greek and Roman occupations looked forward to the end where God's kingdom would be established; and early Christians inherited, transformed, and appropriated for their own purpose the Jewish eschatological expectations of the prophetic and apocalyptic traditions of the Second Temple period. With a conviction in the life, death, and resurrection of Jesus Christ, early Christians, both Jews and gentiles, believed that the eschaton invaded the present age and that they were indeed living in the last days, in which God's kingdom would be ushered in. With a belief in the imminent return of Christ (*parousia*), they looked forward to the final judgment where God through Christ would vindicate the righteous and punish sinners. In the pre-Constantinian era, eschatological hopes and concerns (both apocalyptic and nonapocalyptic) were still strong within various Christian communities in varying degrees and forms. Millennialism, or chiliasm, is the belief in an earthly millennial reign (not necessarily a literal one thousand years, though this is implicit in the meaning) of Christ the Messiah after his return and the resurrection of the just, followed by the final judgment and the ultimate disposition of humanity in heaven or hell. This view expected that the vindication of the righteous entailed the millennial period of peace, justice, and blessedness in this world.[4] Amillennialism, or nonchiliasm, coexisting with millennialism early on and just as fervent as millennialism in eschatological fervor, held the belief in an eschatological return of Christ for the resurrection of the dead and final judgment, followed by eternal life or eternal punishment, without any intervening

2. Cf. E. Ferguson, "Millennial Expectations in Christian Eschatology: Ancient and Medieval Views," in *Apocalypticism and Millennialism: Shaping a Believer's Church Eschatology for the Twenty-First Century* (ed. L. L. Johns; Studies in the Believers Church Tradition; Kitchener, Ontario: Pandora, 2000), 128; B. McGinn, "Apocalypticism and Violence: Aspects of Their Relation in Antiquity and the Middle Ages," in *Scripture and Pluralism: Reading the Bible in the Religiously Plural Worlds of the Middle Ages and Renaissance* (ed. T. J. Heffernan and T. E. Berman; Leiden: Brill, 2005), 209. On definitions of eschatology, apocalypticism, and millenarianism, see also R. Landes, "Lest the Millennium Be Fulfilled: Apocalyptic Expectations and the Pattern of Western Chronography, 100–800 CE," in *The Use and Abuse of Eschatology in the Middle Ages* (ed. W. Verbeke, D. Verheist, and A. Welkenhuysen; Leuven: Leuven University Press, 1988), 205–8.

3. For an overview of patristic eschatology, see B. E. Daley, *The Hope of the Early Church: A Handbook of Patristic Eschatology* (Peabody, MA: Hendrickson, 2003); and C. E. Hill, *Regnum Caelorum: Patterns of Future Hope in Early Christianity* (2nd ed.; Grand Rapids: Eerdmans, 2001).

4. E. Ferguson, *Early Christians Speak: Faith and Life in the First Three Centuries* (vol. 2; Abilene, TX: Abilene Christian University Press, 2002), 338; see also Hill, *Regnum Caelorum*, 5. Representatives include Papias, Justin Martyr, Irenaeus, Tertullian, Commodianus, Novatian, Victorinus, Methodius, and Lactantius. For the treatment of each, see Hill, *Regnum Caelorum*, 21–44.

earthly, golden age.[5] Millennial eschatology, following an earlier Jewish (and Greco-Roman) eschatology, expected that at death all souls, including those of the righteous, would remain in the underworld (hades/Sheol/Inferi) until the resurrection; the millennial kingdom then would prepare the resurrected righteous for God's glory in the eternal heavenly kingdom. In contrast, amillennial eschatology believed that at death the souls of the righteous would go directly to the presence of Christ and of God (paradise); and it regarded the millennial kingdom as rather anticlimactic and superfluous. Regardless of different nuances and understandings of the stages of the eschaton, however, for early Christians, the end (which is the beginning of the new era) was not only the restoration of the pristine past and the *telos* of history, but also the fulfillment of future hope for the righteous in a perfect, bountiful, and just world ruled by God. The eschatological vision for the perfect world to come might encompass a messianic figure, millennial kingdom, heavenly paradise, defeat of the Antichrist, cosmic conflicts and tribulations, cataclysmic events, or apocalyptic transformations veiled in mysterious symbols, images, and code words. Regardless of the varieties of the eschatological vision, it created an alternative reality by which the present world should be perceived and understood, and it projected the hope for ultimate judgment into this world.

Eschatology in the pre-Constantine period, then, carried significant social and moral implications for the corporate lives of early Christian communities that shared that general vision. It provided a social and moral critique and judgment on the present society and status quo (by which they felt disenfranchised or marginalized in one way or another), on the one hand, and put forth an alternative vision and reality of the other world, on the other.[6] It not only created a Christian identity and symbolic universe distinct from the dominant world but also connected this unique sense of group identity and solidarity to the particular behaviors within the community and vis-à-vis the outsiders. For instance, the eschatological scenario of the *Didache* (16.3–8) with a double call to be vigilant and to assemble frequently (16.1–2) functions as a warn-

5. Ferguson, *Early Christians Speak*, 338; Hill, *Regnum Caelorum*, 5–6. Representatives include some of the Apostolic Fathers (e.g., Clement of Rome and *Hermas*), Athenagoras, *Ascension of Isaiah*, *Acts of Thomas*, some of the martyr acts (e.g., *Martyrdom of Polycarp* and *Letter of Vienne and Lyons*), the Montanists, Hippolytus, Clement of Alexandria, Origen, Dionysius of Alexandria, and Cyprian. For the treatment of each, see Hill, *Regnum Caelorum*, 75–201.

6. See, for example, Tertullian, *Apol.* 47.12; *Pat.* 7; *Mart.* 2.5–6; and Lactantius's sharp critique of the Tetrarchy in *Mort.* 7.3 and *Inst.* 7.24.7–8. The words of George W. Nickelsburg on the social aspects of *1 Enoch* are instructive here, "Social Aspects of Palestinian Jewish Apocalypticism," in *Apocalypticism in the Mediterranean World and the Near East* (ed. D. Hellholm; 2nd ed.; Tübingen: Mohr Siebeck, 1989), 645: "In their *response* to this setting of alienation, members of apocalyptic movements create a new symbolic universe that replaces the one dominant in the social system responsible for the alienation. The response of apocalyptic eschatology allows the community to maintain a sense of identity and a vision of their ultimate vindication in the face of social structures and historical events that deny that identity and the plausibility of that vision."

ing to its Jewish Christian community to reinforce righteous living expected in this present age for the retribution at the end of time.[7] And the second-century apologists, in response to the pagan charges of Christian immorality, frequently based the superiority of Christian morality on the Christian hope for eternal life and resurrection, and on God's eschatological judgment: "it is alike impossible for the wicked . . . and the virtuous to escape the notice of God, and . . . everyone goes to eternal punishment or salvation in accordance with the character of his acts. If all people knew this, no one would choose wickedness even for a while."[8] Characteristically, the patristic eschatological emphases were influenced by and responded to practical conflicts, issues, and dilemmas in the life of a believer and the community—such as the conflicts between the rich and the poor.[9] In so doing, patristic eschatology linked ethical behaviors in this world to the final judgment and salvation of God. Whether early Christians understood the *parousia* literally or figuratively, and despite the fact that the imminent *parousia* was apparently delayed,[10] early Christians "live[d] in a community of corporate thought and action befitting those who were called to the superabundant society of the future."[11] Therefore, "various elements of early Christian ethics can best be understood as efforts to capture in the present the conditions of the future."[12] Now we turn to the first main issue of the chapter: material visions of the new age and divine judgment.

2.2. The New Age, Judgment, and Material Kingdom

The writings of the millennialists during this period consistently understand the future messianic age for the resurrected as the time of abundance and

7. For a helpful comprehensive study on the *Didache*, see for instance H. van de Sandt and D. Flusser, *The Didache: Its Jewish Sources and Its Place in Early Judaism and Christianity* (Assen: Royal Van Corgum; Minneapolis: Fortress, 2002); K. Niederwimmer, *The Didache: A Commentary* (trans. L. M. Maloney; Hermeneia; Minneapolis: Fortress, 1998); J. A. Draper, ed., *The Didache in Modern Research* (Arbeiten zur Geschichte des antiken Judentums und des Urchristentums 37; Leiden: Brill, 1996).

8. Justin, *1 Apol.* 12.1–2; see also Aristides, *Apol.* 15; Athenagoras, *Legatio* 33.1–3; *De resurrectione* 18.1–2, 4–5: "Each man will be examined in these matters individually, and reward or punishment will be distributed in proportion to each for lives lived well or badly."

9. E.g., *The Shepherd of Hermas, 1 Clement*, and the *Didache*.

10. Note D. E. Aune's point that "awareness of the delay of the Parousia has in no demonstrable way muted, altered, or transformed imminent eschatological expectations [in early Christianity]" and that "the expectation of the future Parousia was functionally drawn into the present experience of early Christians," in "The Significance of the Delay of the Parousia for Early Christianity," in *Current Issues in Biblical and Patristic Interpretation* (ed. G. F. Hawthorne; Grand Rapids: Eerdmans, 1975), 102, 107.

11. R. C. Petry, *Christian Eschatology and Social Thought* (Nashville: Abingdon, 1956), 77.

12. J. G. Gager, *Kingdom and Community: The Social World of Early Christianity* (Englewood Cliffs, NJ: Prentice-Hall, 1975), 49–50.

bounty. One of the earliest proponents of the millennium, Papias, describes the wonders of the messianic kingdom of renovated earth with vines, grapes, and wheat producing ten thousand–fold and "all other fruits, seeds, and grasses" producing "in like proportions"; moreover, "all animals using for their food what they receive from the earth will become peaceful and harmonious with one another and be subject to human beings with all obedience."[13] This prodigious productivity of the messianic kingdom, which hearkens back to the creation, is also envisioned by Irenaeus in *Against Heresies*, who preserved Papias's description[14] and whose materialistic millennialism was an important part of his antignostic arguments and doctrine of the recapitulation. Inheriting the eschatological hopes of the postexilic prophets and John's Apocalypse, Irenaeus's vision closely parallels those: with all hills leveled to the hill of Zion, which would manifest God's glory with its magnificent new temple, it would tower over all the surrounding area with wealth and prosperity; the former wastelands would be transformed into fertile fields flowing with streams of living water and thus pregnant with abundant fruits and grain; mountains would drip with sweet wine, and animals would live in harmony; Jerusalem would be reestablished in splendor with foundations of sapphire, encircled by precious jewels (e.g., Isa. 2:1–3; 11:6–9; 25:6; 30:23–26; 43:19–20; 65:25; 66:12; Ezek. 43:4–5; 47:12; Joel 3:17–18; cf. Rev. 20:1–6; 21:10–23). The third- and early fourth-century Latin writers such as Tertullian, Commodianus (a poet and apologist), Victorinus of Pettau (who wrote the earliest extant commentary on John's Apocalypse), and Lactantius (apologist and rhetorician) all picture similarly extraordinary fruitfulness and prosperity of the renewed earth under the reign of Christ and the righteous after the destruction of the Antichrist and his followers, as the saints will "drink of this fruit of the vine" (Matt. 26:29).[15]

Lactantius, whose book seven of his grand apology, *Divine Institutes*, is devoted mainly to Christian eschatology, has particularly intriguing visions of the end. Writing during the Great Persecution (303–13 CE), he advances the most vivid and in-depth presentation of apocalyptic expectations about the renewed world in the millennium with blanket backing of Sybil and Virgil (as well as the prophetic texts and John's Apocalypse):

> The earth will disclose its fertility and breed rich fruit of its own accord, the rocks of the hills will ooze with honey, and the rivers will swell with milk; the world itself will rejoice and all nature will be glad at being plucked into freedom from the dominance of evil, impiety, wickedness and error. Wild beast will not feed on blood in this period, nor birds on prey; everything will instead be peaceful and quiet. . . . [Quoting Sybil] "The holy earth, abode of the pious alone, will produce all these things; a stream will flow from a rock dripping honey,

13. Irenaeus, *Haer.* 5.33.3–4.
14. Irenaeus, *Haer.* 5.33.2–3.
15. For a treatment of each of their millennial views, see Hill, *Regnum Caelorum*, 27–43.

and milk too from an immortal spring for all just men." People [the resurrected righteous] will thus live lives of great peace and plenty, and will reign side by side with God. (*Inst.* 7.24.7–8, 15)[16]

For Lactantius, this messianic age is the Golden Age returned, where justice and true piety (i.e., Christian monotheism) once again reign on earth just like the original Golden Age of Saturn. The Golden Age of Saturn was the time of the worship of one God, whose law established justice, particularly fairness or equality (*aequitas*), in sharing of the personal property by the rich with the poor.[17] With worship of one true God, natural justice prevailed and there was neither discord, enmity, nor war (5.5.3–4); people lived in harmony and contentment and shared the God-given land in which "all need was met in common" as intended by God (5.5.5—quoting Virgil).[18] This resulted in an unhindered flow of God's abundance without human greed, in which "all were equally well off because abundant and generous giving was done by those with to those without" (5.5.8). However, the tyranny of Jupiter, who turned people away from monotheism, brought about gross injustice and therefore gross inequality, as indicated by the unbridled manifestation of greed and exploitation by the rich. Subsequently, justice returned with the worship of Christ for the few; but the Golden Age did not return with him since too many were still worshiping the wrong, multiple gods, and even persecuting the true religion (Christianity). The Golden Age of justice (hence *aequitas*) and peace would be restored only with the second coming of Christ who would then judge all of those polytheistic usurpers of power, take control of the whole earth, and root out the evil of idolatry (cf. 4.12.21; 7.2.1).

Compare this extraordinary portrait of the restored Golden Age of the just with the end-time events just prior to and after the millennium, foretold by both pagan and biblical prophets: "they describe a sort of extreme old age for a world exhausted and collapsing. . . . If that is so, then what is left to follow old age but death?" (*Inst.* 7.14.16; 7.15.17). The end of history must correspond to the end of the six-day creation cycle, which represents six thousand years; and Lactantius calculates this end to be just less than two hundred years away (7.25.5).[19] It will be the time of no justice, no generos-

---

16. Translation is from *Divine Institutes* (trans., with an introduction and notes, by A. Bowen and P. Garnsey; Liverpool: Liverpool University Press, 2003).

17. Lactantius consistently assumes that "Christianity, the Religion of the Most High God, is the original and natural religion of all [hu]mankind": O. Nicholson, "*Caelum potius intuemini*: Lactantius and a Statue of Constantine," *StPatr* 34 (2001): 185.

18. That Lactantius did not mean here an absence or eradication of private property is clear in the subsequent lines in his chapter.

19. By Lactantius's time there was a familiar tradition of "the cosmic-week theory" among Christian chronographers (Hippolytus, Julius Afrianus, Cyprian, and even Origen though none of them was a millennialist), according to which history will run its course of six one-thousand-year "days" as God created the world in six days (cf. Ps. 90:4; 2 Pet. 3:8); then as God rested

ity, no shame, and no truth where evil, covetousness, greed, and lust will be rampant and go out of control (7.15.7–9). Then "the Sibyls say openly that Rome will perish, and by judgment of God, because she held God's name in hatred and in her hostility to justice slew the people brought up to truth" (7.15.17). The divine judgment of Rome (represented by the Tetrarchy) by wars and cosmic disturbances will accompany destruction of its cities by fire, sword, earthquakes, floods, chronic disease, and frequent famine as well as drought; certainly for Lactantius, the destruction of Rome represents the end of this age of idolatry and injustice; "and men will have no fruits of the earth: cornfield, orchard and vineyard will bear nothing; they will offer great hope in the flower and betray it in the bud . . . there will be no cattle on earth, no birds in the sky and no fish in the sea" (7.16.5–8, 12).[20] This is a future reversal for the impious in the present, among others "those rich people, laden as they are with a host of vast boxes and bundles, [who] are treading the path of death, which is a very wide path because ruin keeps wide empire upon it" (7.1.21). They are the ones who cannot understand monotheism and therefore justice and piety, whose "minds depraved and vicious, whose sharpness is blunted by their earthly desires, . . . [b]ecause they are aflame with avarice and an insatiable thirst for wealth, because they cannot sell what they love or bestow it around and live a life of straitened means" (7.1.12–13). For Lactantius, impiety (polytheism), greed, and injustice go hand in hand; and God will surely destroy the idolatrous, oppressive, and avaricious ones drunken with Roman luxury and power, who persecute the righteous and lowly, i.e., Christians, who call out to God and beg for his help (7.17.11). While Lactantius does not equate the rich with the wicked, or the poor with the just, as such, his apocalyptic expectation of divine judgment follows the *topos* of the great reversal of fortunes between the wicked and powerful and the innocent and persecuted:

---

on the seventh day, at the end of the six thousand years Christ will return in glory and usher in the eschatological Sabbath rest for his saints (Rev. 20:2–5). O. P. Nicholson, "The Source of the Dates in Lactantius' Divine Institutes," *JTS* 36 (1985): 291–310, shows that Lactantius combined a chronology of Theophilus of Antioch with the cosmic-week theory as a basis for his eschatological scheme of seven millennia.

20. Cf. A. Brent, *Cyprian and Roman Carthage* (Cambridge: Cambridge University Press, 2010), 5–8, 76–116, argues that Cyprian operated within and his eschatology (to an extent) reflected and adopted the contemporary Stoic cosmology and worldview of correspondence between decline and renewal of a moral and social order and that of a natural and physical order. The Stoic historiography and understanding of the golden age with uncorrupted abundance and justice inevitably disintegrating into old age of silver, brass, and iron with moral, legal, and social corruption and decline, only to be reborn again in a renewed golden age with supernatural signs (which was coopted by imperial ideology) was shared and modified by Cyprian in his diagnosis of his contemporary situation and teleological anticipation for the Second Coming of Christ, according to Brent. If this is the case, one can see that Cyprian's conceptualization of Christ's Second Coming in terms of the world's old age by Stoic eschatology is followed and expanded by Lantantius's eschatology analyzed in this section.

People who are in bliss in this corporeal and earthly life are going to be in misery eternally because they have already obtained the goods they preferred; that is what happens to those who worship gods and neglect God. Those who have been in misery in this life by following justice, however, despised and helpless as they are, and often pursued with insult and injury precisely because of their justice, . . . are going to be in bliss for ever, so that they have their enjoyment of good because they have already endured their evil . . . and follow the heavenly religion of God. (7.11.3–4)

Eschatology at the core envisions the ideal, transfigured world and deals with divine justice and judgment at the end. Thus the vindication of the righteous and the condemnation of the wicked takes a form of eschatological bliss and destruction, following the traditional Deuteronomic blessings and curses, based on one's obedience to the divine commandment in this life. At the same time, "the issue of poverty and wealth is inextricably bound up with the question of divine justice and judgment,"[21] as well as in the postexilic theological and social tradition of "the righteous poor" and "the wicked rich,"[22] which still provides a deep undercurrent in early Christianity.

In the Christian apocalyptic literature, the divine judgment and great reversal theme advances material and earthly expectations in close parallel with the tradition of the pious poor and the oppressive rich. As we have already mentioned, in the Apocalypse of John, the "unrighteous rich" *topos* takes the form of a socioeconomic critique of the Roman Empire, the quintessential manifestation of cosmic powers of evil. It urges the faithful in Asia Minor to reject any religious, socioeconomic, and political compromise with Rome and to "come out of Babylon" in a dramatic anticipation of the final judgment and victory of the Lamb over all cosmic evils, with a vision of the new heaven and new earth in extraordinary grandeur and plentitude. In the second-century work *Fifth Ezra*, God's people, Israel (i.e., Christians), are exhorted not to be anxious about the day of the judgment because "others [heathens] will weep and be sorrowful, but thou shalt be gay and rich" (27). In the meanwhile they are commanded to "do right to the widow, assist the fatherless to his right; give to the needy; protect the orphan, clothe the naked; tend the cripple and

21. G. W. E. Nickelsburg, "Revisiting the Rich and the Poor in 1 Enoch 92–105 and the Gospel according to Luke," in *Society of Biblical Literature 1998 Seminar Papers Part Two* (Atlanta: Scholars Press, 1998), 588.

22. For a concise survey of this rich tradition in Jewish and early Christian literature, see P. U. Maynard-Reid, *Poverty and Wealth in James* (New York: Orbis Books, 1987), 24–37; Bammel, *TDNT* 6:885–915; Hengel, *Property and Riches in the Early Church*, 12–41; H.-H. Esser and C. Brown, "Poor" (*ptōchos*), *NIDNTT* 2:821–29; C. Osiek, *Rich and Poor in the Shepherd of Hermas: An Exegetical-Social Investigation* (CBQMS 15; Washington, DC: Catholic Biblical Association of America, 1983), 15–38; M. Dibelius, *James: A Commentary on the Epistle of James* (rev. H. Greeven; trans. M. A. Williams; Philadelphia: Fortress, 1976), 39–45; E. Nardoni, *Rise Up, O Judge: A Study of Justice in the Biblical World* (Peabody, MA: Hendrickson, 2004), precisely relates this tradition to the broader issue of biblical justice and ethics.

the feeble, laugh not at the lame, defend the frail . . ." (20) and be "ready for the rewards of the kingdom" (35) and anticipate the banquet of the Lord (38). While there is no evident identification of "Israel" as the poor here as in Isaiah, this calls for their present social responsibility in anticipation of their future judgment and the dramatic reversal of their fortunes. In the *Sixth Ezra*, written in the context of a persecution, God's fierce judgment on Asia, one of Israel's enemies, "who sharest in the splendor of Babylon [Rome] and in the glory of her station" (46), comes in the form of widowhood, poverty, famine, sword, pestilence, hunger, deprivation of its treasure, and destruction of its splendor (49, 57). While the "sinners" as the recipients of divine woe are not identified as the rich, they are "those who traffic in business . . . as those who plunder" and those who keep "adorn[ing] their cities and houses and their possessions and their persons" to such an extent that they incense God's anger (48); only eschatological shame, humiliation, and destruction are waiting for them (52, 65–68). These texts clearly represent the "typical" this-worldly descriptions of apocalyptic judgment, which will completely reverse the present fortunes of the "righteous poor" and the "wicked rich."

In the Christian *Sybilline Oracles*, the wrath of God will be poured out to those sinners including presbyters and reverend deacons who had more regard for wealth than for the person and did injustice to others,[23] the inordinately proud and usurers heaping up usury out of usury who wrought harm to orphans and widows, and those who gave to widows and orphans from ill-gotten gains (2.260–72). When God the Most High will judge on the throne with his saints, people will finally "cast down their idols and their wealth" (8.224) but will eternally burn in a mighty fire and gnash with their teeth; and God will turn away his face from them. On the other hand, those who practice justice, noble works, piety, and righteousness are destined to the new age of eternal bliss where there are threefold springs of wine, milk, and honey; abundant fruits; common wealth ("unapportioned wealth"); neither paupers nor rich, neither slaves nor kings, and neither buying nor selling (2.313–30). This portrait of the new age at the judgment is repeated elsewhere: with the resurrection of the dead, there will be common sharing of life, riches, and earth, abundant crops and fruits, and springs of sweet wine, white milk, and honey (8.180, 205–12); no slaves, no kings, no ruler judging for money (8.107–121). The coming new age has no social distinctions or disparities, and no private properties—only social equality, abundance, and common sharing of that abundance. As in the case of Lactantius and the *Sixth Ezra*, this is to be taken as a critique of the contemporary (i.e., Roman) social inequalities and private properties as the culprit. The oracles make explicit the end of

---

23. Note the contemporary (second-century) presbyters and shepherds (i.e., bishops?) denounced in the *Ascension of Isaiah* (3.23–25) in an apocalyptic senario as those "who will love office though they are devoid of wisdom, . . . will be lawless and violent . . . [and] exchange the glory of the garment of the saints for the garment of the covetous," loving the worldly honor.

Rome's dominion and its punishment for its presumption and luxury (8.125, 143, 145, 153). The idea of common ownership and use in the Golden Age and the new age would become popular among the church fathers in the fourth and fifth centuries. It is significant that Christian(-ized) visions of the primal past and the ultimate future begin and end "with the communal and cosmic symbol[s] of God's reign of righteousness" in the eschatological kingdom in which "the more-than-enough" of God's grace and riches embraces all of God's people of new creation.[24]

As the visions of the eschatological judgment and new, messianic age became more elaborate and detailed, there developed amplified descriptions of distinctive "tours of hell" in the patristic apocalypses, in which we see sins and eternal punishments matching measure for measure.[25] In *Apocalypse of Peter* and *Apocalypse of Paul*, those who trusted in their wealth (Eth. 9; Gk. 30; *Apoc. Paul*, 37) and did not have mercy on widows and orphans (Eth. 9; Gk. 30; *Apoc. Paul*, 35, 40) are clad in filthy rags and suffer in torment; also those who lent money and took usury are thrown into a place saturated with filth (*Apoc. Pet.*, Eth. 0; Gk. 31). In *Acts of Thomas*, a Syriac Christian novelistic work from the early third century, those hung up by the hands in a chasm are those "who took that which did not belong to them and have stolen, and who never gave anything to the poor, nor helped the afflicted; but they did so because they wished to get everything, and cared neither for law nor right" (56). In these cases, the particular sins that merit corresponding punishments in hell are greed, trust in wealth, and (therefore) ignoring the traditional responsibilities of caring for the poor, widows, and orphans. Here wealth or possessions themselves are not the problem but rather their use and the attitudes toward them; a clear intention is to prompt the *individual believers* to use their wealth to the right end in light of the coming judgment.[26]

2.3. Judgment, the Rich and the Poor, and Almsgiving

What we see mainly developing in the second and third centuries is that, while the theology of the pious poor is still current (in the recognition of God's favor

24. M. D. Meeks, "Being Human in the Market Society," *Quarterly Review* (2001): 264.

25. See M. Himmelfarb, *Tours of Hell: An Apocalyptic Form in Jewish and Christian Literature* (Philadelphia: Fortress, 1983), esp. 68–126.

26. Note a shift in the punishment of the wicked in these works compared to John's Apocalypse, the *Fifth* and *Sixth Ezra*, and the Christian *Sybilline Oracles*: from punishment of wicked nations to individual retribution, and from punishment for the mistreatment of Israel (i.e., people of God) to punishment for individual sins against God's commandments. This would be an example of Aune's observation that "the experience of salvation as conveyed by the doctrine of the immortality of the soul upon personal death became, therefore, a functional substitute for the experience of salvation that was expected to occur upon the event of the Parousia of Jesus," in "Significance of the Delay," 108.

on them and of the efficacy of their intercession), the theology of the wicked rich is increasingly toned down, perhaps for practical reasons. Christianity attracted a greater number of the wealthy and the dignified with high social status, especially in the third century (see the last section of the previous chapter). Both the rich and the poor are members of the Christian assemblies with the former taking an indispensable and substantial role in the assemblies. Therefore, while social tensions between them occasionally do lead to social crises within the church (e.g., neglect of the poor by the rich as in the case of *The Shepherd of Hermas*), the great reversal theme is diminished; for the binary juxtaposition between the pious poor and the wicked rich becomes increasingly untenable. Instead, moral and eschatological discourses shift their focus to moving the rich to change their behavior so that *both* the rich and the poor will pass the coming judgment and receive the heavenly reward *together*. The notion of "redemptive almsgiving" appearing in the Second Temple sapiential texts such as Tobit and Sirach (Ecclesiasticus) receives renewed significance in this context.[27] Hence, the symbiosis or reciprocity theme becomes more dominant than the reversal theme in the second- and third-century Christian writings.[28] Although denunciation of avarice/greed in the apocalyptic framework is just as strong, the righteous rich find hope of eternal life through generous almsgiving. Therefore, future rewards and punishments increasingly correspond to respective categories not between the pious poor and the oppressive rich, but between the righteous rich who are generous in acts of charity and alms and the unrighteous rich who neglect their social responsibilities.

The practical interplay between eschatological judgment and paraenesis for the rich is best demonstrated in *The Shepherd of Hermas*, the second-century Christian apocalyptic literature, by its function.[29] Apocalyptic literature ad-

27. R. Garrison, *Redemptive Almsgiving in Early Christianity* (Sheffield: JSOT Press, 1993), thinks that the early Christian notion of "redemptive almsgiving" emerged as an antidote to anxiety about delay of parousia and the ensuing problem of postbaptismal sin despite Christ's death as sufficient atonement for sin. This, though it has its merit, seems to be a bit too narrow an understanding of "redemptive almsgiving."

28. E.g., *Hermas*; Clement of Alexandria, *Who Is a Rich Man That Is Saved?* See the next section, "Eschatological Dualism and Dualism of Earthly and Heavenly Riches."

29. C. Osiek has successfully shown *The Shepherd of Hermas* as apocalypse in "The Genre and Function of *The Shepherd of Hermas*," in *Early Christian Apocalypticism: Genre and Social Setting* (ed. A. Y. Collins; *Semeia* 36; Decatur, GA: Scholars Press, 1986), 113–21, although scholars still debate *Hermas*'s literary genre, to what extent it is a "genuine" apocalypse, pointing out its lack of revelation about eschatological future, end-time cataclysm, or pessimism in history and the present world order; its content is largely paraenesis on repentance, while it retains an apocalyptic form and style, including visions, parables, allegories, and eschatological urgency and warnings. Cf. P. Vielhauer and G. Strecker, "Apocalypses and Related Subjects: Introduction," in *Writings Relating to Apostles, Apocalypses and Related Subjects* (ed. W. Schneemelcher; vol. 2 of *New Testament Apocrypha*; trans. R. M. Wilson; rev. ed.; Louisville: Westminster John Knox, 1991, 1992), 544–60; N. Brox, *Der Hirt des Hermas* (Kommentar zu den Apostolischen Vätern 7; Göttingen: Vandenhoeck & Ruprecht, 1991), 36–37.

dresses a crisis of some sort, whether political, spiritual, or historical, and whether real, perceived, or imagined, by constructing an alternative vision and exhorting concrete behaviors based on that alternative perception of reality.[30] *Hermas* serves the same function of apocalypse, as it deals with an internal crisis of the local Christian community utilizing apocalyptic form and style. One of the main issues that contributed to the community's internal crisis is the spiritual complacency of certain wealthy believers resulting from their preoccupation with wealth and business activities and the social disparity between the rich and the poor in *Hermas*'s community in Rome. *Hermas*'s concern couched in "otherworldly" discourse is evidently "this-worldly." In a series of visions of the cosmic tower (the eschatological church), the danger of wealth has to do with its attachment to the present world, which takes the faith of the rich away from the Lord in times of persecution (*Vis.* 3.6.5) and keeps them preoccupied with their own security and well-being to the neglect of their social responsibility of caring for the needy (*Vis.* 3.9.2–6). Here eschatological salvation and wealth cannot go together unless the latter is "cut away" from the rich; and in light of the coming judgment, a major warning is directed to those "who exult in [their] wealth" lest they "together with [their] good things be shut outside the door of the tower" (*Vis.* 3.9.5–6).

Later in *Similitude* 9, where this vision of the cosmic tower is revisited with further elaborations, the issue remains the same: the rich represented by the round stones need to be transformed into square ones to be put into the building, which is possible only by massive trimming, i.e., "cutting away" their wealth. However, in both vision and similitude, the tower is still being built; in fact, the tower will not be completed until the master comes and tests the building (*Sim.* 9.5.2); only the completion of the tower with the master's visit brings the eschaton (*Vis.* 3.8.9; *Sim.* 9.5.1). Meanwhile, the earlier-rejected round stones are given a second chance. The rich have a short window of opportunity to be cleaned up and cut off from "this world and the vanities of their possessions" (*Sim.* 9.31.2); the urgency to repent and change lies in the fact that the master might come suddenly and unexpectedly (*Sim.* 9.7.6). Indeed, the danger of wealth has to do with its distraction and entanglement with this world through business affairs and with the rich avoiding their responsibility; however, those who repent "quickly" will enter the kingdom albeit with difficulty (*Sim.* 9.20.1–4). One major difference from the previous vision is that their wealth should be still cut away, but not completely, "so that they might be able to do some good with that which was left to them, and they will live to God" (9.30.5). The goal of these visions and allegories is not to denounce wealth or the rich as such but to move the rich into concrete behaviors for the

---

30. Cf. Osiek, "Genre and Function," 115–18; Osiek, *The Shepherd of Hermas: A Commentary* (Hermeneia; Minneapolis: Augsburg Fortress, 1999), 12.

good of the community (and for their own good). Here the paraenetic nature of eschatological visions and warnings is clearly shown.

The parable of the cosmic willow tree and its various branches recasts the building of the tower with different images (*Sim.* 8.1–11). Among various branches, those half withered and half green represent the *believers* preoccupied with business, and those two-thirds withered and one-third green represent the *believers* who became wealthy, acquired honor and status among the pagans, lived according to their standards, and failed to "do the works of faith" (*Sim.* 8.8.1; 8.9.1). Their explicitly named common problem is double-mindedness (*dipsychia*). Double-mindedness, a major issue and concern in *Hermas*, is a typical characteristic of those with "a divided allegiance . . . doubt, uncertainty with regard to God and salvation, and with regard to their own affairs."[31] It is this double-mindedness, "an earthly spirit from the devil" (*Mand.* 9.11), that absorbs them in "all the vanities of this life" (*Mand.* 9.4) and therefore prevents them from turning to God "unhesitatingly" (*Mand.* 9.2, 4, 6). It invariably causes dissension and division for it leads those affected to disassociate themselves from their Christian community and to ignore acts of charity and hospitality (i.e., "the works of faith") in favor of their own affairs; and in turn, the rich become "double-minded because of their deeds" (*Sim.* 8.8.2–5; 8.9.1–4; 8.10.2–4; cf. *Sim.* 9.20.1–2; *Vis.* 3.6.2; *Mand.* 8.10). This double-mindedness is ultimately a manifestation of pride (cf. *Sim.* 8.9.1) and has communal consequences. Therefore, once again, the call is to swift repentance so that "their home may be within the tower" (*Sim.* 8.8.3; 8.9.4), but "for those who do not repent, persist in their pleasures, death is near" (*Sim.* 8.9.4).

The *Mandates* offer a further antidote to double-mindedness and other vices inspired by the angel of wickedness. It is an exercise of self-control (*enkrateia*) over all evil on the one hand, including "wicked luxury, many kinds of food, the extravagance of wealth" (*Mand.* 8.3) and greed (8.5); on the other hand, one should do what is good (*poiein to agathon*), that is, "serving widows, looking after orphans and those in need, delivering God's servants from distress, being hospitable . . . becoming more needy [*endeesteros*; cf. 11.8] than all other people, . . . [and] not oppressing debtors and all those in need" (8.10)—the classic community responsibility, particularly of the rich.

The second-century homily known as the *Second Clement* addresses greed and almsgiving in the context of apocalyptic dualism and judgment. This age and the coming age are antithetical to each other, as are God and money (6.1–3). The things of this age are insignificant, transitory, and perishable, characterized by immorality, corruption, and greed, whereas those of the

31. J. Reiling, *Hermas and Christian Prophecy: A Study of the Eleventh Mandate* (Supplements to Novum Testamentum 37; Leiden: Brill, 1973), 22–32; quoted by Osiek, *Shepherd of Hermas*, 31.

coming age are good and imperishable (6.4–6). Therefore, since we cannot serve both God and money (cf. 6.1), we must renounce and hate the former in order to experience and love the latter (6.5–6). When we desire to acquire worldly things, we fall away from the way of righteousness (5.7). Double-mindedness is a major problem here as in *Hermas*, for it prevents serving God with a pure heart and enduring in hope for the heavenly reward. There is an implicit reversal theme in addressing the present hardship of God's servants as opposed to wealth of the unrighteous, but there is no correlation throughout the text between "the poor" and God's servants, on the one hand, and "the rich" and the unrighteous, on the other. God will punish the unrighteous whereas the righteous will receive their reward in the life to come (20.1–4). What is more interesting is that the homilist evokes strong apocalyptic imagery and language when exhorting almsgiving. Since "the day of judgment is already 'coming as a blazing furnace,' and 'some of the heavens will dissolve,' and the whole earth will be like lead melting in a fire," every human work will be exposed (16.3). Therefore, "renunciation" or "hatred" of the earthly things turns out to be none other than almsgiving: "almsgiving is good, as is repentance from sin. Fasting is better than prayer, while almsgiving is better than both, and 'love covers a multitude of sins' . . . almsgiving relieves the burden of sin" (16.4).[32] It is the first Christian text that explicitly links 1 Peter 4:8 to almsgiving and almsgiving to pardon of sin. Almsgiving is the ultimate antidote to love of money, the prime act of love and righteousness, and thus the surest way to get ready for the imminent judgment (cf. 12.1; 18.2).

We may find the clearest articulation of this eschatological significance of almsgiving in the writings of Cyprian, bishop of Carthage in the turbulent mid-third century. The political catastrophes, socioeconomic problems, natural disasters, and ecclesiastical crises of his time, including the two imperial persecutions of Decius (250–51 CE) and Valerian (257–58 CE) and the dreadful plague of 252–54 CE, provided the important context for his eschatological sensitivity and social and moral teachings.[33] Cyprian believed (followed by Lactantius) that the six thousand years of history since creation was approaching the end ("old age," *senectus*) and also that the collapse of the Roman Empire was at hand, as foretold by the Scriptures and confirmed by the contemporary calamities.[34] On the one hand, Cyprian is clear that in reply to Demetrianus,

32. Cf. Sir. 3.30; Tob. 4.10; 12.9.

33. J. P. Burns, "Cyprian's Eschatology: Explaining Divine Purpose," in *The Early Church in Its Context: Essays in Honor of Everett Ferguson* (ed. A. J. Malherbe, F. W. Norris, and J. W. Thompson; Supplements to Novum Testamentum 90; Leiden: Brill, 1998), 59–73, shows how Cyprian shifted his eschatology in explaining God's intention and purpose for and through these challenging issues in the specific Carthaginian context while holding on to Christ's return and the final judgment as an overarching framework.

34. *Fort.* 2; *Demetr.* 3; *Mort.* 25; cf. *Ep.* 58.2. See no. 20 and Brent, *Cyprian and Roman Carthage*, 91–109; according to Brent, Cyprian shared with his pagan contemporaries this notion of

the possible local magistrate,[35] who blamed Christians as culprits for the wars, famine, disease, and plagues because of their "atheism" (with respect to the Roman gods), those misfortunes and tribulations are the result of Roman impiety (with respect to the true God) and the sign of God's indignant judgment on the evil.[36] On the other hand, he encourages the faithful to endure these afflictions without anxiety and fear as the sign of the imminence of God's kingdom: "the reward of life, and the rejoicing of eternal salvation, and the perpetual gladness and possession lately lost of paradise, are now coming."[37] Therefore, while Cyprian declares the certainty of God's vengeance on the Roman persecutors,[38] he promises heavenly reward of immediate eternal bliss for those who prove their discipleship by fighting against avarice[39] and "having forsaken and condemned all [their] possessions" through almsgiving, and thus "standing in firmness of the faith and in the fear of God."[40] In this way, upon death, they will reign with Christ along with a heavenly company of the apostles, prophets, martyrs, virgins, and the merciful who "by feeding and helping the poor have done the works of righteousness—who, keeping the Lord's precepts, have transferred their earthly patrimonies to the heavenly treasuries."[41]

As the Decian persecution of 250 and 251 caught the churches off guard and indeed demoralized them to internal chaos and crisis that escalated eschatological anxiety, Cyprian in *On the Lapsed* (251 CE) saw the persecution (however evil and unjust that may be[42]) rather as God's testing of his household that had been growing complacent in the years of peace; it is a heavenly wake-up call to their languid and sleeping faith (5). He attributes the cause of persecution, indeed God's testing, primarily to the faithful's "insatiable greed" (*insatiabili cupiditatis*) and preoccupation with accumulating wealth to the neglect of generous charity for the needy (6). What is more, too many bishops "took up the administration of secular business [*rerum saecularium*]; they left their sees, . . . and toured the markets in other territories on the look-out for profitable deals" (6); while their members in the church went hungry, "they wanted to have money in abundance, they acquired landed

---

the world in a state of "the old age" (*senectus mundi*) waiting for metaphysical transformation or renewal though their remedies for renewal differed.

35. *Demetr.* 10. See M. M. Sage, *Cyprian* (Patristic Monograph Series 1; Cambridge, MA: Philadelphia Patristic Foundation, 1975), 276, for this approximate title for Demetrianus, who judges the designation of Proconsul of Africa by *ANF* 8, 423, far-fetched.

36. *Demetr.* 5, 7, 10; cf. *Mort.* 2.

37. *Mort.* 2; cf. *Mort.* 26.

38. *Demetr.* 17; cf. God's judgment on the Roman Empire in the *Sixth Ezra*, Lactantius, and the Christian Sibylline Oracle in 2.2.

39. *Mort.* 4.

40. *Fort.* 12; cf. *Fort.* 7.

41. *Mort.* 26.

42. *Demetr.* 12, 17.

estates by fraud, and made profits by loans at compound interest" (6). The church's failing in this persecution (i.e., massive apostasy) revealed "the true nature of our malady," which was "a blind attachment to their patrimony [*patrimonii sui amor caecus*]," their enslavement to their earthly riches and property (11, 12). To this the "apostolic solution" is given: scorn the worldly possessions and leave them for the kingdom of God and the heavenly compensation (12). Cyprian frames both the problem and solution in apocalyptic dualism with a sense of exigency, for the end of the world was at hand with the judgment of Christ.[43] The (wealthy) lapsed, as the sign of true repentance, should apply themselves to "good deeds [*iustis operibus*] which can wash away [their] sins, be constant and generous in giving alms, whereby souls are freed from death" (35). Cyprian urges them to invest their earthly goods and riches with the Lord, their coming Judge (35).

2.4. Eschatological Dualism and Dualism of Earthly and Heavenly Riches

The final way that eschatology shaped social and ethical thought on wealth and poverty has to do with the eschatological dualism between heavenly and earthly riches. The parable of the two cities (*Sim.* 1.1–11) in *Hermas* reflects *Hermas*'s concern with the tension between this world and the world to come, a dualism that is both temporal and spatial. These conceptual contrasts—between this world and the next, between heavenly and earthly riches—underline the dangers of wealth and possessions as well as the purpose of wealth. Certainly in the New Testament, the message of "laying up one's treasure in heaven" stands in tension with "laying up one's treasure on earth" (Matt. 6:19–20), with the former promising eternal security and protection. The parable of the rich fool in Luke 12 highlights the imprudence of placing one's security in an abundance of earthly riches as opposed to being "rich toward God" (12:21). *Hermas*'s parable of the two cities, "the author's clearest articulation of his view of the Christian's place in society" according to Osiek,[44] portrays Christian existence as dual residence, one in a foreign country and one in the city of eschatological destiny, each governed by a law incompatible with the other.[45] Accumulation of earthly riches in this temporary foreign city through amassing fields, buildings, and other properties, is a sure sign of foolishness and double-mindedness, for the lord of the foreign city will inevitably expel Christians who are subject to the law of their own city (*Sim.* 1.1–4). Since Christians cannot keep the law of their own city by retaining their worldly possessions, it is in their best interest that they be self-sufficient (*autarkeia*)

43. *Epp.* 57.4.3–5.2; 58.2.1–3, 3.2; 61.4.1; 63.18.4; cf. *Unit. eccl.* 27; *Demetr.* 5, 23.
44. Osiek, *Shepherd of Hermas*, 158.
45. Cf. *Diogn.* 5.4–5.

and be free and prepared to leave the land at any time, and "joyfully conform to the law" of their own city (*Sim.* 1.5–6). It is in this context that Christians should keep God's commandments (*Sim.* 1.7): "instead of fields buy souls that are in distress, as anyone is able, and visit widows and orphans, and do not neglect them; and spend your wealth and all your possessions, which you received from God, on fields and houses of this kind" (*Sim.* 1.8). Once again, these divine commandments articulate the classic (Jewish and) Christian acts of charity as a way of converting earthly temporal riches into heavenly spiritual riches—since it is God's intention and purpose for earthly wealth. God makes one rich for this reason, i.e., for performing "ministries" or "services" (*diakoniai*), and therefore "it is much better to purchase fields and possessions and houses of this kind" (*Sim.* 1.9). Whereas earthly wealth brings grief and fear, heavenly spiritual wealth brings joy; earthly extravagance is unprofitable to the believer, but heavenly extravagance is salvific (*Sim.* 1.10–11). This eschatological motif does not renounce material wealth but affirms it as God's gift, relativizes its earthly significance, and channels it to its proper use of amassing spiritual wealth through acts of charity/ministry.

The famous parable of the elm and the vine is to be seen in relation to this first parable with dualism of earthly and heavenly riches. The affirmation of earthly wealth as God's gift, for which God's specific intent is expressed in his commandments (*Sim.* 1.7–10), thematically leads to the second parable: mutual cooperation and dependence between the rich and the poor in preparation for the world to come. The elm and the vine, representing the rich and the poor,[46] bear much fruit only when they are attached to each other and function together, not on their own. The shepherd, *Hermas*'s revelatory guide, takes for granted the traditional notion that the rich are deficient in the things of the Lord due to their wealth and its attendant problem of distraction, while the poor are rich in intercession and praise with effectual power (*Sim.* 2.5; cf. *Mand.* 10.3.2).[47] Therefore, the rich (should) "unhesitatingly" provide for the needs of the poor and the poor intercede for the rich; in this way they "complete" their work, which is "great and acceptable to God" (*Sim.* 2.6). As Osiek notes, this "is a spiritualization of the institution of patronage: the *obsequium* and *operae* owed by the client to a patron takes the form of intercessory prayer."[48] This mutual partnership between the rich and the poor is spiritualized in view toward the end that both "will be enrolled in the books of the living" (*Sim.* 2.9). The thrust of this parable is that "the rich man understands about his wealth and works for the poor man by using

46. Osiek, in her commentary, *Shepherd of Hermas*, 163, makes the point that although the elm and the vine are traditionally understood as the rich and the poor respectively, this interpretation is not conclusive; according to her, the point of the parable is their interdependence, not exact correlation of symbols. See also C. Osiek, *Rich and Poor*, 86.

47. See the previous section, "Judgment, the Rich and the Poor, and Almsgiving."

48. Osiek, *Shepherd of Hermas*, 163–64.

the gifts of the Lord and correctly fulfills his ministry [*diakonia*]" (*Sim.* 2.7). Those rich who fulfill their God-given ministry/service here and now, and thus secure their heavenly riches, are the ones who overcome double-mindedness and therefore survive the great tribulation (cf. *Mand.* 9.2, 4, 6; *Sim.* 2.7; 8.10.3; 9.24.2; 9.29.2). Hence, the parable concludes with the beatitude for the rich: "Blessed are the rich who also understand that they have been made rich by the Lord, for the one who comprehends this will be able to do some good service" (*Sim.* 2.10; cf. *Sim.* 1.9).

In *On Works and Alms* (*De opera et eleemosynis*), which was probably written during the deadly and devastating plague after the persecution (252–54 CE),[49] Cyprian capitalizes on the appeal of heavenly reward and the contrast between earthly and heavenly riches to entreat the rich members of his church. The Holy Spirit itself exhorts the practice of almsgiving for "everyone who is instructed into the hope of the heavenly kingdom" (4). And the Lord himself will be eager to distribute to their "merits and good works the promised rewards, to give heavenly things for the earthly, eternal things for temporal, great things for small" (26), for "those rich men . . . having pledged or scattered their [earthly] riches, yea, having transferred them, by the change of their possessions for the better, into heavenly treasures" (22; cf. 7; *Hab. virg.* 11). Quoting Tobit 12.8–9, Cyprian stresses the salvific efficacy of almsgiving and connects it to the day of judgment (5, 9). Once again, there is a sense of serious urgency in Cyprian's tone as he admonishes the rich: "Let us, while there is time, take thought for our security and eternal salvation" (24). Furthermore, if one is truly concerned about leaving a secure future for one's heirs, there is no surer way than to "provide for one's pledges for the coming time," i.e., give alms, by "assign[ing] to Him your wealth which you are saving up for your heirs" (19). In proportion as Christians are rich in this world, they may become poor to God (13); if so, why would anyone amass their earthly patrimony for their own eternal punishment (cf. 13, 15)? The rich members should "make Christ a partner with [them] in [their] earthly possessions, that He also may make [them] a fellow-heir with Him in His heavenly kingdom" (13). If they are "lending to God" by giving alms to the poor, "there is no ground for any one preferring earthly things to heavenly, nor for considering human things before divine" (16).[50]

49. This is a traditional dating. For a proposal that this work was probably written during the time of peace *prior to* the Decian persecution, see E. V. Rebenack, "Thasci Caecili Cypriani: *De Opere et Eleemosynis*" (trans., with an intro. and commentary; PhD diss., Catholic University of America, 1962), 1–47; and C. A. Bobertz, "Cyprian of Carthage as Patron: A Social Historical Study of the Role of Bishop in the Ancient Christian Community of North Africa" (PhD diss., Yale University, 1988), 58n18.

50. Based on Prov. 19:17: "Whoever is kind to the poor lends to the LORD, and will be repaid in full." Cf. Luke 6:38. This notion is repeated in Cyprian, *Hab. virg.* 11; *Eleem.* 26; Clement of Alexandria, *Paed.* 2.13; 3.4; *Strom.* 3.6; *Ap. Const.* 3.1.4; 7.1.12.

In a final chapter of his *Divine Institutes*, Lactantius contrasts earthly and heavenly treasures as he urges his readers to "adopt wisdom and true religion together" (7.27.1). True wisdom is despising earthly things, breakable and fragile, and instead aiming for "the everlasting prizes of our treasure in heaven" (7.27.2). People must free themselves from earthly goods—"the prizes of this world"—and not simply ignore them, because ownership of those goods is uncertain, short-lived, and therefore deceptive. Reckoning their own soul is more important—i.e., while "the chance is there," they should turn themselves totally to God and give those goods to the hungry and the thirsty even if they "have license to enjoy them to the last moment" (7.27.9, 10, 12).[51] That is a safe way to wait for the judgment day and thus gain immortality, for which human beings are made. For Lactantius, the dualism of heavenly and earthly wealth also corresponds to the dualism of soul and body; whereas soul benefits by avoiding earthly wealth, body is fed by greed and lust, which pursues temporal riches and pleasures (7.5.23). As long as people are bound by corporeal and earthly goods, they live their earthly life "incapable of aiming at immortality" (7.5.24). No one should put faith in earthly wealth since it makes no one immortal (7.27.15). Instead, people should "use their virtue to trample down the corruptions of the earth" (7.27.14) and to pursue eternal and celestial goods by giving to the blind, the sick, the lame, and the destitute (cf. 6.11.18, 28; 7.27.2), which guarantees heavenly reward.

The *Acts of Thomas* also reflects this dualistic outlook of earthly and heavenly wealth, but with more "radical" imageries.[52] Riches in this world—gold, silver, and jewelry—are corruptible, transient, and attending bodily pleasures (36, 37, 116, 117), but riches in heaven are incorruptible, everlasting, and nourishing to the soul; the former is "entirely useless" for the world above and must be "left behind," but the latter is indispensable and sufficient for the life above (66). Since earthly possessions and riches are part of the present order that will pass away soon, along with bodily pleasures and intercourses, people should free themselves from their possessions and invest in lasting ones (36, 100, 126). Besides "fornication" (any sexual relation both within and without marriage), greed (avarice), covetousness, and gluttony form a triad of sins to be denounced; these sins, all attached to earthly riches, are indeed attributed to the eschatological false apostles and "prophets of

---

51. In *On Resurrection*, an anonymous work conventionally but erroneously attributed to Athenagoras, dualism of soul and body has an interesting take in a context of arguing for a necessity of bodily resurrection; soul has nothing to do with or is innocent of bodily sins such as adultery, theft, robbery, "and in general all covetousness which arises to injure or harm our neighbours" (23.2; cf. 23.5).

52. For comparison between the dualism of earthly and heavenly riches and the dualism of earthly and heavenly marriage, see H. Rhee, "Wealth and Poverty in the *Acts of Thomas*," in *Prayer and Spirituality in the Early Church: Poverty and Riches* (ed. G. D. Dunn, D. Luckensmeyer, and L. Cross; Brisbane: St. Pauls, 2009), 111–18.

lawlessness" (79). On the contrary, heavenly riches are none other than the kingdom of God (66) and eternal life (130, 136). In fact, Christ himself is the "true riches" (136, 145) and a generous dispenser of the heavenly riches, because he is "the judge of the living and of the dead," who, "at his coming and appearance at the end time," will recompense each according to one's works (28; cf. 30). Only those who despise earthly treasures will find everlasting treasures in heaven (130).

The *Acts*, like previous (millennial) works we have discussed, employs opulent imagery and acquisitive language to describe the ascetic model and heavenly riches.[53] In a famous "Hymn of the Pearl" sung by Thomas, the heavenly palace is described as a place of wealth and luxury adorned with gold, silver, and precious stones, and a child (probably an allegory for soul) dressed in a gold-spangled robe (108). In another famous story of Thomas building a palace for king Gundaphorus, heaven is described as full of palaces and mansions; when Gad, king's brother, departs the world and sees different palaces in heaven, the king's palace built by Thomas is so desirable that he bargains to buy it from the king upon returning to life on earth (22–24). Heavenly riches are much to be coveted and desired, and ascetic Thomas is unashamed to preach to Tertia, the king's wife, a "heavenly prosperity gospel": "if you truly believe in him, . . . he will make you great and rich and an heir to his Kingdom" (136). Heavenly reward far outweighs any earthly compensation.

As in *Hermas* and the works of Cyprian and Lactantius, the surest means of acquiring heavenly riches in the *Acts of Thomas* is almsgiving, an act of service. The *Acts* presents a consistent pattern of conversion resulting in almsgiving and vice versa, which is typical in Christian social thought by this time.[54] Thomas's ascetic message of renouncing the world and turning to God who will judge the world leads people to mass conversion (59). Upon their conversion, people bring their money to serve the widows, leaving their home and patrimony (59, 61). Thomas's message to Mygdonia, an encratic heroine of the *Acts*, which leads her to conversion, is that she

> first of all abstain from adultery [marital relation], . . . theft, . . . avarice, . . . and walk in gentleness, helping the poor and satisfying the want of the needy, by bringing your possessions and distributing them to the needy, especially to those who walk in holiness, for this is chosen by God and leads to eternal life. (84–85)

---

53. See 2.2. The *Odes of Solomon*, the Syrian Christian product of the second century, also offer a vision of paradise that is overabundant with trees, vegetation, and fruits, a land of delight and joy, in a general frame of realized eschatology (11.16–24).

54. See, for example, H. Rhee, "Wealth and the Wealthy in the *Acts of Peter*," StPatr 65 (2010): 343–47; cf. "almsgiving as the marker of the doctrinal orthodoxy" in apocryphal acts in R. Finn, *Almsgiving in the Later Roman Empire: Christian Promotion and Practice 313–450* (Oxford: Oxford University Press, 2006), 129–31.

The most intriguing story of almsgiving presents Thomas building a palace for King Gundaphorus. At the request of the king to build an earthly palace, Thomas takes all the money given by the king and distributes it to the poor and needy in the cities and villages. As he keeps providing alms for the poor (the afflicted), orphans, and widows with the king's gold and silver, Thomas assures the king that his palace is being built. When the king finds out what has been happening and demands an explanation, Thomas's answer only enrages the bewildered king further: "Now you cannot see it, but you shall see it when you depart this life" (21). This is the context in which Gad, the king's brother, dies, witnesses the magnificent heavenly palace belonging to the king, and attempts to persuade the king to sell it to him upon returning to earth. Only then the king realizes Thomas's words and actions, seeks forgiveness from Thomas's God, and finally joins him in serving God. Almsgiving here not only obtains one's "eternal benefits" but even works vicariously for an inadvertent giver of alms (24). Hence the prayer of the king: "I may become worthy to be an inhabitant of that house for which indeed I have done nothing, but which you [Thomas], labouring alone, have built for me with the help of the grace of your God" (24). This episode may bear the strongest testimony to salvific efficacy of almsgiving even on behalf of an unbeliever.

Thomas's call for contempt for and renunciation of earthly riches and possessions to gain heavenly riches is thus channeled into almsgiving, and this call is not necessarily meant to be voluntary poverty, renunciation in an absolute sense; the call for material renunciation is not as consistent or radical as that of sexual renunciation in this *Acts*.[55] Upon their conversion, the king and his brother Gad faithfully follow Thomas, "providing for the poor, giving to all, and relieving all" (26); however, there is no mention of them giving *all* and distributing *all* of their possessions to the poor. Conversion of Siphor, a captain of King Misdaeus in India and "one of the wealthiest in India" (62), does not mention dispossessing of his wealth, nor that of wealthy Mygdonia, Tertia, or Vazan, King Misdaeus's son. The danger of earthly riches is real and serious, but ultimately "neither shall riches help the rich, nor will poverty save the poor from judgment" (83). Unlike the universal call to sexual renunciation necessary for heavenly marriage, the call to material renunciation is neither universal nor necessary for heavenly riches but is rather relativized.

The only exception may be Thomas, who fills the role of a mediator and revealer of the one true God, Jesus Christ.[56] Jesus Christ, the "true riches"

55. On the theme of sexual renunciation in the *Acts of Thomas* and other apocryphal Acts, see H. Rhee, *Early Christian Literature: Christ and Culture in the Second and Third Centuries* (London: Routledge, 2005), 125–43.

56. Cf. Hengel, *Property and Riches*, 51–53. Note the similarly ascetic standard of the martyrs during the Great Persecution: "When the persecution was raging under the Emperor Maximian, these women [Agapê, Irenê, and Chionê at Saloniki], who had adorned themselves with virtue, following the precepts of the Gospel, abandoned their native city, their family, property, and

(136, 145), is "Lord of undefiled possessions" (156), a giver of great gifts and abundant riches (120, 142, 149, 159). At the same time, he is also the "poor one" (156) and ascetic (143); he is "hope of the poor" (10), "hope of the weak and trust of the poor, refuge and shelter of the weary" (156); he is "the support of the orphans and the nourisher of the widows and rest and repose to all who are afflicted" (19). As an imitator of Christ, Thomas lives a life of poverty on earth so that he can obtain heavenly riches (61). Just like his twin Lord, Thomas is known for his poverty (66, 96, 136, 139, 149), ascetic practices and preaching (3, 5, 28, 100, 136), and generosity to the poor (19, 20, 62). In fact, it is this imitation of Christ that accords him spiritual authority and mediating power as an apostolic "stand-in" for his "new God," Christ. Thomas regards his earthly poverty as a necessary condition for gaining his heavenly wealth. Therefore, he can claim his heavenly riches with certainty: "for my recompenser is righteous; he knows how I ought to receive my reward; for he is not grudging nor envious, but is rich in his gifts; . . . for he has confidence in his possessions which cannot fail" (159). In this sense, renunciation of earthly riches does serve as an ideal of imitating Christ and affords one a unique status and power for securing heavenly wealth.

2.5. Summary and Conclusion

Eschatology has an important social function. It provides a conceptual and practical framework of the divine judgment and the great reversal at the eschaton, for the present crisis and suffering in the world, with a view toward effecting right conduct and change in action in this world. Visions of the coming kingdom described in this-worldly, material abundance and prosperity point to the hope of communal flourishing and "equality" wrought by God's reign of both justice and grace that would be available for and experienced by all of God's faithful—the rich and the poor together. However, a biblical theme of the eschatological "great reversal," taken up by early Christians, strengthens a dichotomy between the "oppressive" rich and the "righteous" poor. In the Jewish apocalyptic texts and the earlier Christian texts, the association of the wicked rich with the threat of judgment and the pious poor with the promise of justice and reward features prominently. At the same time, it is also in the apocalyptic framework that the rich and the poor are exhorted to support and benefit each other through their respective services for the coming judgment.

---

possessions because of their love of god and their expectation of heavenly things, performing deeds worthy of their father Abraham" (*Martyrdom of Agapê, Irenê, and Chionê* 1.2); also in the *Testament* of the forty soldier martyrs at Sebaste: "For this reason I beg you, brother Crispinus, and make the request that you remain aloof from all worldly error and luxury. . . . Rather should you run to the loving God who offers unfading wealth to those who trust in him" (*Testament of Forty Martyrs* 2.1).

In this context, we have discussed how our sources interpret and reformulate definitions of wealth and poverty in the dualism of earthly and heavenly riches.

The eschatological visions and moral exhortations are also brought together to bear on the *present* earthly issues of social dissonance and stratification in the Christian communities (*Hermas*) and even of disaster relief for the wider communities (*On Works and Alms*). The danger of wealth stems from its earthly attachment, which obscures the desire for gaining heavenly riches. While avarice and luxury are universally denounced in apocalyptic critique, one can discern ambiguity about the renunciation of wealth and Christian commercial activities; renunciation is held as an ideal but relativization of wealth is practiced through almsgiving. We have also seen how the Christian eschatological hopes offered an alterative reality and identity markers in the challenging social contexts of Christians, and how the eschatological discourses both encouraged and constructed Christian social ethics.

According to Abraham Cronbach, the difference between charity and social justice lies in the fact that "charity seems to signify the relieving of poverty without regard to what people may have done to cause the poverty, while social justice holds people—that is, people other than the sufferer—accountable and directs its course accordingly."[57] In one sense, this vision for the eschatological judgment and great reversal could be seen as a way and call to ensure social justice *in this world* by identifying the group responsible for social injustice, oppression, and deprivation ("the wicked rich"), while projecting the ultimate inescapable dualistic fate of people in the world to come. On the other hand, the increasing shift from the great reversal to salvific almsgiving could be seen as steering the focus from social justice to charity (though the former was not lost in sight). Nonetheless, the cumulative effect of ethical paraenesis and eschatological judgment is that they serve as a boundary marker for early Christians as God's eschatological people—they will be judged by what they do to those who are helpless, afflicted, and poor.

Throughout history, Christian eschatology and otherworldliness have been unfortunately used and misused in extreme ways: on the one hand, to justify the sociopolitical and religious status quo (thus being blamed for its tacit neglect of social injustice and for its passivity toward social reforms);[58] on the other hand, to justify sociopolitical and religious radicalism and violence (thus being blamed for its sectarian condemnation of the dominant societies and militant opposition to social process and tolerance).[59] While it is true that the

57. A. Cronbach, "The Social Ideals of the Apocrypha and the Pseudepigrapha," *Hebrew Union College Annual* 18 (1944): 143.

58. See, for example, criticism of G. E. M. de Ste. Croix, "Early Christian Attitudes to Property and Slavery," in *Church, Society and Politics* (ed. D. Baker; Oxford: Basil Blackwell, 1975), 24–38.

59. See, for example, I. Gruenwald's critique of apocalyptic determinism and its ethical dehumanization leading to violence: "A Case Study of Scripture and Culture: Apocalypticism

eschatological orientation and "otherworldliness" of early Christian teachings did not directly deal with or call for larger social change and reform (especially as a tiny minority group in their sociopolitical context of the Roman Empire during the second and third centuries),[60] and while it is also true that there was no lack of the marginal millenarian sects that reaped tragic consequences in efforts to establish God's kingdom on earth by force, such as the revolutionary Anabaptists of Münster in the early sixteenth century, the very eschatological perception of reality and apocalyptic framework did *constructively* guide and shape Christian social thought and concrete Christian practices in the present age for the world to come. In light of this fact, the close mutual impact and effect of eschatological expectations and social messages on the issue of wealth and poverty also bore upon the understanding of salvation, the topic to which we turn in the next chapter.

---

as Cultural Identity in Past and Present," in *Ancient and Modern Perspectives on the Bible and Culture: Essays in Honor of Hans Dieter Betz* (ed. A. Y. Collins; Atlanta: Scholars Press, 1998), 252–80.

60. Cf. J. Viner, "The Economic Doctrines of the Early Christian Fathers," in *Religious Thought and Economic Society: Four Chapters of an Unfinished Work by Jacob Viner* (ed. J. Melitz and D. Winch; Durham, NC: Duke University Press, 1978), 9–18.

3

Wealth, Poverty, and Salvation

If there is a close relation between eschatology and ethics, particularly involving wealth and poverty, as shown in the previous chapter, there is also a firm connection between soteriology and ethics, especially related to wealth and poverty, as well as between eschatology and soteriology.[1] As mentioned in the earlier chapter, there is a synergistic relationship between the notion of one's ultimate destiny (eternal life or eternal punishment through the divine judgment) and the means to obtain that otherworldly salvation through one's praxis with wealth and poverty in this world. This chapter deals with how early Christians developed a concrete use of wealth and a particular understanding of poverty within a paradigm of and toward eschatological salvation, which would begin in this life. As Carter Lindberg puts it, "one of the theological problems that arose in the sociology of the early church was not poverty but wealth" in light of the Gospels' apparent "preferential option for the poor."[2] In the second and third centuries, the question of wealth, poverty, and salvation was contextualized in view of the obvious delay of Christ's return, the thorny problem of postbaptismal sin, and an advance of Christianity into the higher ranks of Roman society. How are the rich to be saved, then, if at all possible? How did "redemptive almsgiving" work? Was the salvation of the poor taken for granted? I will briefly treat the functional relation between

1. As confirmed by John Chrysostom's understanding of redemption and good deeds in R. Brändle, "This Sweetest Passage: Matthew 25:31–46 and Assistance to the Poor in the Homilies of John Chrysostom," in *Wealth and Poverty in Early Church and Society* (ed. S. Holman; Grand Rapids: Baker Academic, 2008), 138.

2. C. Lindberg, *Beyond Charity: Reformation Initiatives for the Poor* (Minneapolis: Fortress, 1993), 22.

early Christian soteriology and ethics and then move on to deal with these questions by focusing on some specific authors and texts in their social and historical contexts.

3.1. Soteriology and Ethics

On the one hand, it is not difficult to find affirmation of salvation by Jesus's atonement through his unique sacrifice in the patristic texts of our period. One of the most eloquent apologies in the early church proclaims the once-for-all and irreplaceable redemptive work of God through Christ in soaring exuberance and awe:

> He [God] . . . Himself in mercy took on Him [Christ] our sins, Himself gave up His own Son as a ransom for us, the holy One for the wicked, the innocent for the guilty, "the just for the unjust." . . . *For what else could cover our sins but his righteousness? In whom was it possible for us, wicked and impious as we were, to be justified, except in the Son of God alone? O the sweet exchange*, O work of God beyond all searching out, . . . that the wickedness of many should be hidden in one righteous Man and the righteousness of the One should justify many wicked! (*Diogn.* 9.2–5 [italics added])

This kind of acclamation would have belonged to emerging mainstream Christian thought on the sufficiency of salvation in Jesus Christ's atoning death and resurrection, which replaced the Jewish sacrificial law and temple (e.g., Origen, *Hom. Lev.* 2.3.3; 2.4.1).[3] Yet there was no firm separation between "salvation by faith in Christ's death" and its manifestation in attendant good works. Salvation is not just a one-time deal with baptism. As a "seal of salvation" that brings about remission of sins, rebirth, and the gift of the Holy Spirit (e.g., *Hermas, Vis.* 3.3; *Sim.* 8.2.2; 9.13; *Mand.* 4.3; Justin, *1 Apol.* 61; Theophilus, *Autol.* 2.16; Origen, *Hom. Lev.* 2.4.5; *Acts Paul* 25; *Acts Thom.* 121), baptism rather marks a new beginning of a lifelong upward journey toward maturity and perfection in imitation of God, which requires constant vigilance, discipline, struggle against vices, and cultivation of virtues until the end.[4] In this sense, ethics is always a part of soteriology since the redeemed, spiritual self entails and demands ethical transformation and internalization of virtues as well as shedding of old vices; salvation is always moral as well as spiritual (theological). The apostle Paul's words, "work out

3. One obvious exception is various gnostic understandings of salvation via the secret knowledge revealed by the "living" Christ.

4. For example, Origen, *Hom. Josh.* 1.6: "Unless you gain the mastery over their vices [e.g., pride, jealousy, greed, and lust] in yourself and exterminate them from your land—which now through the *grace of baptism* has been sanctified—you will not receive the *fullness* of the promised inheritance" (italics added).

your own salvation with fear and trembling" (Phil. 2:12) and "the only thing that counts is faith working through love" (Gal. 5:6), were deeply ingrained in the early Christian psyche; and orthopraxis as well as orthodoxy was always a part and parcel of salvation, especially in the face of the constantly lurking double threats of apostasy and heresy. One does well to remember that apostasy and heresy were judged not only by belief (theology) but also by behavior (ethics). Indeed, early Christian authors are emphatic that just calling Christ Lord alone will not save; it has to be accompanied by keeping his commandments (e.g., 2 *Clem.* 4.1–5; 6.7; cf. Matt. 7:21). Hence, Origen's scolding of those Christians whose good works and moral virtues did not match their professed faith (and desire to serve the church leaders) would have been characteristic across the broad spectrum of the church (*Hom. Josh.* 10.1). "For those . . . our Lord Jesus certainly permits salvation, but their salvation itself, in a certain measure, does not escape a note of infamy" (*Hom. Josh.* 10.1). The fundamental "Two Ways" (way of light/life and way of darkness/death) ethics in the *Didache*, the *Epistle of Barnabas* (second century), the *Didascalia* (third century), and the *Apostolic Constitutions* (fourth century) should be seen in this context and represent not necessarily regression of Christian freedom and *sola fide* of later Protestant construction, but the intricate relation between spiritual and moral transformation and progress, without which salvation is incomplete.

On the other hand, Roman Garrison contends that the early church compromised the exclusive role of Jesus's death as the unique and sufficient means of atonement by adopting and developing the doctrine of redemptive almsgiving (rooted in the Jewish Apocrypha) for postbaptismal sin.[5] Here is another marvelous exchange extolled by Clement of Alexandria:

> What splendid trading! What divine business! You buy incorruption with money [through almsgiving]. You give the perishing things of the world and receive in exchange for them an eternal abode in heaven. Compass the whole earth if need be. Spare not dangers or toils, that here you may buy a heavenly kingdom. (*Who Is a Rich Man That Is Saved?* 32)

This exchange of almsgiving and salvation seems incompatible with the former exchange of Christ's atoning death and salvation and even an egregious violation of the exclusive divine work of atonement, which would present a serious theological departure from and challenge to the Gospel message.[6] The main reason for this compromise, in conflict with Jesus's expiatory death in

5. R. Garrison, *Redemptive Almsgiving in Early Christianity* (Sheffield: JSOT Press, 1993), 60, 75.

6. Some (particularly) Protestant scholars took this view and pointed out a shift to legalism and "works-righteousness" in the second century onward; see, for example, T. F. Torrance, *The Doctrine of Grace in the Apostolic Fathers* (London: Oliver & Boyd, 1948).

Garrison's view, has to do with the crisis in faith provoked by postbaptismal sins, which in turn was incited by delay of the parousia.[7] Implied in this contention is that there took place a momentous shift in patristic soteriology from focusing on the work of Christ to focusing rather on the human work, however much that could be justified by the unexpected social and contextual change.

Still, one cannot help but recognize nearly universal calls to almsgiving for the purpose of forgiveness of sins in the early church,[8] which reflects traditional Jewish piety and its Christian contextualization (in continuity with some of the Second Temple literature and the New Testament passages, both implicit and explicit).[9] For instance, besides the 2 Clement 16.4 quoted in the previous chapter, the Didache commands the Christ followers, "If you acquire something with your hands, give it as a ransom for your sins [eis lutrōsin hamartiōn sou]" (4.6; translation by Ehrman; cf. Barn. 19.10). Polycarp, the revered bishop of Smyrna, exhorted the Philippians not to put off doing good (benefacere) when they were able, "since giving to charity [almsgiving] frees a person from death" (quia eleemosyna de morte liberat—quoting Tob. 4.10).[10] As mentioned in chapter 2, The Shepherd of Hermas attempted to address a dual issue of the problem of postbaptismal sin and of the social conflict between the rich and the poor. Hermas's solution was allowing single repentance for postbaptismal sin and exhorting single-mindedness especially for the rich, which requires cutting away their wealth through almsgiving to the poor (in the community); it would result in the "great exchange" and symbiosis between the rich and the poor: as the rich meet the material needs of the poor through alms, the poor would intercede for the salvation of the rich. By the time of Cyprian in the mid-third century, this notion of almsgiving contributing to eventual salvific effect for the givers would secure its place in a theological trajectory and practical ministries, and Cyprian would develop it further in relation to merit and penance that would sustain salvation of the rich.[11] In the fourth century and onward, "redemptive almsgiving" would be one of the most consistent elements in the sermons and teachings of church leaders.

7. Garrison, Redemptive Almsgiving, 73, 75.

8. Cf. G. A. Anderson, "Redeem Your Sins by the Giving of Alms: Sin, Debt, and the 'Treasury of Merit' in Early Jewish and Christian Tradition," Letter & Spirit 3 (2007): 68.

9. Patristic authors frequently cite passages such as Tob. 4.10–11; 12.9; Sir. 3.30, for scriptural support. Cf. Matt. 6:19–21; 25:31–46; Mark 10:21 and parallels; Luke 16:9, 19–31; 1 Pet. 4:8–9. For parallels from Rabbinic literature, see E. Ferguson, "Spiritual Sacrifice in Early Christianity and Its Environment," ANRW 2.23.2 (1981): 1161–62; A. Cronbach, "The Meʻil Zedakah," Hebrew Union College Annul 11 (1936): 511–49, esp. 525–29.

10. Cf. Cyprian, Eleem. 5, 9. Also note Irenaeus, Haer. 4.12.5: Christ's commandment to a rich young man to sell his possessions and give to the poor and follow him in Matt. 19:17–26 promises the apostolic share (apostolorum partem—its meaning is unclear) to those who obey it and means that Christ's followers can cancel out or annul their former covetousness by almsgiving, as evidenced by Zaccheus's example.

11. See below, "Salvation, Almsgiving, and Penance in Tertullian and Cyprian of Carthage."

Then how could these seemingly contradicting theological views and practices be explained? My aim in this chapter is not to review the whole history of early Christian soteriology but to focus on how their understanding and practice involving wealth and poverty influenced and was in turn influenced by their developing soteriology within their concrete social and historical context.

3.2. Salvation, the Rich, and the Poor—Internalization in Clement of Alexandria, Origen, and Peter of Alexandria

Between *Hermas* and Cyprian's *On Works and Alms* there appeared a pastoral homily by Clement of Alexandria, *Who Is a Rich Man That Is Saved?* (*Quis dives salvetur*),[12] in the late second century. In this work addressed to the affluent and cultured Christian audience in Alexandria,[13] the salvation of the rich who could identify with the "rich young man" in Mark 10:17–31 emerges as a considerable theological and social challenge that needs to be reinterpreted and reapplied. To the rich man's quest for eternal life, Jesus apparently demanded dispossession of his wealth and ultimately declared a virtual impossibility of the rich entering the kingdom of God *as the rich*. Is there hope for the rich? If so, how can they be saved? Clement deals with these questions head-on. This work has been examined by scholars on various occasions. However, I want to revisit this text, paying special attention to Clement's theological reconstruction of wealth, poverty, and almsgiving with regard to his ideal of salvation. In this context, I will examine Clement's notion of salvation and the relationship between the rich and the poor; I will also explore a question of function and motivation for almsgiving, since almsgiving seems to be encouraged more for salvation of the giver than for alleviation of poverty. This unabashed appeal to self-interest appears to be properly legitimized by a developing soteriology and theology of poverty with attendant "utility of the poor."[14] This idea then raises a question of the objects of almsgiving: should the Christian poor, who function as the intercessors for the rich, be the only proper objects? How could a distinction be made between the "worthy" and the "unworthy" poor? In exploring these questions, I will compare the different notions of wealth and its function in the developing soteriology of Alexandrian Christianity.

12. The Greek text and translation used here is Clement of Alexandria, *Exhortation to the Greeks/The Rich Man's Salvation* (trans. G. W. Butterworth; LCL; Cambridge, MA: Harvard University Press, 1919).

13. For literary and inscriptional evidence of an "emergence of urban patron class" in Alexandrian Christian circles as Clement's probable audience and perhaps his own patron(s), see L. M. White, "Scholars and Patrons: Christianity and High Society in Alexandria," in *Christian Teaching: Studies in Honor of LeMoine G. Lewis* (ed. E. Ferguson; Abilene, TX: Abilene Christian University Press, 1981), 331–39.

14. This phrase comes from Lindberg, *Beyond Charity*, 30.

Clement approaches the salvation of the rich out of a pastoral concern and directs his message not to "those [rich] who are uninitiated in the truth" but to "the rich who have learnt of the Saviour's power and His splendid salvation" (2). From the outset, he acknowledges that salvation seems to be more difficult for the rich than the poor, but he wants to show the same *concerned* rich who *have already been initiated* into the salvation process "how that which is impossible with men becomes possible" (2)—with Christ's instruction of the truth and their good works in lifelong perseverance (1). Hence, Clement first unfolds the "truth" of Christ's teachings in Mark 10:17–31 with his figurative interpretation and then guides the audience in how their good works would *secure* their salvation.

For Clement, the "truth" of Christ's instructions to the rich man lies in their "hidden meaning," which can be found with "an effort of mind" (5).[15] The fundamental premise in understanding the Lord's truth is to submit oneself to reason as trainer and to Christ as master of the contest (*agōnothetē*), i.e., salvation (3). The Lord's truth is first and foremost to know God and the Savior (the greatest doctrine), which requires perfection beyond the observance of the Mosaic law; the rich man's fulfillment of the law was good but not perfect.[16] Eternal life is beyond the reach of the law, however; knowing the Savior and eternal life entails inner contemplation, not an outer act (6–10). Therefore, Christ's counsel of perfection to the rich man—to sell his possessions—does not mean any external act of divestment but rather inner detachment: "to strip the soul itself and the will of their lurking passions and utterly to root out and cast away all alien thoughts from the mind" (11). If the Savior's words were to be taken literally, they are no more than an extension of the law, which is external and therefore "no(t) life-giving" (9), and no more than a reiteration of what the Greek philosophers have already done prior to his coming (11). So Christ's teaching *must be* "more divine and more perfect," new and unique, superseding all human teachings before him (12). Thus, it *cannot* mean the literal renunciation of wealth, which points to mere, natural human capacity.

Clement then shows how the external acts of renunciation contradict Christ's other commandments, such as making for ourselves friends with "mammon of unrighteousness" (Luke 16:9 KJV); storing treasures in heaven (Matt. 6.20); feeding the hungry and giving drinks to the thirsty (Matt. 25:41–43) and so on (13). All of these commandments presuppose personal wealth beyond bare necessities of life, which a believer should share with the less fortunate especially when the Lord threatens eternal punishment to those who have

15. E. A. Clark notes that Clement's figurative interpretation of the Markan passage offers a "classic example of how a 'spiritualized' reading might encourage a weakening of the ascetic rigor demanded by a more 'literal' exegesis" in *Reading Renunciation: Asceticism and Scripture in Early Christianity* (Princeton, NJ: Princeton University Press, 1999), 94; for a fuller treatment, see 92–95.

16. Cf. *Strom.* 3.6.55.2.

not obeyed them (13). Thus the commandments like these reveal the intrinsic neutrality and necessity of wealth and correctly highlight its proper utility and instrumentality with right reason and judgment rather than its simplistic abandonment (14). In this context, Clement, using the Stoic vocabulary and principle, places wealth in the external realm of *adiaphora*[17]—things morally indifferent but potentially advantageous depending on their use (15).[18] Receiving an inheritance, saving wealth with frugality, and investing property *prior to* conversion are not morally suspect;[19] rather, he relates these kinds of wealth to the gracious gifts of God, who in his providence distributes fortune to people (26). What is important is how the rich should use wealth to their spiritual advantage and for the benefit of their neighbors (14, 26). We will come back to this point a bit later.

Since Christ's truth regarding salvation "does not depend upon outward things" but upon "soul's virtue" (18), purging oneself of the soul's passions is the key to entering the kingdom of God. The internal nature of salvation demands cultivating pure and passionless souls with God's help, not getting rid of external goods and possessions (cf. 18, 20). Cultivating pure and passionless souls is an essential part of the care of the self that involves continual vigilance, education, training, and discipline in curbing vices of desires, passions, and immoderation.[20] Elsewhere Clement presents Christian salvation more explicitly as a two-stage spiritual *and* ethical process of self-care: first, a struggle with and cure of pleasure (*hēdonē*), passion (*pathos*), and desire (*epithymia*) through purification and self-control (*autarkeia* and *metriopatheia*) (*Strom.* 6.105.1 [2.484.29]),[21] eventually moving on to, second, a perfect state of passionless contemplation and imitation of God (*apatheia*) where the snares and traps of desire are no longer a danger to the soul (*Strom.* 6.7.1 [2.467]; 6.71.3–72.1).[22] With baptism every believer embarks on a long, arduous, and upward journey of healing of passions (*Paed.* 1.36.2.4; 1.43.1; 2.100.3), and an advanced baptized believer should grow and develop to reach the perfect gnostic state. As Harry Maier aptly puts it, for Clement, "the redeemed self is engaged in a life and death struggle [*agōn*] with the old sinful self of the passions" and cultivates freedom by applying the law and Christ's truth;[23] and this struggle itself testifies to the salvation of the self.[24] So even the rich can "enjoy the object of their hope"—the "Savior's prize," i.e., salvation, with "settled purpose" and "hard training and exercises" led

17. See, for example, Seneca, *Ep. 87 (On the Simple Life)*.
18. Plutarch examines this in *On Love of Wealth*, 527.
19. Cf. *Strom.* 3.6.56.1.
20. Cf. H. O. Maier, "Clement of Alexandria and the Care of the Self," *JAAR* 62 (1994): 725.
21. Cf. ibid., 728.
22. Cf. ibid., 734.
23. Ibid., 732.
24. Ibid., 728.

by Christ the instructor and guide (*Quis div.* 3). Hence, in this contest and race toward salvation, it is certainly possible for the rich to cast off inner lust and passions without literal dispossession, Clement writes, because Christ does not envy their wealth, whereas only those who are controlled and overcome by their wealth should leave them (24). In fact, the literal renunciation of wealth does not actually cure the disease of the soul; instead, it could rather create a "double annoyance, the absence of means of support and the presence of regret" simply due to basic human needs (12). Therefore, it could result in false pretension of a cure riddled with even greater passions and anguish. Both voluntary and involuntary poverty have no intrinsic value apart from attendant poverty of the soul, which is available for the rich as well as for the poor.

This internalization of salvation demystifies the traditional assumption of "the pious poor and the wicked rich" and spiritualizes wealth and poverty. As Clement deconstructs the tradition of the pious poor and the wicked rich, he constructs a model of the pious rich and the wicked rich, on the one hand, and the noble poor and the wretched poor, on the other. The pious rich are the ones who are "rich in virtues and able to use every fortune in a holy and faithful manner" (19); they are contrasted with the "spurious rich" who are "rich according to the flesh" but pursuing the life of transitory outward possessions (19). Likewise, the genuine poor (*ptōchoi*) are the ones who are "poor in spirit" with "the inner personal poverty," whereas the spurious poor consist of the poor "in worldly goods, the outward alien poverty" but full of vices (19). Clement in this way connects the true, pious rich with the genuine, spiritual poor and shows how "the same man can be both poor and wealthy" (20). Christ's call to "sell one's possessions" then is a universal call not only to the spurious, outwardly rich but also to the spurious, outwardly poor to detach themselves from the "alien possessions that dwell in [their] soul[s], in order that [they] may become pure in heart and may see God" (19). This is in fact what St. Peter exactly demonstrated in his life. When he said, "Lo, we have left all and followed [Christ]," he meant "by flinging away the old possessions of the mind and diseases of the soul that [the disciples] are following in the track of their teacher" (21). This is indeed how one follows the Savior: that "we seek after [the Savior's] sinlessness and perfection, adorning and regulating the soul before Him as before a mirror and arranging it in every detail after His likeness" (*homoiōsis*; 21).[25] Again, salvation in this paradigm is a continuous, upward progress toward perfection, which is passionless imitation of Christ,[26] overcoming the insidious inner persecutions—godless lusts and manifold pleasures, low hopes and corrupting imaginations, and covetousness (25). This is the life of a true gnostic, which is the costly result of the disciplined care of

25. Cf. *Strom.* 2.97.1; 2.131.5.
26. Cf. *Strom.* 2.326.3.

the self (*heautou epimelomenos*)[27] and can never be achieved by a single act of external renunciation.

Having established the truth of Christ's salvation, Clement then moves to how the rich can arrive at this state *using* their wealth. He first sets the theological ground for good works (almsgiving) in the greatest commandment of loving God (27). Just as knowing God is the foundation of Christ's truth, loving God is the foundation of Christ's love and our striving for good works (cf. 28). The second part of the greatest commandment is loving one's neighbor as oneself. According to Clement's interpretation of the parable of the good Samaritan, our neighbor is none other than Christ himself, who showed us his mercy and heals our wounds of passions (29). How then do the rich love Christ as their neighbor as they love God? It is by loving Christ's disciples, fellow Christians in need. By giving relief to "one of those who have an eternal habitation with the Father" (31), the rich fulfill the Lord's injunction to make friends with unrighteous mammon for their eternal life (Luke 16:9) and secure their heavenly reward (31). In so doing, the rich should not just "yield to a request or wait to be pestered" but "should personally seek out men whom [they] may benefit" for their progress toward salvation, "men who are worthy disciples of the Saviour" (31). Thus, Clement champions the salvific effect of almsgiving in the following way:

> What splendid trading! What divine business! You buy incorruption with money. You give the perishing things of the world and receive in exchange for them an eternal abode in heaven. Compass the whole earth if need be. Spare not dangers or toils, that here you may buy a heavenly kingdom (32).

Giving to the poor Christians promises a sure return of abundant reward and spiritual wealth to the rich to the extent that Clement freely uses an economic language of transaction and exchange—the notion that already heavily featured in the *Shepherd of Hermas*. However, Clement qualifies this great exchange: the rich should see to it that "the Lord did not say, 'give,' or 'provide,' or 'benefit,' or 'help,' but 'make a friend'" (32); indeed, "a friend is made not from one gift, but from complete relief and long companionship" (32). Just as ridding one's soul of passions takes a continual struggle and training, making friends with one's wealth requires sustained work and building relationships with the recipients. Furthermore, in doing so, the rich should not try to distinguish the worthy from the unworthy poor lest they accidentally neglect the former and incur "eternal punishment by fire" (33). They are also not to take offense at the appearance of the needy or to gaze at them with contempt, for God and Christ dwell within the poor (33). What is necessary and important for the rich is to find those among their recipients "who have power to save [them]

27. *Strom.* 7.16.1.

with God" as they give to all who are enrolled as God's disciples, i.e., the Christian poor in general (33).

What is noteworthy is the fact that contrary to his earlier effort to deconstruct the tradition of "the pious poor and the wicked rich" in interiorizing and spiritualizing wealth and poverty, Clement presupposes and counts on that very tradition here in promoting redemptive almsgiving for the rich Christians. The pious poor's role is absolutely vital, and their spiritual services are both specific and comprehensive: "One is able to beg your life from God, another to hearten you when sick, another to weep and lament in sympathy on your behalf before the Lord" (35). Clement loses no time in issuing the clearest call to the rich:

> Enlist on your behalf an army without weapons, without war, without bloodshed, . . . an army of God-fearing old men, of God-beloved orphans, of widows armed with gentleness, of men adorned with love. Obtain with your wealth, as guards for your body and your soul, such men as these, whose commander is God. Through them the sinking ship rises, steered by the prayers of saints alone; . . . [and] the attack of robbers is made harmless, being stripped of its weapons by pious prayers. (34)

If the one-time renunciation would not be a solution for the salvation of the rich, the ongoing generous almsgiving is a palpable way to obtain their salvation. For the redemptive efficacy of almsgiving is rooted in the reciprocal exchange of love among believers, which is in turn rooted in God's love and a reciprocal demand of Christ's sacrifice (37). In this sense, almsgiving is a quintessential, positive *demonstration* of loving God and neighbor as well as of using one's wealth properly. Despite an unabashed appeal to the self-interest of the rich giver, a more fundamental appeal for almsgiving is love of God and love for God, without which no one can gain salvation (cf. 38). Because God receives and forgives everyone who turns to him in genuine repentance, almsgiving is an effective means of repentance and rooting out of the soul the postbaptismal sins leading to death (39).

For Clement, then, almsgiving becomes a necessary part of the care of the self, which is indispensable for the journey of salvation, the path to perfection. As such, it constitutes an essential part of the Christian (perfect gnostic) sacrifice in God's sight (cf. *Strom.* 7.3.14.1; 7.7.49.5).[28] Make no mistake, Clement acknowledges that visible wealth is perilous, beggarly, transitory,

---

28. *Strom.* 7.7.49.3–5: "For so, in the case of the Gnostic, who has unblameably and with a good conscience fulfilled all that depends on him, in the direction of learning, and training, and well-doing, and pleasing God, the whole contributes to carry salvation on to perfection. From us, then, are demanded the things which are in our own power, . . . possession, and use. . . . And what? Does he [the gnostic] not also know the other kind of sacrifice, which consists in the giving of both doctrines and of money to those who need?"

and alien to the soul (cf. 30) and easily leads the soul astray to luxuries and fancy allurements (20). Wealth, like a snake, "twisting in the grasp, whether experienced or not, can cling to the hand and bite unless a man rises superior to it and uses it with discretion" (*Paed*. 3.6.35). Therefore, if the rich know the truth that salvation is internal and belongs to the passionless souls (as they should) and that it is God's love that calls them to love fellow believers, how could they hoard their worldly goods? They can only respond by properly channeling their wealth from the earthly to the heavenly realm, i.e., almsgiving (cf. 20). Through consistent and generous almsgiving, the rich cultivate inner detachment and freedom; for the race to salvation takes a laborious training and perseverance, as in the case with athletes (3; 40).[29] They should even seek a special spiritual director as their "trainer" (*aleiptēs*) and "pilot" (*kybernētēs*)[30] to hold them strictly accountable and to beg for God's mercy on their behalf (41). The rich need and should utilize all the resources they can get to take care of their souls: "God's power, human supplication, the help of brethren, sincere repentance, and constant practice" (40). With all of those resources, "success is achieved" (40); the heavenly Father will give the earnest rich "true purification and unchanging life" (42). Then "when the last trumpet signals the end of the race and [their] departure from the present life as from a course," the rich will "with a good conscience stand before the judge a victor, admitted to be worthy of the father land above, into which angelic crowns and proclamations [they] now ascend" (3). God helps those who help themselves with a given means.

Origen, the fellow Alexandrian of elite culture,[31] also takes a spiritualizing approach to the rich/riches with his similar understanding of salvation and allegorical interpretations, although he did not leave any extensive or consistent teachings on these matters as Clement did. Salvation for Origen is essentially an education in divine training and guidance, in which "God orders every rational soul with a view to its eternal life . . . until it reaches the pinnacle of virtue" with its free will (*Or*. 29.13).[32] Like Clement, Origen is aware that in his time not only rich men but "persons in position of honour, and ladies of refinement and high birth" have favorable regard for the Christian faith, and some of them even become leaders in the church (*Cels*. 3.9). On the one hand, earthly riches ("blind wealth"—*Cels*. 1.24; 7.21) are a stumbling block to salvation, for the rich have greater difficulty controlling their passions (*Comm. Matt*. 15.20, PG) and hinder the rich from bearing the fruits of God's Word (*Cels*. 7.23). In fact, earthly riches belong to the cursed world (*Fr. Luc*. 193; Luke 12:19); thus, for the advanced Christians an ideal is to abandon those

29. Cf. *Paed*. 3.6.34–36.
30. According to White, "Scholars and Patrons," 334, these terms, "trainer" and "pilot," "allude to two common metaphors for moral instruction among the philosophers."
31. On Origen's background and patrons, see Eusebius, *HE* 6.2.12; 6.18.1.
32. Cf. E. de Faye, *Origen and His Work* (New York: Columbia University, 1929), 128.

riches (*Comm. Matt.* 15.16, PG) with a pure heart. Basic needs of physical or material life should not even be of concern to them, because they should live not by literal and physical understanding of God's Word but by its hidden, spiritual meanings.[33] In his treatise on the Lord's Prayer, Origen interprets Jesus's request for daily bread (Luke 11:3) as a request only for God's Word for spiritual nourishment ("supersubstantial bread"), not for material bread for physical nourishment.[34] For the spirit that is completely united to God will transcend any physical and earthly concerns and dealings (*Comm. Rom.* 9.22).

On the other hand, wealth as such is *adiaphoron*, neither good nor evil in and of itself, and therefore what is more important is not literal renunciation but inner detachment and purity, which is attainable only with rigorous discipline and education of the heart and mind (cf. *Comm. Matt.* 10.10). Like Clement, Origen considers rash dispossession of wealth a danger since it might lead to a regret or longing for the lost possessions rather than sublime disentanglement from earthly things (cf. *Comm. Matt.* 15.16; *Comm. Rom.* 9.22); if the former were to happen, it would result in the opposite of salvation—descending to excess of wickedness through carelessness (cf. *Or.* 29.13). When Jesus spoke about the difficulty of the rich entering the kingdom, he meant the rich not as such but the rich who were distracted by wealth or those who were rich in false opinions (*Cels.* 7.23). For that matter, when Jesus pronounced the miserable lot of the rich, he meant not the rich in material wealth per se but those with "a wealth which is without qualification blameworthy," i.e., wealth in vices (*Cels.* 6.16). In the same way, when the Mosaic law promises wealth to the righteous, its promise is not about "blind wealth" in a literal sense, as Celsus foolishly understands, but riches in "things which are genuinely good" such as good works, "all utterance and all knowledge" (*Cels.* 7.21). In the school of salvation, one will ultimately obtain God's blessings by bringing forth the fruit of good works through spiritual labors but will reap God's curse if subject to the "cares of the world, or the desires of pleasures and riches" (*Hom. Lev.* 16.5). As for good works, almsgiving is *a* means to attain virtue, which is the goal of salvation, but only when performed with a pure heart and right intention, i.e., not for vain glory (*kenodoxia*) or love of gain (*philokerdia*) (*Comm. Matt.* 11.15). In fact, for those for whom Christ provided atonement through his unique and all-sufficient sacrifice (i.e., Christians in the school of salvation), the gospel graciously offers no fewer than seven remedies for post-baptismal sins, including almsgiving, only next to baptism and martyrdom in rank (*Hom. Lev.* 2.4).[35] Almsgiving, which the Savior himself commanded for cleansing of sin (cf. Luke 11:41), is apparently the most important Christian

33. Cf. Origen's principles of allegorical hermeneutics in *First Principles* 4.

34. *Prayer* 27.5; cf. *Fr. Luc.* 180, against Marcion's literal interpretation.

35. The whole list is in the order of decreasing importance. The rest of the means of forgiveness include readiness to forgive, converting sinners, fervent love, and penitence; while baptism and martyrdom are nonrepeatable, almsgiving is the first in rank of the repeatable remedies.

sacrifice that is repeatable and is a crucial means to testify to one's progressing (or ongoing) purity from the cares and passions of this world and to receive cleansing from one's postbaptismal sins: "When[ever] you give alms and bestow the love of mercy moved by pity toward those in need, you load the sacred altar with fat goats" (*Hom. Lev.* 2.4.6).[36] Once again, not unlike for Clement, almsgiving for Origen is a necessary part of divine training in salvation.

Origen also deconstructs the tradition of "the pious poor and the wicked rich" in a similar way when he reflects on temptations in his treatise *On Prayer*. Lest people think that the poor are not subject to temptation on account of their poverty, they should note that the devil, the tempter, "does his best to cast down the poor and needy" (29.6). Both the rich and the poor face temptations: the former, the temptation of presumption, lying, and pride, and the latter, that of stealing and forswearing God's name (29.5). Just as the rich who fail to use their earthly riches properly receive the same punishment as the rich man in the Gospel (i.e., the rich man who neglected poor Lazarus in Luke 16:19, 22–24), the poor who bear their poverty "ignobly" and conduct themselves in a more "lowly and servile manner" than is "becoming for saints" fall away from the heavenly hope (29.6). Therefore, Origen implies here that the poor should not take their presumed spiritual status for granted, and yet they have will (capacity) and choice about *how to endure their poverty* (which they did not choose). Unless they resist and overcome these temptations, as do the righteous rich through the care of inner self, they will face the same fate as the wicked rich.

By spiritualizing poverty (and wealth), Clement of Alexandria and Origen underscore two important points: first, they distinguish between worthy and unworthy poverty (and wealth) and between the worthy and unworthy poor (and rich).[37] External poverty in itself is not a spiritual virtue; for that matter external wealth in itself is not sinful. If it were so, Clement retorts,

> those men who have nothing at all, but are destitute and beg for their daily bread, who lie along the roads in abject poverty, would, though "ignorant" of God and "God's righteousness," be most blessed and beloved of God and the only possessors of eternal life, by the sole fact of their being utterly without ways and means of livelihood and in want of the smallest necessities. (*Quis div.* 11)

The kind of poverty that is blessed by the Savior is "poverty in spirit," that is, "poverty for righteousness' sake" (*Strom.* 4.6.25.4; *Quis div.* 17); it is poverty "by choice not by necessity" (*Strom.* 4.6.25.4)—the internal poverty of the

---

36. Cf. *Homilae in Numeros* 11.9: "If one gives to the poor, if one performs any good work [*boni operis*], he has offered to God a present according to the commandment." Consider also the maxim of the Alexandrian *Sentences of Sextus* 47: "The only suitable sacrifice [*thysia*] to God is to do good deeds [*euergesia*] for men because of God."

37. *Strom.* 4.5–6.

true gnostic. Origen echoes this idea by distinguishing between a material poverty and "a poverty that is blessed without qualification," i.e., spiritual poverty accompanied by richness in faith (*Cels.* 6.16; *Homiliae in Genesim* 16.4). He claims that "not even a stupid person would praise the poor indiscriminately; the majority of them have very bad characters" (*Cels.* 6.16).[38] Second, paradoxically, by spiritualizing poverty (and wealth), they extend a possibility and even capacity of moral choice, self-mastery, to the material poor (i.e., the involuntary poor) as well as to the rich.

While it may still be an aristocratic view of poverty (albeit Christianized) and sound condescending to the involuntary poor (from a modern perspective), this is the most powerful portrayal of the poor in this period. Note the way in which Clement highlights the active will of the poor in their ministry on behalf of the rich: they are "*resolved to [pepeismenois]* minister to God, to persuade God, to please God" (35; italics added). In a world where one's moral character and capacity are largely determined by one's socioeconomic and political status, the poor Christians stand alongside the rich Christians as "autonomous" beings with their own volition and value by virtue of their spirituality and service. In this description, they are worthy recipients of alms, clearly deserving the generosity of the rich. In fact, the rich man should "beg" the godly poor man to take his gift, "for he [the poor man] has not been commanded to take, but you [the rich man] to provide" (32). In this way Clement reduces a social distance between the rich and the poor by minimizing "the contempt which otherwise threatens to frustrate the call to almsgiving"[39] and also by accentuating mutual need for each other for their eternal destiny. Both are on the receiving end in different respects, but the needs of the rich are of the more serious kind after all. Origen also states that it is the prayers of the poor that would gradually lead to the perfecting of their benefactor (presumably a rich person) (*Comm. Matt.* 15.17). Richard Finn has recently shown that descriptions of poverty and the poor in Christian texts of late antiquity both revealed and hid the poor to "make them attractive as recipients of alms."[40] We may draw the same conclusion for the depictions of the poor by Clement of Alexandria and Origen.

On the other hand, the descriptions of the poor, however noble and lofty they may be considering the larger (pagan) social context, never appear independently from their expected status and role of being recipients of almsgiving. In this sense, the visibility and portrayal of the poor are always attached to their instrumentality in the salvation of the rich. Clement and Origen raise the

38. Here Origen is simply resorting back to the typical Greco-Roman aristocratic understanding and characterization of the mass, *humiliores*.

39. R. Finn, "Portraying the Poor: Descriptions of Poverty in Christian Texts from the Late Roman Empire," in *Poverty in the Roman World* (ed. M. Atkins and R. Osborne; Cambridge: Cambridge University Press, 2006), 134.

40. Ibid., 144.

question of the salvation of the poor only in deconstructing the pious poor and the wicked rich, which is a way of removing a barrier for the salvation of the rich. Unlike the poor in some of the Jewish Second Temple literature or the New Testament writings, the poor in the second- and third-century works fade in significance as the self-descriptions of distinct chosen groups and/or the active recipients of and participants in God's eschatological salvation and justice (see chap. 1; e.g., *1 Enoch* and DSS for self-descriptions of Jewish groups; cf. Luke 1:53; 6:20; James 5:7).

Lastly, one cannot pass over a later Alexandrian work *On Riches*, attributed to Peter of Alexandria, bishop and martyr (d. 311 CE).[41] In its address to the rich *in* the Alexandrian church, it shares the same concern as Clement of Alexandria—salvation of the rich by their proper use of wealth (14, 18, 43). The familiar theme of the wicked rich is elaborated with its diatribe on the "merciless" and "pitiless" rich man, "the brother-hater" (18), who takes his divine gift of wealth for granted without any concern for the poor (16–18, 20, 23, 41) and therefore without any regard for his own soul (34; cf. 43).[42] While the text castigates the rich for putting their trust only in their wealth and "the things of this age which are like shadows" (33), it turns the Lord's words on the disciples' renunciation in Matt. 19:27–29 (51)[43] into giving a cup of cold water and buying a book for the church (52) and extensively appeals to the biblical examples of the righteous rich by their generous charity, such as Abraham, Job, David, and Solomon (1–2, 18–19, 38–39). The sweet smell of the sacrifice of good deeds by the rich—having "pitied the poor, shown hospitality, and defended orphan(s) and widow(s), (and) torn up every letter, having loved [their] neighbor as [themselves]"—"will travel further in [their] death than in [their] life, and [they] will inherit *with the patriarchs and the apostles* the kingdom of heaven" (47; italics according to the translation).

On the other hand, in its direct address *to* the poor, a rare literary phenomenon in itself in the early church, there is no corresponding piety or spirituality of the poor mentioned; rather it rebukes the poor just as harshly as the wicked rich for their apparent envy and fretting about the rich as well as their ingratitude to the Lord who "made [them] free from all the cares about which the rich man is concerned" (55). The poor man is ignorant of

41. For an argument for a plausible case for Petrine authorship, at least for a "core homily," see *Two Coptic Homilies Attributed to Saint Peter of Alexandria: On Riches, On the Epiphany* (trans. and ed., with an intro., by B. Pearson and T. Vivian, with D. B. Spanel; Roma: C.I.M., 1993), 25–31. All quotations of the text are from the same work.

42. As in Origen, this familiar picture of the wicked rich with a theme of great reversal is taken from the parable of the rich man and Lazarus in Luke 16:19–31.

43. This is the section following Jesus's encounter with the rich young man in the Matthean version: "*Pay attention, my beloved. What is it that he said to him?* 'Everyone,' (Jesus) said, 'who has left behind house or wife (*or*) *father* or mother or child or *money* or everything for my name's sake will receive many times more in the kingdom of heaven and will inherit life forever'" (51). Italics according to the translation.

the destruction of the rich at the end (63) and liberated from any distress that plagues the rich; he should be thankful that his "only care is bread and a garment" (56). Note again that the rich in general are assumed to be the "wicked, merciless rich" unless they are specified as the "merciful and loving" (66). As for the poor, there is no specification of the "pious poor" for their positive or active role either in relation to God or the rich. The author, comparable to and yet somewhat harsher than his Alexandrian predecessors, makes a clear point: "I do not honor the poor by making (them) equal to the rich, nor do I favor (them). Indeed, there is (a kind of) poor man who leaves (his) poverty for another poverty seven times more evil than this"—for instance, an idle poor man, an arrogant one, a treacherous one, and one who steals (58). Unlike the earlier Alexandrians, this text deconstructs the wicked rich (somewhat incompletely) and the pious poor tradition without any attempt to spiritualize wealth and poverty. "Wealth is good for the one who will manage it according to God. Poverty is good for the one who will be able to bear it and be thankful in everything" (66). The rich and the poor, "each one [should] act in a manner befitting God in everything" (69), not in a symbiotic way that mutually ministers with almsgiving and intercession as in the case of *Hermas* and the other Alexandrian authors, but in a way that bears the created social order determined by God (cf. *1 Clem.* 38.2; see chap. 6). The poor in this text, while they may be worthy of direct address and have the moral capacity to bear poverty with thanksgiving, appear only as the passive (and negative) recipients of the alms, even forfeiting their only positive role—in the salvation of the rich.

3.3. Salvation and the Redefinition of Wealth and Poverty in the Christian Apocryphal Tradition

The radical interiorization of salvation in the famous Nag Hammadi text *Gospel of Thomas* takes a poverty motif in another way. In the dualistic worldview of this Gospel, poverty characterizes life in this world,[44] the realm of flesh and body, in contrast to life in the realm of spirit. Saying 3 connects self-knowledge to being "children of the living Father" (i.e., salvation): "But if you do not know yourselves, then you live in poverty, and you are the poverty." Here poverty, ignorance of the self, is an ontological status as well as a negative spiritual condition that self-ignorance entails.[45] According to Saying 29, spirit is identified as wealth, and flesh as poverty, and the true wonder is "how this great wealth has come to dwell in this poverty." The relationship of spirit and body causes marvel because "the wealth of the spiritual realm

44. R. Valantasis, *The Gospel of Thomas* (New Testament Readings; London: Routledge, 1997), 131.
45. Cf. ibid., 59.

lives within the poverty of the world."[46] Yet, the poor are blessed in Saying 54 because heaven's domain belongs to them. Here the poor signify those who live as "passersby" on earth (cf. Saying 42); their material poverty indicates freedom from the cares and involvement of the world (cf. Sayings 36, 42), which is necessary for the seekers of knowledge. Therefore, it takes a more ascetic turn and the material poor (i.e., the voluntary poor here) are indeed the poor "in spirit" in this context.

The well-known *Hymn of the Pearl* in the *Acts of Thomas*, tinged with some gnostic elements like the *Gospel of Thomas* in a similar theological milieu, shares the allegorized understandings of poverty. Broadly, this allegory of salvation describes the soul's (child/prince) descent to this world (Egypt) with a divine mission to fetch a pearl of great price but with an amnesia of heavenly origin; but it is reawakened by a divine revelation of self-knowledge, which helps to fulfill its mission and leads to its return to the heavenly kingdom (the Pleroma).[47] In this hymn, the heavenly world is described with extraordinary wealth and luxury (see chap. 2) once enjoyed by the prince, who must fetch the pearl in an alien world without which the soul cannot return; however, the earthly material world is the foul land of "the yoke of slavery" (44) where the soul falls asleep, forgetting its mission. Here poverty signifies the soul's ignorance of divine status, whereas wealth symbolizes salvation in the Pleroma (with glorious restoration of its royal position) which cannot be attained without the recovery of the pearl—the soul's knowledge of the Pleroma. Thus, poverty in the *Hymn* also refers to the soul's ontological status and its negative spiritual condition in a dualistic worldview.[48]

Another intriguing Nag Hammadi text, the *Acts of Peter and the Twelve Apostles*, has a distinct but related ascetic perspective on poverty and the poor. This text may be a mid-third-century redacted piece of an earlier Christian gnostic allegory of the ascent of the soul, possibly coming from a community

---

46. Ibid., 104.

47. While the precise meaning of this allegory somewhat differs among scholars, some see this as an allegory of humanity's expulsion from and one's return to the paradise of God, describing how a human loses the image of God and one's free will and recovers it, how one becomes mortal and returns to the immortality that God promised humanity in his covenant and holds ready for them; see, for example, H. J. W. Drijvers, "Introduction: The Acts of Thomas," in *Writings Relating to Apostles, Apocalypses and Related Subjects* (vol. 2 of *New Testament Apocrypha*; ed. W. Schneemelcher; trans. R. M. Wilson; rev. ed.; Louisville: Westminster John Knox, 1991, 1992), 332. Others see it as an allegory of the soul's human incarnation, disengagement with the body, and eventual reunion with God; e.g., B. Layton, *The Gnostic Scriptures* (New York: Doubleday, 1987). Still others interpret this as an allegory of a redeemer, Christ, symbolized by the child/son in the *Hymn*. See J. K. Elliott, *The Apocryphal New Testament* (Oxford: Clarendon, 1993), 441.

48. Cf. E. Moore, "Wealth, Poverty, and the Value of the Person: Some Notes on the Hymn of the Pearl and Its Early Christian Context," in *Wealth and Poverty in Early Church and Society* (ed. S. Holman; Grand Rapids: Baker Academic, 2008), 58–60.

in Alexandria that underwent the Decian persecution.[49] In the *Acts*, allegory
of salvation is presented as the "Story of the Pearl Merchant" in which the
merchant (Savior = Jesus = Lithargoel) offers the pearl (here, salvation) that
can be obtained by a soul's laborious journey to Nine Gates (the heavenly
world = the Pleroma) through hostile realms.[50] This journey demands total
renunciation of the world, especially possessions, coupled with daily fasting
(5.21–25), but is achievable for those who rely on Jesus's power. When the
merchant from Nine Gates visits a city of Habitation (the earthly abode) and
offers the pearl, the rich of the city utterly ignore and reject him and his offer
in disdain while the poor invite him to the city. The merchant not only shows
the poor his pearl but also promises to give it to them freely since they are
poor and unable to buy it from him. The poor then rejoice at the merchant's
invitation and promise of the pearl and later become the focus of the ministry
of Peter and the apostles commissioned by Jesus. In this *Acts*, the rich who
rejected Jesus and "reveled in their wealth and pride" are in turn rejected by
Jesus, who does not reveal himself to them and instructs his disciples not to
associate with them (11.26–12.2). The rich mislead people with their partiality and are shown partiality by many who are sinful in the churches (12.3–7).
However, the poor are the object of the physical ministry (i.e., corporal works
of mercy) by the disciples who in fact have renounced the world for Jesus's
sake, as well as the object of Jesus's spiritual ministry, i.e., salvation.[51] As one
can see, the rich and the poor here have both physical and spiritual meanings
and correspond to the "pious poor and the wicked rich" tradition; what is
more, the rich are ignorant of the divine revelation, but the poor are capable of
recognizing it and welcome it.[52] In this context, material poverty has become
a necessary condition for salvation and Christian ministry and is equated as
poverty "in spirit," whereas earthly wealth is not only a harmful hindrance
to the journey into the heavenly kingdom but the cause of exclusion from the
kingdom.

49. See A. L. Molinari, *The Acts of Peter and the Twelve Apostles (NHC 6.1): Allegory, Ascent, and Ministry in the Wake of the Decian Persecution* (SBL Dissertation Series 174; Atlanta,
GA: SBL, 2000). For a different view on the provenance (Syria) and gnostic characteristics, see
H.-M. Schenke, "The Acts of Peter and the Twelve Apostles," in *Writings Relating to Apostles*
(ed. Schneemelcher; trans. Wilson), 412–19.

50. Note the difference from the *Hymn of the Pearl* in which the soul descends to earth before
it ascends to the Pleroma and the pearl is not given freely but has to be fetched; cf. Molinari,
Acts of Peter and the Twelve Apostles, 148–49.

51. Cf. Jesus's instruction to his disciples in 10:8–13: "To the poor of the city give what
they need in order to live until I give them what is better which I told you that I will give you for
nothing." Translation is from Molinari.

52. As the *Acts* itself might have gone through the redaction from an otherworldly allegory
to mysticism based on a historical and concrete *Sitz im Leben*, the rich and the poor refer to
the groups in a literal, material sense as well as in a spiritual sense. Cf. Molinari, *Acts of Peter
and the Twelve Apostles*, 7–9.

3.4. Salvation, Almsgiving, and Penance in Tertullian and Cyprian of Carthage

We now move to the North African scene, where we find Tertullian, the elite Christian apologist and the first Latin theologian at the turn of the third century, and Cyprian, the refined and charismatic bishop of Carthage in the mid-third century. Both were adult converts with high birth, classical education, and significant resources (Cyprian certainly more so than Tertullian), and both were familiar with and participated in sophisticated Roman literary culture in Carthage.[53] While Tertullian shares the broad understanding of salvation as the lifelong journey of "the care of self" and the "education in divine training" of his Alexandrian colleagues, he describes salvation as a consistency between the inner reality and virtue of Christianity and its outer expression and conduct.[54] Christians' fulfilling of God's will on earth through their visible obedience to God's disciplines enables the fulfillment of God's will in heaven and effects their salvation in heaven and on earth (*Or.* 4.2). Therefore, Christian appearance, discipline, good works, and merit as external means of ascertaining Christian truth and faith are crucial indicators of the internal state of the soul and absolutely critical and integral to one's salvation (e.g., *Or.* 4.2; 5.1; *Paen.* 6.4; *Exh. cast.* 2.3; *Marc.* 2.6.7; 4.31.1). For this reason, Tertullian gives meticulous attention to disciplinary matters, even matters of spectacles, modesty, veiling, dress, ornaments, and soldiers' crowns in his treatises.[55] Addressing the wealthy Christian women of Carthage, Tertullian links their dress, cosmetics, and apparel to their salvation: "Salvation . . . not of women only, but also of men, is especially to be procured in the observance of modesty. For, since we are all temples of God because the Holy Spirit has entered into us and sanctified us, modesty is the sacristan and priestess of that temple" (*Cultu fem.* 2.1.1). Indeed, it "is not enough for Christian modesty merely to be, but also to be seen. Its fullness ought to be so great that it flow out from the mind to the dress and erupt forth from the conscience unto the surface, so that even from without it may survey, as it were, its ornament, which may be fit for faith's maintaining forever" (*Cultu fem.* 2.13.3; Groh's translation; cf. 1 Tim. 2:9–10). The salvific faith must show itself in the world and carry exact external or visible form; otherwise it is not faith at all.[56]

---

53. See Brent, *Cyprian and Roman Carthage*, 3–4, 25, 43–44; T. D. Barnes, *Tertullian: A Historical and Literary Study* (Oxford: Clarendon, 1971), 69, 195–96; G. D. Dunn, *Tertullian* (London: Routledge, 2004), 5; and C. A. Bobertz, "Cyprian of Carthage as Patron: A Social Historical Study of the Role of Bishop in the Ancient Christian Community of North Africa" (PhD diss., Yale University, 1988), 51, 75–129; Cyprian as a teacher of rhetoric (*rhetor*) in Jerome, *Vir. ill.* 67; Lactantius, *Inst.* 5.1.24; Augustine, *Serm.* 312.

54. D. E. Groh, "Tertullian's Polemic against Social Co-Optation," *Church History* 40 (1971): 13.

55. Cf. ibid., 13.

56. L. Raditsa, "The Appearance of Women and Contact: Tertullian's *De Habitu Feminarum*," *Athenaeum* 63 (1985): 305.

In this overall theological framework, Tertullian takes up the issue of the rich and the poor in his massive work, *Against Marcion*, where he defends the fundamental unity of God in the Old and New Testaments as both the Creator and the Redeemer against Marcion's dichotomy between the two and radical asceticism in rejection of the material world. Discussing the beatitudes and the woes in the Gospel of Luke (6:20–22),[57] Tertullian affirms that, with the very character and attributes of God the Creator[58] who "always expresses his love for the indigent [*mendicos*], the poor [*pauperes*], the humble, and the widows and orphans, comforting, protecting, and avenging them" (4.14.2; 4.14.13; cf. 5.3.6)[59] throughout the Old Testament (Isaiah in particular), Christ, "the comforter of the indigent" (4.15.8), from the outset identified his ministry as proclaiming the good news to the poor (Luke 4:18), blessed the poor, and pronounced to them the ownership of God's kingdom (4.14.7). At the same time, Christ's disapproval of the rich, expressed in his woes (Luke 6:24), testifies to the Creator's own disapproval of them throughout the Old Testament (prophetic texts in particular) (4.15.6–8). Christ's woe to the rich, which came from the Creator himself, adds a threat against the rich besides his dissuasion from riches (4.15.13). For Tertullian, both Testaments are straightforward with "God's preferential option for the poor." Tertullian (usually) takes for granted the tradition of the pious poor and the oppressive rich[60] and does not allegorize or interiorize wealth and poverty or the rich and the poor, as we have seen in the Alexandrian authors and the apocryphal texts. Thus, Tertullian affirms that Jesus, who himself was poor ("without money"), sets an example of despising wealth and "always justifies the poor and condemns the rich" (*Pat.* 7.3).

Lest people think, however, that this is the last word of the Creator and his Christ on the rich, Tertullian does point out that the Creator, who out of his generosity supplied the Israelites with material provisions and made Solomon rich, also grants riches to his people because the rich get "ease and comfort, and with them are performed many works of justice and charity" (*opera iustitiae*

57. The Lukan Gospel was the only Gospel included (albeit in an abridged form) in Marcion's canon, along with ten Pauline letters (not containing the Pastoral Letters). Hence Tertullian calls the Lukan Gospel "your gospel" (5.3.6).

58. This is typically how Tertullian addresses the God of the Old Testament against Marcion, who believed the creator god in the Old Testament was ignorant, vengeful, and different from the Supreme God, the Unknown Father of Christ the Redeemer, who was purely spiritual and did not create the material world.

59. Note Tertullian's distinction between the indigent (the absolute poor) and the poor (the relative poor), corresponding to the typical distinction in Greco-Roman society. For Clement of Alexandria and Origen, as for most Christian writers, perhaps except *Hermas*, the poor typically meant the indigent (*ptōchoi*), not the "working poor" (*penētēs*).

60. Cf. Note *Marc.* 4.28.11: "I have already in another connection sufficiently proved that boastfulness of riches is condemned by our God, who puts down the mighty from their seat and lifts up the poor from the dunghill" (cf. 1 Sam. 2:8).

et dilectionis; *Marc.* 4.15.8). While God and mammon are antithetical, as the latter is "the author of unrighteousness, and the tyrant of all human society" (14.33.1), and while God does condemn boastfulness of riches (14.28.11), Christ advises us to use worldly wealth to procure ourselves future friendships and support, i.e., eschatological salvation (14.33.1, on Luke 16:1–17). Taking up Luke 17:21, where Jesus tells the Pharisees, "The kingdom of God is within you" (KJV), Tertullian strongly exhorts "everyone" to interpret the phrase "within you" as "'in your hand,' 'within your power,' if you give ear, if you do the commandment [sg.] of God" (4.35.12). Tertullian, who interprets this verse in light of Deuteronomy 30:11–14, says that the kingdom of God is in his commandment and his commandment is in our mouths, in our hearts, and in our hands to *do it* (4.35.13), just as the will of God is to be done and the kingdom is to come *in our capacity* to *do it* (*Or.* 4.2; 5.1). In the words of Ramsey Michaels, "[the kingdom's] presence depends on something they [the Pharisees] must 'do.'"[61]

Then how does Tertullian understand what "the commandment of God" (*dei praeceptum*) is? Commenting on the discourse between Jesus and the rich young man (Luke 18:18–22) who asked Jesus, the "Good Teacher" of God's commandment, how he could obtain eternal life, Tertullian indicates the significance of Jesus's answer in pointing the rich man to the "Creator's *commandments* [pl.], in such form as to testify that by the Creator's *commandments* [pl.] eternal life is obtained" (4.36.4; italics added).[62] To the rich man's answer that he had kept them since his youth, Christ did not rescind those former commandments (the Decalogue) but "both retained these and added what was lacking," namely, selling all that he had and giving to the poor (4.36.4–5).[63] "And yet," Tertullian writes, "even this *commandment* [sg.] of distributing to the poor is spread about everywhere in the law and the prophets," so that it led to "the boastful commandment-keeper's" conviction of "having money in much higher esteem" and, therefore, not to his attainment of salvation (4.36.5; italics added). In this context, Tertullian's precise idea of God's commandment [sg.], without which eternal life could not be obtained, is "distributing [one's possessions] to the poor," and, with that addition, Jesus "both conserved and enriched" the Decalogue and proved that he fulfilled the Mosaic law (4.36.6). By "distributing to the poor" Tertullian does not mean literal abandonment of wealth (voluntary poverty), but almsgiving. Almsgiving, a visible act, fulfills both doing justice and loving mercy in Micah 6:8 and the "one thing" required by Christ for salvation (4.36.7; cf. 4.27.6–9).

61. J. R. Michaels, "Almsgiving and the Kingdom Within: Tertullian on Luke 17:21," *CBQ* 60 (1998): 480.

62. On Tertullian's interpretation of Luke 17:21 and of almsgiving as God's commandment leading to the kingdom/eternal life in the story of a rich ruler in Luke 18, see ibid., 479–83.

63. Compare "all that thou hast" (*quaecunque habes*) in 4.36.4 with "what you have" (*quae habes*) in 4.36.7.

Moving to the mid-third century, there is none who champions this triangular relationship of riches and poverty, almsgiving, and salvation better than Cyprian, bishop of Carthage, who admired Tertullian. Cyprian's biographer Pontius highlights among Cyprian's saintly virtues his generous charity and dedication to care of the poor, which provides special lenses through which Pontius wants his readers to remember the bishop's life. Coming from a wealthy pagan elite background (*honestiores*),[64] Cyprian dispensed "almost all his wealth" for the relief of the poor upon his conversion to Christianity (*Vita* 2).[65] Later, facing his impending martyrdom, Cyprian requested and was granted the delay of his execution so that he as a parting bishop could arrange the care of the poor as his final act of ministry (*Vita* 13). From the beginning to the end, Cyprian is portrayed as a despiser of worldly riches and a "lover of the poor" who takes the biblical mandate to care for the poor seriously and perfectly follows God's will, and as such should serve as an inspiration and example for all Christians who are concerned about their salvation.

Cyprian's own extensive writings attest to his episcopal concerns and activities regarding the care of the poor and dealings with the rich, within the framework of salvation in the difficult situations of persecution, controversies, and schisms. In his first, foundational writing as a Christian, *To Donatus* (*Ad Donatum*, c. 246 CE), Cyprian ascribes salvation not to human virtue but to God's generous munificence (4), from which his mercy and Spirit overflow into our hearts (4, 5); this abundant divine grace is what enlightens and empowers his followers to lead a life marked by "the death of sins" and "life of virtues" (4, 5, 6). In light of this truth of salvation, Cyprian denounces pagan immoralities of both private and public life, including the greed and hoarding of the rich, who shun the poor away (12). Riches bring only anxiety and torments, which could be relieved solely by giving away (12). God makes people rich not with earthly wealth but with celestial food and wealth that last forever (15). In his earliest treatise of his episcopacy, *On the Dress of Virgins* (*De habitu virginum*, 249 CE), Cyprian exhorts wealthy virgins in his church[66] to shun luxury and vanity and to use their wealth for their salvation, i.e., to give generous alms to the poor for forgiveness of their sins: "Let the poor feel that

64. Bobertz, "Cyprian of Carthage as Patron," 51, 75–129, places Cyprian at least in the rank of municipal decurions, belonging to "the highest social and economic aristocracy in the society of Carthage," 87; J. P. Burns, *Cyprian the Bishop* (Routledge Early Church Monograph; London: Routledge, 2002), 16, thinks Cyprian comes from the Roman *honestiores*.

65. In the later chapters of the *Vita* (3, 15) and Cyprian's own letters (esp. *Ep.* 7.2) it becomes clear that Cyprian did not dispossess *all* of his property. And there was no known expectation or tradition in the early church that new converts should renounce and abandon their wealth, as L. W. Countryman reminds us in *The Rich Christian in the Church of the Early Empire: Contradictions and Accommodations* (New York: Edwin Mellen, 1980), 185.

66. G. Dunn, "Infected Sheep and Diseased Cattle, or the Pure and Holy Flock: Cyprian's Pastoral Care of Virgins," *JECS* 11 (2003): 5–12, argues that Cyprian had in mind not just wealthy virgins but Christian women in general.

you are rich; let the needy feel that you are wealthy; through your patrimony make God your debtor; feed Christ" (11; cf. Prov. 19:17). This is how they lay up their treasures in heaven, treasures that are eternal and never corrupt; and this is the only legitimate purpose and use of wealth—so that they could move God by the prayers of the poor on their behalf; in answer to the poor recipients' prayers, God will grant the virgins the glory of virginity (11). Cyprian thus does not suggest total renunciation or divestment of earthly riches for those wealthy virgins (and the wealthy in general) but presents almsgiving as a way of detachment from worldly riches, which is necessary for salvation; in addition, he draws on the "established" symbiotic relation between the rich and the poor in their respective roles. And at the same time, he redefines the true rich also in a term by now familiar: not as the rich in earthly possessions that are to be despised but as the rich in faith and God—the rich in spiritual blessings and the grace of Christ (7, 10).[67]

With the Decian persecution (250–51 CE) mentioned in chapter 2 and the subsequent power struggles and controversies regarding readmission of the lapsed (lapsi), especially the wealthy ones, as well as the devastating plague (252 CE), we see greater rigidity in Cyprian's attitude toward wealth and the wealthy[68] and more pronounced concern for the care of the poor in his writings.[69] Cyprian, who conducted his ministry through letters in a hideout during the persecution (250–51) and returned after the persecution (spring 251), attempted to shore up his challenged authority as bishop by acting as patron of his congregation in control of the church finances for the care of the poor and payment of the clergy (even as he continued to be motivated by the biblical mandate regarding the poor).[70] During the persecution, Cyprian urged his clergy and saw to it that the church's works of charity to the poor and widows (along with the confessors) should continue (Epp. 5.1.2; 7.2; 12.2.2; 14.2.1). However, he specified the kind of poor who could receive the church's assistance: "the poor who, standing steadfast in the faith and fighting valiantly on

67. Cf. the redefinition of the poor by another North African, Minucius Felix, Oct. 36.3–4: "The poor man is he who, having much, craves for more."

68. R. H. Weaver, "Wealth and Poverty in the Early Church," Interpretation 41 (1987): 372.

69. For a thoughtful, accessible study of Cyprian's turbulent episcopacy and socioreligious challenges following the persecution, see Burns, Cyprian the Bishop; for a succinct summary of the socioreligious impact of the Decian persecution among Christians in Carthage and the subsequent controversies and schisms, see esp. 1–24.

70. See Bobertz, "Cyprian of Carthage as Patron," 130–252; Bobertz, "Patronage Networks and the Study of Ancient Christianity," StPatr 24 (1993): 20–27; P. Brown, The Making of Late Antiquity (Cambridge, MA: Harvard University Press, 1978), 24; C. E. Straw, "Cyprian and Matthew 5:45: The Evolution of Christian Patronage," StPatr 18 (1989): 329–39; Dunn, "The White Crown of Works: Cyprian's Early Pastoral Ministry of Almsgiving in Carthage," Church History 73 (2004): 718, 729–33, confines Cyprian's patronal mode of ministry as bishop to the period when the problem of controversies over readmitting the apostates by the confessors and laxist clergy took place after the Decian persecution, against Bobertz's argument that it framed Cyprian's entire episcopal activities even from the outset of his episcopacy.

our side, have not deserted the battlements of Christ" (*Ep.* 12.2.2; cf. 14.2.1; 5.1.2).[71] Here, like (perhaps even more than) Clement and Origen, Cyprian accords to the poor a moral capacity and virtue of free will and of standing firm in their faith against the external pressure and threat of physical pain. These are the deserving, meritorious poor—the steadfast poor in the face of the persecution (*stantes*)—since they set an example of faith for the rest of the poor (*Ep.* 12.2.2)[72] and lest "necessity may force them to do in their difficulties actions which faith prevented them from doing in the storm" (*Ep.* 14.2.1; cf. *Ep.* 12.2.2).[73] This qualification is a significant change from Cyprian's earlier letter where he exhorted his clergy to care for "all the poor" (with no qualification, along with the widows, the sick, and the strangers in want) from his own personal fund (*Ep.* 7.2); it may indicate that between the times of *Ep.* 7 and *Epp.* 5, 12, 14, there were some among the poor who had lapsed[74] and/or that the church's financial resources had been reduced significantly so that Cyprian felt that the church had to prioritize the worthy poor with its limited resources (see below).

Cyprian's stricter attitude toward the wealthy was probably in response to the particular problem of mass apostasy of the wealthy and the ensuing problems of the confessors granting reconciliation to some of those wealthy *lapsi* and the open rebellion of dissenting clergy. Hence in *On the Lapsed* (251 CE), Cyprian blamed a cause of the persecution (God's testing) and mass apostasy on the rich believers' greed and attachment to their possessions (5–8, 11; see chap. 2). Cyprian speaks of them as slaves to profit and money, tethered to the chain of their wealth (12). During the persecution, the enforcement of the Decian edict that had ordered a universal sacrifice (*supplicatio*) to the gods with proof of certificates (*libelli*)[75] affected the rich and the poor in different ways. The wealthy elites (*honestiores*) or the "distinguished individuals" (*personae insignes*) might be subject to confiscation of property[76] and exile minus torture, but the poor lower order (*humiliores*), some of whom would have already been on the church's charity list prior to

71. *Epp.* 5 and 12 are dated earlier than *Ep.* 14.

72. This distinction among the poor clearly suggests the presence of the apostate poor who are undeserving of church support.

73. What Cyprian meant by this is not quite clear. G. Clarke suggests two possible meanings: that "despairing poverty may lead to a loss of faith and hope" or that "penury (unlike persecution) may cause them to sin," in *The Letters of St. Cyprian of Carthage* (vol. 1; trans. and anno. G. W. Clarke; ACW 43; New York: Newman, 1984), 265n16.

74. Ibid., 185n8; cf. Bobertz, "Cyprian of Carthage as Patron," 16–63.

75. Forty-four such *libelli*, dating from June 12 to July 14, 250, have been found in Egypt. For texts and analyses of these *libelli*, see J. R. Knipfing, "The Libelli of the Decian Persecution," *HTR* 16 (1923): 345–90; P. Keresztes, "The Decian *Libelli* and Contemporary Literature," *Latomus* 34 (1975): 761–81; Brent, *Cyprian and Roman Carthage*, 199–213.

76. Cf. Eusebius, *HE* 6.41.11; Origen's own father was martyred and his property was confiscated during the Severan persecution in 202–3 CE—Eusebius, *HE* 6.2.12–13.

the persecution, might be subject to torture or reduced to slavery.[77] However, the poor would not attract the attention of the imperial authorities as much as the rich; indeed, the rich *honestiores* were the more visible target of the authorities because of their sociopolitical position and property especially if the authorities used a census roll with registered property (for tax)—however haphazardly.[78] Nonetheless, they should have confessed Christ by letting go of their properties and withdrawing to exile, Cyprian writes (*Laps.* 10). Yet many wealthy Christians did not follow that expected course of action but instead complied with the edict—some even rushed to the Forum to sacrifice—on behalf of entire households[79] and thereby sought to protect their dependents and properties (8). Others avoided the actual act of sacrifice and therefore regarded themselves guiltless obtaining the certificates of sacrifice (*libelli*) by proxy or bribery[80] by purchasing forged certificates of sacrifice either in person or by agents (27). Apparently, this was an attractive option because it was a clever way to keep their Christian commitment *and* to keep their properties and position—or so they thought. However, Cyprian considered such fictive certificates as "confession of apostasy" and regarded both groups—sacrificers (*sacrificati*) and the certified (*libellatici*)—as the *lapsi* (8, 27).[81] Furthermore, he castigated the wealthy *lapsi* for frequenting the baths and stuffing themselves with sumptuous feasts while neglecting those in need, and the lapsed women in particular for appearing in public in opulent dresses and costly jewels, instead of lamenting their sin of apostasy with fasting and tears of mourning (30).

Among the *lapsi*, some sought immediate reconciliation and readmission to church through certificates of peace (*libelli pacis*) granted by the confessors and martyrs,[82] based on their exalted status and belief that those who suffered for Christ because of their confession of faith were given special anointing and power to obtain forgiveness directly from Christ with their intercession. And the majority of presbyters under Cyprian (five presbyters and the deacon

77. Burns, *Cyprian the Bishop*, 18–19.

78. Probability of the use of Caracalla's citizenship census (*Constitutio Antoniniana*, 212 CE) for taxation purpose is strongly suggested by Brent, *Cyprian and Roman Carthage*, 197–247, and W. C. H. Frend, *The Rise of Christianity* (London: Darton, Longman, & Todd, 1986), 408. *Contra* G. W. Clarke, "Some Observations on the Persecution of Decius," *Antichthon* 3 (1969): 68–73; idem, *The Letters of St. Cyprian of Carthage*, 1.26–28.

79. Cf. Cyprian, *Ep.* 55.13.2; *Laps.* 27–28.

80. Cf. Cyprian, *Ep.* 30.3.1; 55.14.1.

81. Cyprian treated the certified more sympathetically in *Ep.* 55.14.1–2; on the problem of the certified in the Roman church, see *Ep.* 30.3.1.

82. Both confessors and martyrs "confessed" their faith in Christ and remained faithful during the persecutions; confessors came to refer to those who survived the persecution and its attendant punishment (imprisonment, torture, condemnation to mines, etc.), and martyrs were those who perished by capital punishment (decapitation, death by gladiators or beasts) or torture, although the distinction in practice was often blurred.

Felicissimus) supported the *lapsi*'s immediate reconciliation without penance and urged those confessors to issue the certificates of peace against the will of Cyprian, who admonished them to wait until the end of the persecution and wanted to impose traditional penitential discipline on the *lapsi* and to delay their reconciliation until the time of their death (probably except those who were seriously ill). Cyprian's stricter policy provoked these clergy (who in fact had not supported Cyprian's episcopal election two years earlier) and the wealthy *lapsi* to lead an open rebellion and schism against Cyprian and his followers while he was still away. The situation became more complicated when those wealthier *lapsi* paid (i.e., bribed) the confessors for granting the letters of peace. Cyprian remonstrated with those confessors who showed favoritism and made profit out of trafficking their letters of reconciliation (*Ep.* 15.3.2). It seems that the reason or motivation behind the immediate reconciliation and readmission of the wealthy *lapsi* through the confessors' authority and merit, which was strongly urged by those presbyters in defiance of Cyprian's order, was more than theological. Some scholars rightly suggest socioeconomic reasons for their push.[83] The persecution hit the Carthaginian church not only morally but also financially since it was the wealthy in the church who had been major donors of charity and monthly support for clergy (*Laps.* 23).[84] With mass apostasy of the wealthy, the church was getting drained of its resources for caring for the needy, which was the most "public" ministry of the church, as well as for supporting the clergy. The laxist clergy must have been concerned about this particular role of the wealthy *lapsi* since the latter were not eligible to contribute to the care of poor Christians unless they were formally reconciled. As Geoffrey Dunn notes, this "laxist" argument gained much sympathy and popularity in Carthage; "the church needed the wealthy *lapsi* to be readmitted to communion quickly so that they could start making financial contribution to the care of the poor again."[85] Otherwise, the church would face a serious crisis in its ability to care for the needs of the steadfast poor (as well as the clergy).[86] Having lost the majority of wealthy members, this situation presented Cyprian, too, with a real challenge for not only the overall unity of the church around the bishop but also maintenance of the support for the faithful poor (*stantes*) and others. It is at this point that Cyprian began to command unyielding episcopal authority and patronage with more centralized care for the poor by rewarding those who were loyal to

83. Countryman, *Rich Christian*, 189–95; Bobertz, "Cyprian of Carthage as Patron," 57–68, 130–252; Dunn, "White Crown of Works," 733–39.

84. As Countryman, *Rich Christian*, 196, notes, like Tertullian, Cyprian thought of the poor (both the indigent and the "working poor"—people with limited means) not as the givers but as the recipients of charity. On monthly payment of Cyprian's clergy even during the persecution see *Epp.* 1; 34.4.2; 39.5.2; cf. additional provisions in *Epp.* 5.1.2; 13.7; 41.1.2.

85. Dunn, "White Crown of Works," 733n92.

86. Ibid., 734.

him against the laxist faction.[87] We will pursue this issue of patronage and the centralization of almsgiving further in chapter 5.

In this charged context, the true penance for reconciliation and thus for salvation of the lapsed that is authorized by Cyprian, i.e., "making amends through their prayers and good works" (*Ep.* 16.2.3, written as early as May 250 CE; cf. *Ep.* 19.1.1),[88] primarily consisted of almsgiving (cf. Acts 26:20).[89] As Cyprian urged them to give alms "without delay" and generously "to make reparation for the guilt of sin" (*crimen et culpa redimatur*) (*Laps.* 35), he promised that God could extend his mercy to them and turn back his judgment (*Laps.* 36). Cyprian's two treatises written in late 251 and 252, following the persecution and in the midst of the plague, *On the Lord's Prayer* (*De dominica oratione*) and *On Works and Alms* (*De opera et eleemosynis*), articulate "redemptive almsgiving" in the strongest terms. In the former, quoting Tobit 20.8, "Prayer is good with fasting and almsgiving," Cyprian is quite emphatic that prayer alone is "fruitless" and "ineffectual" unless it is accompanied by almsgiving (*Dom. or.* 32). Only prayers with almsgiving "quickly ascend to God which the merits of our labours urge upon God," as shown in the example of Tabatha (*Dom. or.* 32), and in this way almsgiving is spiritual sacrifice to God (*Dom. or.* 33; cf. Clement of Alexandria, *Strom.* 7.3.14.1; 7.7.49.5; Origen, *Hom. Lev.* 2.4).[90] In the latter treatise, already mentioned above, Cyprian repeats the same point that "our petitions become efficacious by almsgiving" (*eleemosynis petitiones nostras efficaces fieri*) as exemplified by another biblical figure, Tobias (*Eleem.* 5).

But Cyprian also augmented his theological argument for almsgiving in light of a new dire situation. Between the compositions of these two works, the dreadful plague swept through Carthage with such great force that a sense

87. Cf. ibid., 732, 734n52; see also Bobertz, "Cyprian of Carthage as Patron," 162–74; and Brent, *Cyprian and Roman Carthage*, 72–74.

88. *Precibus et operibus suis satisfacere*: "good work," *opus* (*operari, operatio*, and *operarius*), in Cyprian's writings refers to almsgiving/charity to the poor and the needy, as shown by E. V. Rebenak, ed. and trans., *Thasci Caecili Cypriani De Opere et Eleemosynis: A Translation with an Introduction and Commentary* (Washington: Catholic University of America Press, 1962), 35–43.

89. In a letter from mid-250 CE (Cyprian, *Ep.* 21.2.2; 21.4.1), written from Rome by Celerinus, the Carthiginean confessor and future lector, to his old friend and also a confessor, Lucianus, in Carthage, we have references to two female *lapsi* in Rome engaged in penance and works of charity (almsgiving) in the hope of receiving forgiveness and readmission to the church. As part of their penance, these wealthy women were taking care of sixty-five people "in every way," (probably) in the same dwelling.

90. Note also the noble martyr Apollonius's association of alms with prayers in *Mart. Apol.* 44: " 'I was hoping, proconsul,' said Apollonius, 'that you would be given a more pious reasoning and that the eyes of your soul would be enlightened by my discourse, so that your heart, bearing fruit, would begin to worship the God who is the creator of all things, and thus by daily alms and a charitable life you would offer prayers to him alone, as a pure and blameless sacrifice to God.' " Also consider the *Sentences of Sextus* 217: "God does not heed the prayer of a man who does not listen to the needy."

of normalcy for both Christians and pagans substantially broke down (summer 252). It was another demoralizing blow to Christians who had just gone through the imperial persecution and especially those Christians who felt that the sweeping deaths by the plague had stripped (or would strip) them of the possibility of either a second chance for salvation (reconciliation) or perfection through martyrdom.[91] Cyprian addressed their anxiety and pessimism and pointed them to another way to purge sin other than martyrdom—not as heroic as martyrdom but certainly effective: almsgiving to the poor (*Eleem.* 6).[92] Out of his great compassion God himself "labored" for our salvation through the advent and death of his Son Christ but his providence also provided for his people remedies for sin "after [they were] already redeemed!" (*Eleem.* 1). For, we all falter and fall short of his "commandment of innocence" even after baptism:

> Nor would the infirmity and weakness of human frailty have any resource, *unless the divine mercy, coming once more in aid, should open some way of securing salvation by pointing out works of justice and mercy*, so that by almsgiving we may wash away whatever foulness we *subsequently* contract. (*Eleem.* 1 [italics added])[93]

Note Cyprian's understanding of the inner logic of salvation and almsgiving. For Cyprian, far from almsgiving being a human work in danger of threatening or supplanting the exclusive divine work of salvation, it was God's own mercy and design that provided for us this particular "way out" of our postbaptismal sins. Almsgiving and Jesus's death never compete with each other, and the former does not undermine the salvific significance or sufficiency of the latter. Both are the expressions of God's abundant grace, condescension, and providence, and it is only by God's grace that almsgiving can be meritorious and satisfactory in his sight (1, 2, 5). In this sense, almsgiving (i.e., "works of righteousness") became "the likeness of baptism" because "in baptism remission of sins is granted once for all" (2). However, the difference between baptism and almsgiving was that the former was nonrepeatable for forgiveness of sins and formal entrance to the church,[94] but almsgiving was not just

---

91. *Mort.* 17. Cf. M. M. Sage, *Cyprian* (Patristic Monograph Series 1; Cambridge, MA: Philadelphia Patristic Foundation, 1975), 273. Although the early church generally opposed voluntary martyrdom, it made an exception for the lapsed Christians who needed to "wash away their former fault" (apostasy) through offering themselves up for martyrdom, and Cyprian himself attested to its occurrence (*Ep.* 24); see also *Ep.* 19.2.3; *Laps.* 36.

92. Cf. Sage, *Cyprian*, 273.

93. *Nec haberet quid fragilitatis humanae infirmitas adque inbecillitas faceret, nisi iterum pietas diuina subueniens iustitiae et misericordiae operibus ostensis uiam quandam tuendae salutis aperiret, ut sordes postmodum quascumque contrahimus eleemosynis abluamus.*

94. Cyprian later changed (at least clarified) his position on the validity of baptism received in a schismatic church (the Novatian church) during his baptismal controversy with Stephen of Rome. Cyprian insisted on "rebaptism" of the schismatic upon their readmission to the Catholic church since they forfeited the Holy Spirit due to their schism; but Stephen recognized the

repeatable but required "constant and ceaseless labour" for remission of sins and readmission to the church (2; "continual labour," 24).[95]

In this way, Cyprian preemptively deals with the rich Christians' possible excuses from and objections to almsgiving and links right motive of almsgiving squarely to their hope of heavenly glory (see chap. 2). Like Clement of Alexandria and the author of the *Acts of Thomas*, Cyprian audaciously describes it as an economic transaction; givers of alms are "merchant[s] of the heavenly grace" whose gain is none other than eternal life (7) in partnership with Christ (13), and who make God their debtor (15, 16, 26). And this God in turn will never fail to pay a divine wage for their labors (23) ("giving a reward for our merits"), that is, "a white crown" in peace as an equivalent to a purple one for martyrdom during persecutions (26). On the flip side, the rich who preserve their worldly wealth while neglecting the poor sin gravely with their covetousness and can only expect eternal loss and punishment like the rich fool in the Lukan Gospel (17). One should remember that Christ himself taught the contempt and perils of riches, as they contained the root of all evils (*Dom. or.* 20). Though Cyprian rarely condemns wealth as such and advocates its divestment, he, like his fellow North African Tertullian, does take Jesus's words to the rich young man (Matt. 19:21) literally, in contrast to the Alexandrians: "the Lord tells us that he becomes perfect and complete who sells all his goods, and distributes them for the use of the poor, and so lays up for himself treasure in heaven" (*Dom. or.* 20). Overall for Cyprian, almsgiving as lifelong penance provided an absolutely necessary (pre-)condition *for and with* the reconciliation of the lapsed; and their "conspicuous almsgiving" would be a means that should sustain the care of the poor in the financially strapped situation of his congregation. Thus, as Countryman fittingly expresses, earthly "riches offered the remedy for the very harm they caused" for the wealthy.[96]

3.5. Summary and Conclusion

The early church proclaimed that Jesus Christ was the Savior, whose revelation of God and sacrifice on the cross provided for his followers the atonement for sin that began a life of faith through baptism. Salvation was an upward spiral or a ladder leading to heaven that required continual upward movement lest one lag behind and regress down toward the bottom. Salvation, a lifelong process, would involve and demand a steady progress in "taking off an old self and putting on a new self" and the persistent cultivation of spiritual and ethical virtues in community. And this moral and spiritual advance and

---

validity of schismatic baptism and required only reconciliation with laying on of hands, since baptism should not be repeated.

95. Cf. Clement of Alexandria, *Quis div.* 32.

96. Countryman, *Rich Christian*, 189.

transformation entails both internal and external works of faith that attest to one's faith in God. In this divine economy of salvation, God has graciously allowed himself to be approached through these works of faith, mainly almsgiving, as a fundamental testimony of one's (especially the rich Christians') commitment and repentance to God (cf. Acts 26:30).[97]

In different regions and specific contexts, works of mercy (i.e., almsgiving) were theologized and practiced as a vital part of the care of the self for salvation;[98] early Christian leaders and texts connected almsgiving to salvation of the giver—the latter as the main motivation for the former. Clement of Alexandria and Origen spiritualized wealth and poverty as well as the rich and the poor through their figurative interpretation of the Scriptures and deconstructed the traditional notion of the pious poor and the wicked rich; both the rich and poor shared the capacity and responsibility of moral choice, of detachment and spiritual freedom, but were also subject to the temptation of greed and attachment to wealth. On the other hand, the Alexandrians also relied on spiritual superiority of the poor and difficulty of salvation for the rich to stress the symbiotic (or patronal) relationship between their respective roles—the rich giving alms generously to the poor who would in turn intercede to God for their spiritual destiny. The apocryphal literature presented both ontological and allegorical understandings of wealth and poverty: wealth as self-knowledge that leads to or represents salvation, but poverty as self-ignorance that leads to or denotes the physical fallen state. At the same time, it also presented a literal and ascetic notion and practice by identifying material poverty with "poverty in spirit," the state of ontological wealth.

In North Africa, for Tertullian, almsgiving was the one commandment of God put forth by Jesus to a rich ruler to compensate for a lack in the Mosaic law, and as such it made one's redemption attainable. For Cyprian, in a specific, turbulent circumstance in the aftermath of the Decian persecution, almsgiving became not only God's benevolent means of penance by which the lapsed giver could be reconciled back to the church but also an episcopal measure through which Cyprian could maintain and control the ecclesiastical care of the poor in his church. The divergent traditions notwithstanding (e.g., the Nag Hammadi texts), overall the early church integrated both individual and corporate understanding and practice of wealth and poverty into the pastoral care of souls within a redemptive context, and almsgiving constituted the spiritual sacrifice acceptable to God for dealing with postbaptismal sins. In the words of Gary Anderson, "alms are not so much a human work as they are an index of one's underlying faith" for those who are already in the path of salvation through Christ's sacrifice.[99]

97. Anderson, "Redeem Your Sins," 64.
98. Cf. Maier, "Clement of Alexandria," 732, 740.
99. Anderson, "Redeem Your Sins," 61.

4

ᐳᐊ

Wealth, Poverty, and Koinonia

As we have seen, salvation for early Christians was a corporate phenomenon in that it occurred within a community context and necessarily entailed social responsibility (as well as cultivated personal virtues) as a testament to faith in God. As Christian communities grew and spread across diverse regions and cross sections of Greco-Roman society in this period, dealing with social differences and meeting the internal needs of diverging Christian communities became increasingly challenging and often provided tests and occasions of genuine Christian fellowship and communion (koinonia). This chapter will explore various ways in which early Christians practiced their fellowship/sharing (koinonia) of wealth in their community contexts. We will first recapitulate early Christian social structure and distinctions (briefly mentioned in chap. 1) and then move on to how they sought to address those issues and problems. In dealing with the internal social disparities, Christians situated their works of charity and koinonia in fulfillment of the Great Commandment of loving God and one's neighbor, which reformulated and transformed Greco-Roman understandings of hospitality and patronage. In these efforts of Christian koinonia, we will also analyze the special roles and contributions of women and how these acts of mercy were regarded as none other than acts of justice.

4.1. Social Composition and Differences within Christian Communities

For the most part early Christians in this period continued to meet in localized households of varying sizes whose relatively wealthy hosts or hostesses acted as patrons of the particular groups,[1] although it seems that in the early third century and on, Christians in some cities also began meeting in "church buildings," initially modified from the private house structures (see chap. 1 and chap. 5). In Asia Minor, Ignatius's letters presuppose the household as the general setting of the meetings and internal divisions (*Smyrn.* 7.1; cf. *Magn.* 4.1; *Eph.* 5.2–3).[2] Also reflecting this historical reality, the apocryphal *Acts of John*, whose provenance and dramatic scenes are set in cities of Asia Minor, describes early forms of worship services in private homes of the wealthy elite converts. The wealthy and prominent householders Lycomedes and Cleopatra, and Andronicus, who provide hospitality to the ascetic, itinerant apostle, function as patrons and leaders of the church at Ephesus and assist the apostle in the care of widows and nurture of new converts of the community (19, 25–26, 30, 34–36, 46, 62, 86, 106–11).

In Rome, smaller localized communities in the mid-second century are illustrated by Justin Martyr's statement that Christians meet (for worship) not in a single house but in multiple homes throughout the city depending on "one's preference and opportunity" (*Acts Just.* 3.1–3), and one of those places included his own place "above the baths of Myrtinus" (*Acts Just.* 3.3 recensions A and B).[3] In another apocryphal work, *Acts of Peter*, the household of a senator Marcellus, staged in Rome, is a juncture of Christian assembly as Peter and Simon Magus (both recipients of Marcellus's hospitality) have contests of miracles and orthodoxy in his house. The portrait of Marcellus—the model Christian benefactor and leader who had once defected by following Simon, then caused schism and havoc, and finally reconverted and resumed his manifold works of charity and unity (8–14, 22)—exemplifies the significant influence of wealthy and prominent householder-patrons and what might have been behind the concerns of *1 Clement* and Ignatius on intracommunity divisions. In *Hermas*'s local community (cf. *oikos* in *Sim.* 8.10.3; 9.27.2), the major groups identified were the poor (*Sim.* 2), the rich (*Sim.* 2; 9.20.1; *Vis.* 3.6.5),[4] those who are "absorbed in business" (*Sim.* 4.5; 8.8.1; 9.20.1), and those "who became rich" (*Sim.* 8.9.1). The latter two (and the rich) are chastised for "much luxury" (e.g., *Mand.* 12.1.3–2.2) and would probably indicate the freedmen whose economic mobility, especially in trade and commerce, and whose conspicuous consumption were known and satirized during that time.

1. A large majority of these patrons belonged to the nonelite order—*humiliores*—which consisted of people with varying economic means but probably belonging to P4/E4-P5/E5; see chap. 1.

2. See H. O. Maier, *The Social Setting of Ministry as Reflected in the Writings of Hermas, Clement, and Ignatius* (Canadian Corporation for Studies in Religion, Dissertation SR 1; Waterloo, ON: Wilfrid Laurier University Press, 1991), 147–56; W. R. Schoedel, *Ignatius of Antioch: A Commentary on the Letters of Ignatius of Antioch* (Philadelphia: Fortress, 1985), 240.

3. This part is corrupt in both recensions.

4. Here the rich and those who are preoccupied with business are identical.

Hermas himself was a freedman with moderate wealth probably through small craft and/or business (*Vis.* 1.1.1),[5] thus representing the very groups about whom the text was particularly concerned in terms of their salvation and communal responsibility. It is especially telling that those entangled in business affairs are criticized for not associating with the "saints" (*Sim.* 8.8.1) and "God's servants" (*Sim.* 9.20.2)[6] and also that the rich are reprimanded for associating with "God's servants only with difficulty, for they are afraid that they may be asked for something by them" (*Sim.* 9.20.2). By forsaking their social responsibility of supporting the poor in their church community, these people avoid church leaders and other Christians and therefore risk their own salvation and break the unity of the church (e.g., *Sim.* 9.20.2–4).

By the third century the Roman community became even more diversified and organized. The church order the *Apostolic Tradition* (attributed to Hippolytus) mentions various occupations impermissible and inappropriate for catechumens, which indicates the possible presence of those in the community with the professions mentioned. Most of them are admittedly socially inferior or questionable ones such as pimps, gladiators, and astrologers; however, also mentioned are high-ranking military and civil officers (those with "the power of the sword" or "civil magistrate[s] wearing the purple," 16.9) and "public official[s] engaged in gladiatorial business" (16.6). The size and financial and organizational strength of the church is illustrated by bishop Cornelius's famous statement about the church supporting more than fifteen hundred widows and people in need as well as more than one hundred forty clergy (Eusebius, *HE* 6.43.2).[7]

The Carthaginian Christian communities in the third century were equally impressive in size, socioeconomic diversity, and organizational strength. Tertullian addresses his treatises to Christians of "birth and wealth," particularly women (e.g., *Idol.* 18.3, 9; *Cultu fem.* 2.9.4–6; *Ux.* 2.3–4, 8), on their conduct; refers to the Christian "women and men of highest rank" (*Scap.* 3.4; 4.5–6; 5.2; cf. *Apol.* 37.4) and slave owners (*Pat.* 10.5; *Paen.* 4.4; *De resurrectione carnis* 57.12; *Marc.* 1.23.7); and favors Christian marriage between social unequals (*Ux.* 2.8). The number of Christians would have been significant by the mid-third century since Cyprian disapprovingly reports that thousands of certificates of forgiveness were dispensed to the *lapsi* every day by

---

5. Cf. C. Osiek, *The Shepherd of Hermas: A Commentary* (Hermeneia; Minneapolis: Augsburg Fortress, 1999), 21; A. Stewart-Sykes suggests business in viticulture in "Hermas the Prophet and Hippolytus the Preacher: The Roman Homily and Its Social Context," in *Preacher and Audience: Studies on Early Christian and Byzantine Homiletics* (ed. M. B. Cunningham and P. Allen; Leiden: Brill, 1998), 45.

6. On this phrase designating Christians in general in *Hermas*, see C. Osiek, "The Ransom of Captives: Evolution of a Tradition," *HTR* (1981): 371.

7. According to Harnack's estimation, the Roman church would have annually spent from 500,000 to one million sesterces on caring for those in need: Harnack, *The Mission and Expansion of Christianity in the First Three Centuries*, 1:195, no. 1.

the confessors during the Decian persecution (*Ep.* 20.2.2). Presence of the indigent, the working poor, and the wealthy in varying degrees is mentioned in the sources, but private homes as their assembly places are hardly indicated.[8] On the one hand, the Christian apologists never apologized for the (working) poor (*pauperes*) and the illiterate in the assemblies and took their presence in Christian congregations for granted and as a factor that made Christianity unique and divine (e.g., Minucius Felix, *Oct.* 36.3; cf. *penētes* in Tatian, *Oratio* 32.1). Most of the membership would have come from the *humiliores* (just like the churches of other regions) to whom these working poor belonged as craftsmen and laborers; and during the Decian persecution Cyprian provided grants for those tradesmen who escaped detection but left behind their tools of trade (e.g., Cyprian, *Ep.* 41.1.2). On the other hand, conspicuous in the church, though in all likelihood a small minority, were the *honestiores* (probably provincial elites, such as Cyprian himself, cf. *Vita* 14; *Ep.* 8.1) and/or wealthy virgins who had their own financial resources (*Hab. virg.*) and the wealthy *lapsi* who had substantial patrimonies and estates to worry about during the Decian persecution (*Laps.* 6). Both the rich and the poor, however, depended on the Roman economy for their livelihood and were assimilated into the Roman social system to that extent.

In Alexandria Clement's and Origen's works attest to a considerable presence of cultured and educated Christians of high society (see chap. 3) and the internal tensions felt between the rich and the poor, as they chastise both the arrogant rich who wallow in their luxurious life without any concern for the needy and the flattering and servile poor who envy and want favors from the rich and yet pass judgment on their spiritual state (e.g., Clement of Alexandria, *Quis div.* 1; Origen, *Prayer* 29.5–6). As in Carthage, Christians of social distinction drew attention from the authorities during the (imperial) persecutions. Dionysius's letter, preserved by Eusebius, describes how Christians of prominence came under particular pressure in the Decian persecution (*HE* 6.41.11): "And of many of the more eminent persons, some came forward immediately through fear, others in public positions were compelled to do so by their business, and others were dragged by those around them." During Valerian's persecution a few years later, Dionysius further records that two presbyters, who were "better known in the world," were forced to wander in the Egyptian desert (*HE* 7.11.24). Valerian's specified punishments (e.g., confiscation of properties, decapitation, exile—*relegatio*), matching for ranks such as senators, high-ranking officials, knights, and matrons, illustrate further the growing penetration of Christians into the upper *ordines* (Cyprian, *Ep.* 80.1.2). As noted in chapter 1, the martyr acts of the imperial persecutions are especially replete with Christians of high status and significant wealth.

8. E.g., Minucius Felix, *Oct.* 16.5; Tertullian, *Apol.* 39.5–6; *Mart. Perp.* 2.1; Cyprian, *Hab. virg.* 7–9; *Laps.* 6, 30; Lactantius, *Inst.* 5.15.5; 7.1.17–19.

4.2. The Great Commandment: Loving God and One's Neighbor

While the previous section examined social diversity and even tensions in Christian communities, this section and the rest of the chapter will explore and underscore some concrete ways that the Christian communities met those challenges and pursued Christian koinonia. In this section we will particularly look at the ways in which they articulated the cross-relationship of loving God and loving one's neighbor in supporting the poor and the needy in their communities (cf. *Did.* 1.2; Clement of Alexandria, *Quis div.* 28–29; Lev. 19:18; Deut. 6:5; Luke 10:27; Gal. 5:14).

One of the grand questions of Christian self-definition posed by the *Epistle to Diognetus* is "how will you love him [God] who so loved you first?" (10.3). Loving God, according to this text, means imitating his goodness, and imitating his goodness means taking on the burden of one's neighbor—that is, benefiting "another who is worse off in something in which he himself is better off" and providing to "those in need things that he has received from God, and thus becom[ing] a god to those who receive them" (10.6). Aristides, another Christian apologist in the early second century, portrays mutual love as the very quality that defines Christians (cf. Heb. 13:1), which manifests itself in the following ways:

> They do not overlook the widow, and they save the orphan. The one who has ministers ungrudgingly to the one who does not have. . . . And if there is any that is a slave or a poor man, they fast two or three days and what they were going to set before themselves they send to them, considering themselves to give good cheer even as they were called to good cheer. (*Apol.* 15.7)

Athenagoras, in his *Plea for the Christians* in the late second century, claims that while among Christians are "the uneducated, artisans, and old women" who are unable to articulate doctrine, they exhibit good works particularly by giving to those who ask of them and loving neighbors as themselves (*Legatio* 11.4). Christians who surely love their God are in fact to love their neighbors more than their lives (*Barn.* 19.5; cf. *Didasc.* 9). Considering that these are apologies with an agenda, they tend to project Christian ideals despite the reality of social differences and conflicts within Christian communities that we have discussed. However, this Christian love in meeting mutual needs and relieving physical distress might not have been a pure rhetoric judged by its consistent testimonies in the sources—Christian and non-Christian. For loving one another in those tangible actions is how one acknowledges Christ (*2 Clem.* 4.3). Tertullian (though certainly not unbiased) also reports that pagans "who hate themselves" marvel at how Christians love one another (*Apol.* 39.7) and describes practical Christian koinonia under this framework. He speaks of "the trust funds of piety" (*deposita pietatis*) to which "everyone" brings "some modest coin," usually once a month or "whenever he wishes," according to one's ability entirely on a voluntary basis (*Apol.* 39.5). Its explicit purpose is "to feed the poor and to bury them, for boys and girls who lack property and parents, and then for slaves grown old and ship-wrecked mariners; and any who may be in mines, islands or prisons, provided that it is for the sake of God's school [*dei sectae*], become the pensioners of their confession" (*Apol.* 39.6). This results in sharing property not in a sense of abandoning private property but in terms of sacrificially benefiting and caring for the needy in their midst (*Apol.* 39.11; cf. Acts 2:44–46; 4:32–37). Though not in a context of a community fund, the same kind of sentiment is expressed in the *Didache*: "You shall not turn away from someone in need, but shall share everything [*synkoinōnēseis de panta*] with your brother, and not claim that anything is your own. For if you are sharers in what is imperishable, how much more so in perishable things" (4.8; cf. *Barn.* 19.8).

The common chest to meet the needs of the poor in the community, which existed from the inception of the early Jesus movement (e.g., Acts 2:44–46; 4:32–37; Gal. 2:10; 1 Tim. 5:9–16; cf. Rom. 15:26–28; 1 Cor. 16:1–2), is attested in other contemporary texts as well. Ignatius, bishop of Antioch, in the first decades of the second century advised Polycarp, bishop of Smyrna, not to ransom slaves from the common treasury (*koinos*), lest they become slaves of greed,[9] but to protect and support the widows presumably from the same common fund (*Polycarp* 4.1–3). Justin, in his detailed account of the type of worship that is common to Christians in house assemblies, highlights voluntary offerings by the well-to-do, collected weekly and then deposited with the "president" or bishop (1 *Apol.* 67.6); most likely these offerings are what Justin has in mind when he states how those who used to value amassing wealth and possessions now bring it into a common treasury as a result of their conversion (1 *Apol.* 14). Again the unequivocal purpose of this common treasury is to share with and provide for "all who are in need"—specified in familiar categories as widows, orphans, the sick, those in prison or other distress (*thlipsis*), and sojourners who are strangers (1 *Apol.* 14; 67.6). The contributions (*ephodia*) sent to "many churches in every city" by the Roman community "since the beginning" that resulted in relieving the poverty of the needy and ministering to those in the mines in all probability came from the common fund(s) mentioned by Justin.[10] Even an unsympathetic and ill-informed pagan observer, Lucian of Samosata, adds a further testimony to this practice in his *Death of Peregrinus*. A religious imposter, Peregrinus Proteus, took advantage

9. This injunction implies the church's practice of using the common chest to free slaves. According to Osiek, "Ransom of Captives," 373, besides this stated reason, the practical reasons for this prohibition might have been: "the strain on church funds and the fear that slaves would become Christians in order to be manumitted."

10. Eusebius, *HE* 4.23.10, in a letter from Dionysius, bishop of Alexandria, to Soter, bishop of Rome, during the reign of Marcus Aurelius, 169–77 CE. Eusebius adds a comment that this custom continued to the Great Persecution of his own time.

of the gullibility and stupidity (from his perspective but certainly sacrificial, mutual love from a Christian viewpoint) of Christians who flocked around him when he was imprisoned in Palestine. Some of these Christians, having come all the way from cities in Asia, were sent "from their common fund to succor, defend, and encourage" him, and he quickly became "exceedingly wealthy" through receiving this money (12–13). In that way, Christians demonstrated in Lucian's mind how "they despise all things equally and consider them a common possession," again in a sense of sacrificially meeting the needs of their fellow believers (rather indiscriminately and recklessly) (13).

An early third-century Christian funerary inscription (ca. 200–210 CE) from Phrygia also records that a tomb for a certain Artemidoros, bishop (*episkopos*) possibly of the New Prophecy, was commissioned "out of the Lord's" (*ek tou kyriakou*). This phrase most likely indicates that the tomb and doorstele were paid for by the common treasury of the church.[11] This system of a common chest in multiple communities in different locales testifies to the degree to which alms and charity were organized and to the process being institutionalized during this period (see chap. 5). Thus by the time of Cyprian in the mid-third century, it is from this common fund channeled from individual gifts and alms that the church (through the bishop) not only sustained the poor, widows, confessors and their families, and even those who had given up unacceptable professions for Christianity (e.g., acting); it also paid salaries of the clergy (*Epp.* 2.2.2; 5.1.2; 7.2; 39.5.2). And the (wealthy) *lapsi* were strongly urged to contribute to this common chest as an important part of their penance to redisplay their loyalty to Christ and the church.[12] Hence, the tension and conflict between Cyprian and the laxist faction during and after the Decian persecution was again not just over different theological ethics and ecclesiology but also over the control of the common chest (*Ep.* 41.1.1–2.1).

Another corporate way that early Christians experienced and expressed the Great Commandment was a "love feast," commonly called *agapē* (Jude 12). In the household setting, Christians shared religious meals (typically in late afternoon or early evening) that included the celebration of the Eucharist at some point. Having a common (religious) meal was not unlike the pagan associations (*collegia*), but it was to be motivated by divine love and mutual love for one another and be accompanied by the proper "table manners" reflecting that love.[13] Even in the earliest Christianity, however, the apostle Paul had to deal

11. W. Tabbernee, *Montanist Inscriptions and Testamonia: Epigraphic Sources Illustrating the History of Montanism* (Patristic Monograph Series 16; Macon, GA: Mercer University Press, 1997), 62–64, no. 3.

12. Cf. Burns, *Cyprian the Bishop*, 13.

13. Well into the second and even early third century, the Lord's Supper and *agapē* were used more or less interchangeably in the literary sources to refer to the community meal; cf. Ferguson, *Early Christians Speak*, 128. As argued by L. M. White, the separation of the liturgical Eucharist from the *agapē* meal coincided with a major development of church buildings

with tensions between the rich and the poor surrounding the Lord's Supper (*agapē*) and sternly rebuked the self-serving rich Corinthians who seemingly not only did not understand the Christological and transforming significance of the meal but also confused it with pagan dinner banquets controlled by patronage where social distinctions and disparities became accentuated rather than neutralized (1 Cor. 11:17–34). Paul appears to have intended that the poor believers in Corinth be included and accepted at the meal on equal terms with their wealthier counterparts, because it should reflect a mutual concern appropriate for their faith in Christ and therefore for the unity of the church. Tertullian, following Paul's intention (and for his apologetic purpose), claims that a Christian supper shows its motive by its name, *agapē*. Contrasting it with pagan banquets of self-serving motives and "vile" and "immodest" table manners, Tertullian defines the nature of Christian *agapē* as a divinely inspired and therefore socially charitable *and* disciplined meal: "Whatever the cost, it is gain to spend in piety's name, for with that refreshment we help the needy . . . because with God there is greater consideration for those of lower degree [*mediocrium*]" (*Apol.* 39.16). Hence, Christians eat enough to satisfy hunger and drink as much as is beneficial to the modest as those who worship the true God (*Apol.* 39.18). Clement of Alexandria echoes Tertullian's points and reproves greed, gluttony, and extravagance at the feast even as he emphasizes the spiritual aspect of *agapē*. Calling *agapē* "truly heavenly food, a rational banquet," he pointedly links it to the Love Commandment and states that "the meal occurs because of love, not love because of the meal, which is a proof of a generous and shared good will. . . . The person who eats of this meal shall obtain the best of the things which pertain to reality, the kingdom of God" (*Paed.* 2.1.4.4). It is an earthly expression of a higher spiritual reality of loving God and one's neighbor, and as such it is to be made for the sake of the poor following the Lord's bidding in the Gospel (*Paed.* 2.1.4.3; cf. Luke 14:12–13).

These writers recognize the importance of *agapē*, a Christian fellowship meal, integral to relief of the poor and thus to Christian worship and piety, for it was indeed the necessary means of charity for wealthier Christians (encouraged and increasingly supervised by church leaders) and the central point of Christian experience for average Christians.[14] Thus, the purity of *agapē*'s koinonia—its dual function of fellowship and charity—had to be guarded all the more with Christian propriety and orderliness (as one can see, this was apparently a persistent issue in various house communities). The wealthier hosts might invite the poor, the sick, widows, virgins, or any of the needy members of the church to the supper (*Ap. Trad.* 23, 28) and send them home with small basketfuls and leftovers (*apophoreta*) and even

---

through renovations of private houses (*domus ecclesiae*): *Texts and Monuments for the Domus Ecclesiae* (vol. 2 of *The Social Origins of Christian Architecture*; Valley Forge, PA: Trinity Press International, 1997), 119–20.

14. Cf. Ferguson, *Early Christians Speak*, 128.

deliver food to those who could not be present (*Ap. Trad.* 28.2–3). Just like the reciprocal symbiosis between the rich and the poor in almsgiving, the invited recipients in the dinner were expected to pray for the wealthier hosts for their spiritual blessings in return. While Clement of Alexandria was concerned that some hosts might think that they could buy the "promise of God" with their dinners (*Paed.* 2.1.4.3), the *Apostolic Tradition* was concerned that the poor guests would not show proper gratitude to the hosts and that their behaviors would become too raucous and rowdy (28.1). Therefore, it gives specific warnings against the guests' drunkenness, noise, and quarrels at the table, all of which disrupt Christian unity and koinonia (28.1, 4). It is worth noting that the giving of meals and small souvenirs for takeaway (*apophoreta*) by wealthy householders to their clients (*clientela*) was a common custom in Roman patronage, which could increase their patronal honor and influence.[15] The distribution of *apophoreta* at dinners symbolized "an extended and encoded social ritual acted out both in the hierarchy of dining and in the social dependency of clientellage."[16] The aforementioned instruction in the *Apostolic Tradition*, then, may be an indication of Christianized patronage exercised by a wealthy and generous Christian host, although the text further says the bishop is to speak and exhort in that setting rather than the wealthy host, possibly as a way to control the influence of the lay host who would be increasingly surpassed by clergy especially in cultic functions (*Ap. Trad.* 28.4–6; cf. Ignatius, *Smyrn.* 8.2).[17] The bishop in particular acted more and more as the head of the household at the love feasts as he also began to take over the church charity and almsgiving.

In addition to *agapē*, sharing food with the needy in general was a natural part of Christian koinonia. Threats of hunger and starvation due to frequent crop failures, wars, and natural disasters such as famine, drought, flooding, etc., were ever present for the vast majority of people in the empire who were living near or on subsistence; and they constituted part and parcel of poverty (however relative that may be) in antiquity and still do even in our contemporary society. Hence, the exhortation and practice of feeding the hungry (*1 Clem.* 59.4; Commodian, *Instr.* 71) and sharing or giving food, both individually and corporately, consistently appear in the sources (*Diogn.* 5.7; cf. *Did.* 1.5; 4.5–8; *Barn.* 19.8, 10–11; Justin, *1 Apol.* 15.10).

15. It is well illustrated in Petronius's satirical portrait of Trimalchio's extravagant dinner parties in *Satyricon* 56–57. Cf. Emperor Vespasian's distribution of *apophoreta* in Suetonius, *Vespesian* 19.

16. L. M. White, "Regulating Fellowship in the Communal Meal: Early Jewish and Christian Evidence," in *Meals in a Social Context: Aspects of the Communal Meal in the Hellenistic and Roman World* (ed. I. Nielsen and H. S. Nielsen; Aarhus, Denmark: Aarhus University Press, 1998), 183. Cf. Martial, *Epigram* 3.60; Pliny, *Ep.* 2.6.

17. A. Stewart-Sykes, *On the Apostolic Tradition: An English Version with Introduction and Commentary* (Crestwood, NY: St. Vladimir's Seminary Press, 2001), 145–46.

If there is a definite connection between meals and charity, so also between fasting and alms. According to *Didache*, Christians fasted on Wednesdays and Fridays (8.1).[18] An earlier quote by Aristides establishes the social responsibility of fasting: Christians willingly give up their meals beyond the designated days for fasting in order to give them to the poor. The *Sentences of Sextus*, a second-century collection of Christian (and Pythagorean) moral aphorisms from Alexandria, approves the practice of fasting in order to provide food for the poor (267).[19] In *Hermas* we see how the traditional piety of fasting, alms, and prayer all come together. The revelatory guide Shepherd commands Hermas to taste only bread and water on the day of fasting[20] and to "estimate the amount of the cost of the food [he] would have eaten on that day on which [he] intended to fast, and give it to a widow or an orphan or someone in need" (*Sim.* 5.3.7). In this way Hermas will become humble-minded and, as a result, "the one who receives [the saved money from fasting] may satisfy his own soul and pray to the Lord on your behalf" (*Sim.* 5.3.7). If Hermas "completes the fast in this way," as the Shepherd commanded him, his "sacrifice [*thysia*] will be acceptable in God's sight, . . . and the service [*leitourgia*] performed in this way is beautiful and joyous and acceptable to the Lord" (*Sim.* 5.3.8). As commented by Osiek, both sacrifice and service here refer to the true fasting done correctly.[21] The right kind of fasting, which should carry social obligations and justice (cf. Isa. 58:6–14) and bring out joy from the performer, will result in spiritual blessings through the prayer of the recipients—again this is a blessed cycle of symbiotic reciprocity. The third-century Syriac church manual *Didascalia apostolorum* and its fourth-century expanded version *Apostolic Constitution* would direct the faithful to fast in order to raise money for alms if one otherwise lacks a means to give (*Didasc.* 19; *Ap. Const.* 5.1.3).[22]

4.3. Hospitality: Christian Reformulations

In this section we will examine the tangible expressions of Christian koinonia, in which early Christians reformulated Greco-Roman customs of hospitality (*philoxenia*; *hospitium*) as a further means to love their neighbors. We will focus our attention on the five distinct modes of Christian hospitality and will follow the order in Aristides's description:

18. This was in contrast to Jewish days of fasting, which were Mondays and Thursdays.

19. Origen also shares this point with a quotation perhaps from the *Sentences* in *Hom. Lev.* 10.2.

20. Cf. Clement of Alexandria, *Strom.* 7.12; Origen, *Hom. Lev.* 10.2; Tertullian, *De jejunio adversus psychicos* 9.13; *Acts Thom.* 20; *Acts Paul* 25.

21. Osiek, *Shepherd of Hermas*, 174.

22. Also noted in ibid., 174.

[1] When they see strangers, they take him under their own roof and rejoice over him as a true brother, for they do not call themselves brothers according to the flesh but according to the soul. [2] And whenever they see one of their poor has died, each one of them according to his ability contributes ungrudgingly and they bury him. [3] And if they hear that some are condemned or imprisoned on account of the name of their Lord, they contribute for those condemned and send to them what they need, [4] and if it is possible, they redeem them. (*Apol.* 15.7)

4.3.1. Entertaining Missionaries and Strangers

We will start with "hospitality proper." The "strangers" mentioned in Aristides's quote above may refer to fellow Christians traveling or visiting places for evangelistic or missionary purpose (brothers "according to the soul"). Travel was common in Roman society, thanks to the *relative* safety on the roads due to Roman engineering skills and military presence, and private hospitality was generally regarded a virtue.[23] Inns, which had been designed to meet the increasing demand of that mobile society, were, however, reputed to provide poor service and to be "centers of all sorts of nefarious activities"[24]; thus, discerning travelers resorted to the hospitality of their acquaintances and business associates whenever possible.[25] Understandably, then, hospitality to traveling Christians ("strangers"), especially as they often carried and disseminated the gospel message, was one of the prime ways that Christians cared for one another through an impressive network of house churches already in the first century, evidenced in the Acts and Pauline and general epistles.[26] In the subsequent centuries clergy in particular were charged with special responsibilities and privileges of offering hospitality to visitors and traveling missionaries, from the common fund under the charge of bishops (Justin,

23. A. Malherbe, *Social Aspects of Early Christianity* (Philadelphia: Fortress, 1982), 94. Traveling of itself was not necessarily a sign of relative wealth and independence as W. A. Meeks, *The First Urban Christians: The Social World of the Apostle Paul* (New Haven: Yale University Press, 1983), 67, understood; on the contrary, as noted by H. W. Pleket, in his review of Meek's *First Urban Christians*, VC 39 (1985): 194, "being itinerant as a craftsman is a sign of economic hardship rather than of prosperity," which would be the case for many traveling Christians.

24. Malherbe, *Social Aspects*, 95.

25. Ibid.

26. For example, Acts 21:4, 7, 16–17; Rom. 15:22–23; 16:1–2; 1 Cor. 16:10–11; Phil. 2:29; Philem. 22; Heb. 13:2; 1 Pet. 4:9; 3 John 12; cf. Rom. 12:13; 1 Tim. 3:2; 5:10; Titus 1:8; 2 John 10. On the connection between early Christian mission and hospitality, see D. W. Riddle, "Early Christian Hospitality: A Factor in the Gospel Transmission," *JBL* 57 (1938): 141–54; on early Christian hospitality in general (though mainly in the NT), see A. Arterbury, *Entertaining Angels: Early Christian Hospitality in Its Mediterranean Setting* (Sheffield: Sheffield Phoenix, 2005)—only 122–29 specifically deal with post–NT period; and C. Pohl, *Making Room: Recovering Hospitality as a Christian Tradition* (Grand Rapids: Eerdmans, 1999), 41–47—the author basically jumps from the NT to the fourth century, bypassing our period.

1 Apol. 67.6; *Didasc.* 8–9).[27] Cyprian stressed the church's continuous support for the strangers (*peregrini*) in need along with the poor during the Decian persecution, even out of his own personal funds either in addition to or in place of the common treasury when it was unavailable (*Ep.* 7.2). Later, the regional councils of Elvira (ca. 306), Arles (314), and Antioch (341) confirmed and enhanced the episcopal authority of extending hospitality to strangers.[28] Jerome subsequently reported that some bishops jealously protected this privilege of dispensing hospitality against the wealthy laymen who usurped their position and entertained strangers who should have been under the charge of clergy (*In. ep. ad Titum* 1.8–9). Bishops and lay people (typically the wealthy or at least wealthier ones) who rendered hospitality performed a critical function of encouraging unity among churches dispersed throughout the empire.[29]

As early as the end of the first century, more defined and detailed guidelines were given for Christian practice of hospitality. The most famous and elaborate guidelines come from *Didache*, which assumes a regular flow of itinerant apostles, prophets, and teachers, as well as ordinary Christians (11–13), into its church community where local, resident leaders—bishops and deacons—are present (15.1–2).[30] In this context, it manifestly deals with apparent abuses of Christian hospitality by some of those Christian travelers and migrants. First of all, the resident Christians are to receive "as the Lord" the apostles (11.4) who are ascetic and itinerant enough, since a true mark of an apostolic life is not residency but itinerancy, preaching to the whole world, not just a local community (perhaps with eschatological urgency).[31] The local Christians are to provide an apostle with hospitality only for a day (or two) and to send him on the next morning with the bare necessities (just enough bread until he finds lodging at night) for continuation of his journey (11.5–6). If an apostle stays more than two days or asks for money (in addition to what he is provided), he is a false prophet; for a true apostolic life is presumably "a life based on a willing abandonment of everything beyond what is really and absolutely necessary" as a sign of one's complete trust in God's provision and care;[32] and the apostle will find another Christian home for hospitality in the

27. H. Chadwick, "Justification by Faith and Hospitality," *StPatr* 4 (1961): 283, specifies presbyters with this role.

28. Cf. Arterbury, *Entertaining Angels*, 128.

29. Osiek, *Shepherd of Hermas*, 250. A converse example of denying hospitality and therefore furthering disharmony and estrangement between Roman and Carthaginian churches during the baptismal controversy is given in Cyprian, *Ep.* 75.25.

30. A steady flow of traveling Christians is also evidenced in Cyprian's letters, such as *Epp.* 8.2; 67.5.

31. Cf. K. Niederwimmer, *The Didache: A Commentary* (trans. L M. Maloney; Hermeneia; Minneapolis: Fortress, 1998), 176; cf. hospitality of wealthy converts receiving ascetic, itinerant apostles in their homes in *Acts John* 19–20, 25, 46; *Acts Pet.* 8, 17, 22; *Acts Paul* 2, 5; *Acts Thom.* 81, 131.

32. Niederwimmer, *Didache*, 176.

evening. As Kurt Niederwimmer suggests, this recalls Jesus's prohibitions against taking purse or money on missionary activity (cf. Mark 6:8; Luke 9:3; 10:4; cf. Matt. 10:9).[33]

Concerning itinerant prophets (i.e., those who "speak in the spirit," 11.7), the resident Christians are to show them proper respect in general but to receive (only) the true ones by comparing their conduct to the Lord's ways and lifestyle (11.7–8): for example, no true prophet who "orders a meal in the Spirit," which is supposedly reserved for the poor in the community, would partake of it.[34] Furthermore, no true prophet would fail to practice the truth he teaches (11.10). Finally, no true prophet would ask for money or something else for himself in the Spirit (as in the same case for the true apostle); yet if a prophet asks the local Christians to give to those in need, he should not be judged (11.12). If an approved genuine prophet (previously itinerant) wants to settle in the local community, resident Christians of that community are obligated to provide a livelihood for that prophet (13.1: "he deserves food"). The prophets are entitled to "all the firstfruits" in terms of wine, bread, oil, and meat from cattle and sheep, for "they are your high priests" (13.3, 5–6). The local Christians are to give them even the firstfruits of money, clothing, and "everything you own," "according to the commandment" but with willingness and generosity ("as it seems good to you") (13.7). If they don't have any resident prophet to receive all these gifts, they should give them to the poor (13.4). Lastly, they should welcome again "as the Lord" those teachers whose correct doctrinal teaching brings about "righteousness and knowledge of the Lord" (11.1–2), for a true teacher also "deserves food" (13.2). As stated by Niederwimmer, *Didache* first recognizes the authority and dignity of these itinerant, charismatic leaders and messengers of the gospel—apostles, prophets, and teachers—as entitling them to the hospitality of local communities as if the Lord himself (11.1, 4, 7); only then it offers the criteria by which the communities can discriminate false prophets from the authentic apostles and prophets.[35]

A similar principle of hospitality applies to all traveling or migrant Christians. Resident Christians should receive "everyone who comes in the name of the Lord" *first* (12.1). Then, they are to distinguish true Christians from impostors by exercising their critical judgment (cf. Lucian, *Death of Peregrinus* 12–13). If a Christian traveler is simply passing through, they should help him "as much as [they] can" (12.2). However, as in the case of true apostles, the traveler should not stay more than two days (three days, if necessary) and should not exploit the hospitality of the local community (12.2). If a migrant or visitor desires to settle in the community as in the case of some prophets

---

33. Ibid., 176–77.

34. Cf. ibid., 79; *The Apostolic Fathers* (ed. and trans. B. E. Ehrman; 2 vols.; LCL 24 and 25; Cambridge, MA: Harvard University Press, 2003), 435n25.

35. Niederwimmer, *Didache*, 182.

and is a craftsman, he should work for his living by his trade (12.3); the community is not further responsible for providing food, lodging, or shelter in that case. If the visitor has no craft, however, the community should collectively determine how he or she would live in the community as a Christian without being idle (12.3–4). This instruction may mean either that the community is responsible that the visitor-now-community-member finds work or that the community should prevent in advance a circumstance in which any idle Christian might live among them. If the person in question is unwilling to work for one's living, that person is a "Christmonger" (*christemporos*), who dishonors and cheats on the Christian name (12.5). The local community should beware of and avoid such people (12.5). Incidentally, this particular teaching highlights the community's understanding of the importance of work and its concern over idleness, already mentioned in the earlier part of the text on giving: acquiring something by manual labor ("by working with your hands") is a legitimate and right way of earning, and out of that they are to give to ransom for their sins (4.6; cf. Acts 20:34–35; Eph. 4:28; 1 Thess. 4:11–12; 2 Thess. 3:12).[36] When combined with the *Didache*'s anxiety about exploitation of Christian generosity in almsgiving (1.5; 4.5–8) and hospitality, this stress on working for one's living against idleness might point to some apprehension about sustaining communal aids and resources for meeting the internal needs of the community, even as it exhorts selfless and cheerful giving (1.5; 4.5–8). The *Didache*'s instruction on hospitality not only shows its concern over liberal but judicious practice of Christian hospitality; but it also shows the link between hospitality and community identity and boundary in terms of orthodoxy and orthopraxy, which is evidenced in its criteria for true and false Christians and itinerant leaders (cf. 2 John 10; 3 John 5–12; Ignatius, *Smyrn.* 4.1; *Eph.* 9.1).

Christians welcomed and received not just traveling co-religionists but also the "strangers" in their local communities to their homes. Clement of Rome praises the Corinthian Christians for the "magnificent character" of their past hospitality (*1 Clem.* 1.2) and names the three scriptural figures—Abraham, Lot, and Rahab—as examples of "faith and hospitality" ("godliness and hospitality" for Lot), through which they were saved (10.7; 11.1; 12.1; cf. 12.3).[37] Clement is keen to promote hospitable practices aimed at unifying the Corinthians (including those in connection to church leadership) as an important part of good works and obedience to the Lord's commandment (13.1–14.1; 33.1–34.4), especially because the Corinthian community was suffering a major

---

36. The implication is that this is the only legitimate source of their earning and giving especially against the backdrop of larger Greco-Roman "work ethic." Acquiring money by inheritance or investment, which was only reserved for the upper order and those with enough assets, is certainly out of question for any member in Didachist community.

37. On justification and hospitality in *1 Clement*, see Chadwick, "Justification by Faith," 281–85.

division and tension between house community leaders.[38] It is not surprising, then, that inhospitality (*aphiloxenia*) completes the list of vices, along with strife and slander (35.5). *Hermas* also counts hospitality among good works to be performed toward one's salvation (*Mand.* 8.10), above all receiving gladly "God's servants" into one's house without hypocrisy (*Sim.* 8.10.3; 9.27.2). Those who are hospitable (*philoxenoi*), along with the bishops who shelter the needy and widows "without ceasing," are promised to "be sheltered by the Lord forever" (*Sim.* 9.27.3) and are praised as the glorious ones in God's sight whose place (in heaven/paradise) is "already with the angels," provided that "they continue serving the Lord to the end" (*Sim.* 9.27.3). *Hermas* shares a similar concern for unity of the community that is experiencing some friction among the different social groups and reserves high praise and reward for those who are fostering a sense of unity among them through hospitality.

4.3.2. Burying the Dead

Roman society, in fact all ancient societies in general, prescribed the greatest moral-religious duty (*pietas*) to providing proper burials for the members of one's family and community and accorded the greatest respect to all buried remains; accordingly, the Roman law, which regarded the tomb a sacred place, dealt severely with those who would disturb tombs and grave sites.[39] While the common Roman funerary practice was cremation, by the late second century CE inhumation became more predominant even in Rome; and this, along with a demographic increase, led to ever-increasing demand for burial space and its rising costs.[40] Cicero (mid-first century BCE) had already observed the high cost and frequent speculation of favorite burial areas around the cities (*Epistulae ad Atticum* 12.21.33). Therefore, although some wealthy urban residents occasionally donated burial plots outside the city for the townspeople for their civic benefaction,[41] there sprang numerous funerary associations or societies (*collegia funeratica*) whose primary purpose was to provide "burial expenses for deceased members and to insure that each member received a

38. Regarding hospitality and internal schism of the Corinthian community, see Maier, *Social Setting of the Ministry*, 92–94.

39. M. J. Johnson, "Pagan-Christian Burial Practices of the Fourth Century: Shared Tombs?" *JECS* 5 (1997): 39; T. J. Harrington, "The Local Church at Rome in the Second Century: A Common Cemetery Emerges amid Developments in This 'Laboratory of Christian Policy,'" *Studia Canonica* 23 (1989): 178.

40. V. F. Nicolai, F. Bisconti, and D. Mazzoleni, *The Christian Catacombs of Rome: History, Decoration, Inscriptions* (2nd ed.; Regensburg: Schnell & Steiner, 2002), 16.

41. C. Osiek, "Roman and Christian Burial Practices and the Patronage of Women," in *Commemorating the Dead: Texts and Artifacts in Context: Studies of Roman, Jewish, and Christian Burials* (ed. L. Brink and D. Green; Berlin: Walter de Gruyter, 2008), 254, citing N. Purcell, "Tomb and Suburb," in *Römische Gräberstrassen: Selbstdarstellung, Status, Standard* (ed. H. von Hesberg and P. Zanker; Munich: Bayerischen Akademie der Wissenschaften, 1987), 25–41.

decent burial."[42] Their members, who assembled regularly and performed customary rites in memory of deceased members, were drawn from among a broad band of urban plebs (minus the destitute), including the "upper levels of the urban plebs" with moderate means (i.e., the middling group), particularly artisans, merchants, craftsmen, and shopkeepers, some of whom were freedmen or slaves.[43] They might at times enjoy the patronage (but not the respect) of the local *honestiores*, and they typically collected monthly contributions for funeral ceremonies and for the maintenance of a burial site that was jointly owned by the members.

Christians shared the general concern for proper funerals and the responsibility to honor the buried (which would later develop into the extensive cult of martyrs).[44] Given the serious and sacred nature of burials, Christians made sure that the poorest members of their communities would be provided with suitable burials (and therefore escape the common fate of exposure and disposal of their corpses, which was left for the destitute and many without means). Burying a Christian poor man in Aristides's quote indicates a collective operation of Christians similar to that of the funerary societies in that "everyone else" in the community pitched in to provide for the deceased poor, but undoubtedly the buried poor could not have paid their "dues" for their funerals while they had been alive. Again, burying the poor was one of the purposes for the common chest (Tertullian, *Apol.* 39.5; *Ap. Trad.* 40). In better-known cases (to us at least), wealthy members of the church communities (patrons) provided their familial or other private burial spaces for the Christian poor of the same communities (see below). Since in Roman society tombs or burial plots were separated by family or agnate kin rather than religion in the first three centuries,[45] many (if not most) Christians shared the tombs and burial grounds (*areae*) with pagans (mainly via kinship) according to whatever was available, whether it was a tomb belonging to an individual or a family, or a tomb belonging to a burial society (see below for Roman law and corporate ownership).[46] Starting from the early third century, "Christian cemeteries" began to emerge in

42. R. L. Wilken, *The Christians as the Romans Saw Them* (New Haven: Yale University Press, 1984), 36.

43. O. M. van Nijf, "*Collegia* and Civic Guards: Two Chapters in the History of Sociability," in *After the Past* (ed. W. Jongman and M. Kleijwegt; Leiden: Brill, 2002), 307; Wilken, *Christians as the Romans Saw Them*, 35.

44. For example, *Acts Just.* B 6.2; Eusebius, *HE* 5.1.61; 7.11.24; *Mart. Lyons* 61; Origen, *Cels.* 8.30; Minucius Felix, *Oct.* 34.10; Cyprian, *Epp.* 8.3.2; 12.2.1.

45. Cf. Osiek, "Roman and Christian Burial Practices," 247; Johnson, "Pagan-Christian Burial Practices," 39–40.

46. The burial societies were de facto recognized as the owners of property by the early third century and could receive donation of property from individuals; cf. Osiek, "Roman and Christian Burial Practices," 265. Aristides does not share with us—probably does not intend to share with us—the kind of tombs in which the poor Christians were buried; the important thing was that Christians provided proper burials for the poor among them.

Carthage, Rome, and Alexandria, as reported by Tertullian,[47] "Hippolytus,"[48] and Origen,[49] respectively (see chap. 1). They most likely refer not to the common cemeteries owned by the respective local churches but to familial tombs owned by the wealthier members of the local churches and made available for the deceased poor members without any means of private burials, since the Roman law did not acknowledge corporate ownership by a legal entity (of course, Christianity was illegal during this time).[50] Nonetheless, while those tombs were legally private property and private burial complexes and though the church did not have a proper legal status as property owner, there was implicit recognition of corporate ownership *in practice* in the course of the third century as local clergy began to take greater control in managing them and the church functioned de facto as a *collegium*, such as a funerary society.[51]

In Rome, one of the well-known examples, already introduced in chapter 1, is the Catacomb of San Callisto on Via Appia Antica, administered by then deacon Callistus (later bishop), commissioned by bishop Zephyrinus (ca. 199–217 CE). As it was a common custom in Roman society to appoint supervisors to manage private tomb properties, the original catacomb of San Callisto might have been the family tomb of bishop Zephyrinus.[52] Out of multiple Christian catacombs surrounding Rome today, this catacomb grew from originally having two nuclei over eighty meters apart to the unprecedented networks of burial complexes extending about twelve kilometers today. The catacombs, which were not Christian inventions, originated because of spatial and economic considerations. The want of space due to the growing trend of inhumation and the skyrocketed premium of burial land led the managers and owners of those burial places to extend their mausolea underground below their own property, and this practice also gained popularity with Christians.[53] This way of extending burial space underground, i.e., carving the horizontal rungs up the ladder (*loculi*) into each side of a hallway or a chamber, up to six feet or so, especially suited Rome, where local *tufa* ("subsoil," soft rock) provided reliable material that is inexpensive and easy to work with. Moreover, visitors

47. *Scap.* 3.1: "our burial fields"—*areae supulturarum nostrarum.*
48. *Ref.* 9.12.14: administration "of the coemeterium"—*eis to koimētērion katestēsen; Liber Pontificalis* 1.141; cf. *Ap. Trad.* 40.
49. *Hom. Jer.* 4.3.16: *apo tōn koimētēriōn.*
50. Osiek, "Roman and Christian Burial Practices," 244; P. Lampe, *From Paul to Valentinus: Christians at Rome in the First Two Centuries* (trans. M. Steinhauser; ed. M. D. Johnson; Minneapolis: Fortress, 2003), 370–71.
51. Osiek, "Roman and Christian Burial Practices," 264–69.
52. P. F. Bradshaw, M. E. Johnson, and L. E. Phillips, *The Apostolic Tradition: A Commentary* (Hermeneia; Minneapolis: Fortress, 2002), 191; Bodel, "From *Columbaria* to Catacombs," 203–5, 230–31; Osiek, "Roman and Christian Burial Practices," 246; Lampe, *From Paul to Valentinus,* 25–28, 369–72; *Liber Pontificalis* 1.139.
53. It is Christians who eventually developed the catacombs into the vast networks of burial systems in the fourth century given the enormous popularity and outburst of the cult of martyrs.

and family seemed to have preferred burial sites "along the main highways leading out of the city [Rome], and as close to the [city] wall as possible" (72), for
subsequent visits to the graves to honor the deceased. Then, the underground
gallery with long horizontal compartments dug in the cheap *tufa* walls (*loculi*),
as near to the city as possible, would have provided an attractive alternative as
the most economical solution in the most compact manner. A directive in the
Apostolic Tradition prohibited overcharging to bury a person in the cemeteries,
"for it is the property of all the poor," but prescribed the wage of the worker
with the price of the tiles (40), which reflects well the Christian Roman burial of
the poor in the catacombs in the third century. The tiles mentioned in this text
are most likely those tiles used in the catacombs to seal up the *loculi* in which
the corpses are placed.[54] Also its charge to the bishop to provide for "those
who are in that place and take care of it" from the common fund points to
the greater episcopal management of the catacombs as their de facto owners.[55]

Interestingly, catacomb archaeologists such as Nicolai, Bisconti, and Mazzoleni highlight the innovative features of the Christian catacombs in terms
of maximizing space extension, "constituted by a series of interconnected
galleries" that are organized, in general, to a regular scheme—a "grid" or a
"fishbone" pattern of *loculi*.[56] The *loculi* were the most common and inexpensive type of burial space, and this kind of design in many of the oldest
catacomb areas (early to mid-third century) is contrasted to the "closed"
scheme of the pagan *hypogeum* ("cavern"). Only a bit later, around 235 CE,
"were five *cubicula* [chambers] opened along one of the two principal" veins;
the private chambers (off a passageway) "would have been the most expensive
type of funerary site to purchase and decorate";[57] these *cubicula* represented
the first 'privileged' spaces, equipped with more monumental tombs (*a mensa*)
and rich pictorial decoration."[58] One of them, the "papal crypt" housed nine
bishops of Rome throughout the third century (starting from 235). Certainly
by the mid-fourth century, catacombs had become much more elaborate and
established different levels of prestige and ranking; high clergy and government officials sought them out for their own burials, especially closer to the
martyrs' tombs for their own spiritual blessings.[59] While tourists and scholars

54. Bradshaw et al., *Apostolic Tradition*, 192.

55. Cf. Cyprian, *Ep.* 80.1.4, mentions the martyrdom of Bishop Sixtus II and his four deacons
"*in cimiterio*" on August 6, 258; most scholars agree that this cemetery refers to "*the* Christian
cemetery in Rome par excellence, viz. that of Callistus": *The Letters of St. Cyprian of Carthage*
(vol. 4; trans. and anno. G. W. Clarke; ACW 47; New York: Newman, 1989), 305n14.

56. Nicolai et al., *Christian Catacombs of Rome*, 16–17.

57. J. H. Tulloch, "Women Leaders in Family Funerary Banquets," in *A Woman's Place:
House Churches in Earliest Christianity* (ed. C. Osiek and M. Y. MacDonald, with J. H. Tulloch;
Minneapolis: Fortress, 2006), 175.

58. Nicolai et al., *Christian Catacombs of Rome*, 17.

59. R. MacMullen, *The Second Church: Popular Christianity AD 200–400* (Atlanta: SBL,
2009), 73.

are drawn to these decorated *cubicula* or other monumental burials (such as niches for sarcophagi), there is a special religious significance attached to this Christian innovation of typological uniformity of thousands of *loculi* along the walls. The structural uniformity could represent a communal and egalitarian characteristic or ethos of the early Christian community, at least as an ideal aspiration, while in reality ever-growing socioeconomic stratification in the community and institutional hierarchy were certainly taking shape, if not already consolidated and taken for granted. Could this represent deliberately putting aside pagan aspirations of ostentatious commemoration of the self, the family, the clan through funerary monuments that were so common in the Roman world?[60] This particular interpretation of archaeological typology of the (early) catacombs is intriguing in that it supports the expressed desire of Christian (literary) self-definition as a distinct community of equals, harmony, and love, while increasing assimilation of the Christian community into the social, cultural, and economic fabric of the Roman world.

In Carthage, "Christian cemeteries" (*areae*), first mentioned by Tertullian, seem to be taken for granted by Cyprian. Cyprian strongly objects to the action of Spanish bishop Martialis, who attended a funerary banquet (*conuiuium*) in honor of a deceased (pagan) friend or relative and allowed his sons to be buried in the cemetery of a pagan burial *collegium* (*Ep.* 67.6.2), probably because he was a member. On the one hand, Cyprian's angry tone suggests that Christians typically would have been buried in separate burial areas by his time; this is supported by a couple of specific references to the "Christian cemeteries" in Carthage. Christians were forbidden to gather at the burial areas (*coemeteria*) by Valerian's second edict in 258 CE (*Acts Cyprian* 1.7), and Cyprian was beheaded and buried in "the cemetery of Macrobius Candidianus the procurator" (*Acts Cyprian* 5.6). During the Great Persecution (303), Bishop Felix of Tibiuca was beheaded and buried "off the highway called the Via Scillitanorum on the property of Faustus" (*Mart. Felix.* 31). On the other hand, Cyprian's impassioned objection, along with Commodian's condemnation of the decisions of those who would be buried in the same way along with pagans (*Instr.* 74) testifies to the (perhaps more common) custom of other Christians who shared the burial plots with pagans, including a bishop.[61]

4.3.3. Caring for Confessors

We now move on to the next in Aristides's list. Christian hospitality also took a form of visiting and caring for those suffering for their faith—the imprisoned and condemned confessors—especially given the church's high

---

60. Nicolai et al., *Christian Catacombs of Rome*, 20; cf. Commodian's denunciation of those who seek funeral pomp in *Instr.* 74.

61. Cf. Osiek, "Roman and Christian Burial Practices," 267.

regard for their extraordinary spirituality and authority. During the sporadic but intense popular and imperial persecutions in various regions in this period, imprisonment, condemnation, and its attending torture and abrasive treatment of Christians (depending on their social ranks to an extent) are well attested in Christian (and a few pagan) sources. Christian confessors included children, youth, women, men, and the elderly, further specified in social status, such as slave, army official, and noble woman, and also in religious status, such as catechumen, deacon, presbyter, and bishop. Unlike today, the ancient prison system was not intended or designed for the long-term confinement of prisoners and was definitely not reputed for its humane treatments or hygienic concerns.[62] Therefore, a prisoner was much more dependent on outside help for the basic necessities of life, such as food and clothing.[63] In this context, Lucian's earlier scornful portrait of Christian credulity and undiscriminating care of the charlatan Peregrinus in prison does illustrate and confirm how seriously Christians took the job of ministering to those imprisoned for faith even in the eyes of an outsider. For Cyprian, along with the poor, the imprisoned confessors were the most important group to be cared for by the church even during the Decian persecution (*Epp.* 5.1.2; 12.1.1; 13.7; 14.2.2).[64]

Many martyr acts report streams of Christian visitors attending their fellow believers in prisons even as they were waiting for their martyrdom. For example, Perpetua and her fellow confessors (d. 203 CE) were visited multiple times while in prison by the Carthaginian faithful, organized by their deacons (Tertius and Pomponius) (3.7). As the deacons bribed the soldiers, who then allowed the confessors to move to a better part of the prison for their refreshment for a few hours (3.7), others brought the confessors meals and provided for even an *agapē*, which the martyrs had as their last meal on the day before their bloody martyrdom (as a replacement of the pagan banquet) (16.4–17.1).[65] Before Felicitas faced her martyrdom soon after her childbirth, one of the women visitors took Felicitas's newborn girl to raise her (15.7); finally, with the help of a sympathetic adjutant who allowed many visitors, confessors and visitors shared mutual spiritual and emotional comfort and encouragement (9.1). Although the presbyter Pionius and his fellow confessors did not accept any gifts brought for them by the faithful out of desire for

62. Ferguson, *Early Christians Speak*, 211. Eusebius reports that during the Great Persecution Diocletian's second edict of imprisonment of clergy was soon followed by his third edict, which commanded release of the imprisoned clergy upon their forced sacrifice because they had filled and shut down the prisons "everywhere": *HE* 8.6.8–10; Tertullian, *Mart.* 2.

63. Ferguson, *Early Christians Speak*, 211.

64. For this reason, Cornelius's testimony against Novatian's unwillingness to care for the confessors in Eusebius, *HE* 6.43.16, was a stinging accusation.

65. Cf. Tertullian, *Apol.* 42.5, who writes about "the Liberalia, which is the habit of the beast-fighters taking their last meal."

self-sufficiency (*Mart. Pion.* 11.2–3),[66] the languishing Montanus and his companions (d. 258/259 CE), who had been suffering from prolonged deprivation and tormenting distress, welcomed and were restored by the food brought by the faithful (*Mart. Mon. and Luc.* 4.7; 9.1–3).

The condemned who were placed on the road for their martyrdom were also visited along the route and cared for. Polycarp thanks the Philippians for welcoming and providing hospitality for Ignatius and his companions as they passed through Philippi on their way from Syria to Rome in chains where Ignatius faced martyrdom (*Phil.* 1.1).[67] From Ignatius's own letters we know that he was visited and refreshed "in every aspect" by delegations of church communities in Asia Minor in or near the cities where his guards sojourned (*Eph.* 1.2–3; 2.1; *Magn.* 1.2; 15.1; *Trall.* 1.1–2; 12.1; 13.1).[68] In western Asia Minor, Ignatius's company took a northern route through Philadelphia to Smyrna and thus bypassed the churches on the southern route (churches of Tralles, Magnisia, and Ephesus); when those churches sent delegations to Ignatius to meet him in Smyrna, he sent a letter to each of the three churches and also to the Roman church (*Eph.* 21.1; *Magn.* 15.1; *Trall.* 12.1; 13.1; *Rom.* 4.1; 5.1; 10.1). During his next sojourn in Troas, he sent letters to churches he had visited (churches of Philadelphia and Smyrna) along with one to Polycarp (*To the Philadelphians* 11.2; *Smyrn.* 10.1; 12.1; 13.1–2; *To Polycarp* 8.1–2).[69] As Riddle aptly calls it, the story of his journey to Rome as we know it is "one long illustration of [hospitality]."[70]

The care was extended as well to those confessors who were condemned to the mines and exile. While in exile at the initial stage of Valerian's persecution (257 CE), Cyprian sent a letter to nine Numidian bishops, presbyters, deacons, and other lay people who were condemned to the mines (Cyprian, *Epp.* 76–79).[71] Condemnation to the mines was considered to be the capital punishment "nearest to death,"[72] and it was notorious and dreaded for its extreme conditions.[73] Some of their company had died presumably as a result

---

66. While his passion account places his martyrdom during the Decian persecution, Eusebius says he faced his martyrdom during the reign of Marcus Aurelius in the late second century: *HE* 4.15.46–47.

67. We are not given any information about the likely deaths of Ignatius's fellow confessors.

68. Smyrnaeans, Philadelphians, Ephesians, Magnesians, and Trallians along with Romans and a letter to Polycarp.

69. See also M. W. Holmes, "Introduction: The Letters of Ignatius, Bishop of Antioch," in *The Apostolic Fathers: Greek Texts and English Translations* (ed. and rev. M. W. Holmes; Grand Rapids: Baker Books, 1999), 128–29.

70. Riddle, "Early Christian Hospitality," 144.

71. Until Valerian's second rescript in the summer of the following year, the punishments were confined to the high clergy—unless others infringed upon the restrictions such as assembly in the cemeteries.

72. *Digesta* 48.19.28, quoted in *The Letters of St. Cyprian of Carthage* (vol. 4), 282n5.

73. For the accounts of Christians condemned to the mines during the Great Persecution, see Eusebius, *HE* 8.13.5; *Mart. Pal.* 13.1–2.

of the acute hardships of the mining or prison conditions (*Ep.* 76.1.2); the surviving confessors were subject to beatings with clubs and other measures designed to inflict wounds and shame on the victims, such as shaving only one side of a head (*Epp.* 76.2.1; 2.4; 77.3.1). Cyprian also mentions the virgins and children who were condemned with them and praises the former for their double glory of virginity and (impending) martyrdom and the latter for having transcended their age with their confession (*Ep.* 76.6.2). These confessors received both physical and spiritual refreshments through the lower clergy (a subdeacon and acolytes) when they delivered them food and contributions from a certain layman Quirinus and Cyprian, along with Cyprian's letter of encouragement (*Epp.* 77.3.1; 78.3.1; 79.1.1). As for Cyprian, during his exile (257–58 CE) he was visited by the many faithful, including his own clergy who must have been in close contact with him and continued to deliver his letters to and from other bishops, presbyters, deacons, and confessors. This kind of visitation and contact was evidently for more encouragement and ministry since he was not in pressing physical or financial need compared to many other confessors; he still kept his private funds (for emergency dispensations for ministry in addition to the common chest evidenced in his letters) and his estate in Carthage (cf. *Ep.* 81.1; *Vita* 15), and among his visitors were "many eminent people of highly illustrious rank and family [knights (*egregii*) and senators (*clarissimi*)], . . . as well as nobles of worldly renown" (*Vita* 14).

As one can see, like other forms of hospitality, caretaking of the confessors operated both individually (informally) and corporately (formally). According to Eusebius, Origen, who himself was imprisoned and tortured during the Decian persecution and died shortly after his release from the effects of the torture, courageously visited incarcerated confessors and accompanied martyrs to their final sentence in his youth (*HE* 6.3.4; 39.5). Tertullian, in his exhortation to the martyrs, also writes how individual (lay) Christians ministered to them out of their own private means (*Mart.* 1.1; 2.7). In his direct letter to the confessors from his hideout, Cyprian informs them he is sending money (250 sesterces) to them from his private fund (in addition to the money from the common fund) and expresses his delight in hearing how individual lay Christians in his church vie with one another to alleviate the confessors' hardships with their own financial resources (*Ep.* 13.7). When clergy was involved in visitations, as some of these martyr acts and the letters of Ignatius and Cyprian testify (see below), the common fund was most likely employed by the clergy so that the benefits were offered in the name of the community (under the direction of the bishop) rather than by individual patrons or givers.[74] The care of the Christians in the mines that was mentioned in Cyprian's letters was done by both the private fund (that of Quirinus) and the common fund, even as Cyprian was in

74. Burns, *Cyprian the Bishop*, 30; see Justin, *1 Apol.* 67.6; Tertullian, *Apol.* 39.6; Lucian, *Mort. Per.* 12–13; Cyprian, *Epp.* 5.1.2; 12.1.1; 13.7; 14.2.2.

exile. However, though he repeatedly advised his clergy to devote themselves to supplying the confessors with "whatever is necessary" in terms of food and clothing (*Ep.* 14.2.2; cf. *Epp.* 5.1.2; 12.1.1; 13.7), because the support came from the common treasury, Cyprian specified the conditions for those confessors on the church roll as in the case of the poor: only those who comply with the moral instruction and discipline of the church and conduct themselves in humility and peace, i.e., those confessors who would acknowledge Cyprian's authority and not join the laxist party (*Ep.* 14.2.2–3.2). The four Alexandrian presbyters who secretly visited fellow Christians, and the deacon Eusebius who served the imprisoned confessors "with all energy" during the Valerian persecution (257–60 CE; mentioned in bishop Dionysius's letter preserved by [a different] Eusebius), probably also ministered out of the community fund (*HE* 7.11.24). Going back to Lucian's account, not just the representatives from the Asiatic cities, but "the aged widows, orphan children, and other church officials" who gathered at the prison to look after Peregrinus also drew on the common chest. The widows and orphans themselves were in all likelihood supported by the common fund, and the church officials (clergy) could actually sleep with Perigrinus inside the prison, having bribed the prison guards.

Bribing the prison guards, which must have cost a certain amount, features frequently enough in the Christian texts.[75] The impressive visiting privileges and hospitality Ignatius enjoyed at Philadelphia and Smyrna with the local Christians and the delegations from three other churches were likely gained by bribery as well.[76] However, Christians at Lugdunum were unsuccessful in obtaining the bodies of the martyrs through bribery (Eusebius, *HE* 5.1.61; *Mart. Lyons* 61). It apparently did not raise any moral qualms among Christians; rather, it constituted a necessary part of supporting the prisoners since it enabled the churches to maintain contact with them (and thus to tend to their needs) and allowed the guards to be more favorably disposed to the Christians. Thus the *Didascalia* (19) and its appropriation into the *Apostolic Constitutions* (5.1–2) ordered the community members to spare no efforts to procure *both* nourishment for the condemned Christian prisoner *and* bribes for the guards so that everything possible might be done for his or her relief.

4.3.4. Ransoming Prisoners and Captives

While early Christians focused more of their energy and resources on caring for the imprisoned, they also sought to free them whenever possible

75. For example, *Acts Paul Thec.* 18 (a silver mirror) and *Acts Thom.* 118 (ten denarii) and 150 (363 silver pieces!); see also *Mart. Perp.* 3.7. Cf. Tertullian's disapproval of a "common" Christian practice of bribing Roman persecutors in *Fug.* 5.3; 12–14. Bribery was a common phenomenon in the Roman imperial operations and the systems of ancient society in general—see also *Letters of St. Cyprian* (vol. 1; trans. and anno. G. W. Clarke; ACW 43; New York: Newman, 1984), 32.

76. Osiek, "Ransom of Captives," 381.

(cf. Lucian, *Mort. Per.* 12). The aforementioned section about sparing no efforts in relieving the condemned Christians in the *Didascalia* and *Apostolic Consitutions* in fact called for almsgiving and fasting even to the extent of sacrificing everything (those who were able) to ransom them from confinement. Although Ignatius enjoyed and thanked the local visitors and delegations from other cities, consisting of the fellow bishops (Polycarp of Smyrna and Polybius of Tralles), deacons, and other laypeople, his exhortation to the Christians in Rome, where he desired and anticipated his martyrdom (by the beasts) is particularly telling. While acknowledging the reputation of the "preeminent love" of Roman Christians, Ignatius pleads with them not to hinder him from achieving the glory of martyrdom by showing "unreasonable kindness" to him (*Rom.* 4.1). Knowing and fearing what their love *could* do, i.e., obtaining his release and thus saving his life (possibly by bribery[77]), Ignatius warns and begs them to "remain silent and leave [him] alone" (2.1; 1.2; 6.2–3). The noted resolve and sacrifice of Roman Christians for the sake of fellow Christians certainly had precedents. Clement of Rome reports that many among them have had themselves imprisoned to substitute for others in prison and that many others sold themselves into slavery and fed the hungry with the price received (55.2). Later in the text Clement offers an intercessory prayer to God who does feed the hungry and release (*lytrōsai*) the prisoners through the very works of Christians (59.4). Using the same term, *lytrōsai*, the common Greek word for releasing of captives by payment of ransom, *Hermas* attests to this practice of freeing the Christian prisoners in exchange for money as the essential work of charity, along with supporting the widows, orphans, and the poor (*Mand.* 8.10). In the Roman tradition, perhaps the most dramatic case of ransom of the condemned Christian would be that of Callistus, the former-slave-turned-bishop of Rome in the early third century. In a biased account of Callistus's life traditionally attributed to a certain Hippolytus, Callistus was condemned to Sardinian mines with other Christians for his confession of faith. The author protests that Callistus's public profession of Christianity was a deceptive ploy to get away with his mishandling of (Christian) investors' funds. However, he ended up joining the rank of confessors when Commodus's concubine Marcia, out of desire to do good for the church, intervened and attained release of all the confessors and Callistus. Although this release was not a Christian initiative per se,[78] Victor, bishop of Rome, actively cooperated to secure that goal.[79]

The other group for which Christians sought release through ransom was Christian captives taken in brigandage (and later piracy and wars as well).

---

77. Suggested by Osiek, "Ransom of Captives," 383–84.
78. Marcia's connection to Christianity is not entirely clear.
79. Hippolytus, *Ref.* 9.12.

Dionysius of Alexandria reports about many Egyptian Christians, including an aged bishop of Nilopolis and his wife, who fled to deserts and the Arabian mountains during the Decian persecution and perished by hunger, thirst, frost, disease, robbers, and wild animals (Eusebius, *HE* 4.42.2). However, among those who took flight to the Arabian mountain, many Christians were taken captive and reduced to slavery by Saracens; some of them were "ransomed for large sums," presumably by fellow Christians, though not without difficulty. Eusebius adds that others have not *yet* been ransomed up to his time as though there might have been continuing efforts and therefore still hope of their ransom in the future (*HE* 4.42.3–4).

In North Africa, after the persecution ceased and the outbreak of the plague subsided, barbarian raiders in Numidian hinterlands carried off a great number of Christians among them as captives, and a group of eight Numidian bishops asked Cyprian for financial assistance for ransoming them (ca. 253 CE; *Ep.* 62). In his response, Cyprian was particularly concerned about the fate of children, wives, and above all virgins who might be subject to abuse and prostitution and therefore lose their purity and honor (*Ep.* 62.2.3).[80] Like his appeal to almsgiving for the poor, Cyprian located biblical and theological bases of ransom of captives in the love and unity of the body of Christ (1 Cor. 12:12–31; 3:16) and the Lord's promise of reward at the last judgment with the hope of salvation (Matt. 25:34–36) and saw Christ in the captive Christians as well as in the poor (*Ep.* 61.1.1–2.2; 3.1). Then he collected a total of 100,000 sesterces in cash from the clergy and laity in Carthage (62.3.2) and sent the money to those Numidian bishops, plus smaller sums collected from other African churches (62.4.2); along with the donation, he also sent a list of contributors so that the recipients could pray for them (62.4.2; this list is lost) as well as instructions to write again if they needed more (62.4.1). The fact that Cyprian mentions a list of individual contributors indicates that the money, indeed a substantial sum, did not come from the regular common fund but consisted of large donations from the limited number of the wealthy.[81] This remarkable collection bears witness to not only Christian readiness to assist but also to "the size, relative prosperity, and financial resilience of the Christianity community in Carthage," especially when one remembers that it was the same amount minimally required for a decurion rank and that it was the rough equivalent of "the average monthly rations of some 3,000 unskilled workmen [which had] been collected [30 sesterces per laborer per month]—enough, therefore, to provide one month's food for their (average) family of four, or sufficient for keeping alive 12,000 people for a month."[82]

80. For Cyprian, virgins represent the collective purity of the church; see his *Hab. virg.*
81. *The Letters of St. Cyprian of Carthage* (vol. 3; trans. and anno. G. W. Clarke; ACW 46; New York: Newman, 1986), 285n12.
82. Ibid., 284n11.

4.3.5. Caring for the Sick

Lastly, nurturing the ill is not mentioned by Aristides but was an important part of Christian hospitality. Christians provided sacrificial care of the sick as they knew how, even as they prayed for healing and exercised the gift of healing. According to the *Apostolic Tradition*, visiting the sick was one of the tests for every catechumen, measuring one's readiness for baptism (15; 20.1); providing meals for the sick, along with the widows and the poor, was a common duty of all the faithful (24). Among the clergy, deacons (and deaconesses, especially in the East) in particular were charged with care of the sick and the infirm, who informed the bishops about their needs so that they could be visited and prayed over by the "high priests," i.e., bishops (34; *Didasc.* 16.3; cf. *Pseudo-Clementines Ep.* 12; *Ap. Const.* 3.19). We also have Polycarp exhorting presbyters to be compassionate and to "visit all the sick" in his letter to the Philippians (*Phil.* 6.1).

This concentric circle of care for the sick in multiple layers prepared the Christians to meet the overwhelming challenge of epidemic in the mid-third century in the most impressive way. Several contemporary accounts, from Carthage and Alexandria, enlighten us with what the contemporaries endured and how Christians provided for care while they were also suffering. The deadly plague, which had originated in Ethiopia in 250 CE, spread quickly throughout Egypt, North Africa, and from there to Italy and the West (as far as Scotland), for the pandemic lasted fifteen to twenty years in intervals.[83] When one was stricken, the symptoms of the plague included diarrhea, sores on the jaws, continual vomiting, and redness of eyes, and in some cases, the loss of limbs and an impairment of hearing or eyesight (Cyprian, *Mort.* 14). Its effects were extensive and destructive with its estimated mortality higher than that of any epidemic previously known (Zosimus, *Historia Nova* 1.26, 37; cf. 1.36, 46). At its height, it is recorded that more than five thousand succumbed to death in one day in Rome alone (*Historia Augusta, Vita Gallieni* 5.6). While Cyprian reported from Carthage in 252 CE that "many of our people are dying from this mortality" (*Mort.* 15), his biographer Pontius elaborated the ravaging and horrifying scene:

> Countless people were seized daily in their own homes by a sudden attack; one after another the homes of the trembling crowd were invaded. Everyone shuddered, fled to avoid contagion, wickedly exposed their dear ones, as if along with the person who was about to die from the plague one could also shut out death itself. (*Vita* 9)

Streets were filled not only with the corpses but also the cries of the diseased and dying who were begging for help (*Vita* 9). Dionysius also recounted the

---

83. M. M. Sage, *Cyprian* (Patristic Monograph Series 1; Cambridge, MA: Philadelphia Patristic Foundation, 1975), 269; G. B. Ferngren, "The Organisation of the Care of the Sick in Early Christianity," in *Actes/Proceedings of the XXX International Congress of the History of Medicine* (ed. H. Schadewaldt and K.-H. Leven; Düsseldorf: Vicom KG, 1988), 193.

terror from Alexandria around 260 CE: "Now indeed all is lamentation, and all men mourn, and wailings resound throughout the city because of the number of dead and of those that are dying day by day" (Eusebius, *HE* 7.22.2). It affected Christians and non-Christians alike, though its fuller impact fell on pagans, as Dionysius reports (Eusebius, *HE* 7.22.6). Modern calculations based on Dionysius's account suggest that two-thirds of ancient Alexandria's population may have perished.[84]

The civil authorities called on the traditional gods by making sacrifices and customary supplications to placate their anger but hardly did anything tangible to alleviate the situation.[85] Classical society lacked any organized program for the treatment of the sick on either a regular or an emergency basis.[86] The Christian churches, by contrast, established rather systematic care of the sick under the leadership of bishops directing relief efforts. According to Pontius, Cyprian gathered his people for the whole city and gave them the theological grounding of their works of charity and mercy (by now we should expect this); based on Christ's example and Scripture, their care of the diseased and the dying would gain merit with God and should be extended to Christians *and* non-Christians alike (*Vita* 9). Cyprian instructed them to go beyond the practice of the "publican or heathen" and to seek perfection "by overcoming evil with good and by the exercise of a divine-like clemency, loving even [their] enemies, and by further praying for the salvation of [their] persecutors, as the Lord advises and encourages" (*Vita* 9). As Christians of all different social ranks assembled to help, their care was given "according to the nature of the men and their rank" (*Vita* 10). Many on account of their poverty who could not contribute wealth for the poor provided their own precious labor while the wealthy donated money (*Vita* 10). Under Cyprian's godly and effective leadership, there was a generosity of overflowing works accomplished for all people, both Christians and non-Christians (*Vita* 10), and these activities of looking after the victims of the plague continued until Cyprian's exile during Valerian's persecution five years later (258 CE) (*Vita* 11).

"What Cyprian encouraged Christians to do, Dionysius said they did,"[87] especially stressing their all-inclusive and sacrificial care: "very many, indeed, of our brothers and sisters through their exceeding love and merciful kindness did not spare themselves but kept close to one another and cared for the sick without taking thought for themselves" (Eusebius, *HE* 7.22.7). These Christians ministered to the victims—again, both Christians and

---

84. A. E. R. Boak, *A History of Rome to 565 AD* (3rd ed; New York: Macmillan, 1947), cited in R. Stark, *The Rise of Christianity* (Princeton, NJ: Princeton University Press, 1996), 77; cf. Eusebius, *HE* 7.21.9.

85. G. B. Ferngren, "Medicine and Compassion in Early Christianity," *Theology Digest* 46 (1999): 318.

86. Ibid., 319.

87. Ferguson, *Early Christians Speak*, 131.

non-Christians—so earnestly and sacrificially that "many who tended the sick and restored them to health died themselves, having transferred to themselves the death that lay upon others" (Eusebius, *HE* 7.22.7). As a result, Dionysius concludes, "the very best of the brothers and sisters among us departed life in this manner—presbyters, deacons, and some of the laity. They are exceedingly worthy of praise, since this kind of death, occurring because of great piety and a strong faith, seems in no way to be inferior to martyrdom" (Eusebius, *HE* 7.22.8). Conversely, "the pagans acted the very opposite" by fleeing and thrusting away from those in the first stages and even their own families and by casting the half-dead to the roads and treating them as refuse (Eusebius, *HE* 7.22.10); these actions are very similar to those in Carthage, described by Pontius, from those who were trying to avoid contagion.

When another plague ravaged the eastern part of the empire in 312 CE, in addition to a famine, an outbreak of another disease ("anthrax"), and a war against Armenia by Maximin—all in the midst of the Great Persecution for Christians (at this point only in the East intermittently)—Christians served the general population in a similarly selfless manner (Eusebius, *HE* 9.8). According to Eusebius, "countless was the number of those who were dying in the cities, and still larger of those in the country parts and villages, . . . the entire population perished all at once through lack of food and through plague" (*HE* 9.8.4–5). In that tragic state of affairs, Christians alone, Eusebius records, exhibited concrete evidence of their sympathy and humanity (*philanthrōpia*): "all day long," some would "diligently persevere in performing the last offices for the dying and burying them (for there were countless numbers, and no one to look after them); while others would assemble the multitude" who were famished all throughout the city and distribute bread to all of them "so that their action was on all men's lips, and they glorified the God of the Christians, and convinced by the deeds themselves, acknowledged that they alone were truly pious and God-fearing" (Eusebius, *HE* 9.8.14).

The compassionate actions of the laity and clergy all accord with the instructions in other sources about their respective roles and responsibilities; and the instructions and conduct taken together give more credence to the portrait of the contrasting conduct between Christians and pagans toward the victims of the epidemics (though not without some idealizations). As shown by Stark, the Christians' organized care of the sick (however rudimentary it might have been), motivated by the higher love, was a factor in a greater survival rate of Christians than pagans during the time of epidemics and other crises and ultimately in the growth of Christianity.[88] And as argued by Gary Ferngren, this Christian response to the plagues might have spurred the church

---

88. Stark, *Rise of Christianity*, 73–94.

to advance in its organized medical charity for those in need (beyond Christian circles), eventually leading to the founding of permanent institutions such as hospitals in the late fourth century.[89]

4.4. Early Christian Women and Acts of Charity

Prominent in these multifaceted aspects of Christian koinonia and hospitality were women, though they were unrecognized and unnamed most of the time. A particular group of women, widows, repeatedly appearing thus far as the major recipients of charity, also played a significant role in giving charity. While the early church continued the classic Jewish piety of supporting widows, along with orphans and the poor, as the socially helpless and needy,[90] widows emerged as a distinct rank or "order" in the pre-Constantine period with specific criteria for ecclesiastical support based on their benevolent activities.[91] Already in 1 Timothy 5:5, 9–10, the foundational criteria are named: she must be sixty years old or older, married only once, known for continual prayers and good works in raising her children, in hospitality, and in helping those in need (cf. moral instruction of younger women in Titus 2:4). With the popularity of asceticism during this period, however, widows included not just those women who had not remarried since the loss of their husbands but also "any woman who has chosen to lead a sexually continent life,"[92] as the oft-quoted greeting by Ignatius to the "virgins who are called widows" in the church of Smyrna also indicates.[93] The aforementioned criteria would turn into the standard duties for the emerging rank of widows, with their growing distinction and honor. They became responsible for prayer and intercession, fasting, moral instruction of younger women (in private), hospitality, and other charitable works such as visiting the sick and the imprisoned, as they themselves received support from the common fund and individual works of mercy.[94] Thus Polycarp exhorts the widows in Philippi to "think soberly about the faith of the Lord and pray unceasingly for everyone and stay far away

89. See G. B. Ferngren, *Medicine and Health Care in Early Christianity* (Baltimore: Johns Hopkins University Press, 2009), 113–39.

90. E.g., Exod. 22:22–24; Deut. 24:17–21; Isa. 1:17; Jer. 7:6; Acts 6:1; James 1:27; 1 Tim. 5:3–8, 16; *1 Clem.* 8.4; Ignatius, *Smyrn.* 6.2; *Polycarp*, 4.1; *Hermas, Mand.* 8.10; *Sim.* 5.3.7; 9.27.2; Justin, *1 Apol.* 67.6; *Acts John* 30, 34–36; *Acts Pet.* 8, 28; *Ap. Trad.* 10, 24, 30; Eusebius, *HE* 6.43.

91. E.g., Ignatius, *Smyrn.* 13.1; Polycarp, *Phil.* 4.3; *Acts Pet.* 29; *Ap. Trad.* 10; *Didasc.* 3.8.1. For a general study on widows in early Christianity, see B. B. Thurston, *The Widows: A Women's Ministry in the Early Church* (Minneapolis: Fortress, 1989).

92. C. Methuen, "The 'Virgin Widow': A Problematic Social Role for the Early Church?" *HTR* 90 (1997): 287.

93. *Smyrn.* 13.1. See also S. L. Davies, *The Revolt of the Widows: The Social World of the Apocryphal Acts* (Urbana: Southern Illinois University Press, 1980), 72–73; cf. Tertullian, *Ux.* 1.6.4; *On the Veiling of Virgins* 9.2.

94. E.g., Tertullian, *Ux.* 2.4.

from all malicious talk, slander, false testimony, love of money, and any kind of evil, knowing that they are God's altar, and that all sacrifices are carefully inspected" (*Phil.* 4.3). The symbolism of the widow as "altar [*thysiastērion*] of God," which became popular in early Christianity, suggests two aspects of the rank. First, it reflects the widows as recipients of charity; since the gifts offered for their support were regarded as a sacrifice, giving to widows was like bringing a sacrifice to the altar. Second, it underlines prayer as the special ministry of widows; prayer was a form of spiritual sacrifice (Rev. 5:8), and widows who were to devote themselves to prayers were the altar where sacrifice was made to God.[95]

When the office of deaconess was established sometime in the third century (at least in Syria), deaconesses took similar but more formal (though still circumscribed) roles in service and also in liturgy, perhaps to check the influence of widows.[96] Paired with male deacons, they were to assist bishops in the baptism of women by anointing the women with oil after they had come up from the water (baptism was administered only by bishop, presbyter, or deacon, however). They also instructed newly baptized female converts and visited the sick among Christian women who lived in "heathen" households (*Didasc.* 16.3).

Returning to the topic of widows, it is significant to note that not all widows were in economic need or dependent on church support. Just as their marital status (or history) became irrespective of their membership to the rank, their socioeconomic status would show a wide range with Christian penetration into the upper order (especially in the fourth century). The very criteria and responsibilities of hospitality and helping those in need may presuppose their (at least modest) economic capacity to do so. In Rome, we know that some widows (and orphans) entrusted their incomes and/or savings to the church, some of which were embezzled by the Roman presbyters Nicostratus and Novatus (Cyprian, *Epp.* 50.1.2; 52.1.2). In fact, Callistus was accused of embezzling sizable deposits similarly entrusted by widows and other Christians when he was a slave (*Ref.* 9.12.1). In Carthage, Tertullian addressed the problem of remarriage of the younger widows for the Carthaginian church in his ostensibly titled *To His Wife* (*Ad uxorem*). Dissuading remarriage, he points out "fleshly" and "worldly" motives for remarriage, for instance, sexual

95. These points are largely drawn from C. Osiek, "The Widow as Altar: The Rise and Fall of a Symbol," *Second Century* 3, no. 3 (1983): 159–60, 166–67; cf. Thurston, *The Widows*, 106–13.

96. Cf. F. Cardman, "Women, Ministry, and Church Order in Early Christianity," in *Women and Christian Origins* (ed. R. S. Kraemer and M. R. D'Angelo; New York: Oxford University Press, 1999), 312. On women officeholders (mostly in the fourth century and later) in general, see U. E. Eisen, *Women Officeholders in Early Christianity: Epigraphical and Literary Studies* (trans. L. M. Maloney; Collegeville, MN: Liturgical Press, 2000); K. Madigan and C. Osiek, *Ordained Women in the Early Church: A Documentary History* (Baltimore: Johns Hopkins University Press, 2005).

desire, glory, greed, ambition, lack of self-sufficiency, conspicuous consumption, and fear of lower status (1.4.6). Obviously, the women addressed are more well-to-do widows than those on the church charity list as he continues to point out (their) wrongful lust for "ponderous necklaces, . . . burdensome garments, Gallic mules, . . . [and] German bearers" (1.4.7).[97] Cyprian wrote his first treatise as bishop to wealthy virgins in his church, exhorting them to turn away from worldly dress and adornments (*Hab. virg.* 5, 12–17 in particular) and to give generously to the poor for their spiritual blessing (*Hab. virg.* 7–11).

In the apocryphal Acts, wealthy women of high status are portrayed as major benefactors of charity. In *Acts of Peter*, Eubola, the noble woman in Judea with "much gold and valuable pearls," gives all of her property to the care of the widows, orphans, and the poor upon her conversion to (orthodox) Christianity by Peter (17). Then the mother of the senator resurrected by Peter donates two thousand gold pieces to Peter to be divided among "the virgins of Christ" (i.e., widows) (29). Even Chryse, the woman of great wealth but with questionable morals, brings ten thousand pieces of gold to Peter for the poor out of fear of Christ (30). In *Acts of Paul*, a wealthy widow, Queen Tryphaena, takes care of Thecla, the condemned Christian virgin (*ad bestias*), and sends "much clothing and gold . . . [to Paul] for the service of the poor" (27, 41).

It is almost certain that these apocryphal accounts corresponded to historical reality, although unfortunately we do not have many specific records of female Christian donors and their charitable activities during *this* period.[98] There are scattered inscriptions and records of wealthy pagan and Jewish female benefactors and their impressive patronage;[99] women's role in Christian

---

97. D. E. Wilhite argues for Tertullian's contextualization of Pauline household economics in 1 Tim. 5 that exhorted wealthy widows to stay single out of concern that their dowries/endowments would no longer support the church if they would remarry: "Tertullian on Widows: A North African Appropriation of Pauline Household Economics," in *Engaging Economics: New Testament Scenarios and Early Christian Reception* (ed. B. W. Longenecker and K. D. Liebengood; Grand Rapids: Eerdmans, 2009), 222–42.

98. We do have a lot more in the fourth century in comparison; for examples of wealthy widows and virgins (via letters directed to them by church fathers) and their Christian euergetism, see J. N. Brenmer, "Pauper or Patroness: The Widow in the Early Christian Church," in *Between Poverty and the Pyre: Movements in the History of Widowhood* (ed. J. N. Bremmer and L. van den Bosch; London: Routlege, 1994), 48–49.

99. For documents and discussions, see, for example, C. Osiek, "The Patronage of Women in Early Christianity," in *A Feminist Companion to Patristic Literature* (ed. A.-J. Levine; London: Continuum, 2008), 173–84; S. Matthews, *First Converts: Rich Pagan Women and the Rhetoric of Mission in Early Judaism and Christianity* (Stanford: Stanford University Press, 2001), 29–50; R. Van Bremen, "Women and Wealth," in *Images of Women in Antiquity* (ed. A. Cameron and A. Kuhrt; Detroit: Wayne State University Press, 1993), 223–42; R. Kearsley, "Women in Public Life in the Roman East: Junia Theodora, Claudia Metrodora, and Phoibe, Benefactress of Paul," *Ancient Society: Resources for Teachers* 15 (1985): 124–37; T. Rajak, "Benefactors in the Greco-Roman Diaspora," in *Geschichte—Tradition—Reflexion: Festschrift für Martin Hengel zum 70*

benefaction would have been similarly impressive and significant, given the fact that Christianity attracted a disproportionate number of higher-status women compared to aristocratic men.[100] Interestingly, the origins of some of the major Roman catacombs are associated with women, who were most likely owners and/or donors of the burial grounds, mausolea, or columbaria at some point in the process: Domitilla, Priscilla, Commodilla, Lucina, and Balbina.[101] And wealthy female heads of households also sponsored and led Christian funerary banquets, as depicted in a number of banquet scenes in the catacomb of SS. Marcellino and Pietro in Rome (the late third or early fourth century).[102] Among Cyprian's targeted audience for his impassioned call to almsgiving during and after the Decian persecution—the wealthy *lapsi*—were wealthy women since he explicitly rebuked their appearance in public in luxurious dresses and expensive jewelries instead of mourning for their sin of apostasy with fasting and tears (*Laps*. 30). Indeed, in a letter from mid-250 CE, written from Rome by one Carthaginian confessor to another, we have references to two female *lapsi*, Numeria and Candida, who in Rome engaged in penance and works of charity in the hope of receiving forgiveness and readmission to the church. As part of their penance, those wealthy women were taking care of sixty-five people and their needs "in every way," (probably) in their own residence (Cyprian, *Ep*. 21.2.2; 21.4.1). Furthermore, in his response to the eight Numidian bishops in ransoming Christians captured by the barbarians, Cyprian mentioned that munificent contributions came from both men and women of the Carthaginian church (*Ep*. 62.4.2), which would suggest that in that community there were women of independent financial resources.[103] Finally, the fact that Valerian's second rescript explicitly called out the matrons (of superior rank by definition) and punished them with confiscation of their property and exile (Cyprian, *Ep*. 80.1) may indicate that they were not only important participants of the church but also valuable contributors to the church for its manifold works of charity.

(vol. 1; ed. H. Cancik, H. Lichtenberger, and P. Schäfer; Tübingen: Mohr Siebeck, 1996), 305–22; S. Dixon, *Reading Roman Women: Sources, Genres, and Real Life* (London: Duckworth, 2001).

100. For documents and discussions of women patrons and benefactors in the NT, see for example, Osiek, "Patronage of Women," 187–91; Matthews, *First Converts*, 72–75, 85–89; C. F. Whelan, "Amica Pauli: The Role of Phoebe in the Early Church," *JSNT* 49 (1993): 67–85; R. Kearsley, "Women in Public Life," 124–37. Note the Roman bishop Callistus's controversial policy that allowed higher-status women to "marry" men of inferior status (Hippolytus, *Ref*. 9.12); it would probably have meant the practice of a freeborn woman of high birth (patron), an *ingenua*, living in concubinage with a freedman, a *libertinus* (often her own), without legally being married, which always raised not a few eyebrows in a conservative Roman society. See also Lampe, *From Paul to Valentinus*, 119–21.

101. Osiek, "Roman and Christian Burial Practices," 246–57.

102. Tulloch, "Women Leaders," 164–93, 289–96.

103. Perhaps the wealthy virgins addressed in *Hab. virg.*? Cf. Dunn, "Infected Sheep and Diseased Cattle," 5n15 and n12.

4.5. Acts of Mercy as Acts of Justice

As one can see, various acts of mercy and charity (whether individual or corporate) were voluntary and meritorious, but in effect obligatory and binding by virtue of the very Christian understanding of the Great Commandment. The acts of mercy, which imply supererogatory and superfluous acts with blessings and reward attached, were in reality the acts of justice, which suggest necessary and mandatory acts with warnings and punishments when not followed (cf. Cyprian, *Eleem.* 1, 17). Hence the blessing promised in the *Didache* to the one who gives generously "to everyone" according to the commandment in the way of life (1.5; *Barn.* 19.11) is followed by the stern warning with implied negative consequences to turn away from the way of death, particularly, "having no mercy for the poor, not working on behalf of the oppressed, . . . turning away from someone in need, oppressing the afflicted, [and being] advocates of the wealthy, lawless judges of the poor" (5.2; cf. *Barn.* 20.2).

For the apologist Lactantius in the early fourth century, the fact that acts of mercy and acts of justice are the two sides of the same coin is clear, and he offers an intriguing explanation of how this relationship works vis-à-vis pagan justice and mercy. Only Christians, who believe in the true God, can understand and practice acts of justice and its derivative, fairness or equality (*aequitas*), as the natural consequences of their true religion. Whereas civil justice derived from relative and utilitarian civil laws is not really justice at all, natural justice, which derives from God's single, uniform rule, is true justice and is wise because of divine reward and retribution at the judgment (*Inst.* 5.18.9). Only natural justice breeds true equality (*aequitas*), which is essentially spiritual and resides therefore only in true religion, Christianity (3.22.4; 5.15.1). For everyone has equal standing before God in the sense that God judges inner disposition and virtues, not outer status markers or forms: "No one is poor in God's eyes except for lack of justice, and no one is rich without a full tally of the virtues; moreover, no one is illustrious except for goodness and innocence" (5.14.18). In other words, equality primarily pertains to people's vertical relationship with God that should impact their horizontal relationships subsequently, but not the other way around. What about the fact that there are Christians who are poor and rich, slaves and masters? Aren't there distinctions among Christians? Lactantius's answer is a resounding no. There is no distinction among Christians because Christians measure everything spiritually and not physically (5.15.2–3). What is remarkable is his translation or projection of spiritual equality into social equality. Among Christians, social distinctions "disappear" and do not constitute injustice or inequality because of spiritual equality, whereas social distinctions among Greeks and Romans testify to their gross injustice and inequality because of the absence of spiritual equality due to their polytheism (paganism). Lactantius sincerely believes that all Christians are equal because physical conditions and riches cause no distinction in God's eyes (5.15.3–4).

Because Lactantius understands private property and economic distinctions to be compatible with Christian justice and *aequitas*, the key to achieving and acting out Christian justice and *aequitas* in the present (in his society) is service to fellow humans. Following true religion, we are called to true compassion, i.e., following the divine law of mutual love and care (i.e., works of charity) grounded in the bond of humanity (*Inst.* 6.10.1–8). Lactantius believes that the common bond of humanity should generate a sense of solidarity and pity (*misericordia*) for one another and is a basis of *aequitas* (6.10.8–9). Since it is unnatural to hurt someone by virtue of their shared humanity, as Cicero says, it is only natural to do good to others (6.11.2, 6). In doing good to others, we should not make any distinction among the worthy and unworthy (6.11.6–7). Here Lactantius debunks a deeply seated Greco-Roman custom of reciprocity and patronage; he essentially links their reciprocity to *utilitas*, the basis of the unjust civil law. People think whatever they give to those in need is a waste and act on their self-interest and immediate advantage so as to target their charity and largesse only to "suitable people," i.e., those who can repay and return the favor (6.11.6–12). Even venerable Cicero insists this, to which Lactantius cries out, "Here you have strayed from true justice, my dear Cicero; you wiped it out with one word, the moment you measured works of piety and humanity by their expediency" (6.11.12). In contrast, Christian generosity and charity should be directed to "the unsuitable" as far as possible, "because a deed done with justice, piety and humanity is a deed you do without expectation of return" (6.11.13). If true virtue pursues duty and not reward, as Cicero himself maintained, then justice, "which is mother and head of the virtues," admonishes Lactantius, should be measured "at its own price and not by its advantage to you; offer it most of all to someone from whom you can expect nothing" (6.11.16). Before the passionate arguments of the Cappadocian Fathers and John Chrysostom in the East, and Ambrose and Augustine in the West, Lactantius champions *humanitas* of "the needy and the useless" (6.11.28):

> Give to the blind, the sick, the lame and the destitute: if you don't, they die. Men may have no use for them, but God has: he keeps them alive, gives them breath and honours them with light. Cherish them as much as you can, and sustain their souls with humanity so that they do not die. Anyone who can help a dying man but doesn't is his murderer. (6.11.18–19)

In light of this fundamental principle of justice and *aequitas*, even civic benefaction and public euergetism fall short of true and just giving (6.12.15). "Anything given for favour's sake to people not in need is wasted, or else it comes back with interest added, and so will not count as a gift. . . . If the good deed is returned, however, it is over and done with" (6.11.27, 6.12.7). Lactantius echoes the concrete examples of the works of justice covered in this chapter: feeding the poor, offering hospitality, ransoming of captives, defending children and widows in need, looking after the sick, and providing burial of strangers and beggars (6.12.5, 15, 21, 24, 25). As Lactantius completes his inversion of pagan reciprocity, he introduces Christian reciprocity. While virtue seeks no reward, there is unexpected return. A return for one's favor comes not from the recipient but from the ultimate provider and judge, God himself (6.12.2). God's universal law prescribes that we provide for others through humanity what we provide for our own family through affection, which is the whole point of justice (6.12.21, 31); it is our duty and obligation to obey this natural justice and yet God reckons our works of justice as works of mercy and rewards them (with remission of sins) (6.12.41). Thus *aequitas* in the present is something that is irrespective of social and economic distinctions but demands that the works of justice be directed to the poor and the desperate ("the needy and the useless")—entirely irrespective of their worthiness and reciprocity.

4.6. Summary and Conclusion

While growing Christian communities with greater assimilation to Roman society experienced internal social differentiations and even strife among those in a wide spectra of the social hierarchy, they also strove to bridge those gaps and foster genuine fellowship by sharing material resources (koinonia) with the needy in their intra-community and inter-communities over distant regions. Based on the Great Commandment of loving God and one's neighbor, two particular customs, common fund (*koinos*) and common meal (*agapē*), adopted from their larger sociocultural context, provided tangible, corporate ways of caring for the poor and the helpless in the communities and also symbolized intra-Christian solidarity among those in different social locations. As presupposed, their primary commitment was to (but not limited to) fellow Christians ("neighbor"), since the sharing—koinonia—was designed to cultivate a greater sense of Christian unity and harmony as well as to provide practical care for those within the local churches (cf. Cyprian, *Unitate*, 26).

Christian hospitality, which reformulated and transformed Greco-Roman hospitality, manifested in five concrete shapes: first, Christian individuals and communities welcomed traveling ministers and fellow believers into their homes (with proper discernment) who often contributed to the spread of the gospel during this time. They also received local strangers with physical nourishment and care. Second, Christians saw to it that they provided decent burials for the poorest of their own through generous donation of private burial places by wealthy members. This eventually led to the church's management and practical ownership of those burial sites even when it was not legally allowed to do so. Third, Christians tended to both physical and emotional needs of those who suffered for the sake of faith—the confessors who were imprisoned and condemned to mines, exile, and death—as these confessors also served the faithful as the inspiration and exemplars of faith. Fourth, Christians, whenever they were able, sought to ransom those confessors and Christian captives with money and other means. Finally, Christians visited and took care of the sick, not only of their own but also of the larger society, especially during the recurring epidemics. In all of these ways of showing Christian hospitality, the faithful were exhorted to be generous and were described as sacrificial; particularly (wealthy) Christian women, though often unrecognized and unnamed, significantly contributed to the tangible care of the afflicted and the poor. By virtue of the Christian love commandment, loving God through loving one's neighbor was not an option but an obligation; acts of mercy were acts of justice (and vice versa), which bound together the whole local community and different regional communities.

This Christian koinonia then testified to the Christian success in creating surrogate families and living out their "family values" by providing "the essentials of social security."[104] The very nature of the way the Christians understood and assumed their community responsibility "made wealth 'for the common good' a practical necessity."[105] Thus, the local churches and clergy regularly tapped into the common funds as these works of mercy and justice became more and more elaborate and extensive. In the next chapter we turn to the increasing institutionalization of charitable works and the economic activities of the church as the clergy took greater control of the common funds and patronage.

104. E. R. Dodds, *Pagan and Christian in an Age of Anxiety: Some Aspects of Religious Experience from Marcus Aurelius to Constantine* (Cambridge: Cambridge University Press, 1968), 137.

105. D. E. Groh, "Christian Community in the Writings of Tertullian: An Inquiry into the Nature and Problems of Community in North African Christianity" (PhD diss., Northwestern University, 1970), 61.

5

ᐳᐸ

Wealth, Poverty,
and Ecclesiastical Control

As Christian koinonia and mutual care grew comprehensive, and as the church experienced increasing structural and cultic institutionalization, especially in the third century, ecclesiastical charity mirrored and corresponded to this process of institutionalization revolving around clerical authority and functions, especially those of bishops. In this chapter, we will examine how the church as a growing institution centralized its charitable ministries under clergy (bishops in particular), and we will consider the process of Christianized patronage through which the clerical control of charity and the episcopal control of clerical salary took place. We will also examine how the church functioned as an economic institution with "corporate" ownership and commercial dealings.

5.1. Christian(-ized) Patronage and the Unity of the Church—Bishop as Patron

The Roman patronage networks worked based on (or because of) structural inequality and limited access to resources. As the patron of superior status bestowed gifts and benefits (*beneficia*) on the client of inferior status, the client in return showed gratitude by loyalty and public praise, which in turn enhanced the honor and status of the patron and thus motivated and obligated him or her to bestow further *beneficia*, and the cycle continued (see chap. 1). Patronage networks therefore functioned as a necessary means of sociopolitical cohesion and control based on the ethics of reciprocity (between unequals). By the third century, with the church as "a society within the society" more or less established,[1] we see the major development of Christian patronage in a context of structured inequality—religious as well as socioeconomic hierarchy—with similar albeit transformed dynamics. Early on, even in the first century, Christians had already adopted the prevailing Roman patronage system and Christianized it over the subsequent centuries as the wealthier lay householders naturally took leadership of the nascent Christian communities by offering their houses for assembly. As we have seen, they also contributed to the care of the needy in their Christian communities with dinners, hospitality, burial plots, and almsgiving, although these works of charity were exhorted to and practiced by the faithful in general and were not confined to the wealthy. However, there is no doubt that the more affluent members were major contributors to the common fund, *agapē*, etc., and felt greater expectation and obligation to share their resources with the poor in their communities; but in return, the poor recipients of alms and other acts of charity were exhorted and obligated to pray for salvation and spiritual blessings for their donors (patrons) in gratitude. This "established" symbiosis between the wealthy and the poor (with theological undergirding and spiritual sanction) shows Christianized patronage at work at the most fundamental level. In the third century, there was a notable shift from patronage of the wealthy lay leaders in household settings to patronage of bishops and other clergy in a more formalized church structure. As church ownership of buildings and other properties increased, the clergy largely took over the official roles of patrons.[2] Once the (wealthier) individuals handed over their gifts to the church (alms for common treasury, burial lands, food, clothing, shoes, etc.) the bishops and other clergy under the bishops' authority replaced the donors as administrators of the properties and exercised full control over their management and distribution (e.g., *Didasc.* 9).

The *Didascalia*, in its rather comprehensive portrait of institutional church life in Syria with extensive (and often repetitive) regulations concerning the liturgy, charitable ministry, clergy, and laity, vividly illustrates this development. Detailing the office, ministry, and qualifications of clergy (bishops in particular), centering on charity, it describes bishops as the high priests placed by God; "set in the likeness of God Almighty, [they] do hold the place of God Almighty" (5). As such, bishops are to their congregations "priests and prophets and chiefs and leaders and kings, and mediators between God and His faithful, . . . witnesses of His will, [and] those who bear the sins of everyone" (8). Opposing bishops is offending the Lord (9). Therefore, the

---

1. *The Letters of St. Cyprian of Carthage* (vol. 1; trans. and anno. G. W. Clarke; ACW 43; New York: Newman, 1984), 163.

2. This does not mean that other forms of patronage by the wealthier lay people suddenly stopped; they might still have been going on informally but certainly became sidelined by the clerical (especially episcopal) patronage.

bishop has "authority to judge those who sin—instead of God Almighty" (5) and to forgive and receive with mercy those who repent "as God Almighty" (6) as the physician of the church (7). He is to "take care of everyone" and "carry the burden of all" (7); for that reason, the bishop is to be honored "as God [is]" and be informed of everything in the congregational life (9). As God's vice-regent on earth, the bishop is most of all to "love the orphans with the widows, and be a lover of the poor and also of strangers" (4; cf. 3.1), for whom he receives from the faithful their firstfruits, tithes, offerings, and gifts (9);[3] his hands should be stretched out to give to all who are in want, but he must discern who is deserving of the church's assistance—any glutton, drunken, or idle person does not deserve alms (4; 8). As God's stewards, bishops' chief responsibilities include excelling

> in dispensing those things that are given and come into the church [i.e., alms and offerings by the faithful] according to the commandment to orphans and widows and those who are afflicted and to strangers, like men who know that [they] have God who will require an account at [their] hands, who committed his stewardship unto [them]. (*Didasc.* 8 [cf. 9])

Note here his role as a mediator not just in a liturgical sense but in terms of being a recipient *and* dispenser of alms. The bishop is the just distributor of what he has received to "each one as it is right for him" since he is required to be "well acquainted with those who are afflicted" as his stewardship demands (9). The people neither have any say in nor can make any judgment on the bishop's dispensation of those alms, which is his God-given prerogative:

> For you [congregation] are commanded to give, but he [bishop] to dispense. And you shall not require an account of the bishop, nor watch him, (as to) how he dispenses and fulfills his stewardship, or when he gives, or to whom, or where, or whether well or ill, or whether he gives rightly. Indeed, he has an inquirer, the Lord God, who delivered the stewardship into his hands and held him worthy of the priesthood of this entire office. (*Didasc.* 9)

Rather, the bishop, with considerable economic power and control, is accountable to God alone but should model munificence, stewardship, and justice in his personal life for the people (5). He should neither love riches, money, nor "dainty meats," nor live in luxury (4; 8; cf. 3; 5); he should in fact be "meager and poor in his food and drink, that he may be able to be vigilant to admonish and discipline those who are undisciplined" (4). Furthermore, he should not show favoritism for persons: he must "not stand in reverence before the rich nor please him beyond what is right. And let him not despise nor neglect the poor nor be lifted up against them" (4). It is worth noting here that his

3. Cf. *Ap. Trad.* 31–32; 23—offering of food for *agapē* meals.

impartiality is in terms of being "a lover of the poor," not in a sense of being a "neutral," detached third party.[4]

The practical outworking of this impartiality toward others involved: taking care of anyone in need ("although she was not a widow") due to illness, infirmity of body, and rearing of children (*Didasc.* 4); nurturing orphans by arranging adoption or by bringing them up himself, including giving girls in Christian marriages and teaching boys trades and seeing to it that they would be able to sustain themselves through trades (so that they would not drain the charity) (17); looking after the condemned or imprisoned confessors with visitations, refreshments, prayers, and their ransom by payments (19); providing shelters for the poor (especially the elderly) from the bishop's congregation "or from another congregation . . . with all [his] heart . . . even if [he has] to sit upon the ground, that [he] be not as one who respects the persons of men, but that [his] ministry be acceptable with God" (12). The practice of the Roman church supporting and caring for more than fifteen hundred widows and people in distress under the episcopal administration indicates similar "established" expectations and responsibilities of the bishop as "a lover of the poor" (Eusebius, *HE* 6.43.2). The multifaceted charitable ministries of Cyprian of Carthage likewise bear witness to this recognized episcopal role. In turn, two things "helped to consolidate permanently the position of the bishop":[5] not only (1) the comprehensive episcopal ministry of charity for the mass of poor (*plerique pauperes*, Minucius Felix, *Oct.* 36.3) who were dependent on the bishop as their breadwinner and patron, and who at the same time stood behind him as his power base of loyal clients, but also (2) the necessary finances centralized in the treasury of the bishop for the poor. This dual phenomenon stabilized the eminent position and ideal of the bishop as the earthly deputy of God to whom the people should give their obedience and loyalty, on the one hand, and as the chief imitator of God's compassion, munificence, and justice, on the other.

Presbyters and deacons, who are likened to the priests and the Levites, respectively, and whose ministries are the extensions of episcopal ministries, are accountable to the bishop and are given specific criteria for their qualifications and roles concerning charity (9; 3.2–4). Qualifications for the presbyterate, which is responsible for teaching and intercession, include that the candidate be "humble, poor, not a lover of money, having labored much in the services of the weak, proven to be pure, . . . if he has been as a father to the orphans,

4. Cf. Deut. 10:17–18; Peter of Alexandria, *On Riches* 71–72: "And if I do not love according to the manner which is acceptable for me, I shall be found beneath all of you. If I show favoritism and perverse justice, I shall be called the judge of injustice. . . . Therefore, it is fitting that every orthodox bishop be a loving person according to the Lord's (command), according to that which is acceptable to him. If he has not done this, he has not given love."

5. P. Lampe, *From Paul to Valentinus: Christians at Rome in the First Two Centuries* (trans. M. Steinhauser; ed. M. D. Johnson; Minneapolis: Fortress, 2003), 407.

if he has served the poor" (3.2).[6] Criteria for the diaconate include that the candidate be the one "who is witnessed of by all the believers, who is not entangled by the business of the world, . . . who has no riches" (3.4). A deacon's service in particular is detailed in close association with episcopal responsibilities and supervision:

> first, those things that are commanded by the bishop so that they only may be done for proclamation, and of all the clergy he shall be the counselor and secret of the church: he who serves the sick, he who serves the strangers, who supports the widows and goes round in all the houses of those who are in want, lest there should be any one in necessity or sickness or in misery. (3.4)

The deacon is also to clothe the dead and bury "strangers, those who are (away) from their dwellings, bypassers or captives" (3.4).[7] He is the practical and "hands-on" manager of the church charity, responsible for relating all necessary information and care to the bishop and congregation (3.4; 9). Cyprian charged his presbyters and deacons with these very tasks with detailed directives during his hideaway (*Epp.* 5.2.1; 13.4.2; 14.2.1), as indeed the *Apostolic Tradition* (Latin version) specified the purpose of a deacon's ordination as "to the service of the bishop, that he may do those things that are ordered by him" (8.2). It seems that the role of deacons as the "personal hands and feet of the bishop" was widely acknowledged by the third century.

Although in previous chapters we had glimpses of the ecclesiastical patronage at work in the *Apostolic Tradition* and through the ministry of Cyprian, we will take this theme of Christianized patronage further to Cyprian's turbulent episcopacy. If you recall, Cyprian (and other church leaders in general) linked almsgiving and other works of mercy (justice) essentially to God's eschatological judgment and the givers' (performers') salvation and penance as signs of their faith in the gracious and munificent God and of their commitment to his church, thus having eternal consequence on their ultimate destiny and affecting their present standing in the church. Using theological and ecclesiastical concepts, Cyprian has defined the charity of individuals and the church as imitation of and response to God's generous *beneficia*. God in his selfless condescension demonstrated his gracious munificence and largesse by giving himself and his *beneficia* to all; imitation of God's generosity takes place in the context of hierarchy of the strong and the weak, the rich and the poor, and the clergy and the laity in the church.[8] As the faithful are called

---

6. Cf. a negative example given in Peter Alexandria, *On Riches* 73.

7. Cf. Deacon Eusebius mentioned by Dionysius in *HE* 7.11.24.

8. Cf. C. E. Straw, "Cyprian and Matthew 5:45: The Evolution of Christian Patronage," *StPatr* 18 (1989): 335; C. A. Bobertz, "Cyprian of Carthage as Patron: A Social Historical Study of the Role of Bishop in the Ancient Christian Community of North Africa" (PhD diss., Yale University, 1988), 71.

to imitate God's munificence, as in the *Didascalia*, the bishop as the earthly head of the church is identified as the supreme imitator of God's munificence. The bishop, appointed by the one God, is the one shepherd of the one church as God wills (*Ep.* 69.5.1), and the church consists of the people who remain united with their bishop (*Ep.* 66.8.3). Then, as God's representative, the bishop "becomes the fountainhead of munificence, the patron of good works in his community."[9] Cyprian characterizes the ministry of charity as the defining feature of the church and his episcopacy (*Epp.* 14.2.2; cf. 5.1.2; 12.1.1; 13.7);[10] and again, we have seen a range of considerable charitable works that Cyprian as the authoritative imitator and redistributor of God's generous bounties[11] has undertaken and directed for those in spiritual and physical need (forgiveness and reconciliation for the *lapsi* and material aid for the poor and the confessors).

Particularly, in his challenging context of theological and moral controversies regarding apostasy and socio-ecclesiastical factionalism for the control of church resources and charity, Cyprian succeeded in establishing himself as patron to his congregation *and* clergy, using both his personal and common funds and laying the theological and ecclesiastical foundation of Christianized patronage that would last for the ages to come. And by acting as patron, he secured political leverage, centralized charity, and therefore enhanced his ecclesiastical authority. While confronting a double challenge of facing opposition by a majority of the presbyters and some lower clergy members and of dealing with mass apostasy and readmission of the (wealthy) *lapsi* in his hideout during the Decian persecution, Cyprian attempted to take control of the situation in his congregation through patronal activities. First, he insisted that only the bishop could dispense the church's spiritual *beneficia* (i.e., reconciliation and readmission) to the lapsed by imposition of his hands based on the criteria approved by him, and he took charge of dispensing the church's material *beneficia* (cash from the common funds, food, and clothing) to those in need of assistance (the poor and the confessors) through his loyal clergy. Note that he limited spiritual *beneficia* only to the *lapsi* (both the sacrificers and the certified) who would submit to the public rituals and disciplines of penance in prayer, fasting, and almsgiving for an appropriate period of time based on the different types and levels of their apostasy (cf. *Epp.* 15.1.2; 16.2.3; 19; 21.2.2).[12] The penitent who is obedient to the precepts and to the "bishops of God . . . earns the Lord's favour by his acts of submission and his just works [*operibus iustis*, e.g., almsgiving]" (*Ep.* 19.1). Those *lapsi* who refused the episcopal imposition of the penitential disciplines were excommunicated

---

9. Straw, "Cyprian and Matthew 5:45," 335.

10. Cf. Straw, "Cyprian and Matthew 5:45," 336.

11. This is also characterized by Pontius as such.

12. A dying penitent with a letter of peace from the martyrs would be received back as an exception—*Ep.* 19.2.1.

along with the laxist clergy who rebelled against Cyprian and demanded immediate reconciliation of the *lapsi* even without penance.

Note also that he confined material *beneficia* only to the deserving and meritorious, i.e., those confessors who would uphold Cyprian's policy of readmission of the *lapsi* and submit to his episcopal authority in humility and loyalty (*Ep.* 14.2.2–3.2; cf. *Epp.* 5.1.2; 12.1.1; 13.7) and the poor who did not apostatize (*stantes*) during the persecution and remained loyal to him (*Ep.* 12.2.2; cf. *Epp.* 14.2.1; 5.1.2). On the one hand, while Cyprian did acknowledge a privileged status of the confessors who would sit at the final judgment as "the Lord's friends" and thus use their spiritual power to intervene with God on behalf of the *lapsi* (e.g., *Epp.* 6.2 ; 15.1–3),[13] he chastised those confessors who collaborated with the laxist faction by writing the wealthy *lapsi* the letters of reconciliation for money without his episcopal authorization (*Ep.* 15.3.2). On the other hand, while he made sure that the confessors in need were generously cared for both from the common fund and his personal resources (*Ep.* 14.2.2; cf. *Epp.* 5.1.2; 12.1.1; 13.7; 77.3.1; 78.3.1; 79.1.1), he at the same time unequivocally reminded those confessors who had received the church's assistance (through his direction and approval) that he was indeed their patron through and through and that they were therefore expected and obligated to obey his will, which in fact reflected God's own (*Epp.* 5.1.2; 12.1.1; 13.7; 14.2.2). After all, the bishop, as God's representative and successor of the apostles, "stands alone" and commands obedience on God's behalf (*Ep.* 66.4.1). If these confessors were to object to his authority and not "conduct themselves humbly, modestly, and peacefully," they would be excluded from his patronage—i.e., the church's assistance (*Ep.* 14.2.2). Since "the bishop is in the church and the church is in the bishop," whoever "is not with the bishop is not in the church" (*Ep.* 66.8.3). Therefore, for Cyprian this seemingly harsh decision would still be justified because those who oppose the bishop "by definition defy the Church and lack charity";[14] for Cyprian, bishop, church, and ministry of charity (to the worthy) always belong together, and the confessors "lack what the bishop has, [i.e.,] the power and organization to perform great eleemosynary works, a history of charitable deeds."[15] It seems that, in the words of Bobertz, "Cyprian believed that in making the confessors clients, he would in turn have a prior claim on the spiritual resources they might control."[16] By his material patronage of the confessors, he tried to curtail and control any spiritual patronage the confessors exercised independently of his supervision, especially in aiding the laxist party toward an open rebellion, and a rival charity toward

13. Already in Tertullian, *Mart.* 2; Origen, *Exhortatio ad martyrium* 30; and Cyprian's contemporary, Dionysius of Alexandria, in Eusebius, *HE* 5.42.5.

14. Straw, "Cyprian and Matthew 5:45," 336; cf. the similar charge against heretics by Ignatius, *Smyrn.* 6.2.

15. Straw, "Cyprian and Matthew 5:45," 336.

16. Bobertz, "Cyprian of Carthage as Patron," 158.

the "other poor" (i.e., the undeserving and unfaithful—the poor *lapsi* and the unruly confessors). The laxist faction likely created (or at least attempted to create) an alternative network of spiritual and material patronage through those confessors who collaborated with them and through the wealthy *lapsi* who would provide resources for the ministry of charity in return for the "fast track" readmission, respectively.[17] Whereas he was willing to compromise the progressive readmission of the *lapsi* in consultation with the episcopal council and his congregation, he would surely not let the confessors dictate the terms, whatever spiritual prerogative they might have. In respect for the confessors, "Cyprian was prepared to accept their *libelli* purely as recommendations to be acted on at his episcopal pleasure."[18] In dispensing and controlling both spiritual and material *beneficia* as the imitator and administrator of God's benefaction, Cyprian consistently stressed the recipients' (clients') submission to the bishop (patron) as a quintessential condition and expectation in reciprocity.

Second, he strove to keep the loyalty of the rest of the clergy and created new "client" clergy in Carthage who would be loyal to and dependent on him (*Epp.* 38–40).[19] For one thing, Cyprian clearly saw the status difference between himself and his clergy as both social and religious; his flight during the persecution was necessitated because he was a person of prominence (*insignis persona*) (*Ep.* 8.1.1), whereas his clergy could carry on their delegated ministry in Carthage since they were not (cf. *Epp.* 5.2.1; 13.4.2; 14.2.1).[20] Cyprian also (though not unusually) expected the proper obedience and subservience of his deacons to episcopal authority and commands befitting their station (*locus*) (*Ep.* 3.1.1; cf. 12.1.1—for a reference to Cyprian's own *locus*).[21] Then, in the face of the major clerical opposition, Cyprian bypassed what was apparently a customary policy of consulting the existing clergy when he unilaterally appointed two young confessors, Aurelius and Celerius, as lectors of the Carthaginian church (*Epp.* 38–39). Moreover, he informed the existing clergy and laity that he "marked them out for the rank of presbyter" (*Ep.* 39.5.2). With these unusual moves, Cyprian was "now not only restoring the depleted ranks of his clergy" but also "drawing into his clerical following what [had] proved to be a source of potential rivalry and rebellion—those blessed with the special graces and spiritual prerogatives of confessors."[22] It is indeed significant that

17. See ibid., 163–91.

18. Brent, *Cyprian and Roman Carthage*, 252.

19. Bobertz, "Patronage Networks," 23; cf. Brent, *Cyprian and Roman Carthage*, 72–74.

20. *Letters of St. Cyprian* (vol. 1), 34; cf. Brent, *Cyprian and Roman Carthage*, 242–46.

21. Cf. *Ep.* 12.1.1 for a reference to Cyprian's own *locus* (station, position) and *gradus* (rank); see Clarke, *The Letters of St. Cyprian of Carthage* (vol. 2; trans. and anno. G. W. Clarke; ACW 44; New York: Newman, 1984), 15: "one gets a sense of the *grand seigneur* prospect from which Cyprian viewed his clerics. They were *ministri*, that is to say, his servants, recipients of the *sportulae* which he dispensed. It was not merely desirable, it was altogether necessary that he should have such clerics at his disposal, for the dispatch of his letters (*Ep.* 29)."

22. *Letters of St. Cyprian* (vol. 2), 178.

these young confessors appear to have been leaders among the confessors who objected to Cyprian by granting their own reconciliation to the *lapsi* (*Epp.* 27.1; 23).[23] Therefore, in order to defend his potentially controversial but politically savvy decision, he went to great lengths to talk about the divine stamp of approval and a vision that guided him as well as the confessors' extraordinary virtues and qualities (e.g., *Epp.* 38.1; 39.1.1–2).[24] In addition, Cyprian enrolled Numidicus, the presbyter and confessor from another community, in the Carthaginian presbyterate with similar praises concerning him (*Ep.* 40). Cyprian insisted that these were necessary appointments because the depleted number of clerics in Carthage was scarcely enough for the daily works (*operis*) of the church (*Ep.* 29.1.1). These new clerical clients of Cyprian's joined the ministry of the existing presbyters and deacons who had been given the charge to care for the poor and the confessors in the absence but on behalf of the bishop and thus to keep material patronage intact in the face of the laxist party led by the deacon Felicissimus (*Epp.* 5; 14; 41.1). Equally significant, Cyprian declared that the new appointees were to receive the equal salary and honor as the current presbyters of Carthage (*Ep.* 39.5). Cyprian, making several references in his letters about the clerical salaries/stipends (*stipendia*), clearly indicated that those were given because the clergy would (and should) devote their full attention to the sacred ministry (*Epp.* 1.1.2; 34.4.2; 39.5.2; cf. *Ep.* 42.2.1). While presbyters and deacons also received allowances (*sportulae*) apparently from the gifts of the faithful, it was the bishop who dispensed those allowances and the monthly stipends (*divisiones*) to them according to various levels of office (*Ep.* 39.5.2; cf. *Ep.* 42.2.1).[25] Thus, the episcopal distribution of clerical *beneficia* (i.e., gifts and payments) put them under the line of Cyprian's patronage, and their reciprocal loyalty was therefore expected in return even as they distributed material *beneficia* as (proxy) patrons to those in need under the direction of and on behalf of the bishop.[26]

The fixed clerical salary, which is a sign of the professionalization of clergy, which was in turn a part of the greater institutionalization of church, was a new development in the proto-orthodox church in the mid-third century. It was initially attested in the late second century within the circle of the sectarian New Prophecy. An anti-New Prophecy writer, Apollonius (recorded by Eusebius), accuses its founder, Montanus, of appointing "collectors of money," organizing "the receiving of gifts under the name of offerings," and

23. Bobertz, "Patronage Networks," 24; Bobertz, "Cyprian of Carthage as Patron," 198–201.
24. Cf. Bobertz, "Cyprian of Carthage as Patron," 193: "it was precisely the act of appointing new clerics for Carthage which would be the most likely to upset the precarious balance of power relations between Cyprian and the clergy."
25. *Letters of St. Cyprian* (vol. 2), 193.
26. Cf. A. Stewart-Sykes, "Ordination Rites and Patronage Systems in the Third-Century Africa," *VC* 56 (2002): 115–30, discusses the function, salary, and ordination rites of presbyters within the context of episcopal patronage.

providing salaries for those preachers of the New Prophecy "in order that its teaching might prevail through gluttony" (Eusebius, *HE* 5.18.1–2). Apollonius goes on to accuse the prophetess Priscilla for receiving "gold and silver and expensive clothes" (Eusebius, *HE* 5.18.4). Along with other confessors of the New Prophecy, these leaders were denounced for their "avarice" of making gain "not only from the rich but from the poor and from orphans and widows" and their disobedience of the scriptural commandment forbidding a prophet from receiving gifts and money (Eusebius, *HE* 5.18.4, 7). Presumably, the followers of the New Prophecy ("the rich, the poor, orphans, and widows") supported their prophets and confessors with gifts and offerings (their common fund?), not unlike the instructions given concerning prophets who wanted to settle in the Didachist community (*Did.* 13.7); but Apollonius's (and also Eusebius's) bias against this "heresy" apparently prompted this unsavory charge and colored his characterization. That the proto-orthodox church employed the accusations of financial scandals of paid leaders/clergy against sectarian and heretical groups is confirmed by other reports by Eusebius and Irenaeus. Eusebius reports that around the same time (late second century) the disciples of Theodotus "the cobbler"—who taught the heresy that Christ was a mere man (adoptionism), and was therefore excommunicated by Bishop Victor of Rome—deceived a certain confessor Natalius to be their sectarian bishop with a fixed salary of one hundred fifty denarii per month (Eusebius, *HE* 5.28.10). Although Natalius eventually repented in public in tears and humiliation after having repeated visions of the Lord warning him of his "covetousness," "he was scarcely admitted into communion" by Zephyrinus, Victor's successor (Eusebius, *HE* 5.28.11–12). Irenaeus, the major heresiologist bishop, linked the reason behind the secrecy of gnostic teachings with gnostic teachers' practice of receiving "a high price" for teaching their mysteries (*Haer.* 1.4.3).

What the proto-orthodox church had thought of as a sectarian and heretical "novelty" of paying their leaders/clergy with gifts and fixed stipends became within a few decades a mainstream, "orthodox" practice and led to a growing hierarchy and disparity between clergy and laity. Thus, in addition to Cyprian's witness, the *Didascalia* states that clergy, following after the Old Testament priests and Levites, are to receive from the people the service of food, clothing, and "other things" (8).[27] And in equal importance, whatever the widow receives from the people, the deacon is to receive double, the presbyter double, and the bishop quadruple (9). "To every [ecclesiastical] position," the laity is supposed to "pay the honor which is right to him, by gifts and honors and with earthly reverence" (9). This discriminating honor and gifts according to one's clerical rank, as in the case of Cyprian's congregation, recalls the contemporary Greco-Roman practice of citizens and members of associations receiving public gifts in proportion to their status (not to their needs) as a

---

27. Cf. *Ap. Trad.* 23; 31–32.

way to confirm and reinforce social hierarchy.[28] Now in a Christian context, "the bishop receiving the largest share with the lower clergy receiving lesser amounts (but always more than the laity, even widows!) would have served to reinforce the hierarchical structure of the Christian community."[29] As in the case of Cyprian, while the congregation is responsible to honor and support clergy with gifts in acknowledgment of their dependent status, the bishop is to dispense to his clergy, thirty-three in total (3.5),[30] from the same offerings and gifts given by people for charity (the common fund) (8). Bishop Cornelius's run-down of 154 Roman clergy suggests that they were also regularly supported by the common chest (most likely in proportion to their rank as well), along with more than fifteen hundred widows and people in affliction (Eusebius, *HE* 6.43.11).

The upshot of all of these developments is the perception and reality that "all good things flowed from the bishop,"[31] while his status was maintained "in relation to lower clergy, lay patrons, and people" in all respects through "the structure and process of the patron-client social exchange."[32] The bishop, now the ecclesiastical benefactor par excellence, both steered and responded to this perception and reality. Richard Gordon has shown how the fusion of Roman public beneficence and the sacrificial system of imperial and civic priesthood (by the same elite individuals) implicitly legitimated "both the divine necessity and the social responsibility of the existing social order."[33] Similarly, the fusion of the marked munificence and sacerdotal authority and distinction of the bishop with theological justification might reflect a Christianized version of that "divine necessity and social responsibility" of the ecclesiastical and social hierarchies within the church. And the church, headed by the bishop and his clergy, functioned as a benefactor to the poor and positioned itself as an advocate of the poor in solidarity with them even as it accumulated wealth and other resources more and more (often in the name of benefaction to the poor).[34] Thus the consolidation of clerical (episcopal) power and the articulation of the church's explicitly self-identifying ministry for the poor occurred concurrently in close relation to each other. This role of the church had an interesting layer of

28. See chap. 1.

29. Bobertz, "Cyprian of Carthage as Patron," 72–73.

30. It mandates the presence of twelve presbyters, seven deacons, and fourteen subdeacons in 3.5.

31. L. W. Countryman, *The Rich Christian in the Church of the Early Empire: Contradictions and Accommodations* (New York: Edwin Mellen, 1980), 162.

32. Bobertz, "Cyprian of Carthage as Patron," 73.

33. R. Gordon, "The Veil of Power: Emperors, Sacrificers and Benefactors," in *Pagan Priests: Religion and Power in the Ancient World* (ed. M. Beard and J. North; Ithaca, NY: Cornell University Press, 1990), 229.

34. For a parallel function of the synagogue as an "economic center" for the organized assistance to the poor during this time, see B.-Z. Rosenfeld and J. Menirav, "The Ancient Synagogue as an Economic Center," *JNES* 58 (1999): 259–76.

complexity against the social background of clergy: while an increasing number of bishops such as Zephyrinus and Cyprian came from a rich, elite background with financial means, most of the clergy came from the lower status and "middling" group, who were still vulnerable to poverty well into the fourth and fifth centuries (cf. Cyprian, *Epp.* 5.2.1; 13.4.2; 14.2.1).[35] With a more manifest ministry of "ecclesiastical redistribution of wealth (which was never questioned as such)," the magnetic power of the church was also exhibited as it attracted those Christian men "who found it difficult enough to support themselves in normal conditions" into the high calling of clerical profession "with gusto."[36]

The church then navigated a balancing act between keeping the faithful (especially the rich) motivated to meet increasingly overwhelming needs and keeping them (the rich) in check and properly respectful of clerical authority and institutional structure, through which the appropriate means of salvation were to be found. Although somewhat simplistic, Countryman's words hold largely true: "the finances of the church were . . . divided between two groups of people: the role of the rich was to give, that of the ministers to spend."[37] Again, the rich were certainly not the only group of the faithful who contributed; however, they were the group most targeted and solicited by the bishop to give and whom the church depended on not only for manifold works of charity but also for the support of clergy now. As the patronage of the Christian wealthy largely shifted to that of the bishop who controlled the church treasury, and as the wealthy increasingly lost control of their donation and influence on the congregation in the traditional mode of Roman patrons, there were occasional tensions between the clergy and their rich members. In the traditional Christian teaching, the rich were constantly urged to give without expecting in return from their recipients here and now (except an eschatological return from God); but at the same time they were given perennial warnings about the danger of their wealth and chastisement for their arrogance and indifference (in continuity with the New Testament). However, the rich could and did at times disregard or show their disapproval of the clergy (i.e., they withheld their loyalty) by refusing to give or by giving only small amounts;[38] some even attempted to influence and control clergy and the

35. P. Brown, *Poverty and Leadership in the Later Roman Empire* (Hanover, NH: University Press of New England, 2002), 20, 48–50. During the Valerian persecution, Cyprian was first condemned to exile (*deportatio*) befitting his higher social status (later executed by sword), while his Numidian bishop colleagues were condemned to the mines (*opus metalli*), which was a plebian punishment (*Ep.* 76). The church, however, especially in the major cities such as Rome, Antioch, Alexandria, and later Constantinople, did *increasingly* recruit its clergy from the "wealthy urban classes of professionals and merchants" in late antiquity. See J. Hillner, "Clerics, Property and Patronage: The Case of the Roman Titular Churches," *Antiquité Tardive* 14 (2006): 68.

36. Brown, *Poverty and Leadership*, 20.

37. Countryman, *Rich Christian*, 162. So far I have found only one text that explicitly exhorts the clergy (presbyter) to give alms: Peter of Alexandria, *On Riches* (74).

38. Cf. Countryman, *Rich Christian*, 162.

episcopal elections[39] and collaborated with clergy whose policies would reflect their interests with their resources (e.g., the wealthy *lapsi* with laxist clergy in Carthage; wealthy laymen usurping the episcopal privilege of hospitality in Jerome, *In. ep. ad Titum* 1.8–9). Conversely, the bishops/clergy could and did promote and plead for more prodigal contributions for the common treasury by theological rationales of the spiritual benefits of alms and by theological threats of divine judgment and punishments (as well as moral/social shaming of selfishness of the rich). The ever-intensifying clerical denunciation of the avarice, luxury, and stinginess of the rich and their correspondingly elaborate promises of spiritual rewards and returns for their willing obedience (i.e., "cheerful giving") well into late antiquity (and beyond) indicate that the balance was indeed a hard act to achieve.

5.2. Church Ownership and Possessions

The institutional and organizational strength of the church during this time is also displayed in the ownership and management of various properties by the church. We have earlier examined the de facto "church ownership" of cemeteries despite its illegal status (see chaps. 1 and 4). In a similar way, from the third century on, we have evidence of local churches *acting* as property owners and managers. The most dramatic properties the church collectively acquired were assembly halls—church buildings. In fact, as early as the turn of the third century, there are a few literary references to church edifices erected for Christian assembly. Clement of Alexandria mentions "a sacred structure raised to God's honor" (*hieron*) though he reserves the word "church" (*ekklēsia*) not for the building but for Christian assembly (*Strom.* 7.5.1); but elsewhere he does use *ekklēsia* to refer to a place of assembly as he writes about proper attire of men and women going to *ekklēsia* (*Paed.* 3.11.79). In North Africa, while Minucius Felix admits that Christians "have no shrines and altars" (*delubra et aras*; *Oct.* 32.1), his contemporary Tertullian also talks about coming and going to the church (*ecclesia*) as the "house of God," a physical structure for assembly (*Idol.* 7.1; cf. *Fug.* 3.2; 14.1; *De pudicitia* 3.4–5; 4.5). In the mid-third century, Cyprian as well refers to the church (*ecclesia*) as the local "house of God" (*Unit. eccl.* 6, 8, 12) and even inadvertently reveals the physical layout of a church building by mentioning the pulpit (*pulpitum*) as the "tribunal of the church . . . the place of highest elevation and conspicuous to the entire

---

39. According to Optatus of Milevis, *On the Schism of the Donatists*, appx. 1, a wealthy widow, Lucilla, secured the election of her candidate as bishop of Carthage by distribution of money to the assembly of bishops apparently for the care of the poor. On the limited role of "popular vote" (*suffragium plebis, populi*, or *omnium*) only in the form of acclamations (devoid of real voice of popular will) in the episcopal elections, see G. E. M. de Ste. Croix, "*Suffragium*: From Vote to Patronage," *British Journal of Sociology* 5 (1954): 35–37.

congregation" and also the designated seating area for the presbytery or clergy
in the context of the ordination of the confessor Celerinus to the office of
reader (*Ep.* 39.4.1; 5.2). Dionysius of Alexandria hints at the Christian assemblies among exiles during the Valerian persecution (257 CE) as he reports
about "a large church [*ekklēsia*]" banding together at Cephro, though this
could refer to a gathering itself rather than a gathering place (Eusebius, *HE*
7.11.12). When Valerian's son Gallienus ended the persecution with his edict
of toleration (261 CE), he also ordered the restoration of Christian places of
worship (as well as their cemeteries) in a letter to the bishops (Eusebius, *HE*
7.13); this indicates the official recognition of church properties well before the
edicts of toleration ordering the restoration of church possessions by Galerius
(311 CE), Constantine and Licinius (313 CE), and Maximin (313 CE).

The earliest *archaeological* evidence of a church building is a modified
house church structure (*domus ecclesiae*) in Dura-Europos, Syria (ca. 240 CE),
which was located down the street from a Jewish synagogue, also renovated
from an existing private house. The elongated assembly hall of this church
was created by renovation of the dining room, which then ceased to have
domestic functions (such as dining or meal preparation), and this church also
contained a baptistery decorated with fresco.[40] Other scattered sources confirm
the existence of church buildings in Syrian cities in the latter half of the third
century. Eusebius reports that after the excommunication of Bishop Paul of
Samosata (for his heresy of adoptionism and alleged misbehaviors) by a synod
of Antioch (268/269 CE), Paul "would in no way relinquish the house of the
church [*tēs ekklēsias oikou*]" (*HE* 7.30.19). However, the emperor Aurelian
responded to the appeal by the Antiochene congregation by ordering transfer
of "the building to those with whom the bishops of the doctrine in Italy and
Rome should communicate in writing" (*HE* 7.30.19). "The house of the church
[*tēs ekklēsias oikou*]" mentioned above might be similar to the remodeled
house church in Dura-Europos[41] and also contained the tribunal and elevated
seat for bishop/clergy as in Cyprian's church, apparently introduced by Paul
of Samosata himself.[42] The similar architectural design may be the case of the
"holy churches" mentioned in the *Didascalia*, in which assemblies should be
held with "all good manners" and decent order (12); the text further designates
a separate area for presbyters to sit with the bishop, who is distinguished by
his chair "in the eastern part of the house," and separates the sitting areas
of laymen from laywomen (12). And as previously mentioned, a pagan critic

40. L. M. White, "Regulating Fellowship in the Communal Meal: Early Jewish and Christian Evidence," in *Meals in a Social Context: Aspects of the Communal Meal in the Hellenistic and Roman
World* (ed. I. Nielsen and H. S. Nielsen; Aarhus, Denmark: Aarhus University Press, 1998), 193.

41. F. Millar, "Paul of Samosata, Zenobia and Aurellian: The Church, Local Culture and
Political Allegiance in Third-Century Syria," *JRS* 61 (1971): 14.

42. The synod of Antioch regarded these features as prideful innovations of Paul of Samosata
(Eusebius, *HE* 7.30.9).

Porphyry jeered at Christians for building splendid templelike structures for their assembly.[43]

Going back to Egypt, several Oxyrhynchus papyri reveal church buildings and property around the turn of the fourth century. A municipal survey of street wardens records two streets known as North-Church Street and South-Church Street (P. Oxy. I, 43).[44] As noted by E. A. Judge and S. R. Pickering, as well as Michael White, it seems to indicate that the streets became associated with the identifiable church buildings since the streets in this list are usually identified by a recognizable building or landmark.[45] In another papyrus a certain Aurelius Ammonius, the lector (*anagnōstēs*) of the *former* village church of Chysis (who was illiterate in Greek), certified on oath the official account of confiscation (February 5, 304 CE) that the church possessed nothing valuable—such as gold, silver, money, animals, slaves, and land—except for the bronze gate already delivered to Alexandria (P. Oxy. XXXIII, 2673). The church (*ekklēsia*) here clearly refers to a church building, which was no longer standing due to the execution of Diocletian's edict to destroy the churches (*ekklēsias*) throughout the empire (303 CE). During the Great Persecution (303–13 CE), Diocletian's first edict included razing the churches along with search and seizure of Scriptures, and one of the first churches to be destroyed was the one situated in the midst of a wealthy residential district, visible from the imperial palace in Nicomedia (*HE* 8.2.4; Lactantius, *Mort.* 12; see also Eusebius, *Mart. Pal.* 1.5.2; *HE* 8.17.9; *Vit. Const.* 2.2). As the above papyrus confirms the specific implementation of this edict, another possible context for the edict is provided by Eusebius, who (with exaggeration for his apologetic purpose) universalizes the existence of church buildings in the empire by the eve of the Great Persecution; Christianity grew so much "in every city" that Christians overflowed "the buildings of olden time, and would erect from the foundations churches of spacious dimensions throughout all the cities" (*HE* 8.1.5). Indeed, judging from the evidence, it seems that by the time of the Great Persecution, church buildings, whose architectural development was already moving toward the basilical structure of formal elongated halls to accommodate assembly,[46] have become well identified and recognized by the government authorities and general populace, and this public notice "ratified the presence of Christian buildings of growing proportions and social prominence."[47]

43. *Adv. Christianos*, fr. 76 in Macarius Magnes 4.21.

44. E. A. Judge and S. R. Pickering, "Papyrus Documentation of Church and Community in Egypt to the Mid-Fourth Century," *JAC* 20 (1977): 60–61.

45. Ibid.; L. M. White, *Building God's Houses in the Roman World: Architectural Adaptation among Pagans, Jews, and Christians* (vol. 1 of *The Social Origins of Christian Architecture*; Valley Forge, PA: Trinity Press International, 1990), 123.

46. White, "Regulating Fellowship," 193.

47. White, *Building God's Houses*, 130.

In addition to church buildings, the church as a corporate entity possessed various resources for charity and liturgy. The property list mentioned in relation to the former village church of Chrysis (P. Oxy. XXXIII, 2673) also "presumably defines the range of property expected to be found in the possession of a church at this time."[48] The official record of Munatius Felix, curator (mayor) of Cirta, Numidia (303 CE), provides a detailed inventory of a search made of a "house church" (*domus ecclesiae*) renovated for specific cultic and charitable functions:

> two gold cups, six silver cups, six silver pitchers, a small silver kettle, seven silver lamps, two wax candles, seven small bronze lamps with their wicks, eleven bronze lamps with chains, eighty-two women's tunics, thirty-eight *mafortea* [a woman's headdress or veil], sixteen men's tunics, thirteen pairs of men's shoes, forty-seven pairs of women's shoes, and nineteen crude thongs. (*Gest. ap. Zenoph.*, CSEL 187–88)

The church also contained a library with cupboards and barrels and a dining room with four large jars and six barrels, in addition to "one exceedingly large volume" of Scripture. The clothing and shoes items, too numerous for private possession, likely "represent the charitable store of the Christian community" for distribution.[49] In the same year (303 CE), the basilica of Abthungi was found to possess supplies of oil and corn presumably also for charity (CSEL 26.200), and the church in Carthage provided food, clothing, and cash for the needy and the confessors from its common stocks as already witnessed in Cyprian's letters (e.g., *Epp.* 5.1.2; 12.2.2). Finally, a comprehensive tax register of buildings in Panopolis, Egypt (*P. Gen. inv.* 108, ca. 298 CE), included a house that had most likely belonged to the local *ekklēsia* ("the house which is the such-and-such of the church," *oikia ētoi ekklēsia s[. . .]*) as it mentions the names of several property owners with ecclesiastical offices, such as *diakonos* (twice) and *anagnōstēs*.[50] Though it is not entirely clear from the document, it is probable that the house and/or the church might also have had charitable stocks of food and clothing items in store, as did the churches elsewhere during this period.[51]

48. Judge and Pickering, "Papyrus Documentation," 59.

49. White, *Building God's Houses*, 122.; cf. W. H. C. Frend, *Martyrdom and Persecution in the Early Church* (Oxford: Blackwell, 1965), 372–73; A. H. M. Jones, *Constantine and the Conversion of Europe* (1948; Toronto: University of Toronto Press, 1978).

50. Judge and Pickering, "Papyrus Documentation," 61; White, *Building God's Houses*, 122–23.

51. An Oxyrhynchus papyri of late fifth or early sixth century records an instruction to Victor, the steward or overseer of wine stores employed by the church, to distribute wine to the widows of the church (P. Oxy. XVI, 1954–56); cf. A. Serfass, "Wine for Widows: Papyrological Evidence for Christian Charity in Late Antique Egypt," in *Wealth and Poverty in Early Church and Society* (ed. S. R. Holman; Grand Rapids: Baker Academic, 2008), 88. It is also attested that

5.3. The Economic Activities of the Church and Clergy

Going beyond owning and managing properties, the church as an institution was engaged in financial functions beginning in the mid-third century. As mentioned in chapter 4, the church of Rome took the role of depository to which some widows and orphans entrusted their income/savings (Cyprian, *Epp.* 50.1.2; 52.1.2). In Alexandria, bishop Maximus (264–82 CE), the successor of Dionysius, and his assistant presbyter (acting as a financial secretary?), Theonas, who later succeeded Maximus as bishop (282–300 CE) and built a church building,[52] served as depositaries for Christian businessmen (P. Amherst I, 3).[53] A fragmentary papyrus from (probably) Fayum, Egypt, perhaps the earliest autograph letter of a known Christian,[54] contains a number of requests sent by an unnamed Christian in Rome to a Christian community in the Arsinoite nome (a regional administrative unit) regarding the sale of goods that the community had produced. Apparently, the writer is concerned about a payment due to a certain Primitinus, probably a shipper,[55] and asks the community to deliver money to him, as he will soon be in Alexandria. The Arsinoite community should be able to deposit money enough for the payment through the sale of barley, bread, and linens. Here, Maximus "the papa" is to receive a certain sum that is to be handed over to Primitinus, and another sum is to be given to Theonas, who is to hold it for the writer. This letter, though fragmentary, gives some insight into the socioeconomic situation of the Alexandrian church and the economic role the Alexandrian higher clergy played, especially in expediting financial transactions and holding deposits.[56] Later in the early fourth century and on, the Alexandrian bishops would become increasingly involved in controlling the Mediterranean grain shipment and trade with their growing wealth and political influence, apparently for mobilizing funds for the relief programs in the charged context of church politics.[57]

In Carthage, however, Cyprian, based on a conciliar decision, repeatedly denounced any clerical involvement in "earthly and worldly affairs," such as

---

even the rural churches in Egypt (Oxyrhynchus) in late antiquity had stores of goods, particularly food items such as wine, oil, bread, and grains, for charitable distribution and that churches owned vineyards and bakeries that produced those products (Serfass, "Wine for Widows," 94). See further Serfass, "Wine for Widows," 88–102.

52. Eusebius, *HE* 7.32.30.

53. On discussion of this papyrus, see A. Deissmann, *Light from the Ancient East* (trans. L. R. M. Strachan; rev. ed.; New York: Harper, 1927), 205–13; H. Musurillo, "Early Christian Economy: A Reconsideration of P. Amherst 3(a)," *Chronique d'Egypte* 31 (1956): 124–34; M. J. Hollerich, "The Alexandrian Bishops and the Grain Trade," *JESHO* 25 (1982): 188–90; G. F. Snyder, *Ante Pacem: Archaeological Evidence of Church Life before Constantine* (Macon, GA: Mercer University Press, 1985, 1991), 152–53.

54. Deissmann, *Light from the Ancient East*, 205.

55. Identified as such by ibid., 207.

56. Snyder, *Ante Pacem*, 153.

57. See Hollerich, "Alexandrian Bishops and the Grain Trade," 187–207.

serving as a guardian of children and trustee of estates, and in profit-making by dealings of "secular business [*rerum saecularium*]" (*Ep.* 1.2; *Laps.* 6). He complained that too many bishops, out of desire "to have money in abundance," left their sees and people in hunger and "acquired landed estates by fraud, and made profits by loans at compound interest" in foreign provinces (*Laps.* 6). Despite Cyprian's outcry, this kind of selfish episcopal practice allegedly went on not just in Carthage but also elsewhere. About a half-century later, the Council of Elvira in Spain prohibited bishops, presbyters, and deacons from leaving their sees and parishes or traveling in the provinces in order to engage in profitable ventures (canon 19). However, the council advised them to "send a son, a freedman, an employee, a friend, or someone else" if it was "an economic necessity" and also ordered them to "engage only in business activities within their own area" (canon 19)—an indication that the economic activities and secular employment of bishops had become a growing trend by the early fourth century even with (or despite) consolidation of episcopal position and power.

5.4. Summary and Conclusion

The church, as an institution with increasing financial resources, made its formidable presence and strength felt both within the Christian communities and the larger society in several ways. First of all, the church centralized its charitable ministry under the authority and administration of the bishop, who emerged as God's earthly representative and a preeminent imitator of his benefaction, justice, and mercy by contextualizing the existing patronage networks revolving around him. The boundless spiritual and material munificence of God, the ultimate patron *and* father, was mediated through the spiritual and material *beneficia* dispensed by the bishop according to his unique prerogative, merciful discretion, and righteous judgment. As a chief of clergy, he was distinguished among the rest of the clergy in responsibilities, honor, and gifts. And the clergy as a whole was set apart from the laity, whose influence diminished in proportion to cultic and structural hierarchy. The greater the social and material needs of those in the church, the more necessary it became for the clergy to take charge of ministry of charity; and the greater the social and material needs of those in the church, the more necessary it became for the clergy to turn to the wealthier members to contribute more for the good of many, including their own. The bishop used his spiritual *beneficia* and punishments to "encourage" the wealthy to give sacrificially for distribution of his material *beneficia*, so that "the giving and the spending were the responsibilities of two distinct groups of people."[58] This resulted at

---

58. Countryman, *Rich Christian*, 162.

times in tensions between bishop (clergy) and wealthy laity as the transfer of patronage (and therefore power) from the latter to the former reinforced and became almost complete in the context of the larger institutionalization of the church.

Second, the church to a greater extent enjoyed de facto ownership and management of many properties—from liturgical items of value such as chalices of gold and silver, to female tunics and oils for charitable store, and to impressive physical structures for Christian assembly—to the point that its members, their non-Christian neighbors, and the government officials all came to notice and at times to expect the church's possession of valuables and considerable wealth by the time of the Great Persecution. Finally, the church and clergy played an economically significant role by serving as depositories, banks, and trustees for its members and even engaged in trades apparently as "fundraisers for charity" and business affairs for profits. While leaders responded to these innovative and ambivalent activities in different ways, these ecclesiastical engagements demonstrated the interconnectedness of the complex ministries and identities of the church as well as perhaps the blurring of a Christian identity at the highest level—the topic of our next chapter.

6

ͰⵔͰⵔͰⵔͰⵔͰⵔͰⵔͰⵔͰⵔͰⵔͰⵔͰⵔͰⵔͰⵔͰⵔͰⵔͰⵔͰⵔͰⵔ

Wealth, Poverty, and Christian Identity

In one sense, we have been dealing all along with how early Christian communities constructed their identities in relation to wealth and poverty. Nonetheless, we devote this chapter to focusing on the explicit social and theological construction of Christian identities with regard to perceived threats that would blur those identities as well as both negative and positive boundary markers. Picking up on the discussion of clerical engagement in business and commercial activities at the end of the previous chapter, we first proceed with the perceptions and reality of the commercial and business activities of lay Christians. Then we will move to Christian denunciation of avarice and luxury as negative markers of Christian identity, and affirmation of almsgiving and charity as positive markers. Finally, we will conclude the chapter with how the Constantinian revolution and the development of monasticism affected the existing identity construction and practices of the church involving wealth and poverty.

6.1. Wealth, Business Activities, and the Blurring of Christian Identity

While Christians formed their distinct socioeconomic enclaves and koinonia even in the face of persecution and personal sacrifice during this period, they had always been integrated into the larger Roman society. Obviously, the more financially resourceful the members were—i.e., the middling group such as merchants, artisans, and skilled workers with their own businesses, and those in the upper rank of the society, now with a greater burden and responsibility to support the poorer members and clergy in their communities—the more integrated they were and the more they had at stake. Honor, inheritance, power, property, and prestige—the usual building blocks that constitute one's social standing in a larger society—were not supposed to work in the same manner in Christian communities. However, we have already seen that these were not simply to be rejected or given up (see below for a discussion of renunciation of wealth) since wealth and power were useful in serving the Christian communities when properly controlled and channeled with the right motivations. This presented those with the greatest financial burdens with the problem of maintaining their Christian identity while keeping their socioeconomic standing, not to mention aspiring to upward social mobility.

The extant Christian texts are almost unanimous in disapproving and warning of the dangers of business affairs because they were thought to obscure Christian identity and responsibilities. As discussed earlier, *Hermas* censures particularly those who are "absorbed in business" (*Sim.* 4.5; 8.8.1; 9.20.1)[1] and those "who became rich" (*Sim.* 8.9.1), probably through business ventures. To these very ones who are guilty of "desire for gain" and hypocrisy, (one-time) repentance was offered (*Sim.* 8.8.2; 9.19.3). While many heeded the commandments and repented, however, others "fell away completely . . . for on account of their business affairs (*dia tas pragmateias*) they blasphemed the Lord and denied him" (*Sim.* 8.8.2). In times of peace their "excessive involvement in business" (*tōn pollōn praxeōn*) pulled them away from the church community and the Lord (*Sim.* 4.5), leading them to helpless self-absorption with riches and evasion from due service to their own Lord, i.e., avoiding almsgiving and sharing with the poorer members in community (*Sim.* 4.5). In times of persecution, they are especially prone to apostasy "because of their riches and their business affairs" (*Vis.* 3.6.5). Thus, those involved in business "a great deal" sin "a great deal" (*Sim.* 4.5).[2] Much like the seeds that fell on the thorny soil in the Gospel parable (Mark 4:7, 18–19; Matt. 13:7, 22; Luke 8:7, 14), their concerns in "business affairs and wealth and pagan friendships" prevent their minds from understanding the truth, and "the parables about the Deity," choke their faith and leave them in spiritual barrenness and ruin (*Mand.* 10.1.4). This triad of business affairs, wealth, and pagan friendships, which forces them to commit hypocrisy out of "desire for gain," is indicative of how powerful and critical the social connections are for the social climbers and the rich addressed here; the way to stay afloat in their social circle and to climb up the social ladder through accumulating riches, if possible, is by connecting with and maintaining "the right company" through patronage. Those preoccupied with business and wealth avoid offending their pagan

1. In *Vis.* 3.6.5–7 the rich and those who are preoccupied with business are the same group.
2. Christian widows are forbidden to engage in business in *Ap. Const.* 3.7.

friends (which is interpreted by the author of *Hermas* as hypocrisy) and end up following "the desires of sinful men," i.e., their pagan friends (*Sim.* 9.19.3). They fail to comprehend their true identity and act hypocritically toward it; thus they are always on the verge of sliding back to the world. They want to have the goods of both worlds but are incapable of attaining the heavenly good due to their double-mindedness and the murky and distracted state of their souls (cf. *Sim.* 9.20.1). They remain in danger of lapsing into worldliness until they get rid of enough wealth and put aside *excessive* business activities (*Vis.* 3.6.5–6; 3.9.5–6; *Sim.* 4.5) and "do some good with that which was left to them" (*Sim.* 9.30.5)—i.e., share with those in need (*Vis.* 3.9.4; *Sim.* 2.5, 10; 10.4.2). Note that the way for the rich to be useful to God is to cut away their wealth (*Vis.* 3.6.7), though not entirely, but just enough to make them "fit for the Kingdom of God" through removing "the vanities of their possessions" (*Sim.* 9.31.2) while keeping enough to "seek out the hungry until the tower is finished" (*Vis.* 3.9.5).

Buying and selling, and trade in general, are even more suspect for Irenaeus, bishop of Lyons (ca. 180 CE), who regards wealth, including that of Christians, as the product of unrighteousness through commercial activities: "For in some cases there follows us a small, and in others a large amount of property which we have acquired from the mammon of unrighteousness" (*Haer.* 4.30.1). Whether that property may be a house, clothing, vessels, or "everything else ministering to our every-day life, . . . we acquired by avarice [before conversion], or received them from our heathen parents, relations or friends who unrighteously obtained them" (*Haer.* 4.30.1). This is in fact the case "even now" (i.e., after conversion) because business and trade, in which Christians are engaged, are *by nature* motivated by "desire for gain," to use *Hermas*'s phrase: "For who is there that sells, and does not wish to make a profit from him who buys? Or who purchases anything, and does not wish to obtain good value from the seller? Or who is there that carries a trade, and does not do so that he may obtain a livelihood thereby?" (*Haer.* 4.30.1). Irenaeus then paints a picture of commerce and business as a whole in a negative light, from which all Christians (not just the rich or those who run businesses) can hardly claim innocence as long as they participate in them. However, he does not call for total asceticism or partial renunciation as a remedy; somewhat (but not entirely) similar to *Hermas*, he advises use of those goods "acquired from unrighteousness" for righteousness, i.e., caring for the needy and giving alms for the poor as in the words of the Lord (*Haer.* 4.30.3; cf. Matt. 6:3; 25:35–36; Luke 16:9).

Didascalia, like *Hermas*, sees the danger of engaging in business as its blurring of participants' Christian identity. Once they enter the world of business and trade, its "desire for gain" is so consuming that it is difficult for them not to get entangled or absorbed and thus to mix up their priorities and identity. Those who are engaged in business are strongly reminded that "the handicrafts of the faithful are called works of superfluity. Indeed, their true work is religion" (*Didasc.* 13). Therefore, the faithful are to pursue their "worldly affairs," that is, trade and business, only as a "work of superfluity" so as to obtain their provision, but no more than that (13). Practically, this means that they "endeavor never to withdraw from the assembly of the church" on the Lord's Day; they are to "leave everything," including their crafts and commercial activities, and "run eagerly to [their] church" (13).[3] Using the threat of everlasting fire on the day of judgment, the text goes on to warn the faithful repeatedly not to leave the church and attend the assembly of the gentiles, i.e., the theatre, spectacles, and festivals, "because of the idols" (13). Attendance at these public events, which were ubiquitous and deemed indispensable in Roman society, is considered not only to confirm their care for the world and concern for materialism ("affairs of living"), presumably because of trade and commercial activities conducted in those places, but also to commit idolatry and therefore pollute Christian identity (13). Thus, the text poses an eventual and inevitable tension between business/commercial affairs and purity of Christian identity and is anxious to draw a clear boundary between them—an indication that in reality this kind of tension was likely "smoothed out" by the faithful in an undesirable way—i.e., they did mix up and harmonize their trades/businesses with Christian faith without many qualms.

Tertullian certainly understood the seriousness of this tension and pressed this issue further in a similarly dichotomizing way. In his earlier apology supposedly addressing a pagan audience, he stressed Christians' "full participation" in Roman society and daily interactions with their "gentile" neighbors in the forum, meat market, baths, shops, factories, inns, weekly market, and "the rest of the life of buying and selling" (*Apol.* 42.2). He denies that Christians are ascetics or unprofitable in business because "we sail ships, . . . [go] to market with you . . . and our living depends on you" (*Apol.* 42.3).[4] In his more "rigorous" treatises addressing Christians, however, he saw right through the dilemmas of Christian traders and businessmen whose business transactions and Christian commitment could not be neatly compartmentalized or harmonized. In his treatise *On Idolatry* (*De Idololatria*), while giving Christians strict guidelines on arts and crafts concerning idolatry (*Idol.* 5–8), Tertullian directly deals with the question of whether trade (*negotium*) is a fitting occupation for a Christian (*Idol.* 11).[5] Like the other contemporary Christian authors, Tertullian clearly sees the fundamental motive of trade as covetous-

3. Note that Sunday (the Lord's Day) was not made the public day of rest until by Constantine in 325.

4. Tertullian emphasizes Christians' reliability and success in banking business in *Scap.* 4.7: "we never deny the deposit placed in our hands."

5. This is another indication of the presence of those Christians in Carthage who were engaged in making idols or the "attributes" of the idols and in providing supplies related to sacrifices to the idols (whom Tertullian attempted to dissuade from those activities).

ness (*cupiditas*; *pleonexia* in Greek), which is the root of all evil (1 Tim. 6:10; cf. 1 Tim. 1:19) and also called idolatry (Col. 3:5) according to the apostle Paul (*Idol.* 11.1). If covetousness, which is accompanied by mendacity and perjury, disappears, Tertullian asks, "what is the motive for acquiring? When the motive of acquiring ceases, there will be no necessity for trading" (11.1). However, suppose that there might be some righteous pursuit of gain just for the sake of argument; trade is still guilty of idolatry if it supplies any items used for sacrifices to the pagan deities, however indirectly it may be, such as frankincense and public victims (11.2–7); for it creates the possibility of and agency for idolatry. Not all trade might be combated in this way (11.2), but "no craft, therefore, no profession, no form of trade contributing anything to the equipment or formation of idols will be free from the charge of idolatry" (11.8).

Furthermore, many of the business/commercial dealings took place in and around pagan temples and places of spectacles filled with pagan deities. Even if one may grant that Christians of sociopolitical standing or with businesses could enter those places for their official duties and proper business (since there is no law forbidding Christians from the mere places), however, they are still exposed to religious pollution because the things done in those places, including business dealings, "belong to the idol-patrons to whom the very places are sacred" (*Spec.* 8). A case in point is the fact that normal commercial or business contracts are written in the name of pagan deities (*Idol.* 23). Tertullian presents a plausible situation: in "borrowing money from heathen under pledged securities, Christians give a guarantee (*cavent*) under oath, and deny themselves to have done so" (*Idol.* 23.1). Their guarantee under oath by pagan gods is in writing, not in speech; so these Christian businessmen or traders insist that since "it is the tongue, not the written letter, which kills" in light of Christ's prescription against swearing, they have not denied their Christian name and faith (*Idol.* 23.2). Nevertheless, Tertullian points out that one cannot write something without inner consciousness and participation (*Idol.* 23.2–5). Christ, in his judgment seat, sees through the unspoken consent, and Christian borrowers' consciences are compromised when they silently meant to swear in their heart (which is required for the guarantee to take effect). "Thus, in his pen there speaks a hand clearer than every sound, in his waxen tablet there is heard a letter more vocal than every mouth" (*Idol.* 23.4). They cannot justify signing a guarantee based on ignorance or unwillingness: "For when you gave the guarantee, you were conscious of it, and when you were conscious of it, you were, of course, willing" (*Idol.* 23.5). Therefore, they commit idolatry "both in deed [writing] and in thought " (*Idol.* 23.5). Tertullian prays that Christians would never face any necessity for that kind of (business) contract under pagan deities; and he continues that "if it should fall out, may He [Christ] give our brethren the means of helping us [i.e., Christians lending Christians the necessary money], or give us constancy to break off all such necessity, lest those denying letters, the substitutes for our mouth, be brought forward against us in the day of judgment, sealed with the seals, not now of witnesses, but of angels!" (*Idol.* 23.7). The implication is rather unmistakable: Christians should preemptively avoid business or commercial dealings (with pagans) that necessitate or even raise any occasion for such tacit compromise of Christian identity.

Indeed, for those Christians with wealth and high birth, i.e., the Roman and civic elite and the rich in general, the social tension and dilemma would have been urgent and pressing. The very social, religious, and political roles (all intertwined) that they were expected to play through patronage and euergetism, which were part and parcel of holding public office and power—such as offering sacrifices, keeping up the temples, funding spectacles, theaters, festivals, baths, and even judging—endangered polluting their Christian identity (cf. *Idol.* 17.2–3). "All the powers and dignities of this world are not only alien to, but enemies of God," spurted Tertullian (*Idol.* 18.8). These Christians might protest that those functions were simply part of their societal responsibility due to their birth and that therefore there was no way to avoid those civic obligations (cf. *Idol.* 18.1, 4, 9). By implication, they were demanding that their inseparable civic and social ties and functions should be separated from their Christian (religious) identity. To that, Tertullian answers that the attire (priestly insignia) and pomp of these offices are already tainted with idolatry and thus make these functions closed to Christians (*Idol.* 18.1–4). As a matter of fact, Christ, our example, rejected worldly glory (*gloria saeculi*), honor, and dignity, "which He did not want, and He condemned what He rejected, and what He condemned, He consigned to the pomp of the devil" (*Idol.* 18.7). Thus, "for avoiding it, remedies cannot be lacking; since, even if they be lacking, there remains that one by which you will be made a happier magistrate, not in the earth, but in the heavens [i.e., martyrdom]" (*Idol.* 18.9). On the one hand, for Tertullian, the interlocking web of socioeconomic and political position and pagan idolatry, the very way the Greco-Roman society operates, deceives Christians into insidious enslavement to the present world as though they could settle for compartmentalizing their Christian identity without having to renounce and separate from the whole system. On the other hand, other Christians would attempt to disentangle perfunctory religious customs ("idolatry") from those interwoven socioeconomic and political fabrics of society so that they could maintain their faith without jeopardizing their sociopolitical livelihood and standing *and* serve their Christian communities utilizing their "worldly" and "unrighteous" resources and influences.

The choice between these two options would not have been so stark and acute if ordinary Christians were not forced to make these decisions during the occasional persecutions. While Cyprian was more aligned with Tertullian's stance before the Decian persecution (cf. *Don.*), others in his congregation, including many of the wealthy and some of his clergy, were not, as is illustrated by the mass apostasy of the wealthy and its attendant controversy with the laxist faction over their readmission during the persecution (see chaps. 3–5 above). Cyprian saw the muddying of Christian separation from the world due to "a blind attachment to their patrimony" (*Laps.* 11, 12) as the pernicious consequence of the imperial persecution and yet had to concede, to an extent reinstating the wealthy *lapsi* based on the severity of their apostasy and penance (especially almsgiving) in light of the practical problems created by the loss of the wealthy for the preservation of the common chest and ecclesiastical charity.

While these literary texts reveal certain biases against the business and commercial activities of the faithful with concerns, along with the commercial activities of the clergy mentioned in the previous chapter, we have some interesting epigraphic indicators and indirect inferences of Christian businesses in the period from the mid-third to early fourth century that mainly catered to Christian needs in funerary monuments. In a classic study conducted on early Christian monuments in Phrygia, Anatolia, Elsa Gibson has identified a group of thirteen burial monuments in similar formulaic design and execution as products of the same workshop of stonecutters who might have been Christian.[6] Relatively recent follow-up studies carefully confirm the Christian identity of those masons (as well as the purchasers).[7] Twelve out of the thirteen epitaphs explicitly commemorate Christian burials—eight of them utilizing the now famous formula, "Christians for Christians" (*Christianoi Christianois*) and three of them using the word "Christian(s)," though one is lost—all decorated with the similar stylized vine and grape patterns, wreaths, and crosses.[8] These panel steles with the epitaphs also feature standardized funerary motifs (of the region) such as images of oxen and agricultural tools (on nine of the monuments) and gender-specific symbols: pruning hooks and whips for males, and baskets, combs, distaffs, and spindles for females.[9] Judging from the uniformity of motifs and symbols of this workshop and the display of "mass-produced" quality with specific alterations made (e.g., erasure of a cross), Gary Johnson suggests that this workshop apparently prefabricated burial monuments (apart from epitaphs) for Christian use and subsequently altered some motifs for sale to non-Christian clientele.[10] If this is true, this seemingly active role of the workshop in the production and marketing of

6. E. Gibson, *The "Christians for Christians" Inscriptions of Phrygia* (Harvard Theological Studies 32; Missoula, MT: Scholars Press, 1978).

7. E.g., G. J. Johnson, "A Christian Business and Christian Self-Identity in Third/Fourth Century Phrygia," *VC* 48 (1994): 341–66; W. Tabbernee, *Montanist Inscriptions and Testamonia: Epigraphic Sources Illustrating the History of Montanism* (Patristic Monograph Series 16; Macon, GA: Mercer University Press, 1997), 133–339.

8. A vine and grape pattern represents the importance of viticulture, and the wreath is a known funerary symbol of victory at death: Tabbernee, *Montanist Inscriptions*, 298, 253. Only a cross indicates unique Christian identity.

9. Johnson, "Christian Business," 344.

10. Ibid., 350.

the distinctively Christian funerary monuments strongly indicates not only the Christian self-identity of the stonecutters who have designed them (even more than that of the Christian customers) but also a departure from usual Anatolian practice, which did not express religious affiliation in epitaphs.[11] The concentration of crosses in these monuments in light of the fact that use of crosses as Christian symbols in Anatolian iconography was rare even in the fourth century only reinforces the plausibility of this case.[12] Furthermore, inclusion of a Christianized curse formula in some of these epitaphs in case of violation of the tomb—the most famous one, "the Eumeneian Formula," warning the violator that he "will reckon with God" (*estai autō pros ton theon*)—strengthens the case.[13] Despite unusually heavy Christian presence in this rural area and this remarkable professional Christian self-identification, however, the workshop is less likely to have been exclusively Christian during the third century but probably employed Christians as well as non-Christians, as it did business with both Christians and non-Christians.[14] Also, this workshop, comprising at least some Christians, would have surely been engaged in business dealings with the regional economic institutions (non-Christian) created by the lines of distribution of raw stone.[15] Finally, these funerary monuments, which are "handsome and expensive," also reveal the socioeconomic level of the Christian clients, who are most likely from the agrarian population (inferred by the common funerary representations) with "a level of income sufficient to afford some kind of stone burial monument," i.e., the middling group with relative wealth.[16]

Overall, as Christianity moved up the social ladder in this period, the Christian texts repeatedly disapproved of business affairs and commercial activities, linking them to the inordinate acquisitiveness of the (Christian) rich and *those who tried to be rich*, i.e., the middling group who could have had a hope and chance of upward social mobility through those engagements.[17] The messages of not seeking to gain wealth and not envying the rich (e.g., Clement of Alexandria, *Quis div.* 2; Peter of Alexandria, *On Riches*, 55) that accompanied disapproval of business and avarice (see below), as well as the assumption that positions of honor and power (e.g., Tertullian, *Idol.* 18) were un-Christian activities, would have discouraged social mobility.[18] Yet it could have also been a reaction/response to the social reality of a strong presence

11. Ibid., 351.
12. Ibid., 352.
13. Ibid., 356–57.
14. Cf. Tabbernee, *Montanist Inscriptions,* 250.
15. Johnson, "Christian Business," 357.
16. G. J. Johnson, *Early-Christian Epitaphs from Anatolia* (SBL Texts and Translations 35; Early Christian Literature Series 8; Atlanta, GA: Scholars Press, 1995), 79.
17. Again, those who put confidence in "the [business] transactions that have made them rich" are condemned in *On Riches*, 37, attributed to Peter of Alexandria.
18. Cf. R. M. Grant, *Early Christianity and Society* (San Francisco: Harper & Row, 1977), 123.

of those socially mobile populations in local Christian assemblies.[19] With the possible exception of Irenaeus, for Christian leaders, wealth itself is morally neutral (though clearly dangerous), and following the cultural understanding, inheritance is the superior form of acquiring wealth to trade or business, which reveals their idea about socioeconomic order (cf. Eusebius, *HE* 8.14.10). Indeed, while Christianity attracted not insubstantially the socially mobile groups, upon becoming Christians, they would have to give up aspirations for upward social mobility (through accumulation of earthly fortunes). As we have seen in the case of Christians who were engaged in business activities, this implicit and explicit message against social mobility was not likely followed by those who were able in reality. Moreover, the church and clergy also played an economically significant role by serving as depositories, banks, and trustees for its members and even engaged in trades apparently as "fundraisers for charity" and business affairs for profits (especially in the later period). However, the leaders' vision of a society was largely conservative and static; they believed that people's stations (*loci*) were ordained by God (e.g., *1 Clem.* 38.2; Clement of Alexandria, *Quis div.* 3, 26; Peter of Alexandria, *On Riches* 66; Cyprian, *Epp.* 3.1.1; 8.1.1; cf. 12.1.1; Tertullian, *Cultu fem.* 2.9.1) and even that all worldly powers and honors were to be rejected as the enemies of God (Tertullian, *Idol.* 18.8). Thus, "while the concerns of blurring Christian identity projected an irreconcilable incompatibility between social mobility and Christian community—between the opportunities and status of human community and the commitment to divine community"[20] in rhetoric, the Christian engagement in business and commercial activities from the low to high level revealed certain disparities in image and reality and demonstrated the complex negotiations and identities in relation to the larger culture and society. While Christian identity was partially and indirectly associated with social immobility, Christianity of this period unprecedentedly penetrated into the circles of the socially mobile, the prominent, and the elite.

6.2. Christian Identity—Denunciation of Avarice and Luxury

In light of the generally negative tone of early Christian texts about business and commercial activities (perceived to be) motivated by unnatural greed, one can easily imagine that they would strongly denounce avarice and luxury (cf. chap. 2). This was not at all unique in a Christian circle. As mentioned in chapter 1, Greco-Roman and Jewish moralists characteristically condemned the twin

19. This kind of message would be repeated by the bishops throughout late antiquity; e.g., John Chrysostom, *Homilae in epistulam i ad Corinthios* 15:6.

20. D. E. Groh, "Christian Community in the Writings of Tertullian: An Inquiry into the Nature and Problems of Community in North African Christianity" (PhD diss., Northwestern University, 1970), 69.

vices of love of money and luxury. Nonetheless, Christian authors characterized the problem of avarice (love of money: *pleonexia*, *philarguria*, *avaritia*, *cupiditas*) essentially as idolatry (i.e., a theological problem even more than a moral problem, though they are usually intertwined; cf. Col. 3:5; Tertullian, *Idol*. 11.1) and thus as something intrinsically antithetical to Christian identity. The earliest extant sermon warns that "when we desire to acquire these [worldly] things, we fall away from the way of righteousness" (*2 Clem*. 5.7); and with dominical sayings on the impossibility of serving both God and money (cf. Luke 16:13; Matt. 6:24), it goes on to put them in an opposing relationship (6.1–5). Polycarp also admonishes the Philippians that unless they avoid avarice, they will be "polluted by idolatry, and will be judged as one of the Gentiles, who are ignorant of the Lord's judgment" (*Phil*. 11.2), and Origen likewise repeats this close link between avarice and idolatry (*Hom. in Judices* 2.3; *Hom. in Exodum* 8.4).

In the context of addressing Christian patience in the face of many ills in life, including the loss of property, Tertullian frames his argument after the dominical example of indifference toward money (*Pat*. 7.2). The Lord "has set disdain for wealth ahead of the endurance of losses, pointing out through His rejection of riches that one should make no account of the loss of them" (*Pat*. 7.3). Tertullian interprets a familiar maxim of "the desire [*cupiditas*] of money [as] the root of all evils" (cf. 1 Tim. 6:10), to mean that desire of money here refers to "the desire for that which belongs to another" (*concupiscentia alieni*) and "even that which seems to be our own belongs to another" since God is the owner of all things (*Pat*. 7.5). Thus, if Christians fret and are impatient for their material loss, they "will be found to possess a desire for money, since [they] grieve over the loss of that which is not [their] own" (*Pat*. 7.6). When Christians are unable to bear their material loss, they sin against God Himself and behave like pagans by confusing the priority of heavenly goods over earthly ones (*Pat*. 7.7, 11). Just consider to what extent the pagans would go in order to pursue wealth: "they engage in lucrative but dangerous commerce on the sea; . . . they unhesitatingly engage in transactions also in the forum, even though there be reason to fear loss; they do it, in fine, when they hire themselves out for the games and military service or when, in desolate regions, they commit robbery regardless of the wild beasts" (*Pat*. 7.12). In contrast, in view of Christian identity, it befits Christians "to give up not our life for money but money for our life, either by voluntary charity or by the patient endurance of loss" (*Pat*. 7.13).

As (pagan) impatience over material loss reveals one's inordinate desire for and attachment to wealth, which was inspired by none other than Satan (*Pat*. 5.3–4), this idolatrous desire is closely associated with the two Latin words, *ambitio* and *gloria*, with which Tertullian further probes the fundamental problem of human avarice.[21] Reflecting the current use of these terms

21. This paragraph is partially dependent on Dennis Groh's fine study: Groh, "Christian Community."

in wider literature, for Tertullian, *ambitio* is "desire without proper limits," which manifests itself in the immoderate desire for or the unrestrained use of wealth.[22] In his treatise *On the Apparel of Women* (*De cultu feminarum*), in which he addresses the wealth of Christian women that manifests in their extravagance and luxury of dress and adornment (cf. *Or.* 20.1–2), Tertullian defines *ambitio* as a vicious cycle of an unending movement with boundless desire: from scarcity (of goods/material, not its origin or use) is born the "desire to possess" (*concupiscentiam . . . habendi*); from this desire to possess comes *ambitio*, that is, immoderate desire (*immoderate habendi*) (*Cultu fem.* 1.9.1–2). Then from this unlimited *ambitio* is born "a desire of glory" (*gloria*), a "grand desire" for magnificence and self-exaltation, which in turn does not come from nature or truth but from "a vicious passion [*concupiscentia*] of the mind" (*Cultu fem.* 1.9.2; 2.9.5). Then, the insatiable desire for wealth (*ambitio* and *cupiditas*) and the unrestricted desire for self-aggrandizement (*gloria*) feed upon each other and, along with the "want of sufficiency" (*insufficientia*), result in the "worldly concupiscence" (*concupiscentia saeculi*) of striving for visible honors, dignity, and power of this passing world under God's wrath (*Ux.* 1.4.6; cf. *Cultu fem.* 2.3.2; *Idol.* 18). *Gloria* and *ambitio* drive and characterize Roman social, political, religious, and intellectual life with pursuit of public ostentation, praise, vanity, and "conspicuous consumption" (e.g., *Cultu fem.* 2.9.5; 2.10.1; 2.11.1; *Marc.* 4.34.17; *Apol.* 38.3; *Pal.* 4.6; *De anima* 52.3; *Spec.* 25.3). And although Christ abolished the worldly glory (*Idol.* 9.4), they tempt and contaminate (wealthy) Christian women in particular in the latter's efforts of "glorying in the flesh" and the world as the opposites of Christian humility (*Cultu fem.* 2.3.2; 2.9.5), sufficiency, modesty (*Ux.* 1.4.7), and frugality (*Spec.* 7.5).

If avarice, the acquisitive spirit for earthly goods, confuses and undoes Christian identity for lay people, how much more for the leaders, who were apparently so vulnerable to this temptation? Even in the Pastoral Letters, one of the repeated qualifications for the leaders was that they be "not a lover of money" (1 Tim. 3:3, 8; Titus 1:7; cf. 2 Tim. 3:2). Polycarp, dealing with the problem of an avaricious presbyter, Valens, in his letter (*Phil.* 11.1–4) reiterates this same qualification for deacons and presbyters as well as others, including widows (4.3; 5.2; 6.1). As the *Didache* commands the faithful to shun a prophet who demands money (11.12), the *Ascension of Isaiah* decries many elders (presbyters) and shepherds (bishops) who "exchange the glory of the robes of the saints for the robes of those who love money" in the "last days" (i.e., the current days of the Christian redactor, ca. 100 CE) (24–26). The pre-Constantine proto-orthodox church accused sectarian and heterodoxical leaders of greed as a way

22. Ibid., 72; D. E. Groh, "Tertullian's Polemic against Social Co-optation," *Church History* 40 (1971): 9. For examples of these terms in the Latin texts, see Groh, "Christian Community," 72–73, 152–54; Groh, "Tertullian's Polemic," 9nn14–15; 10nn23–25.

to distinguish them from the "authentic," "orthodox" Christians (Eusebius, *HE* 5.18–19; 7.30–31). For example, Eusebius reports that according to Apollonius, confessors of the New Prophecy are impostors (not unlike Peregrinus in Lucian's account) who, driven by their covetousness, "exchanged prison for wealth" and would fail "the test of fruits of prophets" by engaging in such activities as lending money, loving ornaments, and gambling (*HE* 5.18.5–9). Eusebius also underscores that Paul of Samosata, "though he was formerly poor and penniless," has come "to possess abundant wealth, as a result of lawless deeds and sacrilegious plundering and extortions exacted from the brethren by threats" (*HE* 7.30.7). Paul's insatiable greed manifests in how he "promises to help them for money, yet breaks his word"; and Paul's basic attitude to ministry is that he "considers that godliness is a way of gain" (*HE* 7.30.7).

Avarice, the idolatrous and irrational lust of money or wealth, goes hand in hand with luxury (*tryphē*), an idolatrous and irrational display of one's wealth. Clement of Alexandria, addressing his cultured audience, indulges in describing a "disease" of avarice and outrageous and even comical displays of luxury among the refined elites, from clothing, food, vessels, crowns, shoes, to jewelries and ornaments (e.g., *Paed.* 2.3, 8, 11–13). Christians who are serious about salvation must understand and settle the first principle in their minds "that all that we possess is given to us for use, and use for sufficiency, which one may attain to by a few things" (*Paed.* 2.3.39), whereas those with love of money, "the stronghold of evil," from that greed "take delight in what they have hoarded up" (*Paed.* 2.3.39). The latter will "never reach the kingdom of heaven, sick for the things of the world, and living proudly through luxury" (*Paed.* 2.3.38). Clement highlights the unnatural and thus degenerate nature of avarice and luxury: "Love of wealth displaces a man from the right mode of life, and induces him to cease from feeling shame at what is shameful" (*Paed.* 3.7.37). Luxury deranges all things and disgraces a person; "a luxurious niceness seeks everything, attempts everything, forces everything, coerces nature" (*Paed.* 3.3.21). A Christian who lives in luxury (which itself is an oxymoron) commits not only a "sin of commission" (avarice, vanity, self-love, and attachment to the world) (cf. *Paed.* 3.6.34–36), but also a "sin of omission" by neglecting the commandment of loving one's neighbor (*Paed.* 2.13.120). "It is monstrous for one to live in luxury, while many are in want. How much more glorious is it to do good to many [i.e., giving alms], than to live sumptuously!" says Clement (*Paed.* 2.13.120). The very existence of the needy and the poor (yes, there are many who are in want) testifies to the outrage of luxury, especially in its social ramification. God created all things for all people; for the rich to hoard and appropriate an undue share of goods and wealth beyond what is necessary and useful, is to oppose God's very creative purpose and intent (*Paed.* 2.13.120).[23]

---

23. Clement's understanding of natural or proper wealth based on its "use" and "necessity" in contrast to unnatural or irrational wealth, i.e., superfluity with illiberality (nonuse) or luxury

Thus avarice and luxury result in eternally damning consequences in both vertical relationship with God and horizontal relationship with humanity. Note further how Clement's argument for common use of property as a principle against avarice and luxury is informed by his doctrine of creation:

> God created our race for sharing [*koinōnia*] beginning by giving out what belonged to God, God's own Word [*logos*], making it common [*koinos*] to all humans, and creating all things for all. Therefore all things are common [*koina*]. . . . To say therefore, "I have more than I need, why not enjoy?" is neither human nor proper to sharing [*koinōnikon*]. . . . For I know quite well that God has given us the power to use; but only to the limit of that which is necessary; and that God also willed that the use be in common. (*Paed.* 2.13.120, PG [trans. Gonzalez])

The purpose of God's creation of humanity is for sharing, which is demonstrated first by God's sharing of the divine logos. What makes us human is our sharing in this logos; hence, for anyone not to share with others what is meant to be shared, i.e., "all things" created, rebels against the very *koinonia* that is a foundation and principle of our creation.[24] Although we are created for a higher order than mere material things of the world that are transient, God has made them for our use, and *all humans* are given access to these material things as means of necessary sustenance (*Strom.* 4.13). Thus, our "right" of property is limited by the legitimate use made of it—i.e., meeting our needs *and* the needs of fellow humans—"avoiding all excess and inordinate affection" (*Strom.* 4.13; cf. *Quis div.* 14, 26).[25]

6.3. Christian Identity—Almsgiving as Christian Freedom, Obligation, and a Boundary Marker

If renunciation of avarice and luxury constituted a negative boundary marker for Christian identity, almsgiving and sharing constituted Christians' positive

---

(misuse), is very much like Plutarch's line of argument in his *On Love of Wealth*, who in turn follows that of classical authors.

24. Lactantius acknowledges the Golden Age (with the rule of Saturn) as the time of worship of one true God, where people lived in harmony and contentment and shared the God-given land in which "all need was met in common" as intended by God (*Inst.* 5.5.5, quoting Virgil). However, for Lactantius, the justice and *aequitas* that marked the Golden Age did not mean doing away with private property or social distinction but entailed voluntary sharing of goods by the rich with the poor (*Inst.* 5.5.7–8). Here Lactantius sets up a primeval social paradigm to which he will later return for envisioning a Christian social ideal in the present.

25. Cf. Peter of Alexandria, *On Riches* 14: "He [God] did not give it [wealth] to you [a rich man] for you to revel in it with worthless men and frivolous people or mocking theater performers. Nor did he give it to you so you could hide it in the earth, nor did he give it to you so you could spend it on large houses beyond the standard of life of the men of old. But he has given it to you so you (could) eat and give to the poor with it and those who are in need."

boundary marker. We can see three modes of this theological and rhetorical construction. First, Christians highlight a general dichotomy between greed/luxury and almsgiving/charity, implicitly associating the former with non-Christian disposition and behavior and the latter with Christian ones. This antithesis appears in the teachings of the Two Ways in the *Didache*, *Epistle of Barnabas*, and *Hermas*. While avarice is a staple in the list of the way of eternal death and punishment (*Did.* 5.1; cf. 2.6; 3.5; *Barn.* 20.1), the way of life and light involves generous and cheerful almsgiving to those in need in *Didache* (1.5–6; 4.5–8) and *Epistle of Barnabas* (19.8, 9, 11). *Hermas*'s version of the Two Ways includes two kinds of angels (*Mand.* 6.2), self-control (*Mand.* 8.1–11), desire (*Mand.* 12.1.1–3.1), and luxury (*Sim.* 6.1–5). As one might imagine, to the angel of wickedness belong "extravagant kinds of foods and drink, . . . various kinds of unnecessary luxuries, . . . and greed" and to the angel of righteousness, contentment, and every righteous deed (*Mand.* 6.5, 3), which is specified throughout the book especially as "serving widows, looking after orphans and those in need, delivering God's servants in distress, being hospitable, . . . becoming more needy than all other men, . . . not oppressing debtors and those in need, and whatever else is like these" (*Mand.* 8.10). Hermas is commanded not to exercise self-control regarding doing good works such as those listed above but to be self-controlled regarding evil, including "wicked luxury, many kinds of food and the extravagance of wealth, . . . greed, . . . and whatever else is like these" (*Mand.* 8.3). The same kinds of vices and virtues correspond to the destructive evil desires that should be rejected ("extravagance of wealth, and many needless things to eat and drink, and many other foolish luxuries") and the desire of righteousness that must be clothed, respectively (*Mand.* 12.2.1; 12.3.1). The two kinds of luxury eventually parallel the two desires but require spiritual discernment and determination: Destructive luxury is forgetting God's commandments and living according to the worldly passions and pleasure. Indistinguishable from the life of non-Christians, this luxury is deceptive because it initially comes with apparent attraction to those who are insensitive (*Sim.* 6.5.5). But those who are engaged in salvific luxury indulge in "doing good" in obedience of God's commandments.[26] Ultimately, wicked luxuries bring about self-inflicted this-worldly afflictions and torments such as illnesses, losses, and deprivations of worldly things, whereas redemptive luxuries carry the practitioners away with the distinctively Christian pleasure of doing good (*Sim.* 6.5.7; 6.3.4). Once again, these catalogs of virtues and vices that mark Christian identity positively and negatively are concrete and socially oriented practices with eternal consequences.[27]

Other Christian texts contrast Christian almsgiving and care of the poor explicitly with pagan avarice and enslavement to earthly goods. Tertullian, as

26. Cf. Clement of Alexandria, *Paed.* 2.13.120.
27. C. Osiek, *The Shepherd of Hermas: A Commentary* (Hermeneia; Minneapolis: Augsburg Fortress, 1999), 130.

he mocks the begging of pagan gods for alms, boasts of Christian compassion, which discerns the truly needy and provides them with practical help: "our compassion spends more street by street than your religion temple by temple" (*Apol.* 42.8). Pagans' notion of sharing property is so skewed that they share their own wives with friends, but Christians share property—everything except their wives—to meet the needs of those suffering (*Apol.* 39.11–13).[28] In the previously mentioned treatise, *On Patience*, Tertullian further states that contrary to pagans who are obsessed with seeking and hoarding wealth and cannot bear its loss (*Pat.* 7.11–12), Christian ability to endure loss of property ultimately points to Christian liberty and willingness to give and share with the poor: "Patience to endure, shown on occasions of loss, is a training in giving and sharing. He who does not fear loss is not reluctant to give" (*Pat.* 7.9). As a matter of fact, the *Apostolic Tradition* prescribes that candidates for baptism (a central boundary rite for Christians as it formally separates Christians from non-Christians) be examined publically on whether they honored the widows (see 1 Tim. 5:3), visited the sick (see Matt. 25:36), and were thorough in performing good works (20.1). Christian identity is predicated upon these acts of orthopraxis as much as their orthodoxy, as the next point further confirms.

Second, caring for and sharing possessions with the less fortunate is what distinguishes the "authentic" and "orthodox" Christians from the sectarian and "heretical" so-called Christians. Ignatius of Antioch, in his opposition to the docetists who deny the physical reality of Jesus Christ, including his passion, warns the Smyrneans that they also deny tangible love and physical care for those afflicted (as opposed to orthodox Christians): "They [the docetists] have no concern for love, none for the widow, none for the orphan, none for the oppressed, none for the prisoner or the one released, none for the hungry or thirsty" (*Smyrn.* 6.2).[29] While the *Didache* links the judgment scene of Matt. 5:25–26[30] to almsgiving where the recipient without real need who takes advantage of the community's generosity would be under judgment (*Did.* 1.5),[31] the

28. Cf. Lactantius's criticism of Plato's idea of communism, including sharing of wives, in *Inst.* 3.21.

29. Note Jesus's rejection of the traditional triad of piety in the *Gospel of Thomas*, Saying 14: "If you fast, you will bring sin upon yourselves, and if you pray, you will be condemned, and if you give to charity, you will harm your spirits." Compare Saying 6: "His disciples asked him and said to him, 'Do you want us to fast? How should we pray? Should we give to charity? What diet should we observe?' Jesus said, 'Don't lie, and don't do what you hate, because all things are disclosed before heaven. After all, there is nothing hidden that won't be revealed, and there is nothing covered up that will remain undisclosed.'"

30. "Come to terms quickly with your accuser while you are on the way to court with him, or your accuser may hand you over to the judge, and the judge to the guard, and you will be thrown into prison. Truly I tell you, you will never get out until you have paid the last penny."

31. "But the one who receives without a need will have to testify why he received what he did, and for what purpose. And he will be thrown in prison and interrogated about what he did; and he will not get out until he pays back every last cent."

Carpocratians, a little-known gnostic sect, interpret these verses as referring to death and reincarnation, according to Irenaeus (*Haer.* 1.25.4).[32] Also, Clement of Alexandria takes issue with communism of property by the Carpocratians, who followed Plato's model, including sharing of wives (criticized by Tertullian earlier), as opposed to private property and almsgiving, which were deemed authentic Christian practices (*Strom.* 3.6.54–56). If Clement's doctrine of creation is a basis of his argument against avarice and luxury (as well as lust), it also serves as the basis of his argument against wrongful renunciation of God-given private property (and chaste marriage) (cf. *Quis div.* 11–13). The Carpocratians' "righteousness" in their communism is in fact "sharing in a fellowship of immorality" since it hinders one from possessing one's own goods and thus prevents one from giving, doing good to, and sharing with those in need as the Scripture commands (*Strom.* 3.6.54.1–4). Personal possessions, whose purpose is to do good to the poor, are presupposed in many scriptural commands in order to give and share earthly, temporal property with the poor with the promise of eternal reward in heaven; in the Lord's own identification with "one of the least of these" who received acts of mercy in Matt. 25:35–40 ("The Sheep and the Goats"); and in his words of judgment against those who ignored these Christian acts of justice (*Strom.* 3.6.54.3–56.3; cf. *Paed.* 3.6.36; cf. *Quis div.* 14, 26; Cyprian, *Don.* 11); for the world consists of "those who give and those who receive" (*Strom.* 3.6.55.1). The problem of the rich young man (Mark 10:19 and parallels) was not that he was rich per se but that his obedience to the law did not in fact fulfill the commandment of loving his neighbor as himself with his riches (*Strom.* 3.6.55.2). Thus, *both* the heretics who shun personal property, rejecting the goodness of material creation, *and* those who pursue "unjust and insatiable acquisition" of material wealth, lacking self-control, miss the mark and sin against God's justice and grace (*Strom.* 3.6.56.1–57.2).

Moreover, Irenaeus, in the context of refuting Marcion's charge that Christ did away with the Mosaic law, shows that Christ rather fulfilled and perfected it by extending its application. Thus, going beyond the law of tithes, Christ enjoined his followers "to share all our possessions with the poor"; and he taught "not to love our neighbors only, but even our enemies; and not merely to be liberal givers and bestowers, but even that we should present a gratuitous gift to those who take away our goods" (*Haer.* 4.13.3). As Irenaeus is careful to stress the continuity between the Mosaic law and Christ's reinterpretation of the law against Marcion, he also makes clear that Christians are to be defined by this perfected law of Christ.[33]

32. Cf. Grant, *Early Christianity and Society*, 129.

33. Apologist Theophilus of Antioch underscores the harmony and consistency between "the teaching of the [OT] prophets and the gospels" concerning the law of justice "because all the inspired men made utterances by means of the one Spirit of God" (*Autol.* 12). He then quotes a number of prophetic texts commanding doing justice to the weak and the poor by showing acts

In the *Acts of Peter*, along with miracles and sexual abstinence (especially of high-ranking Roman matrons), charity constitutes a crucial part of true Christian identity, particularly in the events surrounding conversion of the wealthy. The wealthy and the privileged—i.e., senators, knights, wealthy women and matrons (30)—consistently appear not only as the recipients of the Christian message but also as witnesses of *and* participants in a contest of power between the Christian God, mediated by the apostle Peter, and the devil, mediated by Simon Magus. And their use of wealth attests to either their true conversion and the validity of Petrine Christianity or their false conversion and the momentary triumph of the counterfeit Simonian cult. I will now zoom in on four specific characters in the *Acts* for their use of wealth in relation to their authentic Christian self-definition.

The first character is Senator Marcellus, a prominent convert, whose charity and hospitality accorded him distinction in the Roman Christian community—well, until he follows Simon through his magic (*Acts Pet.* 8). He housed widows, fed orphans, acted as a patron for the poor, and protected the pilgrims and the poor (8); he was a chief benefactor of the Christians even to the extent that the emperor complained that Marcellus would "rob the provinces to benefit the Christians" (8). However, his charity and hospitality take a sharp turn to the opposite direction once he is won over by Simon Magus. Marcellus not only "repents" (*paenitetur*) of his previous good deeds but also considers them a waste and loss, lamenting, "So much wealth have I spent for such a long time in the foolish belief that I spent it for the knowledge of God" (8). He even beats a pilgrim in rage and drives him off by saying, "If only I had not spent so much money on those imposters" (8). These two quotes reveal an "established" contemporary theological assumption that is positively affirmed later in the *Acts*: one could, in fact should, spend wealth for the knowledge of God *by* spending it on the needy and the helpless. How people, particularly the wealthy, spend their wealth has direct implications for their salvation, as we discussed above in chapter 3. While Marcellus is furious about the apparent "fraud" and "cheating" of Christian charities, he redirects his hospitality to Simon by hosting him in his house and erecting a statue to him. When confronted by Peter's presence, however, Marcellus comes to his senses and repents of his sins with this confession: "If I knew, Peter, that you could be won over with money, I would give my whole fortune; I would have given it to you and despised it, in order to regain my soul. . . . [Simon] seduced me only because he said that he was the power of God" (10). After witnessing the power of God through Peter's miracles, Marcellus then attacks Simon,

---

of mercy, such as Isa. 58:6–7: "Dissolve . . . every bond of iniquity, loosen the knots of violent dealings, send away the wounded with forgiveness, and tear asunder every unjust contract, break your bread for the hungry, and bring the homeless poor into your house; if you see someone naked, clothe him, and do not despise your own relatives" (This Isaiah translation comes from Theophilus's *Ad Auto*.).

labeling him as a "destroyer" (corruptor) of Marcellus's soul and a deceiver, and his servants beat Simon and drive him off (14). This episode discloses an interesting dynamic among the power of God, salvation, and the use of wealth. Whereas Simon's magic and pretension as the power of God deceived Marcellus to follow him and thus to withdraw his charity and reverse his hospitality, the true power of God displayed by Peter's miracles leads Marcellus to reconvert; but his authentic reconversion to true Christian faith is only demonstrated by redirection of his hospitality and restoration of his charity. Therefore, after "purifying" his house from the vestige of Simon, Marcellus invites widows and elders to his house and promises each of them a piece of gold "for the sake of their ministry" (*ministerii*) as they pray for Marcellus (19); Peter is invited to pray with them and to "grace their prayers" for Marcellus (19). Marcellus is reminded of "right use of money" one last time. After his crucifixion and costly burial provided by Marcellus, Peter appears in Marcellus's dream and chastises him: "What you spent on the dead is lost. For though alive you were like a dead man caring for the dead" (40). This word stands as a poignant contrast to what Marcellus had once thought a waste and loss: charity and hospitality. Even honoring Peter, the mediator and bearer of God, in decent burial becomes a loss when compared to the acts of hospitality and charity to the poor (the living); they are fundamental to being a Christian.

The second character is introduced by Peter when he recollects his earlier confrontation with Simon in Judea (*Acts Pet.* 17). Simon stayed in the house of a wealthy woman of distinction, Eubola, but stole all of her gold through his magic. Eubola, unaware of Simon's deception and scheme, instead tortured her servants for robbery. Nevertheless, when Peter learns of this incident through a dream, he exposes to Eubola Simon's ploy to get profit from selling her stolen gold. As Peter instructs her to true Christian faith, his promise of full restoration of her property comes with a clear mandate that "she renounces the present world and seeks an everlasting comfort" (17); the purpose of the restoration of her property is so as to give it to the care of the poor. Interestingly, Peter attributes the cause of Simon's robbery to Eubola's impiety and idolatry: "For when you meant to celebrate a festival and put up your idol and veiled it and put out all the ornaments upon a stand, he [Simon] had brought in two young men whom none of you saw; and they made an incantation and stole your ornaments and disappeared" (17). Eubola's turning from "wickedness and perversion to the God" (*impie et contrario contra deum*) of all truth and righteousness involves belief not in "words, but in works and deeds" (*fides, sed in operibus et factis*) (17). Eubola's promise of right use of wealth (here understood as renunciation of the world) precedes, and its fulfillment follows, her conversion to true faith; in fact, the *Acts* describes this relationship in a succinct, telling way: "Eubola, after recovering her property, gave it for the service of the poor [*ministerium pauperorum*]; she believed in the Lord Jesus Christ and was strengthened; she despised and renounced this world, supported the widows and orphans, clothed the poor, and after a long time fell asleep" (17). Once again, genuine Christian conversion accompanies almsgiving and charity while idolatry and perversion of faith can actually lead to loss of wealth.

The contest of miracles between Peter and Simon over resurrection provides a specific context for the use of wealth by the third character. The mother of a senator, Nicostratus, implores Peter in the public spectacle to raise her dead son. Peter then asks the Roman multitude to be the judge and challenges Simon, who once enjoyed their hospitality, to restore the senator. Simon on his part incites the crowd to cast Peter out of the city when he succeeds. However, Simon succeeds only in making the son's head move and his eyes open. Peter exposes it as a magical sham and Simon as a "sorcerer" (*Acts Pet.* 28) and a "messenger of the devil" (32). Raised by Peter, the senator says to him, "I beg you . . . let us go to our Lord Jesus" (28). Here, what is striking is Peter's request to the mother immediately before he raises the senator: first, the freed slaves remain free even after the resurrection of the senator; second, they receive their financial subsistence as before; third, they remain with the senator, i.e., continue to serve him as their patron.[34] The mother concedes to Peter's request (28); but Peter goes even further: "Let the remainder be distributed to the widows" (28). Thus, this story ends with the donation of two thousand gold pieces by the mother and four thousand gold pieces by the senator for the widows; the senator here makes sure that he offers "the double gift" of his mother's since it is he who has experienced the power of God. The intricate dynamic of miracle (i.e., power of the Christian God), conversion, and use of wealth is powerfully displayed once again. The genuine Christian identity of the wealthy is only authenticated by their acts of charity.

We can highlight how the use of wealth by these three rich converts becomes a critical identity marker, in contrast to the use of wealth by Simon Magus, our fourth character, who is clearly an antagonist and perverter of true Christianity in the *Acts*. Its portrayal of Simon as a deviant, deceiver, sorcerer, son of the devil, etc., is directly connected to his avarice and wrongful use of wealth. In contrast to Peter, Simon attempts to buy the power of miracle (23; cf. Acts 8:18), sells his "salvation" and magic for money for himself (10, 32), and exploits his converts' hospitality with magic for his personal gain as in the cases of Marcellus and Eubola (cf. 8, 17); furthermore, he shamelessly diverts the charity and hospitality of his wealthy followers for the poor to himself (cf. 8, 17). Thus, Simon, the epitome of a manipulative heretic, demonstrates his treachery and magic through his love of money.[35]

This brief examination shows that in the *Acts of Peter*, as in other early Christian texts, charity and hospitality are indispensable and determinative

---

34. P. Lampe, *From Paul to Valentinus: Christians at Rome in the First Two Centuries* (trans. M. Steinhauser; ed. M. D. Johnson; Minneapolis: Fortress, 2003), 124.

35. See Lucian, *On the Lover of Lies* 14–15, for a connection between magic and money; cf. 1 Tim. 6:10.

features of authentic Christian self-definition and identity, especially for wealthy converts. And if one can save one's soul by right use of money, the reverse is also true; one can destroy one's soul and lead others astray by wrong use of money. This portrayal is part of a Christian ideal—that the Christian attitude toward and use of wealth was a critical identity marker that distinguished genuine Christians from false Christians.

Ultimately, charity is a fundamental marker for Christian identity because it is an imitation of God's character—generosity and *philanthrōpia*. According to *1 Clement*, Christians should be eager and zealous to accomplish "every good work" (*pan ergon agathon*)—prominently almsgiving and care of the poor[36]—following after God, who rejoices in his works and formed humans "as a representation of his own image" (33.1–34.4). The *Epistle of Diognetus* singularly defines an imitator of God as a Christian who takes up a burden of a "neighbor," who wants to help those in need using one's own abundance, or who provides for the destitute from one's God-given possessions (10.6)—this is how one becomes a "god" to those who receive the *beneficia* (10.6) in contrast to those who oppress one's neighbors, desire to have more than the weak, or coerce those who are in need using wealth (10.5). Cyprian looks back in nostalgia at the early Christian practice of selling one's possessions and cheerfully presenting the apostles with the proceeds to be distributed to the poor so as for the community to share all things "in common" with "one heart and one soul" (Acts 4:32; *Eleem.* 25). Cyprian exclaims this as a transformation of becoming "sons of God by spiritual birth," which demonstrates how the spiritual transformation and material sharing go together in a Christian community. This is "to imitate by the heavenly law the equity of God the Father" (*Eleem.* 25). Similar to Clement of Alexandria's argument for common use of God's created goods, but in a different context (almsgiving as an imitation of God), Cyprian goes on: "For whatever is of God is common in our use; nor is any one excluded from His benefits and His gifts, so as to prevent the whole human race from enjoying equally the divine goodness and liberality" (25). That Cyprian, like Clement and Lactantius, did not mean abolition of private property by common use is clear by his examples of "common property": sun, rain, wind, sleep, stars, and the moon. However, common access to and common use and enjoyment of these natural resources is an example of God's equity,[37] and the Christian "who labour[s] charitably," i.e., the one who "shares his returns and his fruits with the

---

36. Cf. *Hermas*, *Vis.* 3.5.4; 3.9.5; *Mand.* 2.4; 8.10.

37. Lactantius's understanding of God's equity is that God created all to be wise, bestowed fairness and virtue on all people, and promised all of them immortality (5.14.16–17); he divides his light equally between all and supplies food and sleep to all and therefore "no one is cut off from God's celestial benevolence" (5.14.16, 17). We are "all his children with equal rights" because God is "the same father to everyone" (5.14.17). Like Cyprian, here the kind of *aequitas* that Lactantius has in mind turns out to be God's general providence and provision for humanity and our equal access and rights to God as his children.

fraternity, while he is common and just in his gratuitous bounties, is an imitator of God the Father" (*Eleem.* 25, 26). As for Clement and Lactantius, for Cyprian imitation of God's equity and justice does not mean social egalitarianism with distribution of equal portions to everyone, but means meeting the differing needs of others with God-given resources (which implies unequal distribution due to different needs) so as to ensure that every needy person in the community is included in the sharing (distribution) of God's gracious gifts and plentitude.

6.4. The Constantinian Reformation—Church, Wealth, and Public Service

When Constantine seized the imperial power (in the West) with the power of the Christian God (312 CE), the church had been functioning as a formidable social and economic institution with massive operation of charity, as we have seen. Constantine's unprecedented imperial patronage of the church did not prompt a brand-new theological base for the work the church had been doing, which by then had been securely established, but it transformed the scale of the church's charity and wealth and the impact they had on Roman society. His joint edict of toleration with Licinius (the so-called Edict of Milan, 313 CE) officially acknowledged what had been a de facto reality of the church's ownership of buildings, cemeteries, gardens, and other movable and immovable properties throughout the third century by ordering their restoration (Lactantius, *Mort.* 48; Eusebius, *HE* 10.5.9–11). Then he granted the churches and bishops financial assistance (3,000 *folles*) that would turn into regular support (cf. Eusebius, *HE* 10.2.2; 10.6) and clerical exemption from all compulsory public services and personal taxes so that they could devote themselves to worshiping their God on behalf of their communities and the empire (Eusebius, *HE* 10.12; *Cod. theod.* 16.2). Although in these measures—religious freedom, financial subsidy, and clerical exemption—Constantine did not necessarily go beyond extending to Christian churches the privileges that the official cults of the empire enjoyed, with further "pro-Christian" policies before and after his sole reign of the empire in 324 CE, their overall impact was nothing less than revolutionary. He exempted church lands and other properties, which would keep growing from pious endowments, from taxation, and in fact, he himself endowed lands in Italy, Africa, Crete, and Gaul that produced more than two hundred pounds of gold a year.[38] He also established "a system of gifts of food to churches, grain allowances to nuns, widows, and others in church service,"[39] presented extensive gold and silver ornaments to the church of Rome (*Liber Pontificalis* 34), and in sum provided the church with "the abundance of good things" (Eusebius, *HE*

---

38. Grant, *Early Christianity and Society*, 152.
39. R. MacMullen, *Christianizing the Roman Empire (AD 100–400)* (New Haven: Yale University Press, 1984), 49.

10.8.1). Furthermore, Constantine created an ecclesiastical court for appeals cases, open to both Christians and non-Christians, especially for the poor and the powerless, that granted bishops the final judicial authority in arbitrating civil suits (*episcopalis audientia*; *Cod. theod.* 1.27.1).[40] The most well-known support for Christianity is Constantine's extraordinary church buildings throughout the empire, particularly in Rome, Antioch, Constantinople, and the Holy Land: for example, St. Peter's and the Basilica of St. Laurentius (outside the walls) in Rome, the Golden Church in Antioch, the Church of the Twelve Apostles in Constantinople, and churches on the supposed sites of Golgotha, of Christ's resurrection, and at Mamre for the theophany to Abraham (Eusebius, *Life of Constantine* 3.25–43, 48, 51–53). And under his reign, numerous "festivals of dedication in the cities and consecrations of the newly-built houses of prayer," though not all imperially funded, were celebrated (Eusebius, *HE* 10.3.1).

All of these remarkable imperial benefactions on behalf of the Christian church (restricted to the Great Church, not extended to schismatics and heretics), however, came with some strings attached. Aside from other political reasons and purposes, with imperial largesse, Constantine made the church not only officially visible (much more so than before) but also accountable to the public for the very public gifts it received. Up to this point, the church received offerings from the faithful, especially the middling group and the wealthy, because it primarily cared for the poor of its own, i.e., Christians. Theoretically, the clergy were accountable to the bishop as the bishop was ultimately accountable to God alone for the handling of those offerings, although practically, the faithful, especially those who had wealth and high birth and contributed sizable sums, would attempt to keep the bishops and the rest of the clergy in check; the bishops would try to negotiate their patronal power over the common chests with those faithful even as they securely controlled the whole operation of charity and financial flows of the church. As Peter Brown has argued and shown, "by a slight but significant shift of emphasis, traditional Christian charity to fellow believers within the Christian community came to be regarded as a public service, as a more general 'care of the poor' performed in return for public privileges."[41] With this shift, Christian identity was all the more linked to the church's care of the poor in Roman society, both Christians and non-Christians, as "the rich must assume the secular obligations and the poor must be supported by the wealth of the churches" (*Cod. theod.* 16.2.6); the church would literally act as a mediator between the rich and the poor of the society. While the church and clergy acted as patrons of

40. Scholars differ on assessing the functionality and effectiveness of this bishops' court. Peter Brown is more positive, even using the phrase, "advocacy revolution," in *Poverty and Leadership in the Later Roman Empire* (Hanover, NH: University Press of New England, 2002), 69–70, 80–83, whereas P. Allen, B. Neil, and W. Mayer are more skeptical in *Preaching Poverty in Late Antiquity: Perceptions and Realities* (Leipzig: Evangelische Verlagsanstalt, 2009), 226–27.

41. Brown, *Poverty and Leadership*, 31.

their community, especially in relation to the poor and other dependents, they acted "as megaclients" with respect to the empire and the emperors, "begging on behalf of the poor, the hungry, the sick, prisoners for whom [they] paid ransoms, all ideally with no strings attached."[42] The church and clergy would then be directly accountable to the imperial authority for this task "as challenges to the privileges of the clergy," and the bishop became primarily identified as the "lover of the poor" and the "governor of the poor" par excellence in late antiquity.[43] Thus, Constantine delegated distribution of grain dole and clothing to the bishops for the continuing care of widows, orphans, the elderly, and the poor who were registered on the church lists as the "official" poor; and the church in Antioch, for example, received thirty-six thousand measures of grain, an amount sufficient for supporting a thousand people for a year.[44] Moreover, Constantine made burial services available free of charge under the direction of the clergy.[45] For this sort of support and responsibility, the clergy (bishops) would have to be ready to give an account of the use of those resources on behalf of these publically registered poor people.[46] A negative case involved Athanasius of Alexandria, the champion of the Nicene party, who was accused by his Arian enemies of selling the grain received from Constantine (supposedly headed for Libyan and Egyptian widows) in the private market and keeping the funds, while he apparently tried to have that grain reach the orthodox faithful, not Arians.[47] Conversely, Athanasius accused the Arians, who were supported by Constantius, of failing to care for the destitute and widows as well as mistreating those who showed mercy and looked after the poor.[48]

As the institutional and public responsibility of the church for the care of the poor in exchange for imperial and private gifts and privileges became clear to those inside and outside the church, this did not certainly mean that the faithful were off the hook from their obligation of almsgiving and charity. Although there was hardly a new theological basis of almsgiving that had not already been

42. Allen, Neil, and Mayer, *Preaching Poverty*, 220.

43. Brown, *Poverty and Leadership*, 32, 1, 45. We have discussed the bishop as the "lover of the poor" already in the third century in chapter 5.

44. Theophanes, *Chronicle* 29; Eusebius, *Life of Constantine* 4.28; Grant, *Early Christianity and Society*, 144; Finn, *Almsgiving in the Later Roman Empire*, 32, 108–15. Constantine legislated two laws on the indigent (315 and 322 CE): the first on providing the indigent parents of newborns with food by the imperial officer upon request; the second on providing the indigent parents with grain to prevent selling their children into slavery (*Cod. theod.* 11.27.1–2).

45. P. Brown, *Power and Persuasion in Late Antiquity: Toward a Christian Empire* (Madison: University of Wisconsin Press, 1992), 102.

46. Brown, *Poverty and Leadership*, 32.

47. *Apol. sec.* (*Defense against Arians*) 18.2; see T. D. Barnes, *Athanasius and Constantius: Theology and Politics in the Constantinian Empire* (Cambridge, MA: Harvard University Press, 1993), 37–38, 177–78.

48. *Historia Arianorum* (*History of the Arians*), 7.61.

addressed, church leaders tirelessly exhorted the faithful to almsgiving and charity with further theological augmentation. Familiar (and interconnected) themes
continued to appear in the writings of the Latin, Greek, and Syriac Fathers now
as the established church tradition (e.g., Ambrose, Jerome, Augustine, Basil the
Great, Gregory Nazianzen, Gregory of Nyssa, John Chrysostom, and Ephrem
the Syrian): for instance, earthly wealth versus heavenly wealth; almsgiving as
effecting atonement for sin and pious lending to God; the symbiotic exchange
between the rich and the poor; the pious poor and the wicked rich; God's creative intent of common use for humanity; and identification of the poor with
Christ. The last point, which had been seen in Clement of Alexandria (*Quis
div*. 33; *Strom*. 3.6.54.3) and Cyprian (*Eleem*. 23), received particular attention
and underwent significant development in the post-Constantinian period and
beyond.[49] Based on Matthew 25:31–45, a classic message now with universal
application would be set for the rest of Christian history: in *every* poor person
(regardless of one's Christian faith), Christ is fed, given to drink, and welcomed
as a guest, so that "whatever is given to the poor is given to him [Christ]."[50] The
poor person identified with Christ may be Christian or non-Christian in light
of the public interest the church is serving. It is significant that only in the post-
Constantinian era with the public service of the church that the non-Christians
were *explicitly* included as legitimate recipients of alms by the church.[51] By the
time of Augustine, non-Christians apparently took this "universal" service of
the church for granted: "How many people there are nowadays who are not yet
Christians who run to church and ask for the Church's assistance! They want
temporal help for themselves, although as yet they don't want to reign with us
in eternity."[52] Thus, we see once again how theology influences, supports, and
accommodates the changing social reality and practices.

6.5. Monasticism, Poverty, and Public Service

The Constantinian reformation not only brought about a new era of peace,
privilege, and responsibility for the church but also ushered in (organized)

49. See B. Ramsey, "Almsgiving in the Latin Church: The Late Fourth and Early Fifth Centuries," *TS* 43 (1982): 226–59.
50. Pelagius, *2 ep. ad Cor*. 8.9–10 [PL 21.1157]. Ambrose also stated, "Minister to a poor
person and you have served Christ" (*De uiduis* 9.54 [PL 16.251]).
51. Possibly an exception may be Tertullian's imaginary scenario in his discussion of idolatry:
"To be blessed in the name of the gods of the heathens is to be cursed in the name of God. If I
give someone an alms or confer a benefit on him, and that man prays that his gods or the genius
of the colony may be propitious to me, my gift or benefit will therewith be a homage to the idols
in whose name he returns to me his blessing, which is his thank. But why should he not know
that I acted for the sake of God, in order that it is rather God who is glorified, and that it is not
the demons who are honoured by that which I have done for the sake of God?" (*Idol*. 22.1–2).
52. Augustine, *Enarrationes in Psalmos* 47 [46], 5 (CCSL 38.532).

monastic movements against the backdrop of imperial Christianity—a mixed bag of opportunism, nominalism, coercion, and genuine spiritual and ecclesiastical growth and influence on society. With the unprecedented development and popularity of the monastic lifestyle and movement, a new group of "the poor" emerged: the ascetics who practiced voluntary poverty by renouncing one's private property (as well as social and familial ties) and/or sharing possessions in common with monastic colleagues in communities. Ascetics were not a new group of Christians in the time of Constantinian peace but constituted a "new" formidable Christian elite who came to be both entitled to alms and dispensers of alms in complement and competition with the clergy at times.[53] While these monks individually renounced all worldly attachments, including possessions, many, if not most, cenobitic monastics could count on sufficient shelter, clothing, regular meals, and "excellent" health care for the rest of their lives due to the economic stability of monastic communities.[54] The monastic brotherhood usually engaged in local enterprises of various goods, for example, the production of oil in northern Syria or around Bethlehem;[55] and according to Egyptian papyri the monks were involved in extensive economic activities with the secular world they were supposed to leave behind and kept close contact with local elites.[56] Some, such as the Pachomian and White monastery federations in Egypt, operated as substantial financial enterprises in agriculture and in trading goods such as mats, baskets, ropes, and sandals, with considerable impact on the local economy.[57] The financial stability of cenobitic communities was, like that of churches, almost guaranteed by the Constantinian privileges and benefactions because of "the exemptions, revenues, and constant donations that recognized the spiritual and social role henceforth played by the monks," like that of the clergy as well.[58] In addition, semi-eremitical monks clustered around particular *abbas* in northern Egypt (Nitria, Kellia, and Sce-

53. These ascetics were already regarded as "spiritual elites" and "divine men" in the second and third centuries as shown in the apocryphal Acts of Paul, Peter, John, Andrew, and Thomas. It should be noted that from the mid-fourth century on, an increasing number of bishops (e.g., the Cappadocian Fathers, Augustine, and John Chrysostom) would have experienced monastic life and come from the monastic ranks, thus leading to greater cooperation between clergy/church and monks/monasteries.

54. D. Brakke, "Care for the Poor, Fear of Poverty, and Love of Money," in *Wealth and Poverty in Early Church and Society* (ed. S. R. Holman; Grand Rapids: Baker Academic, 2008), 76.

55. E. Patlagean, "The Poor," in *The Byzantines* (ed. G. Cavallo; trans. T. Dunlap, T. L. Fagan, and C. Lambert; Chicago: University of Chicago Press, 1997), 22.

56. See E. A. Judge, "Fourth-Century Monasticism in the Papyri," in *Proceedings of the Sixteenth International Congress of Papyrology* (Chico, CA: Scholars Press, 1981), 613–20.

57. J. E. Goehring, *Ascetics, Society, and the Desert: Studies in Early Egyptian Monasticism* (Harrisburg, PA: Trinity Press International, 1999), 47–48; Brakke, "Care for the Poor," 77; S. Rubenson, "Asceticism and Monasticism I: Eastern," in *Constantine to c. 600* (vol. 2 of *The Cambridge History of Christianity*; ed. A. Casiday and F. Norris; Cambridge: Cambridge University Press, 2007), 648, 650.

58. Patlagean, "The Poor," 22.

tis) supported themselves with self-managed finances through farming and crafts;[59] even "radical" hermits living in the Egyptian deserts and remote areas ("Desert Fathers" and "Desert Mothers") survived by similar labors of trade, gardening, and agriculture, however rudimentary they might have been, and their solitude and separation from villages or towns were "only relative."[60] In fact, archaeological studies on the early monastic dwellings of northern Egypt (Nitria, Kellia, and Naqlun) and the early monasteries of Syria and Palestine reveal that the early monks enjoyed a high standard of building materials and dwellings.[61] Moreover, the Sayings of the Desert Fathers (*Apophtheg-mata patrum*) and other sources contain references to monks owning servants, books, garments, and vessels, as well as references to hospitality, thieves, char-ity, wages, bakeries, and winepresses, which indicate private resources and business activities of even anchorite and semi-anchorite monks.[62] The model hermit, Anthony, portrayed by Athanasius, despite earlier divestment of his property eventually practiced economic self-sufficiency through producing his own bread and vegetables, and he repeatedly provided alms for the poor and hospitality for his visitors supposedly throughout his life (*Life of Anthony*, 50.4–6). Another famous (semi-)anchorite, Evagrius Ponticus, worked as a calligrapher and owned a decent library, and other monks were engaged in the business activities of plaiting ropes and weaving baskets, for instance.[63] Thus, whether one was an anchorite, semi-anchorite, or a cenobite, a monk did not necessarily live in destitution with "total" renunciation of private property, although other wandering monks in Syria who lived off of begging did choose a life of destitution with severe economic vulnerability. The monastic poverty in reality was more patterned after economic self-sufficiency than destitution.

On the one hand, a monk's relative security and latitude regarding personal possessions and finances rather complicated one's attitude and relationship to possessions and poverty.[64] The fact that Evagrius often advised the monks to renounce possessions (which are dangerous and distracting but not evil in

59. Cf. Brakke, "Care for the Poor," 77.

60. Patlagean, "The Poor," 22. Speaking of the social and economic interaction of the monk and the world, Goehring, *Ascetics, Society, and the Desert*, 41, says, "Such interaction was not only possible; it was inevitable. The desert in Egypt, while sharply distinct from the inhabited land, was not remote."

61. S. Rubenson, "Power and Politics of Poverty in Early Monasticism," in *Poverty and Riches* (vol. 5 of *Prayer and Spirituality in the Early Church*; ed. G. D. Dunn, D. Luckensmeyer, and L. Cross; Strathfield, Australia: St. Pauls, 2009), 94–95. See also P. Rousseau, *Pachomius: The Making of a Community in Fourth-Century Egypt* (Berkeley, CA: University of California Press, 1985), especially on Pachomian monasteries.

62. Rubenson, "Power and Politics," 96.

63. L. Regnault, *The Day-to-Day Life of the Desert Fathers in the Fourth-Century Egypt* (trans. E. Poirier; Petersham, MA: St. Bede's Publications, 1999), 99–102; Goehring, *Ascetics, Society, and the Desert*, 45–46.

64. Brakke, "Care for the Poor," 77.

themselves) and that avarice (*philargyria*) and vanity were consistent points of concern in the Sayings of the Desert Fathers and other monastic literature, including Evagrius's works, is telling.[65] Evagrius's advice on the renunciation of possessions and on choosing poverty meant economic self-sufficiency for the monks through manual labor and the practice of inner detachment from desire and care of possessions—all as a demonstration of their dependence on God and their purity of heart. This stance was much like the position of Clement of Alexandria earlier: "Give thought to working with your hands, and further that you may be able to offer donations, as the holy apostle Paul advised (1 Thess. 2:9; 2 Thess. 3:8)."[66] The ideal monk (whether a hermit or cenobite) should *possess* just enough to support oneself and to give alms (still out of surplus, however small that may be) to the economic poor, as almsgiving was a monastic obligation. At issue was how to balance wealth and charity in light of and in relation to their voluntary poverty (i.e., simplicity) and freedom from the worldly concerns and passions. However, due to the business affairs in which they were engaged as a way to support themselves, monks were still vulnerable to love of money (which precipitated repeated teachings against avarice and vanity). So in buying or selling, Evagrius advises "to take a small loss on the just price, lest you get caught up by meticulousness in the ways of greed regarding the price and fall into dealings that cause harm to the soul" (*Foundations of the Monastic Life*, 8). And in the case of avarice creeping in under the pretext of having money to distribute to the poor, "Do not desire to possess riches in order to be able to make donations to the poor, for this is a deception of the evil one, and often leads to vainglory," admonishes Evagrius (*Foundations of the Monastic Life*, 4). For these reasons, there was also a certain ambivalence with regard to monastic almsgiving and even reluctance to give to the poor—out of fear that charity might take a priority over prayer and knowledge of God.[67]

On the other hand, on account of both institutional (communities') wealth and financial revenues, and individual freedom from worldly attachment (at least in theory), the monks acted as key players in serving the poor of society. They lived "the life of an angel" here on earth due to their spiritual disciplines and voluntary poverty and therefore emerged as new "mediators of salvation through alms and intercession" like the radical, charismatic ascetics in the pre-Constantine period (e.g., Apostle Thomas in the *Acts of Thomas* and Peter in the *Acts of Peter*).[68] While their spiritual prowess made them impervious to

65. See *Evagrius of Pontus: The Greek Ascetic Corpus* (trans. R. E. Sinkewicz; Oxford Early Christian Studies; Oxford: Oxford University Press, 2003); *The Desert Fathers: Sayings of the Early Christian Monks* (trans. and intro. by Benedicta Ward; London: Penguin Books, 2003).

66. *Foundations of the Monastic Life* 8 (from *Evagrius Pontus: The Greek Ascetic Corpus*); cf. Brakke, "Care for the Poor," 82.

67. Brakke, "Care for the Poor," 84–86.

68. Patlagean, "The Poor," 24.

their own needs but particularly sensitive to the needs of the poor, free from any self-interest (cf. Cassian, *Conlat.* 21.33 [CSEL 13.609–10]), charity for them was also a means of fighting against their passions, such as avarice and irascibility, and displaying their inner freedom.[69] The monks and the poor had "mutual attraction"; while monks liberally and "cheerfully" reached out to the vulnerable, the sick, and the poor by establishing the poorhouses, orphanages, hostels for lodging, hospitals for palliative care (not necessarily for cure), and regular distribution of food and clothing, the able-bodied poor also migrated to the cities and the regions of monastic developments, especially the Holy Land and northern Syria.[70] Indeed, the theological construction of the poor person as Christ in disguise and charity as the imitation of Christ reinforced this mutual attraction.

Some of these ascetics, increasingly coming from aristocratic backgrounds especially in the West (and even Egypt), still maintained their financial independence and civic standings while having "renounced" possessions. A number of the church fathers kept close correspondences with these wealthy aristocratic ascetics, especially females, exhorting and affirming their ascetic lifestyle with generous almsgiving *befitting* their social status.[71] The wealthy aristocratic women, typically young widows, such as Marcella, Paula, Melania the Elder, Macrina (sister of Basil the Great and Gregory of Nyssa), and Olympias, functioned as significant patrons of their male spiritual advisers, monastic communities, and churches, providing spectacular gifts and the establishment of monasteries in addition to extravagant alms to the poor. Just to name a few examples briefly, Paula and Marcella, noted for their patrician family and wealth by Jerome, were set apart, upon their embrace of asceticism, by their exceeding generosity to the poor, giving money "to each according as each had need, not ministering to self-indulgence but relieving want" out of careful management of their wealth (Jerome, *Epp.* 108.16; 127.4); Paula also built monasteries in Bethlehem, one for men and one for women. Melania the Elder donated three hundred pounds of silver to the Desert Fathers at Nitria, Egypt, took care of the needs of more than a dozen exiled bishops and priests in Palestine, and also built monasteries in Jerusalem (Palladius, *Lausiac History* 46). Olympias, the deaconess from Constantinople with a vast inherited fortune, supported John Chrysostom's ministry, paid for his private expenses

69. Evagrius, *Chapters on Prayer* 17; *To Monks* 30; cf. Rubenson, "Power and Politics," 106–7.

70. See Patlagean, "The Poor," 21, 24. On "the similarities between the monastic health care system and the late antique hospital," see A. T. Crislip, *From Monastery to Hospital: Christian Monasticism and the Transformation of Health Care in Late Antiquity* (Ann Arbor, MI: University of Michigan Press, 2005), 101–38.

71. For example, John Chrysostom and Olympias (*Vita Olymp.*); Jerome and Marcella (Jerome, *Epp.* 46, 54, 127); Paula and Eustochium (*Epp.* 22, 108); Rufinus and Melania the Elder. On the general issue of voluntary poverty and ecclesiastical attitude toward it in late antiquity, see Allen, Neil, and Mayer, *Preaching Poverty*, esp. 82–100 (on John Chrysostom), 130–46 (on Augustine), and 188–96 (on Leo I).

and ransomed him from exile, and donated to the church of Constantinople her estates in Galatia, Cappadocia Prima, Bithynia, and Thrace, in addition to giving money, lands, food, and lodging to numerous bishops, monks, virgins, and the poor (*Vita Olymp.* 5–8). The fact that these ascetics remained capable of giving extensive alms and donations from their personal wealth throughout their lives testifies to their ongoing financial independence (with substantial resources still intact) *while* practicing rigorous asceticism. These ascetics of elite status shifted their munificence from the classic civic benefaction (sponsorship of games, construction of baths, aqueducts, libraries, theaters, etc.) to ecclesiastical and monastic benefaction—church buildings, monastic communities, funding of bishops and other ascetics, alms for the poor, etc.[72] In the words of Wendy Mayer, their asceticism was "associated not with the blanket disposal of wealth but with a shift from generosity toward citizens of the *polis*, to giving generously to the church and its clients, contributing via the church and the poor to the spiritual capital in heaven."[73] Thus, the voluntary poverty of the aristocratic ascetics and the monks in general rather conformed to the classical ideal of noble self-sufficiency coupled with generosity, and was (meant to be) clearly distinguished from the economic destitution of the involuntary poor.[74] For it was not poverty in itself that was praised, or considered a virtue, even for ascetics; rather, it was what poverty signified and made possible—freedom, prayers, and charity.[75] Hence, the ascetic rule of thumb was once again the twin principles of self-sufficiency and charity, similar to the general rule of thumb for Christian life, but ascetics actually embodied that rule with much greater success, for which they were praised and admired, though not imitated, by the vast majority of the faithful.

6.6. Summary and Conclusion

Early Christians consciously and intentionally constructed their self-definition revolving around their understanding and practice of wealth and poverty, which encompassed activities such as basic commercial and business dealings on individual, professional, and corporate levels. By and large Christian texts were apprehensive about and negative toward businesses and trades since they were thought to compromise the Christian identity of those participating; this negativity partly reflected the general aristocratic attitude toward trade but especially was due to the idolatrous nature of avarice—insatiable desire

72. W. Mayer, "Poverty and Generosity toward the Poor in the Time of John Chrysostom," in *Wealth and Poverty in Early Church and Society* (ed. S. R. Holman; Grand Rapids: Baker Academic, 2008), 144.

73. Ibid., 145.

74. Ibid., 151, 154; Rubenson, "Power and Politics," 104.

75. Rubenson, "Power and Politics," 104.

for wealth—that was supposed to be behind all business affairs, as well as idolatrous aspects of business and commercial enterprises that were typically conducted in the pagan temples and under the names of pagan gods. While Christian leaders recognized the difficulties in separating their faithful from the ways in which the larger Greco-Roman society operated in a complex socioeconomic and religiopolitical web of public activities, civic responsibilities, and social pressures (especially for those with some social standing), they nonetheless drew theologically unequivocal, though practically ambiguous, boundaries for Christians and discouraged Christians from seeking upward social mobility through acquisition of wealth. Despite their endeavors to sever the tie between Christian identity and business/trade, Christian businesspeople apparently fused the two without many misgivings in practice, enjoying the clientele of both Christians and non-Christians.

Although condemnation of avarice and luxury was a familiar topic in Greco-Roman moral writings, Christian authors built a negative self-definition around these twin sins as the manifestations of idolatry. As such, both irrational love of wealth and irrational show of wealth bar and move one away from the core of Christian commitment: loving God and loving one's neighbor. As symptoms of self-love, they drive one further into insidious self-absorption and rebellion against God's creative design for humanity: common use of common resources for common flourishing. Common use of resources and properties as God's intent of creation did not mean renunciation of private properties, practice of communism, or erasure of socioeconomic distinctions, but meant generous almsgiving and sharing of one's God-given possessions with those in need, primarily fellow Christians (though not limited to them). Thus almsgiving and sharing formed positive markers of Christian self-definition. Christian apologists and heresiologists regularly contrasted the liberality and charity of Christians with (1) the greed and slavery to materialism of pagans and (2) the lack of charity and avarice of schismatics and heretics. Ultimately, Christian sharing and almsgiving mark necessary imitation of God's own generosity, munificence, and equity.

With the dawn of a new era of peace and prosperity for the church under Constantine and his successors, the church had to deal with a new reality of imperial patronage and favors; bishops as the guardians and protectors of the poor were now obligated to care for the poor of the church *and* society in view of not only the eschatological judgment but also the imperial judgment. At the same time, the church saw the emergence of a new kind of poor: the ascetics whose voluntary poverty was largely reconciled with adequate supplies of necessities and even financial independence. In the paradoxical coexistence of corporate dependence on imperial and pious benefactions and individual self-sufficiency, and sometimes vice versa (i.e., collective independence due to monastic trades and individual dependence on the institutional resources and alms), the ascetics were likewise obligated to and champions of charity but at the same time vulnerable to love of money and vanity. Ascetic poverty, to be guarded against both destitution and avarice, was modeled after the classical, but Christianized, ideal of self-sufficiency (simplicity) and generosity and contributed to the two-tier Christianity in practical terms since most of the Christian faithful admired but did not live up to this ideal.

Christian identity in terms of wealth and poverty in the Constantinian era reflected the growing bifurcation of reality after all: the church getting richer and richer in earthly splendor while theologizing poverty (simplicity, not necessarily destitution) more and more as a Christian virtue to imitate. While the earthly grandeur fittingly reflected the heavenly glory, and while material wealth manifested unspeakable spiritual truth, Christian self-definition also corresponded to the Christianization of civic benefaction, on the one hand, and Christianization of poverty, on the other, which would eventually pave the way for medieval *pauperes Christi*.

7

ᐅᐊᐅᐊᐅᐊᐅᐊᐅᐊᐅᐊᐅᐊᐅᐊᐅᐊᐅᐊᐅᐊᐅᐊᐅᐊᐅᐊᐅᐊᐅᐊᐅᐊᐅᐊᐅᐊ

Wealth, Poverty, and Christian Response in Contemporary Society

So what now? We've studied early Christian beliefs, attitudes, and practices on wealth and poverty, but we must ask: How are they relevant now? Is it possibile for contemporary Christians in North America to extrapolate and appropriate the early Christian teachings and practices in this global age?[1] It is one thing to examine the socioeconomic and theological dynamics of wealth and poverty and their impact on early Christianity but quite another to attempt to relate and apply the early Christian teachings and practices to our contemporary situation since our (post-)modern outlooks, global economy, social structure, and cultural assumptions are radically different from those of ancient Christians. Besides the dangers of well-intended anachronism and uncritical assimilation of patristic texts into contemporary situations,

---

1. On the broad theme of the relevance, use, and function of patristic texts on contemporary Christian ethics (especially on Catholic Social Teaching) and their attendant challenges, see for example, R. Bieringer, "Texts That Create a Future: The Function of Ancient Texts for Theology Today," in *Reading Patristic Texts on Social Ethics: Issues and Challenges for Twenty-First-Century Christian Social Thought* (ed. J. Leemans, B. J. Matz, and J. Verstraeten; Washington, DC: Catholic University of America Press, 2011), 3–29; P. Allen, "Challenges in Approaching Patristic Texts from the Perspective of Contemporary Catholic Social Teaching," in *Reading Patristic Texts* (ed. Leemans, Matz, and Verstraeten), 30–42; T. Hughson, SJ, "Social Justice in Lactantius' Divine Institutes: An Exploration," in *Reading Patristic Texts* (ed. Leemans, Matz, and Verstraeten), 185–205; B. Matz, "The Use of Patristic Socioethical Texts in Catholic Social Thought," in *Wealth and Poverty in Early Church and Society* (ed. S. R. Holman; Grand Rapids: Baker Academic, 2008), 287–93.

in our hyperspecialized academia, I may be entering dangerously into the territory of someone else's specialized field, say that of Christian ethics or even economic ethics, without proper training and credentials in that field, and therefore risking a "right" to be heard. In that case, I may end up as just another moralizing, simplistic voice lacking proper nuances and complex perspectives. Notwithstanding these challenges, however, I will venture this very thing in a limited way. Christians in every era and generation throughout the last two millennia drew on the tradition and wisdom of the previous generation(s)—patristic works in this case—and contextualized what they thought to be biblical and theological mandates and practices on this issue, though in greatly diverse ways.

My attempt in this chapter is very modest. I will not engage in various theories or analyses of modern free-market economics and global economy or theories of ethics, which are beyond my expertise and the scope of this chapter. However, I will draw out some implications from the previous chapters as to how we might consider and attempt to contextualize those lessons, confining myself to brief reflections on the following areas.

7.1. Contextualizing Attitude, Use, and Distribution—Sufficiency, Materialism, and Simplicity

Early Christians, both the biblical writers and the patristic authors, operated within a socioeconomic framework in which wealth was predominantly associated with accumulation and consumption rather than production (creation) and investment. Therefore, their concern was more about attitude toward and use and distribution of wealth within the conceptual world of limited goods and a subsistence economy. The contextual and structural distance of our modern context—where we take productive capital and wealth creation for granted (at least in the industrialized parts of the world)—helps us relate to the early Christian perspectives on wealth consumption and distribution better (or more directly) than to those on wealth creation and productive capital, though without dismissing the latter as irrelevant, outdated, or unauthoritative.[2] Obviously, these issues of attitude, use, and distribution of wealth do matter for Christians today (as well as creation and investment of wealth). Our attitudes (understanding of ownership, stewardship, attachment, or detachment) govern our use and lifestyle (conspicuous consumption, miserliness, simple living, or generous giving) and distribution (hoarding or sharing; justice and equity). At the same time, our individual and collective use of wealth impacts distribution of wealth in personal choices and public (social, economic, and political) policies. This triad should lead us to consider

2. Cf. J. Halteman, "Productive Capital and Christian Moral Teaching," *Faith and Economics* 44 (2004): 26–38.

questions of how wealth and property are produced and acquired in light of patristic teachings on the common good.

Let's start with an attitudinal/motivational issue. In light of God's creation of the material world and his absolute ownership of the created world, human ownership of material things is only derivative and relative ("stewardship"). While early Christians in general hardly denied the legitimacy of private property, they considered it a share of the common creation that was intended for the common use and the common good; all material goods (which were never a substitute for spiritual goods and virtues but could be vehicles of spiritual goods) are God's gracious gifts intended for sustenance and sufficiency of all humans through common access.[3] Therefore, human possession of earthly goods is good when it fulfills God's creative purpose—sufficient provision of one's needs and the needs of others for common enjoyment and flourishing. On the one hand, this basic affirmation validates the material dimension of complex human needs and legitimates the appropriateness and necessity of sufficiency and common enjoyment of earthly goods (but in subordination to heavenly goods, our ultimate priority and object of love). Our need to delight in God includes our creaturely need to enjoy his creation and abundance through material means,[4] as God's shalom, wholeness, is all-encompassing—material as well as spiritual. In this sense, material things, when properly enjoyed, serve as channels through which God manifests his goodness and are intended to point us toward God, reflecting his beauty, generosity, and glory.

On the other hand, it also means that the needs of others do matter in our stewardship of God-given possessions and that they should influence our decisions about our money and property. Our ownership is always conditional in light of God's absolute ownership and creative purpose (the common good). However impractical or unreasonable it may sound, this would mean that, at least theologically and ethically, meeting basic human needs (others' and our own) in terms of providing real access to means of sustenance should be a fundamental ground and goal for economic and sociopolitical choices, activities, and systems.[5] This principle also implies that the concern to meet others' needs takes priority over accumulation of my surplus assets or display

3. This was passed on as the common good, "universal destination of goods," and "social mortgage" in Catholic Social Teaching; cf. Pope Pius XI, *Quadragesimo Anno* (1931), 84; Pope John XXIII, *Mater et Magistra* (1961), 78–80; John XXIII, *Pacem in Terris* (1963), 53–59; John Paul II, *Centesimus Annus* (1991), 30; Catholic Catechism #2420; D. A. Hicks, *Money Enough: Everyday Practices for Living Faithfully in the Global Economy* (San Francisco: Jossey-Bass, 2010), 74.

4. Cf. M. Volf, "In the Cage of Vanities: Christian Faith and the Dynamics of Economic Progress," in *Rethinking Materialism: Perspectives on the Spiritual Dimension of Economic Behavior* (ed. R. Wuthnow; Grand Rapids: Eerdmans, 1995), 188; J. R. Schneider, *The Good of Affluence: Seeking God in a Culture of Wealth* (Grand Rapids: Eerdmans, 2002), esp. 41–64.

5. Cf. N. Wolterstorff, "Has the Cloak Become a Cage? Charity, Justice, and Economic Activity," in *Rethinking Materialism* (ed. Wuthnow), 151.

of my refined taste in luxury items. Beyond sufficiency and common enjoyment, we do not have a "natural right" to accumulation of wealth, attachment to wealth, and conspicuous display of wealth—all of which are symptoms of the love of wealth—because our possessions, even as fruit of our labor, are always contingent upon our social responsibility and creaturely witness to God's ownership. Furthermore, while all wealth ultimately comes from God, it does accompany real and powerful temptations, danger, and deceitfulness, which is actualized in those manifestations of avarice, as early Christians repeatedly have warned us.

Going back to the positive aspect of our conditional ownership and God's creative purpose, while this affirmation of our delight in God's created world is fundamental, it is difficult to define concretely what sufficiency and appropriate enjoyment would look like. Free-market capitalism in the West and globalization revolutionized people's habits and systems of wealth acquisition by creating "new wealth" that had not existed before rather than by taking it away from someone else as it had been thought in ancient societies of limited goods and zero-sum game.[6] Creative ingenuity and entrepreneurship, along with investment in technology, have raised the standard of living to an unprecedented level (especially in the West), and "democratic capitalism" created a modern middle class, "allowing the common man to escape from poverty and live in relative comfort."[7] Furthermore, the United States (even with its recent economic crisis) succeeded in creating "the first mass affluent class in world history."[8] What used to be luxury items even a generation ago—a DVD player, a camera phone, an iPod, and a giant flat-screen television—have become "regular" household items today. And what used to be the items of affluence several decades ago—microwave ovens, (multiple) cars, washing machines, color televisions, refrigerators, cell/landline phones, and even computers—have now become the items of "necessity" for most of the American households, even for those who live under the national poverty threshholds,[9] thanks to ever-developing technology and globalization in production and consumption. Surely the rich are getting richer, but the poor are also getting richer, though not in the same terms or at the same pace.[10] With an increase in the total amount of wealth in many households over time, upward social mobility has become

6. Cf. Schneider, *Good of Affluence*, 30–35; D. D'Souza, *The Virtue of Prosperity: Finding Values in the Age of Techno-Affluence* (New York: Free Press, 2000), 71–72, 124–27; J. W. Richards, *Greed, Money, and God: Why Capitalism Is the Solution Not the Problem* (San Francisco: HarperOne, 2009), 7–8, 89–104.

7. D'Souza, *Virtue of Prosperity*, 16.

8. Ibid., 16.

9. The official poverty level for 2010 is an annual income of $11,139 for an individual (unrelated) and $22,314 for a family of four according to US Census Bureau (released on Sept. 13, 2011).

10. D'Souza, *Virtue of Prosperity*, 71–72; cf. Schneider, *Good of Affluence*, 34. The US Census Bureau report for 2010 reveals that the overall poverty rate climbed to 15.1 percent, or 46.2 million, up from 14.3 percent in 2009. The 46.2 million now living in poverty is the largest

common not only in the United States but also in the international scene, especially in countries like China and India.[11] In fact, Andrew Carnegie praised the salutary effect of industrialization at the turn of the twentieth century in much the same way: "The poor enjoy what the rich could not before afford. What were the luxuries have become the necessities of life. The laborer has now more comforts than the farmer had a few generations ago. The farmer has more luxuries than the landlord had, and is more richly clad and better housed."[12] On a social front, "average" people in developed *and* developing countries have come to enjoy and even take for granted occasional eating out; urban amenities and entertainments such as movies, plays, concerts, museums, and sporting events; vacations; and domestic and international trips, certainly not as an extravagant lifestyle but as affordable and "necessary" leisure. Ability to have and enjoy delicious food, spacious houses, fashionable clothing, and diverse cultures and natural beauties through travels, has defined sufficiency in this new "culture of affluence."[13] Thus, the notion of sufficiency, or for that matter of necessities, has been evolving and contextualized—inevitably so; and this in one sense is a sign of the remarkable progress and positive contribution of wealth creation by democratic capitalism, which has enabled so many people worldwide to come out of poverty, experience upward social mobility, and "enjoy" the benefits of these goods and services.

However, this relative and fluid sense of sufficiency, necessities, and material enjoyment blurs and softens what used to be thought of as avarice and materialism (which nurture and are in turn fueled by consumerism). A vast majority of Americans, who belong to the top 5–10 percent of the richest people in the world by a global standard,[14] identify themselves as the middle class yet without a firm sense of economic security or contentment. With the recent economic recession and the ever-growing costs of health care (or "sick care"), child care, and education, the middle-class Americans feel ever so strapped and squeezed in their pocketbooks just to "stay afloat" in the sea of "sufficiency," not to mention the lower class and the poor.[15] But why do they (we) feel so discontent and insecure about "not having sufficient stuff"

on record since the census was tracking the poverty level first taken in 1959 (http://www.census.gov/hhes/www/poverty/about/overview/index.html).

11. Cf. Richards, *Greed, Money, and God*, 91; see www.gapminder.org.

12. A. Carnegie, "The Problem of the Administration of Wealth," in *The Gospel of Wealth and Other Timely Essays* (New York: Century, 1900), from *On Moral Business: Classical and Contemporary Resources for Ethics in Economic Life* (ed. M. L. Stackhouse et al.; Grand Rapids: Eerdmans, 1995), 292.

13. This phrase is from Schneider, *Good of Affluence*, 20.

14. See Hicks, *Money Enough*, 4 and 183n3. For example, based on figures from the World Bank Development Research Group, an annual income of $25,400 USD places one in the top 10 percent of the richest people in the world, $33,700 in the top 5 percent, and $47,500 in the top 1 percent according to "How Do We Calculate It?" at http://globalrichlist.com/how.html.

15. See n10 above.

to make a living despite the fact that we indeed have more than enough by any global standard if we are honest? Would there be an end to our pursuit of "the middle-class sufficiency" to our satisfaction? Our determined pursuit of sufficiency has become our pursuit of materialism, i.e., our concern for and devotion to material needs and desires, and in its due course this pursuit has exposed our hidden avarice, i.e., our insatiable passion and preoccupation with more wealth for a "better life." Materialism sneaks up through smoke screens of apparently legitimate and thoughtful concerns in life. Obsessing over name-brand goods (e.g., automobile, clothing, jewelry) for status enhancement, embezzling company funds for personal gain, measuring people by income levels, or daydreaming about the lifestyle of the rich and famous might be too easy to detect and feel embarrassed about. Yet many North Americans, while bemoaning the control of materialism over our values and society, "devote ourselves wholeheartedly to earning as much money as we can" and "to the pursuit of material interest" on the seemingly innocent and even financially responsible level:[16] for example, tracking the latest electronic gadgets and appliances for efficiency and performance, remodeling one's house for greater hospitality and comfort, buying more expensive furniture and goods for better quality and convenience, contributing to one's 401(k), IRA, and pension for future financial security, working multiple jobs to own a home, relocating cross-country for a higher-paying job, working overtime to send a son or daughter to a college, and moving to a "better" or "safer" neighborhood in suburbia for kids' schools and education. How does one distinguish these concerns and decisions from proper sufficiency and enjoyment, or should we? Are these acts of prudence and responsibility or acts of insecurity—or even distrust in God's provision for the future? The very idea and tireless pursuit of an "American dream" may be a hopeful inspiration for success for the socially mobile (as often roused by politicians), yet could it also be a masked allurement to vanity and legitimation of greed and materialism for what it promises?

Moreover, our greed and materialism find a great ally in consumerism. The current market economy is structured to maximize consumption of goods by individual preferences and wants. Instead of making any moral judgment on the kinds of purchases the "rational" consumers make or on our innate bent toward materialism, our neoliberal capitalism thrives on our insatiable desire for goods and our "rational choices" to satisfy our preferences with maximum efficiency and instant gratification.[17] It deceives us into thinking that the sort of product we prefer and purchase defines our identity, representing our social rank, worth, and significance in society; therefore, each class strives to emulate

16. R. Wuthnow, "A Good Life and a Good Society: The Debate over Materialism," in *Rethinking Materialism* (ed. Wuthnow), 4–5.

17. Cf. K. A. Van Til, *Less Than Two Dollars a Day: A Christian View of World Poverty and the Free Market* (Grand Rapids: Eerdmans, 2007), 31–33; R. J. Sider, *Rich Christians in an Age of Hunger: Moving from Affluence to Generosity* (4th ed.; Dallas: Word, 1997), 23–26.

the class above it and to purchase the goods that could get them to the step above their place in the social hierarchy (e.g., from the lower to the lower middle; from the middle to the upper middle; and with the rich[18] emulating the celebrities and the super rich). The whole advertising and marketing industry is based on this social psychology and premise. However, it is crucial that the desires or wants of the consumers are never fully or permanently met or satisfied but only seem to be so in order that the advertising and marketing industries can constantly create new promises and wants, which successfully keep the cycle of consumerism going and leave us with greater and deeper holes and desires. Perhaps we should acknowledge that we all are much more active participants in this intricate web and societal structure of materialism and consumerism than we are willing to admit or could justify our economic practices. For that matter, love of wealth, i.e., avarice, and its attendant companions, materialism and consumerism, are easier to denounce in abstract but much harder to identify and deal with in concrete terms. In one way or another, many of us American Christians are partakers of "pious materialism," a "genteel affirmation of a 'normal' American life."[19]

Given these ambiguities and complexities, how do we fight against this formidable triad of avarice, materialism, and consumerism? We are reminded that early Christians in general did not endorse total renunciation or divestment of personal wealth as a solution to these fundamentally internal and spiritual problems, even for monastics; material divestment in itself does not address the deeper problem. However, they did exhort *qualified* renunciation as evidence of an inner freedom from the grip of material things and therefore as a way of reorienting desire for spiritual good. They consistently saw through the real danger of wealth and its power to corrupt souls. From the *Shepherd of Hermas* and Clement of Alexandria to Cyprian of Carthage, renunciation or cutting away of *some* (even substantial) earthly riches (in the forms of simple living and generous almsgiving) appears as a *partial* antidote to dealing with insatiable desire for, attachment to, and pursuit of earthly riches. The virtue of internal freedom and contentment cannot be cultivated without actual cutting away or giving away of external goods because of the force and deceitfulness of wealth and our fallenness. We as fallen creatures "want to grasp and retain, to store up rather than receive daily, to turn from what is given to what is desired—and for such creatures the movement of negation built into the dialectic of creation must often be experienced as painful renunciation."[20] Note, however, that renunciation makes sense only

---

18. In current American political debates on tax increase and tax breaks (2010–11), the rich are "defined" as those whose annual income is $250,000 or more.

19. R. Wuthnow, "Pious Materialism: How Americans View Faith and Money," *Christian Century*, March 3, 1993, 238–42; M. G. Witten, "'Where Your Treasure Is': Popular Evangelical Views of Work, Money, and Materialism," in *Rethinking Materialism* (ed. Wuthnow), 140.

20. G. Meilaender, "To Throw Oneself into the Wave: The Problem of Possessions," in *Preferential Option for the Poor* (ed. R. J. Neuhaus; Grand Rapids: Eerdmans, 1988), 84.

in the context of enjoyment of creation—the movement of affirmation.[21] The qualified renunciation serves as a corrective to the exaggerated and inordinate affirmation and enjoyment of the created things. Our qualified renunciation of material things involves both negative (simplicity) and positive (generous giving) movements, as the latter complements the former.

The first form of renunciation, simplicity, calls for the discipline of taking *regular* inventory of one's possessions and cutting away one's excess goods; too much (and also too little) does corrupt and enslave the soul. These possessions are to be freely given away or donated, not sold for profit through garage sales, eBay, or Craigslist (unless those proceeds are to be freely given away to help the needy). This aspect of simplicity is "essentially a reminder that we are seldom as generous as we think, as we could be, as we ought to be."[22] Simplicity also calls for vigilance and discernment in identifying our needs and sufficiency in stricter terms than our culture of affluence leads us to believe in comparison with those in a similar social location with us ("the middle-class sufficiency" or "keeping up with the Joneses"). Admittedly, notions of simplicity, needs, and sufficiency are fluid, and we run into difficulty in determining precise or absolute criteria in tangible terms, as we have mentioned.[23] In this sense, simplicity demands more than rigid legalism; it demands a discipline of contentment, which is a faithful and grateful response to God's abundance and provision, and contentment in turn nurtures and fosters simplicity. Nonetheless, it would still require a practice of restraint—saying no to the advertising phrases such as, "I deserve this" or "I'm worth it," and severing a tie between identity or self-worth and particular goods of desire. Finally, a lifestyle of simplicity entails making ourselves accountable to others (perhaps in family, church home groups and even the whole congregation, close friends, like-minded people in our neighborhood, and even Facebook friends) for our consumption patterns: the kinds of goods we prefer and want and the ways in which we acquire those goods. This means that the discipleship of simplicity goes beyond personal and private virtues and carries the kind of influence that shapes communal ethos and values. In our contemporary consumer culture, this dimension of simplicity might present the greatest challenge to practice since we regard our "consumption rights" as almost sacred and too personal/private. However, note that if we can practice this, we are creating a new kind of fictive kinship and solidarity that forms alternative economic units (however small that may be) that could go against the tides of our own desire and consumer culture. In all of these forms of simplicity, we are to be guided by "a cheerful nonconformity," as R. T. France calls it.[24]

21. Ibid.

22. Ibid., 80.

23. Cf. Richards, *Greed, Money, and God*, 160–61; Schneider's critique of Sider's "arbitrary" distinction between "necessities" and "luxuries" and of Blomberg's notion of sufficiency as the biblical ideal ("neither poverty nor riches"), *Good of Affluence*, 98–103.

24. R. T. France, "God and Mammon," *Evangelical Quarterly* 51 (1979): 20.

Yet since the problem with idolatrous avarice, materialism, and consumerism is also misdirected love, devotion, and trust from the Creator to created things, renunciation of external goods cannot be the only or ultimate remedy or weapon. It must be accompanied by renunciation of the self that keeps trusting and going after the created things even when knowing these do not last and cannot fill our void and yearning for security.[25] This double renunciation—showing "contempt" for transient and corruptible earthly riches via inner discipline and outer acts, and denial of the self—is in turn to be accompanied by our committed reorientation of love for, devotion to, and trust in God and his kingdom—i.e., placing our hope in and actively looking forward to heavenly riches as our true riches and security. This "heavenly" pursuit calls for a cultivation of eschatological hope and a reorientation of our values, which requires at the same time spiritual imagination and faith. The more we become steeped in the reality of the eschatological judgment and reward beyond this world and the value of heavenly riches, the more convinced we become in practicing our internal and external renunciation here and now. I am talking not about becoming an otherworldly quietist but about how we order our socioeconomic worldviews, habits, and lives in anticipation of the already and not-yet kingdom of God and its values (such as abundance and justice through mutuality, sharing, generosity, etc.). Thus, our fight involves both action *and* attitude: real giving up of the self and something material, and active yearning for something spiritual, not just either/or. This dual approach helps us develop genuine Christian simplicity and freedom as opposed to Stoic indifference. Early Christians did not shy away from appealing to heavenly riches, heavenly reward, and heavenly treasures, which were part of the biblical promise and hope. Though spiritualizing true riches (and true poverty) could potentially become an excuse and justification for keeping one's property intact and maintaining a status quo here on earth (it certainly has been throughout history), it does have a proper place in Christian discipleship and service.

These affect not just individuals but communities, societies, cultures, nations, and even our world as a "global village" as the concentric circles become larger and more complex. Despite the incredible connectedness through globalization, the irony is in the ever-increasing impersonalization of a "global village." Whereas "traditional Christian morality in economic life is based on *interpersonal* relations among neighbors, . . . our contemporary global economy is based on impersonal exchanges around the world."[26] Perhaps one way of drawing from early Christian concerns on this aspect is to attempt to acknowledge, recover, and remind ourselves of this organic link among these ever-expanding social and economic units and to (re-)personalize these

25. Cf. Meilaender, "To Throw Oneself into the Wave," 84.
26. D. A. Hicks and M. Valeri, "Introduction: Christian Faith and the Global Market," in *Global Neighbors: Christian Faith and Moral Obligation in Today's Economy* (ed. D. A. Hicks and M. Valeri; Grand Rapids: Eerdmans, 2008), xix (italics original).

circles that have been impersonalized in the process of industrialization and globalization. That is, not only to believe that how I as an individual regard personal possessions and what I do with them does matter for larger communities and societies, but also to act consistently and constructively in alternate communities to which we belong and create, believing that small things add up to change.

7.2. Use and Distribution of Wealth, and Poverty Relief—Generosity, Church, and Justice

Let's now delve into the issue of proper use of possessions and take up the second form of renunciation: generous (alms-)giving. The discipleship of simplicity is not the same as the discipleship of giving or generosity; if simplicity involves more inward orientation and disciplines, generous giving entails more outward disposition and actions; simplicity frees up resources for generosity. If we are not careful, generosity can be self-serving, self-righteous, and egocentric on the motivational and attitudinal level, as it was practiced in Greco-Roman patronage (and arguably in certain early Christian appeals). Nonetheless, rooted in God's own self-giving generosity, beneficence, and purpose of creation, the call for generosity is our response to and imitation of God's character and gracious act toward us. As Douglas Hicks reminds us, Christian economic attitudes and practices are grounded in "the joyful, grateful response to the God of grace," who gives life abundant.[27] "The proper response to the challenge of global poverty, and to giving in general, is gratitude for God's grace. We cannot earn our eternal life through our actions and we will not attain moral perfection. But we can embody gratitude in our lives. That approach then shapes more generous actions."[28] Clement of Alexandria and Cyprian did ground almsgiving fundamentally in God's gracious love, which resulted in the giving of Christ and his life abundant "not because we deserve but only because of our need."[29] Cheerful giving (2 Cor. 9:7) in the Christian tradition comes from this gratitude for God's giving, a fundamental "disposition for sharing."[30] Thus, early Christians were exhorted to not be modest in giving to and sharing with the needy, since our giving would (should) reflect God's own giving and our fundamental Christian identity and orientation in life.[31]

In practicing generosity, it is important to keep in mind that while the call for generosity is binding for all Christians in light of Christian identity and

27. Hicks, *Money Enough*, 167.
28. Ibid., 170.
29. A. D. Meeks, "Being Human in the Market Society," *QR* 21 (2003): 262.
30. Hicks, *Money Enough*, 171.
31. Meeks, "Being Human in the Market Society," 262.

self-definition, the specific ways in which Christians enact this call may be multidimensional, diverse, and particular to one's vocation, work, and context, such that no single way can be universally prescribed.[32] Hence, Christian giving and generosity is much larger than giving of material things, of course, but generosity as a form of renunciation should include these material things. In that vein, the discipleship of generosity calls for creativity, planning, and a thoughtful strategy for giving of our material possessions. We are to ask and consider to whom we should give, for what we should give, and how we should give. In terms of the recipients of our generosity, we might naturally include our family, neighbors, friends, church members, local and regional charities, etc.—people in a circle of our proximate relationships (our "neighbors" limited by time, place, and opportunities),[33] but we must not stop there especially considering the "universal destination of goods."[34] "Our neighbors" should also include the "strangers" who are more removed from us in terms of relationship or national boundaries, including not only the domestic poor and the victims of disaster (e.g., Hurricane Katrina) but also the global poor (e.g., Guatemalan day-laborers, HIV-positive orphans in Sudan, earthquake victims in Haiti) and the global victims of disaster (e.g., flood victims in Australia and tsunami/earthquake victims in Southeast Asia and Japan).[35] Here "our neighbors" obviously include all who are suffering and afflicted, Christians as well as non-Christians. We could give to organizations that work for short-term relief for immediate and urgent needs (e.g., sheltering the homeless, feeding the hungry, clothing the naked, and caring for the sick in inner cities or disaster zones), to which the traditional charity organizations tend to respond, and/or for social change and development organizations that work toward long-term, structural, and institutional changes and policies for the betterment of the poor and the underprivileged (e.g., basic education and literacy, affordable housing, living wage campaign, judicial justice, micro-lending, asset-based community development, and health care programs).[36] In light of God's creative intent—sufficiency for all humanity through common access to the created world, i.e., productive means—our support for the latter seems

32. Cf. Meilaender, "To Throw Oneself into the Wave," 80–81; France, "God and Mammon," 20.

33. See E. Gregory, "Agape and Special Relations in a Global Economy: Theological Sources," in *Global Neighbors* (ed. Hicks and Valeri), 31–42; Schneider, *Good of Affluence*, 87–89, 212; cf. Richards, *Greed, Money, and God*, 49–51, on a problem of impersonal and nonspecific government-run welfare programs.

34. Cf. K. A. Van Til, "Poverty and Morality in Christianity," in *Poverty and Morality: Religious and Secular Perspectives* (ed. W. A. Galston and P. H. Hoffenberg; Cambridge: Cambridge University Press, 2010), 79; contra Schneider, *Good of Affluence*, 87–89, 212.

35. Cf. Van Til, *Less Than Two Dollars a Day*, 140–41; T. W. Walker, "Who Is My Neighbor? An Invitation to See the World with Different Eyes," in *Global Neighbors* (ed. Hicks and Valeri), 3–15.

36. C. Collins and M. Wright, *The Moral Measure of Economy* (Mary Knoll, NY: Orbis Books, 2007), 181–83.

particularly significant so that those who cannot or do not have access to the productive means on their own could have opportunities through these means and services.[37] We could also consider whether the agencies or organizations are distinctively Christian and also faithful to Christian visions and values, e.g., missionaries/mission organizations who work with and for the poor and the disadvantaged. We could concentrate on one or two people or organizations for regular support or spread out to several more spontaneously and flexibly. Not as a rule but as a suggestion, it might be helpful to seek a balance in supporting different needs and different kinds/levels of aids and remedies.

For consideration of how much we should give, one helpful and challenging way could be practicing the "graduated tithe" as evangelical scholars Ron Sider and Craig Blomberg have suggested.[38] While the principle of tithe (giving 10 percent to the works of God) was established in the Old Testament, taken for granted by Jesus (and the New Testament), and continuously practiced in the early church (though not mentioned much), the emphasis in the New Testament and the early church (and churches throughout history) has been on generous and sacrificial giving and sharing beyond the law of tithe (cf. Irenaeus, *Haer.* 4.13.3). Sider's example consists of giving a tithe on a "base figure" ("sufficiency" figure for his family cognizant of the current United States poverty thresholds) and then giving a graduated tithe (15 percent or more) on income above that (5 percent increase on each thousand dollars above his base).[39] Blomberg, though he does not provide precise charts or figures for his calculation, follows a principle of increasing his giving beyond a tithe as his income has grown—to the extent of 30 percent of the total income of his household.[40] Their exact or specific percentage or figures need not alarm or confine us, but this principle of giving in proportion to an increase in one's income accords with the practices of early Christians and offers us a tangible goal or guidance in practice. In this plan, we might allocate different percentages to agencies or organizations that provide various kinds of services and development.

Another, simpler example also comes from early Christian practices: socially responsible fasting and hospitality. It is more and more difficult to find a discipline of fasting regularly practiced among American Christians (especially

---

37. Recent books by R. D. Lupton, *Toxic Charity: How Churches and Charities Hurt Those They Help (And How to Reverse It)* (San Francisco: HarperOne, 2011) and B. Fikkert and S. Corbett, *When Helping Hurts: Alleviating Poverty without Hurting the Poor . . . and Yourself* (Chicago: Moody, 2009) drive this point home. See below on distributive justice. The distinction between the charity organizations and social change/development organizations may be somewhat artificial and fluid; larger charity organizations such as World Vision usually operate in both levels and capacities.

38. Sider, *Rich Christians*, 187–90; Blomberg, *Neither Poverty Nor Riches*, 247–49.

39. See Sider, *Rich Christians*, 188, for his calculation of a "base figure," and 188–89, for a table on a graduated tithe.

40. Blomberg, *Neither Poverty Nor Riches*, 248.

Protestants). During Lent, the traditional season when fasting (in varying degrees) and almsgiving are practiced among Catholic and Orthodox (and some Protestant) Christians, and even during Advent in which the "spirit of giving" is often appealed to, one could combine fasting, alms, and hospitality that would benefit those in need. Instead of engaging in fasting just as an individualistic "spiritual" discipline, we could calculate the cost of a meal, set aside money for the number of meals (or content of meals) for the period of fasting, and then give it to those in need or one of those charity and social change organizations. Or we could invite the afflicted into our homes, churches, neighborhood, and communities and share meals with them consistently throughout the period. Individual households could take turns in providing meals and getting to know the invitee(s) and form sustaining relationships and friendships (cf. Clement of Alexandria, *Quis. div.* 32). This hospitality of sharing meals humanizes and personalizes both the givers/hosts and the recipients/guests. If we could establish this as a "spiritual" lifestyle for these seasons (and beyond) when the advertisers and market want us to be consumed with shopping for ourselves and our circle of friends and family the most, we could be countercultural against our culture of greed and consumerism and also experience the horizontal (as well as vertical) impact of our fasting and hospitality (cf. Isa. 58:6–12). Again, in this practice, simplicity and generosity go hand in hand.

Like the case for simplicity, the discipline of generosity is meant to be practiced not just by individuals but also by groups or communities of solidarity with accountability, i.e., churches, Christian interest groups, social networks, and small groups at work, in the neighborhood, or through a church. Again, these fictive kinship groups can exercise alternative economic behaviors in anticipation of the coming kingdom of God; and the hard and strategic work of discernment of whom, what, and how also applies to the communal or corporate giving—perhaps even more so.

At this point, I would like to reserve some space to address the role of the church in care of the poor in particular. Perhaps the clearest principle and application we can draw from early Christianity is that the church was at the center of providing relief for the poor and the afflicted. Grant that the government (the Roman Empire) did not have well-organized social welfare programs and that the early church, as a persecuted minority with limited resources, took care of primarily its own poor (i.e., the Christian poor), not necessarily the poor of the society in general—until it was "imposed" by Constantine in return for its public favors and privileges. However, just as there was no dichotomy drawn between spiritual and material dimensions and responsibilities in the faith of an individual Christian, there surely was no dichotomy in the mission of the church on whether to attend to either the "spiritual" or the "material/social" needs of the community. In a sense, precisely because of its "spiritual" vision and message, the church saw to it that "material" care and ministry would not be neglected. The task of caring for the "widows, orphans and the poor" and other socioeconomically marginalized groups (such as the disabled, the elderly, the sick, etc.) constituted faithfulness to the gospel and was never separated from the essential self-definition and mission of the church. The gospel proclaimed and the gospel embodied were never pitted against each other, nor did they compete for the loyalty of the faithful; it was the same gospel preached and practiced to and by the same communities of faith. Furthermore, the role and authority of clergy (especially bishops as the "lovers of the poor") was unequivocally defined by not only their liturgical/ sacramental ("spiritual") function but also their social ("material") function of spearheading and operating extensive services and charities for the poor, the infirm, the elderly, the disabled, and the helpless.

Although some Christians believe that poverty relief has to be always voluntary, never "coerced" or "mandated" by the church,[41] as we have seen, it was not an altruistic option but a mandatory obligation of the faithful by virtue of the gospel message and Christian identity. The works of charity— almsgiving, sharing, hospitality, caretaking of the poor, the afflicted, and the helpless—were not supererogatory "add-ons" but the works of justice and equity grounded in *koinonia* of God's creation and *imago Dei*. Without them Christians could not claim their spiritual security and maturity in Christ but could incur the eschatological judgment of God due to their failure to love their neighbors. Protestants would have some uneasiness about linking ultimate salvation with "doing good" in any way as though it would undermine "salvation by grace through faith alone." Yet this dichotomous grid is no longer helpful or sound; grace is opposed to the attitude of earning, not the action of doing good.[42] "Doing good" is always part and parcel of salvation, which is God's gracious, unconditioned gift, *and* which we are to work out with fear and trembling willed and enabled by God and already living in but also looking forward to his kingdom (see Phil. 2:12). Again, there are different options among the specific kinds and ways of works of charity and justice that Christian communities may choose, but the ecclesial duty to engage in such works seems nonnegotiable.

Throughout history, the church has been more or less faithful to this call and responsibility. Nonetheless, in the confluence of several circumstances at the turn of the twentieth century in modern American churches, especially in evangelical circles (e.g., the traumatic experience of the fundamentalist-modernist controversies and the Social Gospel movements in the context of conservative-liberal clashes, as well as the influence of dispensational premillennialism), the unwarranted and unfortunate wedge between these "spiritual" and "social"/"physical" ministries of churches has been running deep—as

41. Cf. Wuthnow, *God and Mammon*, 218–21.
42. Cf. D. Willard, Mayterm Faculty Seminar, Westmont College, May 26, 2011.

though the churches have to choose either one or the other as their "primary" mission, or as though the churches should devote their ministries entirely to "spiritual life" rather than to paying attention to material needs.[43] This is a concept foreign to early Christianity, and in an ironic way it recreates a gnostic, dualistic approach to the gospel, undermining the materiality of the creation and redemption through the gospel. If we affirm the physicality of the creation, we will have to affirm the physicality of redemption, which entails physical or material wholeness as well as spiritual care and restoration. Meeting the basic physical/material needs of the poor and the helpless then does (should) not supplant or replace the spiritual ministry but is a part and parcel of proclaiming to the created world the already and not-yet kingdom: God's reign and restoration of shalom. The church is then uniquely positioned to recognize and deal with both material and nonmaterial dimensions and multiple levels of poverty: nonaccess or lack of access to material necessities—economic, educational, social, political, medical, and spiritual resources and care. In this, the church is to be careful not to romanticize poverty or patronize the poor as the early church did, however; for that matter, the church should not adulate wealth or castigate the wealthy but foster redemption of wealth. In this task, the church should be at the forefront, and the clergy should lead the way as "lovers of the poor" although the church's role does not negate the need for or importance of other agents and the government in providing for systemic and structural justice and basic social safety nets. The church can (and should) collaborate with the charity and development organizations and the government agencies in working for and with the poor.

While the church's role in charity and justice is crucial, and while the church should even reclaim that responsibility, ecclesial and other organized charity and justice alone (not to mention private simplicity and generosity) is obviously not enough to deal with the staggering poverty in our day and age; in reality, they have never been sufficient and never will be. Thus far, I have addressed simplicity and generosity as qualified renunciation for Christian attitude and use of possessions based on God's creative purpose. Our responsibility to help the poor, the vulnerable, and the helpless for the basic sustenance and common flourishing of all humanity and for the alleviation of socioeconomic inequality goes beyond the realm of attitude and use to distribution (and production) of resources. Individual and ecclesial (corporate) simplicity and generosity certainly involve distribution of goods to the needy to an extent, but our contextualization of biblical and patristic distribution also has to do with economic fairness and justice on the level of structure and policy—in not only a national but also an international context. Free-market capitalism, the dominant economic structure of our world, among all the other economic systems, provides a social framework that rewards free exchanges, individual initiatives and responsibility,

43. Cf. Wuthnow, "Pious Materialism," 241; *God and Mammon*, 218.

investments, and entrepreneurship.[44] It creates wealth (at least in theory) for those who participate in the market with their "initial endowments" (the "given" assets of individuals brought to the market such as birth, inheritance, education, opportunities, and capital for production, etc.),[45] based on market competition and driven by self-interest.[46] However, it does not address or respond to the basic needs of those who lack the "initial endowments" to begin with[47] and thus has and works under built-in structural imbalances. Countless able-bodied adults in the underdeveloped and developing countries and even among the domestic poor in the United States are deprived of these "initial endowments" that the market takes as the given, not to mention inadequate food, water, and medical care, and inaccessible land and property rights. Consider the fact that the median income in the world (after adjustments in different purchasing power in different nations) is less than $2,000 a year[48]—which puts the official poor in the United States high on the economic scale by comparison.[49] With the world population having reached seven billion (2011), a billion live on less than $1 a day, another more than 1.4 billion live on less than $1.25 a day, and half of the world's population lives on less than $2 a day; these are the numbers on absolute poverty according to the World Bank (2008).[50] According to its "Poverty & Inequality Analysis,"

> from 1981 to 2005 [the most recent year for which comprehensive estimates are available], the number of people living on less than $1.25 per day (PPP adjusted in 2005 USD) has fallen from 1.9 to 1.4 billion. During this same period, the proportion of the world's population living below the $1.25 poverty line has declined from 52 percent to 26 percent. It is estimated that the number of people living on less than $2 per day has increased slightly over this period, from 2.5 to 2.6 billion people, although the proportion living below the poverty line has declined from 70 percent to 48 percent [mainly due to China's development].[51]

44. On positive contributions of free-market capitalism see among others M. Novak, *The Spirit of Democratic Capitalism* (New York: Simon & Shuster, 1982); M. Novak, *In Praise of the Free Economy* (trans. S. Gregg; Smithfield, Australia: Center for Independent Studies, 1999); Richards, *Money, Greed, and God*, esp. 59–182; D'Souza, *Virtue of Prosperity*; Schneider, *Good of Affluence*; V. V. Claar and R. J. Klay, *Economics in Christian Perspective: Theory, Policy and Life Choices* (Downers Grove, IL: InterVarsity, 2007).
45. See Van Til, *Less Than Two Dollars a Day*, 49–51.
46. Cf. Richards's distinction between self-interest and selfishness/greed, *Greed, Money, and God*, 111–33.
47. Cf. ibid., 127, admits that "after all, before you can exchange, you must have something to exchange."
48. Hicks, *Money Enough*, 4.
49. See n9 above.
50. World Bank, "Measuring Poverty at the Global Level," http://web.worldbank.org/WBSITE /EXTERNAL/TOPICS/EXTPOVERTY/EXTPA/0,,contentMDK:22397595~pagePK:210058 ~piPK:210062~theSitePK:430367,00.html.
51. World Bank, "Poverty & Inequality Analysis," http://web.worldbank.org/WBSITE /EXTERNAL/TOPICS/EXTPOVERTY/EXTPA/0,,contentMDK:20205999~menuPK:435780 ~pagePK:148956~piPK:216618~theSitePK:430367,00.html.

For this distressing number of people in abject poverty who tragically remain faceless to most of us, each day presents a life-or-death challenge.

Distributive justice calls for distribution of resources according to human needs, not price-based, "effective demand" of the market by those who have purchasing power, since the market responds only to ability to pay, not the needs of the poor who are excluded from the system itself.[52] Distributive economic justice *"demands that every person or family has access to the productive resources (land, money, knowledge) so they have the opportunity to earn a generous sufficiency of material necessities and be dignified, participating members of their community."*[53] In reality, this distributive justice aims to provide basic "initial endowments" for the weak and the vulnerable and thus to "get them in" to the market to participate in the system so that they could earn and *retain* the minimum means of sustenance such as food, shelter, clothing, health care, living wage, and a safe environment. Note that distributive justice presupposes a fundamental idea of wealth creation and entrepreneurship and the capacity of the poor to become self-sufficient through their entrepreneurial participation in the market; once again, then, individuals, churches, organizations, and governments can partner together in directing giving, charity, and development efforts moving from crisis management toward this goal of enabling the poor to earn and maintain self-sufficiency with dignity.[54] The same principle of justice is expressed by the evangelical document. The Oxford Declaration on Christian Faith and Economics (1990):

> Justice requires conditions such that each person is able to participate in society in a way compatible with human dignity. Absolute poverty, where people lack even minimal food and housing, basic education, health care, and employment, denies people the basic economic resources necessary for just participation in the community. Corrective action with and on behalf of the poor is a necessary act of justice. This entails responsibilities for individuals, families, churches, and governments. (40)[55]

At the same time, this justice aims to guarantee basic sustenance for another group of those who are unable to provide and care for themselves—orphans, the elderly, the disabled, the mentally ill, and so on. As justice requires special attention to people who cannot help themselves in the most basic level,

---

52. Van Til, *Less Than Two Dollars a Day*, 52–53.

53. S. Mott and R. J. Sider, "Economic Justice: A Biblical Paradigm," in *Toward a Just and Caring Society* (ed. D. P. Gushee; Grand Rapids: Baker, 1999), 40 (italics original).

54. Both Lupton, *Toxic Charity*, 61–163 and Fikkert and Corbett, *When Helping Hurts*, 103–200, in particular, critique need-based and crisis-based charity and giving for breeding dependency and strongly advocate asset-based (community) development for, with, and by the poor by investing in them to create wealth for themselves through training, employment, lending, and investing.

55. "The Oxford Declaration," *Transformation* 7, no. 2 (April–June, 1990), 13.

distributive justice in this sense is partial; but this particular attention to the poor and needy follows the biblical picture of God's justice and love as well as early Christian ideals and practices: i.e., "the preferential option for the poor." Distributive justice recognizes the inequitable distribution and imperfection of the unchecked free-market system and addresses systemic problems of devastating income and wealth inequality both within and between nations, the crisis of foreign debt of poorer countries, the concentration of economic and political power on the few and its power structure that privileges the rich and the powerful (such as tax exemptions and loopholes), and exploitation of the poor through market speculations, out-of-control consumerism and materialism, etc.[56] The most capable (though not most effective, unfortunately) agents of distributive justice, then, are the government institutions whose activities and policies wield enormous impact on people not only in the United States but also in many other countries. They could provide ways to help fund assistance and services to the extreme poor and disadvantaged both in the United States and around the world.[57] It is a part of Christian responsibility to discern, support, engage in, and advocate the kinds of domestic and international policies that could make a positive difference in the lives of billions of people. Note here for the Christians, the common good of all humanity, material and spiritual, rather than the national interest is to dictate and guide our concern and support for the public policies at home and abroad.[58]

Distributive justice then can correct capitalism as an unbridled economic system of "the survival of the fittest" but can also protect capitalism as free enterprise of human ingenuity and creativity by calling for the important role of the wider community—of faith and civil society—and by offering "a viable moral, religious, and sociopolitical framework for its operation."[59] The synergistic relationship between distributive justice and capitalism can also be seen in the Catholic Social Teaching, which has identified subsidiarity and solidarity as the core, complementary principles of the common good— the goal of human economic life. Subsidiarity calls for the autonomy of the church and "subordinate groups" and "various associations" under the state (such as family, neighbors, civic or community organizations, and local or regional governments)[60] as "principled or institutional pluralism."[61] Solidarity as Christian virtue and determination to see the "other" (person, people, or

56. Cf. John Paul II, *Laborem Exercens* (1981), 14; *Centesimus Annus* (1991). Commutative justice, which has to do with fairness in market exchange, concerns unfair international trade, which affects income and wealth inequality between nations.

57. R. M. Blank, "A Christian Perspective on the Role of Government in a Market Economy," in *Global Neighbors* (ed. Hicks and Valeri), 246.

58. Cf. Blomberg, *Neither Poverty Nor Riches*, 252.

59. A. Yong, *In the Days of Caesar: Pentecostalism and Political Theology* (Grand Rapids: Eerdmans, 2010), 288; cf. Pope John Paul II, *Centesimus Annus* (1991).

60. Pope Pius XI, *Quadragesimo Anno* (1931), 80.

61. Yong, *In the Days of Caesar*, 290.

nation) as a neighbor, helper, and sharer of God's life, not as an instrument of exploitation, calls for committing oneself to the common good both at local and global levels.[62] In light of these twin principles, the late Pope John Paul II writes:

> The State must contribute to the achievement of these goals [the common good] both directly and indirectly. Indirectly and according to the *principle of subsidiarity*, by creating favorable conditions for the free exercise of economic activity, which will lead to abundant opportunities for employment and sources of wealth. Directly and according to the *principle of solidarity*, by defending the weakest, by placing certain limits on the autonomy of the parties who determine working conditions, and by ensuring in every case the necessary minimum support for the unemployed worker.[63]

This Catholic Social Teaching brings us back to the key role of the church (along with the state and individuals), not only in working toward the common good, including poverty relief and social justice, but also in shaping and "redeeming" the market economy by providing an "alternative *telos*" to consumerism, materialism, and the absolutism of the market.[64] The church "as a people of God who live *in* a free market economy but are not *of* such an economy" is called to "inspiring a distinctively ecclesial set of economic practices that look back to the Jubilee doctrine and yet anticipate the future economy of the kingdom, even while working as a leaven within the present market system."[65] A "pneumatological economy of grace," as Amos Yong calls it (drawing on Douglas Meeks's trinitarian economy of grace),[66] in contrast to the economy of "effective demand" or maximum profits, mirrors what early Christians practiced (at least what they were called to practice): "charity (giving without anticipation of return), forgiveness (not only of sins but also of debts), and solidaristic fellowship [koinonia] (nurtured through interpersonal relations, common meals," common chest, hospitality, care of the sick, and interdependent interactions).[67] This economy of grace allows the recipients of the goods to be visible and attended to in relationship while recognizing their personhood and equal significance in God's kingdom; it also allows the sharers and givers to redeem their material goods in solidarity with the recipients while recognizing their common bond with the recipients as equal partners in God's kingdom and also as equally needy in Christ. This economy of grace works as a leaven for those who embrace it but will not

62. Pope John Paul II, *Sollicitudo Rei Socialis* (1987), 38–39.
63. John Paul II, *Centesimus Annus* (1991), 15.
64. Yong, *In the Days of Caesar*, 294.
65. Ibid., 294, 303, respectively.
66. Meeks, "Being Human in the Market Society," 261–63; see also M. D. Meeks, *God the Economist: The Doctrine of God and Political Economy* (Minneapolis: Fortress, 1989), 170–71.
67. Yong, *In the Days of Caesar*, 306–7.

necessarily bring ultimate justice to the national and world economy, which belongs to God and his coming kingdom alone. Nonetheless, it does foster greater sensitivity to the works and vision of justice and serves as a witness to God's creative intention and purpose: the common good and well-being of all people and of the creation.[68] If charity and generosity were to take an effect, justice has to be at work concurrently, which has to do with working for and establishing a local, national, and global infrastructure and system "that allows all people to contribute their talents and creativity to the common good."[69] While this justice seems to work typically in impersonal ways through the system and structure, it is also "deeply personal, in the sense that it can shape every human relationship."[70] Therefore, justice and charity are the two sides of the same coin in the mission of the church, as they were for the early church: "If we love others with charity, then first of all we are just toward them. Not only is justice not extraneous to charity, not only is it not an alternative or parallel path to charity: justice is inseparable from charity, and intrinsic to it."[71] Indeed, "if we are to show love toward neighbors, we must work for justice for all neighbors."[72]

7.3. What about the Prosperity Gospel Movement?

By highlighting the critical role of the church in constructing and practicing an economy of grace especially in "privileging" and protecting the weak and the poor and "redeeming" the market economy, how are we to understand the so-called prosperity gospel movement in some Christian circles? It may seem odd to bring up the prosperity gospel/theology in this context, since it is widely criticized in mainstream Christianity.[73] This issue of the prosperity movement is particularly poignant, however, because prosperity is a "central feature of the globalization of Pentecostalism"[74] and has a tremendous appeal and growth in the global South where poverty and suffering often define people's (Christians') day-to-day existence. This movement provides one surprising and controversial example of how the current church is attempting to contextualize the "economy of grace" and

68. Cf. Hicks, *Money Enough*, 172.

69. Ibid., 155.

70. Ibid.

71. Benedict XVI, *Caritas in Veritate* (2009), 6, quoted in Hicks, *Money Enough*, 156.

72. Hicks, *Money Enough*, 156.

73. See, for example, D. R. McConnell, *A Different Gospel: A Historical and Biblical Analysis of the Modern Faith Movement* (Peabody, MA: Hendrickson, 1988); G. D. Fee, *The Disease of the Health and Wealth Gospels* (Beverly, MA: Frontline, 1985); B. Barron, *The Health and Wealth Gospel* (Downers Grove, IL: InterVarsity, 1987); W. C. Kaiser Jr., "The Old Testament Promise of Material Blessings and the Contemporary Believer," *Trinity Journal* 9 (1988): 151–70.

74. Yong, *In the Days of Caesar*, 15.

address the problem of poverty while co-opting the contemporary features of global capitalism.

The prosperity movement traces its origin and history to Pentecostal and certain charismatic sectors as well as New Thought metaphysics in the United States at the turn of the twentieth century. The contemporary movement, coming out of the Pentecostal faith-healing movement, the Word of Faith, began to spread in the 1960s and 1970s and through the 1980s to this day via a number of charismatic proponents and television evangelists, such as Oral Roberts, Kenneth Hagin, and Kenneth and Gloria Copeland. Seizing on the biblical passages such as 3 John 2 that "Beloved, I wish above all things that thou mayest prosper and be in health, even as thy soul prospereth" (KJV), they all emphasized that physical healing and material blessings were part and parcel of salvation wrought by Jesus Christ. Also influenced by E. W. Keynon, who had been inspired by New Thought metaphysics and taught "positive confession of the Word of God" (based on Mark 11:24) and the predetermined "law of faith," they advocated the universal "success formula" from the Bible, such as the promise of a hundredfold return based on Mark 10:29–30; and they claimed that financial success would be guaranteed to those who have the faith and claim it for themselves as they give sacrificially to God, i.e., the ministries run by the prosperity preachers. Oral Roberts introduced the "Blessing-Pack" with a promise of financial blessing for the supporters of his ministry with a $100 donation (1954) and developed a "seed-faith" concept that the Old Testament tithe (giving out of obligation to God) was replaced by the New Testament version (giving in order to expect a blessing); thus one could plant a "seed" (i.e., donation to his ministry) and expect God's abundant material blessings in return.[75] According to Kenneth Hagin, "God has a certain law of prosperity and when you get into contact with that law . . . it just works for you—whoever you are."[76] Kenneth Copeland also writes, "Do you want a hundredfold return on your money? Give and let God multiply back to you."[77]

While these (white) preachers, who reached worldly success coming from humble and poor backgrounds, appealed to those who were seeking a similar release from socioeconomic disenfranchisement with divine help and increasingly catered their messages to the middle class, African American Pentecostal and charismatic preachers adopted and tailored the prosperity gospel to meet the particular needs of the black communities against the backdrop of the pursuit of equality, respectability, and social status by the civil rights movement

75. See S. Coleman, *The Globalisation of Charismatic Christianity: Spreading the Gospel of Prosperity* (Cambridge: Cambridge University Press, 2000), 41–42; D. Hollinger, "Enjoying God Forever: An Historical/Sociological Profile of the Health and Wealth Gospel," *Trinity Journal* 9 (1988): 142.

76. K. Hagin, "The Law of Faith," *Word of Faith* (November 1974): 2.

77. K. Copeland, *The Laws of Prosperity* (Fort Worth: Kenneth Copeland, 1974), 67.

and even black liberation theology.[78] Thomas Dexter Jakes (T. D. Jakes), the pastor of the Potter's House in Dallas, Texas, with over thirty thousand members, without qualms heads commercialized, ever-expanding enterprises (TDJ Enterprises) for profit, preaches the personal and economic betterment and principle of profitability, and displays his God-given, conspicuous wealth and the wealth of his church as a sign of divine presence and favor.[79] At the same time, however, his message of personal prosperity is "only a starting point rather than a goal in itself for his vision of transforming the black community."[80] He distinguishes profitability, which means "adding value to the Kingdom of God, to oneself, to one's family, and to all humanity" from just "getting rich" and worldly success.[81] Profitability requires hard work and the discipline of living within one's means, saving, and investing for holistic restoration while breaking the generational and communal curses of slavery, fatherlessness, passivity, and defeatism; and there is no profitability without faith and obedience to God.[82] His church and T. D. Jakes Ministries (nonprofit) play a crucial role in fulfilling God's vision of restoration and provide rather comprehensive social ministries and networks for the poor, the elderly, children, and other marginalized people. The organization's services range from a residential center, school, literacy program, and prison ministry, to assistance to pregnant teens and prostitutes.[83] His vision also included "alleviating poverty in southwest Dallas through real estate development, cooperative programs, and regional planning" and saw its fruition with establishment of an intergenerational community center, a Christian school, an independent living center, a business resource network targeting minority businesses, a performing arts center, a shopping center, and even a golf course.[84] Thus "if the civil rights movement made possible black upward mobility, Jakes and others have taken the initiative to realize these as actualities."[85]

The prosperity gospel has become another export of American Christianity to the "global market" but as the case of African American contextualization in conjunction with the civil rights movement, it has quickly found its strong

78. See a helpful book, S. Y. Mitchem, *Name It and Claim It? Prosperity Preaching in the Black Church* (Cleveland: Pilgrim, 2007), 103–45; cf. Yong, *In the Days of Caesar*, 265.

79. See a biography by S. Lee, *T. D. Jakes: America's New Preacher* (New York: New York University Press, 2005), esp. 84–157; Mitchem, *Name It and Claim It?* 103–23.

80. Yong, *In the Days of Caesar*, 267.

81. H. Morken, "Bishop T. D. Jakes: A Ministry for Empowerment," in *Religious Leaders and Faith-Based Politics* (ed. J. R. Formicola and H. Morken; Lanham, MD: Rowman & Littlefield, 2001), 35.

82. Ibid., 36, 49, respectively.

83. Yong, *In the Days of Caesar*, 267; see further S. Pappu, "The Preacher," *Atlantic Monthly* 297, no. 2 (2006): 92–103.

84. Morken, "Bishop T. D. Jakes," 40, 44.

85. Yong, *In the Days of Caesar*, 267n29; see further J. L. Walton, "Empowered: The Entrepreneurial Ministry of T. D. Jakes," *Christian Century*, July 10, 2007, 25–28.

niche and has become "indigenized" in particular socioeconomic, cultural, and historical contexts of African, Latin American, and some Asian countries.[86] For example, in Zimbabwe, the Zimbabwe Assemblies of God Africa (ZAOGA), founded by Ezekiel Guti, witnessed a spectacular success and claims to have about 10 percent of the national population.[87] Guti, having studied "Charismatic Oriented Biblical Studies," in the Christ for the Nations Institute in Dallas, Texas, returned to Zimbabwe and founded ZAOGA and transformed it into a "respectable bourgeois movement," tapping into his social and political capital as well as networks he had kept from the United States *and* the existing "deep African roots" in concern for betterment.[88] The church wields formidable social and political influence by promoting economic ethics that construct and channel Zimbabwean nationalism, liberation theology, and pan-African black pride (which drew on African American sources but was contextualized) into engendering social mobility, avoiding destitution, and dealing with modernity and benefiting from it.[89] ZAOGA conducts annual "penny capitalism" projects in which "indigenous business women" sell cheap foodstuffs (peanuts, chips, cakes, sweets, etc.) and clothes inside and outside the church community to finance its expansion; these projects systematize women's production and establish the participants as self-reliant entrepreneurs with provision of start-up grants and coaching of budgeting and market niches. After six months, the money earned by the projects is collected with much celebration and the participants give testimonies about "how God helped them make money and each person's earnings [which are significant] are read out."[90] ZAOGA also conducts periodic "resisting the 'spirit of poverty' initiatives" among its members.[91] The doctrine of the "spirit of poverty" explains the root cause and condition of poverty in Africa not because of structural injustice but because of a "spirit of poverty" passed on through ancestral spirits and traditions. Therefore, release from the "spirit of poverty" entails rejection of the negative ancestral habits, rituals, and sins such as debt and waste, witchcraft, polygamy, and violence on women, and adoption of the new, positive (economic) virtues and practices such as personal

86. See S. Brouwer, P. Gifford, and S. Rose, *Exporting the American Gospel* (New York: Routledge, 1996).
87. On ZAOGA and its transnational success and impact, see D. Maxwell, *African Gifts of the Spirit: Pentecostalism and the Rise of a Zimbabwean Transnational Religious Movement* (Athens: Ohio University Press; Harare, Zimbabwe: Weaver; London: James Currey, 2007); on its economic ethic, see Maxwell, *Christians and Chiefs in Zimbabwe* (Edinburgh: Edinburgh University Press, 1999); Maxwell, "Delivered from the Spirit of Poverty," *Journal of Religion in Africa* 28, no. 3 (1998): 350–73.
88. D. Martin, *Pentecostalism: The World Their Parish* (Oxford: Blackwell, 2002), 146; Maxwell, "Delivered from the Spirit of Poverty," 351–52.
89. Martin, *Pentecostalism*, 146–47; Maxwell, "Delivered from the Spirit of Poverty," 351–52.
90. Maxwell, "Delivered from the Spirit of Poverty," 355–56.
91. Ibid., 357–61.

financial responsibility, self-reliance, thriftiness, hard work, trustworthiness, literacy, being courteous to women, and mutual assistance in employment and welfare.[92] Thus, prosperity preached and practiced by and in ZAOGA takes a form of "re-socialization" that "makes the born-again believer more industrious and socially mobile than many of their 'unsaved' neighbours" in the various ways mentioned above.[93] As for the leaders, at least in teaching, if not in practice, conspicuous consumption as a display of God's blessings in their lives must be matched by conspicuous giving and charity.[94]

In Ghana, Mensa Otabil, pastor of the six-thousand-member International Central Gospel Church (ICGC), strikes a chord among the urban educated, English-speaking, upwardly mobile youth with his message of "releasing the power of the person and Black pride" for and with personal and national prosperity.[95] His message is not just about receiving fish but how to fish for oneself, so to speak: that is, not just about desiring, accumulating, and enjoying the benefit of wealth but also learning how to work toward success, how to manage one's resources, how to have control over wealth but not be controlled by it, and how to contribute building a prosperous economy of a larger society.[96] Like many other prosperity preachers, Otabil presents himself as the exemplar of a successful entrepreneur who embodies those virtues and qualities and continues to experience God's faithfulness to his promises, and thus as the fulfillment of his followers' faith-inspired aspirations. He broadens his appeal and vision to the whole of Africa, arguing for equality between blacks and whites and urging fellow Africans to take control of their lives and destinies so that they may be a blessing to others as God has intended.[97] "Herein the message of prosperity, dominion, and production interfaces with a vision for a revitalized African economy, one that allows the nations of Africa to participate in and contribute to the global market rather than be a dependent recipient of first world aid."[98] As in the case of Guti's (ZAOGA) message in the Zimbabwean and southern African context, when set in Ghanaian and western African context, "Otabil's Afrocentrism is a theology of hope—of health, wholeness, empowerment, and prosperity—that has individual, social, national, and even continental aspirations."[99]

In Latin America, the Brazilian-based, controversial Universal Church of the Kingdom of God (*Igreja Universal do Reino de Deus*, IURD) "made the

92. Ibid., 358–61; Martin, *Pentecostalism*, 146–47.

93. Maxwell, "Delivered from the Spirit of Poverty," 353.

94. Ibid., 363; Martin, *Pentecostalism*, 147.

95. Coleman, *Globalisation of Charismatic Christianity*, 33, following P. Gifford, *African Christianity: Its Public Role* (London: Hurst, 1998), 82.

96. Yong, *In the Days of Caesar*, 272–73; see further Gifford, *African Christianity*, 140–60.

97. See M. Otabil, *Beyond the Rivers of Ethiopia* (Bakersfield, CA: Pneuma Life; Accra-North, Ghana: International Central Gospel Church, 1993).

98. Yong, *In the Days of Caesar*, 274.

99. Ibid., 275.

prosperity message central to its mission and evangelistic agenda"[100] as "an enormous money machine."[101] With three to six million members at its height before its downturn in 2000, it has its own political party, one of the largest television stations in Brazil, and a professional football team.[102] As it has become a "transnational organization" with churches set up in North America, Africa, Europe, and Asia, it adopted the "consumer advertising" of global capitalism and contextualized the prosperity gospel according to "the global economy of migration" that to "those in the lower classes the focus is on economic survival, while to those in the middle and upper classes the emphasis is on economic success."[103] As in the other prosperity churches, in the context of the giver's relationship with God, tithing and giving to the church—its "lifeblood"—is the most significant investment and the key to unlocking the reciprocity of material blessings from God;[104] conversely, withholding the tithe is a serious violation in the contractual agreement (with God) that may result in spiritual degeneration and material depravity.[105] Despite the abuses, in the context of popular religiosity in Brazil and in light of its majority of members, drawn from "the underworld sector of the underclass,"[106] this almost sacred focus on tithing empowers the poor as the givers, creditors, and contributors to the "lifeblood" of their church.[107] At the same time, IURD enthusiastically promotes the virtues of entrepreneurship for the "prosperity campaigns" based on the social space and networks within the church.[108] IURD members and the many poor of other Pentecostal congregations in Brazil and Chile are instructed to shun destructive habits (alcohol, drugs, tobacco, promiscuity), to invest and resocialize in home and church, and to take two or three jobs, receiving training in skills ranging from building and driving to managing household accounts.[109] Prosperity Pentecostal communities across Latin America are concerned about both accumulating wealth for the kingdom and equipping the members with economic disciplines and competitiveness, along with providing a range of social services to help them face and confront the pressures of modernization.[110]

100. Ibid., 18.

101. B. Furre, "Crossing Boundaries: The 'Universal Church' and the Spirit of Globalization," in Spirits of Globalization: The Growth of Pentecostalism and Experiential Spiritualities in a Global Age (ed. S. J. Stålsett; London: SCM, 2006), 46, quoted in Yong, In the Days of Caesar, 18.

102. P. Jenkins, The Next Christendom: The Coming of Global Christianity (rev. ed.; Oxford: Oxford University Press, 2007), 74.

103. Yong, In the Days of Caesar, 18–19.

104. R. A. Chestnut, Born Again in Brazil: The Pentecostal Boom and the Pathogens of Poverty (New Brunswick, NJ: Rutgers University Press, 1997), 117–19.

105. Chestnut, Born Again in Brazil, 119.

106. Martin, Pentecostalism, 80.

107. Chestnut, Born Again in Brazil, 118–19.

108. Ibid., 116–17.

109. Martin, Pentecostalism, 80–81.

110. See D. Petersen, "Latin American Pentecostalism: Social Capital, Networks, and Politics," PNEUMA: The Journal of the Society for Pentecostal Studies 26 (2004): 293–306.

In the Philippines, the El Shaddai movement founded by "Brother Mike" Velarde, with seven million adherents across the nation and twenty-five chapters worldwide (2007), represents a Catholic charismatic expression of the prosperity gospel. "El Shaddai's Master Plan" for people, according to Velarde, is "prosperity, good health, and success in this life" since ultimately "He [God] wants us to be a part of His plan to build His Kingdom on earth" with the qualification that worldly prosperity is "not for yourself but to use . . . for the glory of God."[111] Velarde's teachings (e.g., the "seed-faith principle" and "positive confession") are influenced by American prosperity preachers like Oral Roberts, Kenneth Hagin, and Pat Robertson but are adapted to a Filipino context. Reflecting the current composition of the churches with prosperity appeal in the world, a vast majority (up to 80 percent) of its members are those who live below the nation's poverty thresholds but who expect that someday their monetary "seeds" of faith (i.e., prayer requests with tithe and gifts to the El Shaddai radio station, foundation, and its Golden Rule company) will bring about the miraculous returns of God's earthly blessings.[112] Because the cause of suffering and poverty is a person's disobedience of God's will or principles (not necessarily systems of injustice beyond people's control), the way to alleviate or rid oneself of suffering and poverty is by following God's principles that include tithing, saving, and striving to improve one's lot, as well as abstinence from drugs, gambling, drinking, smoking, borrowing money, and adultery.[113] This living by God's principles is accompanied by El Shaddai's social services that include "consumer cooperatives, livelihood assistance (for natural disaster victims), medical and dental services, disaster relief, educational assistance, and legal help."[114] In addition, people are asked to bring any objects they want blessed by Velarde (especially for healing, jobs, or finances) to rallies, and "when brought into the El Shaddai ritual sphere, [those 'blessing objects'] become catalysts for upward mobility."[115] For instance, wallets, bank savings books, job applications, or healing oil are opened up to the sky;[116] some worshipers raise their passports to be blessed to secure that they will get visas for working overseas. As a symbolic gesture of catching the abundant earthly blessings coming from on high, many also open umbrellas and turn them upside down.[117]

On the one hand, there is no doubt that this gospel of health and wealth is fraught with hermeneutical, theological, and ethical abuses, and with the

111. K. L. Wiegele, *Investing in Miracles: El Shaddai and the Transformation of Popular Catholicism in the Philippines* (Honolulu: University of Hawaii Press, 2005), 23.
112. Yong, *In the Days of Caesar*, 17; Wiegele, *Investing in Miracles*, 81, 27, respectively.
113. Wiegele, *Investing in Miracles*, 18–22.
114. Ibid., 33–34.
115. Ibid., 32–33.
116. Ibid., 33.
117. Jenkins, *Next Christendom*, 77.

problems of commercialized "anti-gospel of greed"[118] and egotism, and that these ultra-mega-prosperity churches and preachers have exploited the poor and vulnerable with magical formulas, manipulation, and business schemes while amassing their own kingdoms and family enterprises. They distort the gospel of the Christ crucified and reduce the mysterious workings of God to a predictable giant vending machine, and their embarrassing scandals and failures of expectations are too numerous to count. On the other hand, within the specific socioeconomic and cultural situations in which these movements spread among the disinherited (in the global South), these prosperity movements could be and have been the agents of social and economic transformation in a qualified sense. In Donald Miller and Tetsunao Yamamori's study on global Pentecostalism, a Filipino observer (not a participant) of the prosperity gospel aptly captures the critical problem of poverty: "the biggest problem that poor people face is that they have no hope for future advancement."[119] Prosperity gospel preachers, in their promotion of worldly success and material blessings, rather than "pie-in-the-sky-in-the-sweet-by-and-by," raise the hope and expectations of the hopeless about the possibility of a better life with the fight against a "demon of poverty" and "provoke people to think in new ways, and while members may be disappointed if they are expecting a quick fix, they may also start organizing their lives in ways that allow for upward social mobility."[120] As we have encountered, some of these prosperity gospel preachers take on a role of financial planners and lifestyle coaches and offer sound, pragmatic advice concerning budgeting, family planning, lifestyle change, and business investment.[121] Thus, while liberation theology advocated a preferential option for the poor, the poor themselves opted for the prosperity gospel (and Pentecostalism) in Latin America and elsewhere.

Indeed, Pentecostal churches "function as alternative social and economic networks, with congregations providing local apprenticeship systems for members, especially in terms of knitting together people into communities with 'mutual obligations and shared concerns.' "[122] In other words, they function to provide the "initial endowments" for the poor so that they can participate in the communally monitored market. Formation of a new social network in the church "that breaks with the street, cherishes the home, and promotes thrift, discipline, mutual respect among spouses, trust, honesty, self-confidence, hard work, and sobriety" (in the context of male irresponsibility mixed with machismo in Guatemala City, for instance), brings about not only individ-

---

118. This phrase is from Yong, *In the Days of Caesar*, 264; cf. Maxwell, "Delivered from the Spirit of Poverty," 366–69.

119. D. Miller and T. Yamamori, *Global Pentecostalism: The New Face of Christian Social Engagement* (Berkeley: University of California Press, 2007), 176.

120. Miller and Yamamori, *Global Pentecostalism*, 176.

121. Ibid., 167.

122. Yong, *In the Days of Caesar*, 24.

ual transformation but social transformation among the poor, who exercise responsibility and develop a sense of being able to take charge of one's own life and that of a community.[123] Then, prosperity Pentecostal communities as "new forms of solidarity" exhibit Yong's "pneumatological economy of grace" in unexpected though ambivalent ways. Conversion to Pentecostalism interestingly correlates with socioeconomic advancement (or at least hope for advancement) in places where painful social and economic transitions are taking place and where global capitalism and consumer culture are on the rise.[124] David Martin's assessment of a powerful emerging culture of Pentecostal, prosperity-influenced evangelical Protestants in Latin America can be generalized to an extent in the global South:

> It is a culture which has enabled many to survive who would otherwise have sunk into abject immiseration, and has aided many to ride the sea of economic change with some success. It has created social capital where none existed and has motivated and sustained a labor force which shifted from being pre-modern to post-industrial often in one traumatic step. Without the Pentecostal movement the transition might have been less successful and involved far more violent social disruption.[125]

In this way, the Pentecostal/charismatic prosperity gospel does resonate positively with a free-market economy with entrepreneurial spirits and modes of operations, and it results in tangible upward mobility for some, if not many, of its adherents. Prosperity-pursuing Pentecostals/Charismatics adopt the kinds of discipline that enhance a sense of self-esteem and the integrity and economy of the family, foster supportive self-help groups that contribute to the social welfare of their members, and promote independent initiative, interdependent businesses, and equality within the social space provided by the church in the very social and cultural contexts where new opportunities for those expressions are regularly denied for the poor and disadvantaged.[126] It exhibits seemingly contradictory, yet fitting, capitalist modes of economic ethics: simplicity, disciplined consumption, and diligence and honesty at work, on the one hand, and "holy materialism" and "sanctified consumerism," on the other, as blessings that come with salvation and as divine validation of the adherents' faith.[127] In this era of globalization, Pentecostalism "has

123. Martin, *Pentecostalism*, 85–86. See H. Gooren, *Rich among the Poor: Church, Firm, and Household among Small-Scale Entrepreneurs in Guatemala City* (Amsterdam: Thela Thesis, 1999), 23–229, esp. 149–97, 214–29.

124. Martin, *Pentecostalism*, 14–15, 77–88, 139–40; Miller and Yamamori, *Global Pentecostalism*, 33; cf. Maxwell, "Delivered from the Spirit of Poverty," 369. This is the same kind of transformation that Lupton, *Toxic Charity*, as well as Fikkert and Corbett, *When Helping Hurts*, point to as a result of the asset-based community development.

125. Martin, *Pentecostalism*, 82.

126. Cf. ibid., 144; Petersen, "Latin American Pentecostalism," 296.

127. Cf. Martin, *Pentecostalism*, 88; Yong, *In the Days of Caesar*, 19.

become the religion of choice in part because it promotes values that enable transition into and survival within the market economy."[128] Thus, prosperity Pentecostalism and contemporary capitalism are related by way of "a complex symbiosis,"[129] and the "pious poor" look forward to being transformed into the pious rich with a hundredfold return of their spiritual and material investment "in Christ."

7.4. Last Words

As we leave this final chapter, it is apparent that I have not touched many important topics. However, from the limited topics addressed in this chapter, I hope I have shown that early Christian texts and practices concerning wealth and poverty still offer to us relevant, referential, and illuminating frameworks, principles, perspectives, and practices for our contemporary dealings with wealth and poverty and their attendant opportunities and challenges—enormous historical and sociocultural distance and "otherness" notwithstanding.[130] Just as early Christians consciously constructed their self-definition(s) using wealth, responding to poverty, and understanding the responsibilities of the rich and the poor in light of God's creative purpose, Christians today are inescapably called to and have been forming and reforming Christian identity in relation to our attitude, use, and distribution of wealth and dealing with poverty for the common good, individually and corporately. Based on the continuing work of the Holy Spirit in creating, guiding, and "perfecting" Christian communities throughout history, Christians near and far have been engaged in these endeavors of constructing and reconstructing collective identity as lovers of God and neighbors through collective engagement in socioeconomic beliefs and practices by reading, interpreting, and translating past practices into their present ultimately in light of the collective vision and projection of the future—the eschaton when God's perfect love, justice, and abundant life will reign. In this sense, the relevance, usefulness, and guidance of early Christian texts and practices for the present is because of their eschatological orientation, their future-orientedness even as the Christians in the present are reminded of and look forward to the future through the mediated past.[131] The distinct economy of grace practiced by the church, however imperfectly

---

128. Yong, *In the Days of Caesar*, 21.

129. B. Martin, "New Mutations of the Protestant Ethic among Latin American Pentecostals," *Religion* 25 (1995): 101.

130. Despite Allen, "Challenges in Approaching Patristic Texts from the Perspective of Contemporary Catholic Social Teaching," in *Reading Patristic Texts on Social Ethics: Issues and Challenges for Twenty-First-Century Christian Social Thought* (ed. J. Leemans, B. J. Matz, and J. Verstraeten; Washington, DC: Catholic University of America Press, 2011), 40.

131. Cf. R. Bieringer, "Texts That Create a Future: The Function of Ancient Texts for Theology Today," in *Reading Patristic Texts* (ed. Leemans, Matz, and Verstraeten), 14–23.

throughout history as a leaven in this world, will find its perfect manifestation in God's kingdom even as we strive to embody this here and now, certainly in contrast to the worldly ways, structures, and systems in one respect but in conjunction or cooperation with them in another respect.

Consider the words of Boniface Ramsey on the church fathers' appeal to apparent self-interest of givers/donors (e.g., salvation, heavenly rewards, perfection, etc.) for their distribution of wealth to the needy:

> The Fathers may have been crass to a certain extent in speaking as they did of spiritual rewards, but they also understood human nature and were ultimately only translating scriptural data into more graspable terms. . . . Their intention was, after all, not theoretical so much as practical: to provide for the feeding and clothing of the poor.[132]

We are called to continue this task of "translating scriptural data into more graspable terms" in our context though not without mistakes, misgivings, and blind spots. The poor will always be with us, but precisely because that is so, God commands, "open your hand to the poor and needy neighbour in your land" (Deut. 15:11)—until Christ comes again.

132. B. Ramsey, "Almsgiving in the Latin Church: The Late Fourth and Early Fifth Centuries," *TS* 43 (1982): 259.

Bibliography

Primary Sources

The Amherst Papyri. Part 1 of *The Ascension of Isaiah, and Other Theological Fragments*. Edited by W. A. T.-A. Amherst, B. P. Gremfell, and A. S. Hunt. London: H. Frowde, 1900.

The Apostolic Fathers. Edited and translated by B. E. Ehrman. 2 vols. LCL. Cambridge, MA: Harvard University Press, 2003.

The Apostolic Fathers with Justin Martyr and Irenaeus. Edited by A. Roberts and J. Donaldson. Ante-Nicene Fathers 1. Edited by A. C. Coxe. New York: Charles Scribner's Sons, 1908.

Brandt, S., and Laubmann, G. *L. Caeli Firmiani Lactanti Opera Omnia*. CSEL 19 and 27. Prague, Vienna, Leipzig, 1890–93.

Charlesworth, J. H., ed. *The Old Testament Pseudepigrapha*. 2 vols. New York: Doubleday, 1983.

Chrysostom, J. *On Repentance and Almsgiving*. Edited by G. G. Christo. Washington, DC: Catholic University of America Press, 1998.

Cicero. *De Officiis*. Translated by W. Miller. LCL. London: Heinemann, 1938.

Clement of Alexandria. *Clementis Alexandrini Paedagogus*. Edited by M. Marcovich. VCSup 62. Leiden: Brill, 2002.

———. *Clementis Alexandrini Protrepticus*. Edited by M. Marcovich. VCSup 34. Leiden: Brill, 1995.

———. *Exhortation to the Greeks/The Rich Man's Salvation*. Translated by G. W. Butterworth. LCL. Cambridge, MA: Harvard University Press, 1919.

———. *Les Stromates: Stromate VI*. Edited and translated by P. Descourtieux with an introduction and notes. Sources Chrétiennes 446. Paris: Éditions du Cerf, 1999.

———. *Stromata III and VII*. Translated by H. Chadwick. Edited by J. E. L. Oulton and H. Chadwick. *Alexandrian Christianity*. Library of Christian Classics 2. London: SCM, 1954.

———. *Stromateis: Books 1–3*. Translated by J. Ferguson. FC 85. Washington, DC: Catholic University of America Press, 1991.

Connolly, R. H. *Didascalia Apostolorum: The Syriac Version Translated and Accompanied by the Verona Latin Fragments.* Oxford: Clarendon, 1929.

Cyprian. *De Lapsis and De Ecclesiae Catholicae Unitate.* Text and translation by M. Bevenot. Oxford: Clarendon, 1971.

———. *The Letters of St. Cyprian of Carthage.* Translated and annotated by G. W. Clarke. 4 Vols. ACW 43-44, 46-47. New York: Newman, 1984–88.

———. *Saint Cyprian: Treatises.* Translated and edited by R. J. Deferrari. FC 36. New York: Fathers of the Church, 1958.

———. *Sancti Cypriani Episcopi Opera. Pars II: Ad Donatvm, De mortalitate, Ad Demetrianvm, De opera et eleemosynis, De zelo et livore.* CCSL. Turnholti: Typographi Brepols Editores Pontificii, 1976.

The Didascalia Apostolorum in Syriac. Translated by A. Vööbus. 2 Vols. Corpus Scriptorum Christianorum Orientalium. Louvain: Secrétariat du Corpus SCO, 1979.

Ehrenberg, V., and A. M. Jones, eds. *Documents Illustrating the Reigns of Augustus and Tiberius.* Oxford: Clarendon, 1955.

Elliott, J. K. *The Apocryphal New Testament.* Oxford: Clarendon, 1993.

Epictetus. *The Discourses as Reported by Arrian, the Manual and Fragments.* Translated by W. A. Oldfather. 2 Vols. LCL. 1928. Repr., Cambridge, MA: Harvard University Press, 1978.

Eusebius of Caesarea. *The Ecclesiastical History.* Translated by K. Lake. LCL. Cambridge, MA: Harvard University Press, 1926–32.

———. *Eusebius' Ecclesiatical History.* Translated by C. F. Cruse. New updated edition. Peabody, MA: Hendrickson, 1998.

Evagrius Ponticus. *Evagrius Ponticus: Ad Monachos.* Translated by J. Driscoll. ACW 59. New York: Newman, 2003.

Evagrius of Pontus: The Greek Ascetic Corpus. Translated by R. E. Sinkewicz. Oxford Early Christian Studies. Oxford: Oxford University Press, 2003.

The Fathers of the Second Century: Hermas, Tatian, Athenagoras, Theophilus, and Clement of Alexandria (Entire). Edited by A. Roberts and J. Donaldson. Ante-Nicene Fathers 2. Edited by A. C. Coxe. New York: Charles Scribner's Sons, 1908.

The Fathers of the Third Century: Hippolytus, Cyprian, Caius, Novatian, Appendix. Edited by A. Roberts and J. Donaldson. Ante-Nicene Fathers 2. Edited by A. C. Coxe. Grand Rapids: Eerdmans, 1951.

Gibson, E. *The "Christians For Christians" Inscriptions of Phrygia.* Harvard Theological Studies 32. Missoula, MT: Scholars Press, 1978.

Heck, E., and A. Wlosok. *Epitome Insitutionum Divinarum.* Teubner: Stuttgart, 1994.

Hippolytus. *On the Apostolic Tradition.* Translated, with an introduction and commentary, by A. Stewart-Sykes. Crestwood, NY: St. Vladimir's Seminary Press, 2001.

Holmes, M. W., ed. *The Apostolic Fathers: Greek Texts and English Translations.* Updated edition of *The Apostolic Fathers: Greek Texts and English Translations of Their Writings.* 2nd ed. Edited and translated by J. B. Lightfoot and J. R. Harmer. Grand Rapids: Baker Books, 1999.

Irenaeus of Lyons. *St. Irenaeus of Lyons Against the Heresies, Book I*. Translated by D. J. Unger and Rev. J. J. Dillon. ACW 55. New York: Paulist Press, 1992.

Johnson, G. J. *Early-Christian Epitaphs from Anatolia*. SBL Texts and Translations 35. Early Christian Literature 8. Atlanta: Scholars Press, 1995.

Junod, E., and J.-D. Kaestli, eds. *Acta Iohannis*. Corpus Christianorum Series Apocryphorum 1 and 2. Brepols, 1983.

Justin Martyr. *Dialogus cum Typhone*. Edited by M. Marcovich. PTS 47. Berlin: Walter de Gruyter, 1997.

———. *The First and Second Apologies*. Translated, with an introduction and notes, by L. W. Barnard. ACW 56. New York: Paulist Press, 1997.

———. *Iustini Martyris Apologiae pro Christianis*. Edited by M. Marcovich. PTS 38. Berlin: Walter de Gruyter, 1994.

Juvenal. *Juvenal and Persius*. Translated by G. G. Ramsay. LCL. New York: G. P. Putnam's Sons, 1918.

Lactantius. *Divine Institutes*. Translated, with an introduction and notes, by A. Bowen and P. Garnsey. Liverpool: Liverpool University Press, 2003.

———. *Lactantius: De Mortibus Persecutorum*. Edited and translated by J. L. Creed. Oxford: Oxford University Press, 1984.

Lewis, Naphtali, and Meyer Reinhold, eds. *The Empire*. Vol. 2 of *Roman Civilization: Selected Readings*. 3rd ed. New York: Columbia University Press, 1990.

Lipsius, R. A., and M. Bonnet, eds. *Acta Apostolorum Apocrypha*. 3 Vols. Leipzig: Mendelssohn, 1891–1903.

Lucian of Samosata. *Lucian*. Translated by A. M. Harmon, K. Kilburn, and M. D. Macleod. 8 Vols. LCL. Cambridge, MA: Harvard University Press, 1921–67.

Lutz, C. E. *Musonius Rufus: The Roman Socrates*. Yale Classical Studies 10. New Haven: Yale University Press, 1947.

MacKenzie, I. M. *Irenaeus' Demonstration of the Apostolic Preaching: A Theological Commentary and Translation*. Aldershot, UK: Ashgate, 2002.

Malherbe, A. J. *Moral Exhortation, A Greco-Roman Sourcebook*. Library of Early Christianity. Philadelphia: Westminster, 1986.

Minucius Felix. *Octavius*. Translated by G. H. Rendall. LCL. Cambridge, MA: Harvard University Press, 1931.

———. *The Octavius of Marcus Minucius Felix*. Translated by G. W. Clarke. ACW 39. New York: Newman, 1974.

Musurillo, H., ed. *The Acts of the Christian Martyrs*. 1972. Repr., Oxford: Oxford University Press, 2000.

Origen. *Commentary on the Epistle to the Romans, Books 6–10*. Translated by T. P. Scheck. FC 104. Washington, DC: Catholic University of America Press, 2002.

———. *Commentaire sur l'évangile selon Matthieu*. Tome 1 (Livres X et XI). Introduction, translation, and notes by R. Girod. Paris: Éditions du Cerf, 1970.

———. *Contra Celsum*. Translated by H. Chadwick. Cambridge: Cambridge University Press, 1953.

———. *Contra Celsum*. Edited by M. Marcovich. Boston: Brill, 2001.

———. *Homilies on Genesis and Exodus*. Translated by R. E. Heine. Washington, DC: Catholic University of America Press, 1982.

———. *Homilies on Joshua*. Translated by B. J. Bruce. Edited by C. White. Washington, DC: Catholic University of America Press, 2002.

———. *Homilies on Leviticus, 1–16*. Translated by G. W. Barclay. Washington, DC: Catholic University of America Press, 1990.

———. *Homilies on Luke; Fragments on Luke*. Translated by J. T. Lienhard. Washington, DC: Catholic University of America Press, 1996.

———. *Prayer; Exhortation to Martyrdom*. Translated by J. J. O'Meara. Westminster, MD: Newman, 1954.

"The Oxford Declaration." *Transformation* 7, no. 2 (April–June, 1990): 7–18.

Peter of Alexandria. *Two Coptic Homilies Attributed to the Saint Peter of Alexandria: On Riches, On the Epiphany*. Translated and edited, with an introduction, by B. Pearson and T. Vivian with D. B. Spanel. Rome: C.I.M., 1993.

Phan, P. C. *Social Thought*. Message of the Fathers of the Church 20. Wilmington, DE: Michael Glazier, 1984.

Pliny, Caecilius Secundus. *Letters*. 2 Vols. Translated by W. Melmoth. Revised by W. M. L. Hutchinson. LCL. Cambridge: Harvard University Press, 1961, 1963.

Plutarch. *On Love of Wealth*. Vol. 7 of Plutarch's Moralia. Translated by P. H. De Lacy and B. Einarson. LCL. Cambridge, MA: Harvard University Press, 1959.

Robinson, J. M. *The Nag Hammadi Library in English*. Translated, with an introduction, by Members of the Coptic Gnostic Library Project of the Institute for Antiquity and Christianity, Clarement, CA. 3rd ed. Afterword by R. Smith. San Francisco: HarperSanFrancisco, 1988.

Schneemelcher, W. *Writings Relating to Apostles, Apocalypses and Related Subjects*. Vol. 2 of *New Testament Apocrypha*. Translated by R. M. Wilson. Rev. ed. Louisville: Westminster John Knox, 1991, 1992.

Seneca. *Volume 4: Epistles 66–92*. Translated by R. M. Gummere. LCL 76. Cambridge, MA: Harvard University Press, 1925.

———. *Moral Essays: On Beneficiis*. Translated by J. Bascore. LCL 310. Cambridge, MA: Harvard University Press, 1935.

The Sentences of Sextus. Edited and translated by R. A. Edwards and R. A. Wild, SJ. Chico, CA: Scholars Press, 1981.

Shelton, J.-A. *As the Romans Did: A Sourcebook in Roman Social History*. 2nd ed. New York: Oxford University Press, 1998.

Shewring, W., ed. *Rich and Poor in Christian Tradition*. London: Burns Oates & Washbourne, 1948.

Stackhouse, M. L., D. P. McCann, and S. J. Roels, eds. *On Moral Business: Classical and Contemporary Resources for Ethics in Economic Life*. Grand Rapids: Eerdmans, 1995.

Stewart-Sykes, A. *On the Apostolic Tradition: An English Version with Introduction and Commentary*. Crestwood, NY: St. Vladimir's Seminary Press, 2001.

Tabbernee, W. *Montanist Inscriptions and Testamonia: Epigraphic Sources Illustrating the History of Montanism*. Patristic Monograph Series 16. Macon, GA: Mercer University Press, 1997.

Tatian. *Oratio ad Graecos and Fragments*. Edited and translated by M. Whittaker. OECT 8. Oxford: Clarendon, 1982.

Tertullian. *Apology and De Spectaculis*. Translated by T. R. Glover. LCL. Cambridge, MA: Harvard University Press, 1931.

———. *Tertullian: Adversus Marcionem*. Edited and translated by E. Evans. 5 vols. OECT. Oxford: Clarendon, 1972.

———. *Tertullian: Apologetical Works and Minucius Felix: Octavius*. Translated by R. Arbesmann, E. J. Daly, and E. A. Quain. FC 10. New York: Fathers of the Church, 1950.

———. *Tertullian: Disciplinary, Moral, and Ascetical Works*. Translated by R. Arbesmann, E. J. Daly, and E. A. Quain. FC 40. Washington, DC: Catholic University of America Press, 1959.

———. *Tertullian: De Idololatria*. Translation and commentary by J. H. Waszink and J. C. M. Van Winden. Leiden: Brill, 1987.

———. *Tertulliani Opera. Pars I: Opera Catholica Adversus Marcionem*. CCSL. Turnholti: Typographi Brepols Editores Pontificii, 1954.

———. *Treatises on Marriage and Remarriage: To His Wife, An Exhortation to Chastity, Monogamy*. Translated and annotated by W. P. Le Saint. ACW 13. Westminster, MD: Newman, 1956.

Theophilus of Antioch. *Ad Autolycum*. Translated by R. M. Grant. OECT 10. Oxford: Clarendon, 1980.

Secondary Sources

Adamson, J. B. *James: The Man and His Message*. Grand Rapids: Eerdmans, 1989.

Alföldy, G. "The Crisis of the Third Century as Seen by Contemporaries." *Greek, Roman and Byzantine Studies* 15 (1974): 89–111.

———. *The Social History of Rome*. 2nd rev. ed. Baltimore: Johns Hopkins University Press, 1988.

Allen, P. "Challenges in Approaching Patristic Texts from the Perspective of Contemporary Catholic Social Teaching." Pages 30–42 in *Reading Patristic Texts on Social Ethics: Issues and Challenges for Twenty-First-Century Christian Social Thought*. Edited by J. Leemans, B. J. Matz, and J. Verstraeten. Washington, DC: Catholic University of America Press, 2011.

Allen, P., B. Neil, and W. Mayer. *Preaching Poverty in Late Antiquity: Perceptions and Realities*. Leipzig: Evangelische Verlagsanstalt, 2009.

Allison, P. "Roman Households: An Archaeological Perspective." Pages 112–46 in *Roman Urbanism: Beyond the Consumer City*. Edited by H. M. Parkins. London: Routledge, 1997.

Alston, R. *Aspects of Roman History, AD 14–117*. London: Routledge, 1998.

Anderson, G. A. "Redeem Your Sins by the Giving of Alms: Sin, Debt, and the 'Treasury of Merit' in Early Jewish and Christian Tradition." *Letter & Spirit* 3 (2007): 39–67.

Arterbury, A. *Entertaining Angels: Early Christian Hospitality in Its Mediterranean Setting*. Sheffield: Sheffield Phoenix, 2005.

Atkins, Margaret, and Robin Osborne, eds. *Poverty in the Roman World*. Cambridge: Cambridge University Press, 2006.

Aune, D. E. "Eschatology (Early Christian)." Pages 594–609 in vol. 2 of *ABD*. Edited by D. N. Freedman. New York: Doubleday, 1992.

———. "The Significance of the Delay of the Parousia for Early Christianity." Pages 87–109 in *Current Issues in Biblical and Patristic Interpretation*. Edited by G. F. Hawthorne. Grand Rapids: Eerdmans, 1975.

Avilla, C. *Ownership: Early Christian Teaching*. Maryknoll, NY: Orbis Books, 1981.

Baker, D. *Tight Fists or Open Hands? Wealth and Poverty in Old Testament Law*. Grand Rapids: Eerdmans, 2009.

Balch, D. L. "Rich and Poor, Proud and Humble in Luke-Acts." Pages 214–333 in *The Social World of the First Christians: Essays in Honor of Wayne A. Meeks*. Edited by L. M. White and O. L. Yarbrough. Philadelphia: Fortress, 1995.

Bammel, F. "*ptōchos*." Pages 888–915 in vol. 6 of *TDNT*. Edited by G. Friedrich. Translated by G. W. Bromiley. Grand Rapids: Eerdmans, 1968.

Barclay, J. M. "Money and Meetings: Group Formation among Diaspora Jews and Early Christians." Pages 113–27 in *Vereine, Synagogen und Gemeinden im kaiserzeitlichen Kleinasien*. Edited by A. Gutsfeld and D.-A. Koch. Tübingen: Mohr Siebeck, 2006.

———. "Poverty in Pauline Studies: A Response to Steven Friesen." *JSNT* 26 (2004): 363–66.

Barker, I. V. "Charismatic Economics: Pentecostalism, Economic Restructuring, and Social Reproduction." *New Political Science* 29, no. 4 (2007): 407–27.

Barnard, L. W. "The 'Epistle of Barnabas' and Its Contemporary Setting." *ANRW* 2.27.1 (1993): 159–207.

Barnes, T. D. "Lactantius and Constantine." *JRS* 63 (1973): 29–46.

———. *Tertullian: A Historical and Literary Study*. Oxford: Clarendon, 1971.

Barron, B. *The Health and Wealth Gospel*. Downers Grove, IL: InterVarsity, 1987.

Barrosse, T. "The Unity of the Two Charities in Greek Patristic Exegesis." Pages 69–102 in *Christian Life: Ethics, Morality, and Discipline in the Early Church*. Edited by E. Ferguson. Vol. 16 of *Studies in Early Christianity: A Collection of Scholarly Essays*. New York: Garland, 1993. Repr. from *TS* 15 (1954): 355–88.

Bartchy, S. Scott. "Community of Goods in Acts: Idealization or Social Reality?" Pages 309–18 in *The Future of Early Christianity: Essays in Honor of Helmut Koester*. Edited by B. A. Pearson. Minneapolis: Fortress, 1991.

Bassler, J. M. *God and Mammon: Asking for Money in the New Testament*. Nashville: Abingdon, 1991.

Batey, R. *Jesus and the Poor*. New York: Harper & Row, 1972.

Bauckham, R. "The Economic Critique of Rome in Revelation 18." Pages 47–90 in *Images of Empire*. Edited by L. Alexander. JSOTSup 12. Sheffield, UK: Sheffield Academic Press, 1991.

————. "The Great Tribulation in the Shepherd of Hermas." *JTS* 25 (1974): 27–40.

Bauer, W. *Orthodoxy and Heresy in Earliest Christianity.* London: SCM, 1972.

Behr, J. *Asceticism and Anthropology in Irenaeus and Clement.* Oxford: Oxford University Press, 2000.

Beisner, E. C. "Justice and Poverty: Two Views Contrasted." Pages 57–80 in *Christianity and Economics in the Post–Cold War Era: The Oxford Declaration and Beyond.* Edited by H. Schlossberg, V. Samuel, and R. J. Sider. Grand Rapids: Eerdmans, 1994.

Berger, K. "Almosen für Israel." *NTS* 23 (1977): 180–224.

Bernstein, A. E. *The Formation of Hell: Death and Retribution in the Ancient and Early Christian Worlds.* Ithaca, NY: Cornell University Press, 1993.

Bieringer, R. "Texts That Create a Future: The Function of Ancient Texts for Theology Today." Pages 3–29 in *Reading Patristic Texts on Social Ethics: Issues and Challenges for Twenty-First-Century Christian Social Thought.* Edited by J. Leemans, B. J. Matz, and J. Verstraeten. Washington, DC: Catholic University of America Press, 2011.

Bird, F. B. "A Comparative Study of the Work of Charity in Christianity and Judaism." *JRE* 10 (1982): 144–69.

Blasi, A. J., J. Duhaime, and P.-A. Turcotte, eds. *Handbook of Early Christianity: Social Approaches.* Walnut Creek, CA: Altamira, 2002.

Blomberg, C. *Neither Poverty Nor Riches: A Biblical Theology of Material Possessions.* Grand Rapids: Eerdmans, 1999.

Boatwright, M. T. "Plancia Magna of Perge: Women's Roles and Status in Roman Asia Minor." Pages 249–72 in *Women's History and Ancient History.* Edited by S. B. Pomeroy. Chapel Hill: University of North Carolina Press, 1991.

Bobertz, C. A. "Cyprian of Carthage as Patron: A Social Historical Study of the Role of Bishop in the Ancient Christian Community of North Africa." PhD diss., Yale University, 1988.

————. "The Development of Episcopal Order." Pages 183–211 in *Eusebius, Christianity and Judaism.* Edited by H. W. Attridge and G. Hata. Leiden: Brill, 1992.

————. "Patronage Networks and the Study of Ancient Christianity." *StPatr* 24 (1993): 20–27.

————. "The Role of Patron in the Cena Dominica of Hippolytus' Apostolic Tradition." *JTS* 44 (1993): 170–84.

Bodel, J. "From Columbaria to Catacombs: Collective Burial in Pagan and Christian Rome." Pages 177–242 in *Commemorating the Dead: Texts and Artifacts in Context: Studies of Roman, Jewish, and Christian Burials.* Edited by L. Brink and D. Green. Berlin: Walter de Gruyter, 2008.

Boerma, C. *Rich Man, Poor Man—and the Bible.* London: SCM, 1979.

Bradshaw, P. "Continuity and Change in Early Eucharistic Practice: Shifting Scholarly Perspectives." Pages 1–17 in *Continuity and Change in Christian Worship.* Edited by R. N. Swanson. Suffolk: Boydell, 1999.

Bradshaw, P. F., M. E. Johnson, and L. E. Phillips. *The Apostolic Tradition: A Commentary.* Hermeneia. Minneapolis: Fortress, 2002.

228

Brakke, D. "Care for the Poor, Fear of Poverty, and Love of Money." Pages 76–87 in *Wealth and Poverty in Early Church and Society*. Edited by S. R. Holman. Grand Rapids: Baker Academic, 2008.

Brändle, R. "This Sweetest Passage: Matthew 25:31–46 and Assistance to the Poor in the Homilies of John Chrysostom." Pages 127–39 in *Wealth and Poverty in Early Church and Society*. Edited by S. Holman. Grand Rapids: Baker Academic, 2008.

Bremmer, J. N. "Pauper or Patroness: The Widow in the Early Christian Church." Pages 31–50 in *Between Poverty and the Pyre: Movements in the History of Widowhood*. Edited by J. N. Bremmer and L. van den Bosch. London: Routlege, 1994.

———. "Why Did Early Christianity Attract Upper-Class Women?" Pages 37–47 in *Fructus centesimus: Mélanges G. J. M. Bartelink*. Edited by A. A. R. Bastiaensen, A. Hilhorst, and C. H. Kneepkens. Steenbrugge: In abbatia S. Petri; Dordrecht: Kluwer, 1989.

Brent, A. *Cyprian and Roman Carthage*. Cambridge & New York: Cambridge University Press, 2010.

———. *Hippolytus and the Roman Church in the Third Century: Communities in Tension before the Emergence of a Monarch-Bishop*. VCSup 31. Leiden: Brill, 1995.

Bridge, S. L. "To Give or Not to Give? Deciphering the Saying of Didache 1.6." *JECS* 5, no. 4 (1997): 555–68.

Brown, P. *Poverty and Leadership in the Later Roman Empire*. Menahem Stern Jerusalem Lectures. Hanover, NH: University Press of New England, 2002.

———. *Power and Persuasion in Late Antiquity: Toward a Christian Empire*. Madison: University of Wisconsin Press, 1992.

———. "The Study of Elites in Late Antiquity." *Arethusa* 33 (2000): 321–46.

Brox, N. *Der Hirt des Hermas*. Kommentar zu den Apostolischen Vätern 7. Göttingen: Vandenhoeck & Ruprecht, 1991.

Bruck, E. F. "Ethic vs. Law: St. Paul, the Fathers of the Church, and the 'Cheerful Giver' in Roman Law." *Traditio* 2 (1944): 97–121.

Budde, G. J. "Christian Charity: Now and Always." *Ecclesiastical Review* 85 (1931): 571–73.

Buell, D. K. "Ambiguous Legacy: A Feminist Commentary on Clement of Alexandria's Works." Pages 26–55 in *A Feminist Companion to Patristic Literature*. Edited by A.-J. Levine. London: Continuum, 2008.

———. " 'Sell What You Have and Give to the Poor': A Feminist Interpretation of Clement of Alexandria's *Who Is the Rich Person Who Is Saved?*" Pages 194–213 in *Walk in the Ways of Wisdom: Essays in Honor of Elisabeth Schüssler Fiorenza*. Edited by C. Kittredge, S. Matthews, and M. Johnson-DeBaufre. Harrisburg, PA: Trinity Press International, 2003.

Burns, J. P. *Cyprian the Bishop*. Routledge Early Church Monograph. London: Routledge, 2002.

———. "Cyprian's Eschatology: Explaining Divine Purpose." Pages 59–73 in *The Early Church in Its Context: Essays in Honor of Everett Ferguson*. Edited by A. J. Malherbe, F. W. Norris, and J. W. Thompson. Supplements to Novum Testamentum 90. Leiden: Brill, 1998.

Cardman, F. "Women, Ministry, and Church Order in Early Christianity." Pages 300–329 in *Women and Christian Origins*. Edited by R. S. Kraemer and M. R. D'Angelo. New York: Oxford University Press, 1999.

Chadwick, H. "Justification by Faith and Hospitality." *StPatr* 4 (1961): 281–85.

———. *The Sentences of Sextus: A Contribution to the History of Early Christian Ethics*. Cambridge: Cambridge University Press, 1959.

Charry, E. T. "When Generosity Is Not Enough." *QR* 21 (2003): 266–78.

Chestnut, R. A. *Born Again in Brazil: The Pentecostal Boom and the Pathogens of Poverty*. New Brunswick, NJ: Rutgers University Press, 1997.

Chow, J. K. *Patronage and Power: A Study of Social Networks in Corinth*. JSNTSup 75. Sheffield: JSOT Press, 1992.

Claar, Victor V., and Robin J. Klay. *Economics in Christian Perspective: Theory, Policy and Life Choices*. Downers Grove, IL: InterVarsity, 2007.

Clark, E. A. *Reading Renunciation: Asceticism and Scripture in Early Christianity*. Princeton, NJ: Princeton University Press, 1999.

Clarke, G. "Christianity in the First Three Centuries: Third-Century Christianity." Pages 589–671 in *The Crisis of Empire, A.D. 193–337*. Edited by A. K. Bowman, P. Garnsey, and A. Cameron. Vol. 12 of *The Cambridge Ancient History*. 2nd ed. Cambridge: Cambridge University Press, 2005.

———. "Some Observations on the Persecution of Decius." *Antichthon* 3 (1969): 68–73.

Clarke, W. K. L. *Almsgiving*. London: SPCK, 1936.

Clements, R. "Poverty and the Kingdom of God—an Old Testament View." Pages 13–27 in *The Kingdom of God and Human Society*. Edited by R. S. Barbour. Edinburgh: T&T Clark, 1993.

Cohick, L. H. *Women in the World of the Earliest Christians: Illuminating Ancient Ways of Life*. Grand Rapids: Baker Academic, 2009.

Coleman, S. "The Faith Movement: A Global Religious Culture." *Culture and Religion* 3 (2002): 3–19.

———. *The Globalisation of Charismatic Christianity: Spreading the Gospel of Prosperity*. Cambridge: Cambridge University Press, 2000.

Collins, C., and M. Wright. *The Moral Measure of Economy*. Maryknoll, NY: Orbis Books, 2007.

Collins, J. J., B. McGinn, and S. Stein, eds. *The Encyclopedia of Apocalypticism*. 3 vols. New York: Continuum, 1998.

Conzelmann, H. *Acts of the Apostles*. Hermeneia. Philadelphia: Fortress, 1987.

Countryman, W. *The Rich Christian in the Church of the Early Empire: Contradiction and Accommodations*. New York: Edwin Mellen, 1980.

———. "Welfare in the Churches of Asia Minor under the Early Roman Empire." Pages 131–46 in *Society of Biblical Literature 1979 Seminar Papers*. Edited by P. J. Achtemeier. Missoula, MT: Scholars Press, 1979.

Crislip, A. T. *From Monastery to Hospital: Christian Monasticism and the Transformation of Health Care in Late Antiquity*. Ann Arbor: University of Michigan Press, 2005.

Cronbach, A. "The Me'il Zedakah." *Hebrew Union College Annual* 11 (1936): 503–67.

———. "The Social Ideals of the Apocrypha and the Pseudepigrapha." *Hebrew Union College Annual* 18 (1944): 119–56.

Curran, J. R. *Pagan City and Christian Capital: Rome in the Fourth Century.* Oxford: Clarendon, 2000.

Dahl, N. A. "Paul and Possessions." Pages 22–39 in *Studies in Paul: Theology for the Early Christian Mission.* Edited by N. A. Dahl. Minneapolis: Augsburg, 1977.

Daley, B. E. *The Hope of the Early Church: A Handbook of Patristic Eschatology.* Peabody, MA: Hendrickson, 2003.

Daniélou, J. *Gospel Message and Hellenistic Culture.* Vol. 2 of *A History of Early Christian Doctrine before the Council of Nicaea.* Edited and translated, with a postscript, by J. A. Baker. London: Darton, Longman & Todd, 1973.

Danker, F. W. *Benefactor: Epigraphic Study of a Graeco-Roman and New Testament Semantic Field.* St. Louis: Clayton, 1982.

Davids, P. H. "James and Jesus." Pages 63–84 in *Jesus Tradition outside the Gospels.* Edited by D. Wenham. Sheffield: JSOT Press, 1985.

———. "The Test of Wealth." Pages 355–84 in *The Missions of James, Peter, and Paul: Tensions in Early Christianity.* Edited by B. Chilton and C. Evans. Supplements to Novum Testamentum 115. Leiden: Brill, 2005.

Davies, S. L. *The Revolt of the Widows: Social World of the Apocryphal Acts.* Urbana: Southern Illinois University Press, 1980.

Decret, F. *Early Christianity in North Africa.* Translated by E. Smither. Eugene, OR: Cascade, 2009.

De Faye, E. *Origen and His Work.* New York: Columbia University Press, 1929.

Deissmann, A. *Light from the Ancient East.* Translated by L. R. M. Strachan. Rev. ed. New York: Harper, 1927.

De Ligt, L. "Restraining the Rich, Protecting the Poor: Symbolic Aspects of Roman Legislation." Pages 1–43 in *After the Past: Essays in Ancient History in Honour of H. W. Pleket.* Edited by W. Jongman and M. Kleijwegt. Leiden: Brill, 2002.

De Soto, H. *The Mystery of Capital: Why Capitalism Triumphs in the West and Fails Everywhere Else.* New York: Basic, 2000.

D'Souza, D. *The Virtue of Prosperity: Finding Values in the Age of Techno-Affluence.* New York: Free Press, 2000.

De Ste. Croix, G. E. M. "Suffragium: From Vote to Patronage." *BJS* 5 (1954): 33–48.

De Vinne, M. J. "The Advocacy of Empty Bellies: Episcopal Representation of the Poor in the Late Empire." PhD diss., Stanford University, 1995.

Dillon, J. *The Middle Platonists: 80 BC to AD 220.* Ithaca, NY: Cornell University Press, 1977.

Dixon, S. *Reading Roman Women: Sources, Genres, and Real Life.* London: Duckworth, 2001.

Dodds, E. R. *Pagan and Christian in an Age of Anxiety: Some Aspects of Religious Experience from Marcus Aurelius to Constantine.* Cambridge: Cambridge University Press, 1968.

Donahue, J. R. "Two Decades of Research on the Rich and Poor in Luke-Acts." Pages 129–44 in *Justice and the Holy: Essays in Honor of Walter Harrelson*. Edited by D. A. Knight and P. J. Paris. Atlanta: Scholars Press, 1989.

Dover, K. J. *Greek Popular Morality in the Time of Plato and Aristotle*. Berkeley: University of California Press, 1974.

Downey, G. "Who Is My Neighbor? The Greek and Roman Answer." *ATR* 47 (1965): 3–15.

Downs, D. *The Offering of the Gentiles: Paul's Collection for Jerusalem in Its Chronological, Cultural, and Cultic Contexts*. WUNT II/248. Tübingen: Mohr Siebeck, 2008.

Draper, J. A., ed. *The Didache in Modern Research*. Arbeiten zur Geschichte des antiken Judentums und des Urchristentums 37. Leiden: Brill, 1996.

Drijvers, H. J. W. *East of Antioch: Studies in Early Syriac Christianity*. London: Variorum Reprints, 1984.

Dunbar, D. G. "The Delay of the Parousia in Hippolytus." *VC* 37 (1983): 313–27.

Duncan-Jones, R. *The Economy of the Roman Empire*. Cambridge: Cambridge University Press, 1974.

———. "Wealth and Munificence in Roman Africa." *PBSR* 31 (1963): 159–77.

Dunn, G. D. "Cyprian and His Collegae: Patronage and the Episcopal Synod of 252." *JRH* 27 (2003): 1–13.

———. "Cyprian and Women in a Time of Persecution." *JEH* 57 (2006): 205–25.

———. "Infected Sheep and Diseased Cattle, or the Pure and Holy Flock: Cyprian's Pastoral Care of Virgins." *JECS* 11 (2003): 1–20.

———. *Tertullian*. London: Routledge, 2004.

———. "The White Crown of Works: Cyprian's Early Pastoral Ministry of Almsgiving in Carthage." *Church History* 73 (2004): 715–40.

———. "Widows and Other Women in the Pastoral Ministry of Cyprian of Carthage." *Augustinianum* 45, no. 2 (2005): 295–307.

Dunn, J. D. G. *Unity and Diversity in the New Testament: An Inquiry into the Character of Earliest Christianity*. Philadelphia: Westminster, 1977.

Dunn, M. "Asceticism and Monasticism, II: Western." Pages 669–90 in *Constantine to c. 600*. Edited by A. Casiday and F. Norris. Vol. 2 of *The Cambridge History of Christianity*. Cambridge: Cambridge University Press, 2007.

Dunning, J. H., ed. *Making Globalization Good: The Moral Challenges of Global Capitalism*. Oxford: Oxford University Press, 2003.

Edwards, M. J. "Satire and Verisimilitude: Christianity in Lucian's 'Peregrinus.'" *Historia: Zeitschrift für Alte Geschichte* 38 (1989): 89–98.

Eichler, J., et al. "Possessions, Treasure, Mammon, Wealth." Pages 829–47, 852–53, in vol. 3 of *NIDNTT*. Edited by C. Brown. Grand Rapids: Zondervan, 1978.

Eisen, U. E. *Women Officeholders in Early Christianity: Epigraphical and Literary Studies*. Translated by L. M. Maloney. Collegeville, MN: Liturgical Press, 2000.

Elliott, J. H. "Patronage and Clientism in Early Christian Society." *Forum* 3 (1987): 39–48.

Elsner, J. *Art and the Roman Viewer: The Transformation of Art from the Pagan World to Christianity*. Cambridge: Cambridge University Press, 1995.

———. *Imperial Rome and Christian Triumph: The Art of the Roman Empire AD 100–450*. Oxford History of Art. Oxford: Oxford University Press, 1998.

Esler, P., ed. *The Early Christian World*. 2 Vols. London: Routledge, 2000.

———. "Poverty and Riches in the Bible and the Third World." Pages 145–79 in *Christianity for the Twenty-First Century*. Edited by P. Esler. Edinburgh: T&T Clark, 1998.

Esser, H.-H., and C. Brown. "Poor." Pages 820–29 in vol. 3 of *NIDNTT*. Edited by C. Brown. Grand Rapids: Zondervan, 1978.

Fahey, M. A. *Cyprian and the Bible: A Study in Third-Century Exegesis*. Tübingen: Mohr Siebeck, 1971.

Fee, G. D. *The Disease of the Health and Wealth Gospels*. Beverly, MA: Frontline, 1985.

Ferguson, E., ed. *Acts of Piety in the Early Church*. Vol. 17 of *Studies in Early Christianity: A Collection of Scholarly Essays*. New York: Garland, 1993.

———. "Divine Pedagogy: Origen's Use of the Imagery of Education." Pages 343–62 in *Christian Teaching: Studies in Honor of LeMoine G. Lewis*. Edited by E. Ferguson. Abilene, TX: Abilene Christian University Press, 1981.

———. *Early Christians Speak: Faith and Life in the First Three Centuries*. 3rd ed. Abilene, TX: Abilene Christian University Press, 1999.

———. *Early Christians Speak: Faith and Life in the First Three Centuries*. Vol. 2. Abilene, TX: Abilene Christian University Press, 2002.

———. "Millennial Expectations in Christian Eschatology: Ancient and Medieval Views." Pages 127–57 in *Apocalypticism and Millennialism: Shaping a Believers Church Eschatology for the Twenty-First Century*. Edited by L. L. Johns. Studies in the Believers Church Tradition. Kitchener, Ontario: Pandora, 2000.

———. "Spiritual Sacrifice in Early Christianity and Its Environment." *ANRW* 2.23.2 (1981): 1152–92.

———. "Women in the Post-Apostolic Church." Pages 493–513 in vol. 1 of *Essays on Women in Earliest Christianity*. Edited by C. D. Osburn. Joplin: College Press, 1993.

Ferguson, J. *Clement of Alexandria*. Twayne's World Authors Series. New York: Twayne, 1974.

Ferngren, G. B. "Medicine and Compassion in Early Christianity." *Theology Digest* 46 (1999): 315–26.

———. *Medicine and Health Care in Early Christianity*. Baltimore: Johns Hopkins University Press, 2009.

———. "The Organisation of the Care of the Sick in Early Christianity." Pages 192–98 in *Actes/Proceedings of the XXX International Congress of the History of Medicine*. Edited by H. Schadewaldt and K.-H. Leven. Düsseldorf: Vicom KG, 1988.

Finley, M. I. *The Ancient Economy*. 1973. Updated ed., with a forward by I. Morris. Berkeley: University of California Press, 1999.

———, ed. *Studies in Roman Property*. Cambridge Classical Studies. Cambridge: Cambridge University Press, 1976.

Finn, R. "Almsgiving for the Pure of Heart: Continuity and Change in Early Christian Teaching." Pages 419–29 in *Severan Culture*. Edited by S. Swain, S. Harrison, and J. Elsner. Cambridge: Cambridge University Press, 2007.

———. *Almsgiving in the Later Roman Empire: Christian Promotion and Practice 313–450*. Oxford: Oxford University Press, 2006.

———. "Portraying the Poor: Descriptions of Poverty in Christian Texts from the Late Roman Empire." Pages 130–44 in *Poverty in the Roman World*. Edited by M. Atkins and R. Osborne. Cambridge: Cambridge University Press, 2006.

Finn, T. M. "Mission and Expansion." Pages 295–315 in vol. 1 of *The Early Christian World*. Edited by P. Esler. London: Routledge, 2000.

Fiorenza, E. S. "The Phenomenon of Early Christian Apocalyptic: Some Reflection on Method." Pages 295–316 in *Apocalypticism in the Mediterranean World and the Near East*. Edited by D. Hellholm. Tübingen: Mohr Siebeck, 1983.

Fisher, A. L. "Lactantius' Ideas Relating Christian Truth and Christian Society." *JHI* 43, no. 3 (1982): 355–77.

Fitzgerald, A. "Almsgiving in the Works of Saint Augustine." Pages 445–59 in *Signum pietatis: Festgabe für Cornelius Petrus Mayer zum 60 Geburstag*. Edited by A. Zumkeller. Würzburg: Augustinus-Verlag, 1989.

Ford, J. M. "Three Ancient Jewish Views of Poverty." Pages 39–55 in *The New Way of Jesus*. Edited by W. Klassen. Newton, KS: Faith and Life, 1980.

France, R. T. "God and Mammon." *Evangelical Quarterly* 51 (1979): 3–21.

Frend, W. H. C. "Early Christianity and Society: A Jewish Legacy in the Pre-Constantinian Era." *HTR* 76, no. 1 (1983): 53–71.

———. *Martyrdom and Persecution in the Early Church*. Oxford: Blackwell, 1965.

———. *The Rise of Christianity*. London: Darton, Longman, & Todd, 1986.

Friesen, S. J. "Injustice or God's Will? Early Christian Explanations of Poverty." Pages 17–36 in *Wealth and Poverty in Early Church and Society*. Edited by S. R. Holman. Grand Rapids: Baker Academic, 2008.

———. "Injustice or God's Will? Early Christian Explanations of Poverty in Proto-Christian Texts." Pages 240–60 in *Christian Origins: A People's History of Christianity*. Edited by R. Horsley. Minneapolis: Fortress, 2005.

———. "Poverty in Pauline Studies: Beyond the So-Called New Consensus." *JSNT* 26 (2004): 323–61.

Furre, B. "Crossing Boundaries: The 'Universal Church' and the Spirit of Globalization." Pages 39–51 in *Spirits of Globalization: The Growth of Pentecostalism and Experiential Spiritualities in a Global Age*. Edited by S. J. Stålsett. London: SCM, 2006.

Gager, J. G. *Kingdom and Community: The Social World of Early Christianity*. Englewood Cliffs, NJ: Prentice-Hall, 1975.

Gamble, H. Y. *Books and Readers in the Early Church: A History of Early Christian Texts*. New Haven: Yale University Press, 1995.

Garnsey, P. *Famine and Food Supply in the Graeco-Roman World: Responses to Risk and Crisis*. Cambridge: Cambridge University Press, 1988.

————. *Food and Society in Classical Antiquity.* Cambridge: Cambridge University Press, 1999.

————. "Legal Privilege in the Roman Empire." Pages 141–65 in *Studies in Ancient Society: Past and Present Series.* Edited by M. I. Finley. London: Routledge and Kegan Paul, 1974.

————. *Social Status and Legal Privilege in the Roman Empire.* Oxford: Clarendon, 1970.

Garnsey, P., and R. Saller. *The Roman Empire: Economy, Society and Culture.* London: Duckworth, 1987.

Garnsey, P., and W. Scheidel, eds. *Cities, Peasants and Food in Classical Antiquity: Essays in Social and Economic History.* Cambridge: Cambridge University Press, 1998.

Garnsey, P., and G. Woolf. "Patronage of the Rural Poor in the Roman World." Pages 153–70 in *Patronage in Ancient Society.* Edited by A. Wallace-Hadrill. New York: Routledge, 1989.

Garrison, R. *Redemptive Almsgiving in Early Christianity.* Sheffield: JSOT Press, 1993.

Georgi, D. *Remembering the Poor: The History of Paul's Collection for Jerusalem.* Nashville: Abingdon, 1992.

Gifford, P. *African Christianity: Its Public Role.* London: Hurst, 1998.

Goehring, J. E. *Ascetics, Society, and the Desert: Studies in Early Egyptian Monasticism.* Harrisburg, PA: Trinity Press International, 1999.

González, J. L. *Faith and Wealth: A History of Early Christian Ideas on the Origin, Significance, and Use of Money.* San Francisco: Harper & Row, 1990.

Gooren, H. *Rich among the Poor: Church, Firm, and Household among Small-Scale Entrepreneurs in Guatemala City.* Amsterdam: Thela Thesis, 1999.

Gordon, B. *The Economic Problem in Biblical and Patristic Thought.* VCSup 9. Leiden: Brill, 1989.

Gordon, R. "The Veil of Power: Emperors, Sacrificers and Benefactors." Pages 199–231 in *Pagan Priests: Religion and Power in the Ancient World.* Edited by M. Beard and J. North. Ithaca, NY: Cornell University Press, 1990.

Gowan, D. E. "Wealth and Poverty in the Old Testament." *Interpretation* 41 (1987): 341–53.

Grant, R. M. "Early Christianity and Capital." Pages 7–29 in *The Capitalist Spirit: Toward a Religious Ethic of Wealth Creation.* Edited by P. L. Berger. San Francisco: Institute for Contemporary Studies, 1990.

————. *Early Christianity and Society.* San Francisco: Harper & Row, 1977.

Greene, K. "Technological Innovation and Economic Progress in the Ancient World: M. I. Finley Re-considered." *EHR* 53 (2000): 29–59.

Gregory, E. "Agape and Special Relations in a Global Economy: Theological Sources." Pages 16–42 in *Global Neighbors: Christian Faith and Moral Obligation in Today's Economy.* Edited by D. A. Hicks and M. Valeri. Grand Rapids: Eerdmans, 2008.

Griffiths, B. "The Challenge of Global Capitalism: A Christian Perspective." Pages 159–80 in *Making Globalization Good: The Moral Challenges of Global Capitalism.* Edited by J. H. Dunning. Oxford: Oxford University Press, 2003.

Groh, D. E. "Christian Community in the Writings of Tertullian: An Inquiry into the Nature and Problems of Community in North African Christianity." PhD diss., Northwestern University, 1970.

———. "Tertullian's Polemic against Social Co-Optation." *Church History* 40 (1971): 7–14.

Groody, D. G., ed. *The Option for the Poor in Christian Theology.* Notre Dame: University of Notre Dame Press, 2007.

Gruenwald, I. "A Case Study of Scripture and Culture: Apocalypticism as Cultural Identity in Past and Present." Pages 252–80 in *Ancient and Modern Perspectives on the Bible and Culture: Essays in Honor of Hans Dieter Betz.* Edited by A. Y. Collins. Atlanta: Scholars Press, 1998.

Hackett, R. I. J. "The Gospel of Prosperity in West Africa." Pages 199–214 in *Religion and the Transformations of Capitalism: Comparative Approaches.* Edited by R. H. Roberts. London: Routledge, 1995.

Halteman, J. "Productive Capital and Christian Moral Teaching." *Faith and Economics* 44 (2004): 26–38.

Hamel, G. *Poverty and Charity in Roman Palestine: The First Three Centuries CE.* University of California Near Eastern Studies 23. Berkeley: University of California Press, 1990.

Hamman, A. *Riches et pauvres dans l'Eglise ancienne.* Paris, 1962.

Hands, A. R. *Charities and Social Aid in Greece and Rome.* London: Thames & Hudson, 1968.

Hanks, T. D. "Poor, Poverty." Pages 403–24 in vol. 5 of *ABD*. Edited by D. N. Freedman. New York: Doubleday, 1992.

Hanson, K. C. "Greco-Roman Studies and the Social-Scientific Study of the Bible." *Forum* 9 (1993): 63–119.

Hanson, K. C., and D. Oakman. *Palestine in the Time of Jesus: Social Structures and Social Conflicts.* Minneapolis: Fortress, 1998.

Harland, P. A. "Connections with Elites in the World of the Early Christians." Pages 385–408 in *Handbook of Early Christianity.* Edited by A. J. Blasi, J. Duhaime, and P.-A. Turcotte. Walnut Creek, CA: AltaMira, 2002.

Harnack, A. *The Mission and Expansion of Christianity in the First Three Centuries.* Translated by J. Moffatt. 2 Vols. New York: G. P. Putnam's Sons, 1908. Repr., Gloucester, MA: Peter Smith, 1972.

Harrington, T. J. "The Local Church at Rome in the Second Century: A Common Cemetery Emerges amid Developments in This 'Laboratory of Christian Policy.' " *Studia Canonica* 23 (1989): 167–88.

Hauck, F. "*penēs.*" Pages 37–40 in vol. 6 of *TDNT*. Edited by G. Friedrich. Translated by G. W. Bromiley. Grand Rapids: Eerdmans, 1968.

———. "*ptōchos.*" Pages 885–87 in vol. 6 of *TDNT*. Edited by G. Friedrich. Translated by G. W. Bromiley. Grand Rapids: Eerdmans, 1968.

Hauck, F., and W. Kasch. "*ploutos.*" Pages 318–32 in vol. 6 of *TDNT*. Edited by G. Friedrich. Translated by G. W. Bromiley. Grand Rapids: Eerdmans, 1968.

Harris, W. V. "Between Archaic and Modern: Some Current Problems in the History of the Roman Economy." Pages 11–29 in *The Inscribed Economy: Production and Distribution in the Roman Empire in the Light of Instrumentum Domesticum.* Edited by W. V. Harris. Ann Arbor: Journal of Roman Archaeology Supp 6, 1993.

Hellerman, J. H. "Wealth and Sacrifice in Early Christianity: Revisiting Mark's Presentation of Jesus's Encounter with the Rich Young Ruler." *Trinity Journal* 21, no. 2 (2000): 143–64.

Hengel, M. *Property and Riches in the Early Church.* Philadelphia: Fortress, 1974.

Hicks, D. A. *Money Enough: Everyday Practices for Living Faithfully in the Global Economy.* San Francisco: Jossey-Bass, 2010.

Hicks, D. A., and M. Valeri. "Introduction: Christian Faith and the Global Market." Pages xviii–xxv in *Global Neighbors: Christian Faith and Moral Obligation in Today's Economy.* Grand Rapids: Eerdmans, 2008.

———, eds. *Global Neighbors: Christian Faith and Moral Obligation in Today's Economy.* Grand Rapids: Eerdmans, 2008.

Hiers, R. H. "Friends by Unrighteous Mammon: The Eschatological Proletariat (Luke 16:9)." *JAAR* 38 (1970): 30–36.

Hill, C. E. *Regnum Caelorum: Patterns of Future Hope in Early Christianity.* 2nd ed. Grand Rapids: Eerdmans, 2001.

Hillner, J. "Clerics, Property and Patronage: The Case of the Roman Titular Churches." *Antiquité tardive* 14 (2006): 59–68.

———. "Families, Patronage and the Titular Churches of Rome." Pages 225–61 in *Religion, Dynasty, and Patronage in Early Christian Rome, 300–900.* Edited by K. Cooper and J. Hillner. Cambridge: Cambridge University Press, 2007.

Himmelfarb, M. *Tours of Hell: An Apocalyptic Form in Jewish and Christian Literature.* Philadelphia: Fortress, 1983.

Hitchner, R. B. "'The Advantage of Wealth and Luxury': The Case for Economic Growth in the Roman Empire." Pages 207–22 in *The Ancient Economy: Evidence and Models.* Edited by J. G. Manning and I. Morris. Stanford: Stanford University Press, 2005.

———. "Olive Production and the Roman Economy: The Case for Intensive Growth in the Roman Empire." Pages 71–83 in *The Ancient Economy.* Edited by W. Scheidel and S. von Reden. New York: Routledge, 2002.

Hobson, D. "Women as Property Owners in Roman Egypt." *TAPA* 113 (1983): 331–21.

Hollerich, M. J. "The Alexandrian Bishops and the Grain Trade." *JESHO* 25 (1982): 187–207.

Holman, S. "Constructed and Consumed: Everyday Life of the Poor in 4th Century Cappadocia." Pages 441–64 in *Social and Political Life in Late Antiquity.* Edited by W. Bowden, A. Gutteridge, and C. Machado. Late Antique Archaeology 3. Leiden: Brill, 2005.

———. "The Entitled Poor: Human Rights Language in the Cappadocians." *Pro Ecclesia* 9 (2000): 476–89.

———. *God Knows There's Need: Christian Responses to Poverty.* Oxford: Oxford University Press, 2009.

————. *The Hungry Are Dying: Beggars and Bishops in Roman Cappadocia*. Oxford Studies in Historical Theology. Oxford: Oxford University Press, 2001.

————, ed. *Wealth and Poverty in Early Church and Society*. Grand Rapids: Baker Academic, 2008.

Hopkins, K. "Christian Number and Its Implications." *JECS* 6, no. 2 (1998): 185–226.

————. "Élite Mobility in the Roman Empire." Pages 103–20 in *Studies in Ancient Society*. Edited by M. I. Finley. London: Routledge and Kegan Paul, 1974.

————. "Rome, Taxes, Rents and Trade." Pages 190–230 in *The Ancient Economy*. Edited by W. Scheidel and S. Von Reden. New York: Routledge, 2002.

————. "Taxes and Trade in the Roman Empire [200 B.C.–A.D. 400]." *JRS* 70 (1980): 101–25.

Hoppe, L. J. *There Shall Be No Poor among You: Poverty in the Bible*. Nashville: Abingdon, 2004.

Horrell, D. *The Social Ethos of the Corinthian Correspondence: Interests and Ideology from 1 Corinthians to 1 Clement*. Edinburgh: T&T Clark, 1996.

Horsley, R. A. *Jesus and the Spiral of Violence*. San Francisco: Harper & Row, 1987; Minneapolis: Fortress, 1993.

Hughson, T. S. J. "Social Justice in Lactantius' Divine Institutes: An Exploration." Pages 185–205 in *Reading Patristic Texts on Social Ethics: Issues and Challenges for Twenty-First-Century Christian Social Thought*. Edited by J. Leemans, B. J. Matz, and J. Verstraeten. Washington, DC: Catholic University of America Press, 2011.

Hunt, E. D. "The Church as a Public Institution." Pages 238–76 in *The Late Empire, AD 337–425*. Edited by A. Cameron and P. Garnsey. Cambridge Ancient History 13. Cambridge: Cambridge University Press, 1998.

Jeffers, J. S. *Conflict at Rome: Social Order and Hierarchy in Early Christianity*. Minneapolis: Augsburg Fortress, 1991.

Jenkins, P. *The Next Christendom: The Coming of Global Christianity*. Rev. ed. Oxford: Oxford University Press, 2007.

Johnson, G. J. "A Christian Business and Christian Self-Identity in Third/Fourth Century Phrygia." *VC* 48 (1994): 341–66.

Johnson, L. T. *Sharing Possessions: Mandate and Symbol of Faith*. Philadelphia: Fortress, 1981.

Johnson, M. J. "Pagan-Christian Burial Practices of the Fourth Century: Shared Tombs?" *JECS* 5 (1997): 37–59.

Johnson, T., and C. Dandeker. "Patronage: Relation and System." Pages 219–41 in *Patronage in Ancient Society*. Edited by A. Wallace-Hadrill. New York: Routledge, 1989.

Jones, A. H. M. *Constantine and the Conversion of Europe*. 1948. Toronto: University of Toronto Press, 1978.

————. "Church Finance in the Fifth and Sixth Centuries." Pages 334–44 in *Acts of Piety in the Early Church*. Edited by E. Ferguson. Vol. 17 of *Studies in Early Christianity: A Collection of Scholarly Essays*. New York: Garland, 1993. Repr. from *JTS* 11 (1960): 84–94.

———. *The Later Roman Empire, 284–602.* Oxford: Blackwell, 1964.

Jongman, W. "Hunger and Power: Theories, Models and Methods in Roman Economic History." Pages 258–84 in *Interdependency of Institutions and Private Entrepreneurs: Proceedings of the Second MOS Symposium, Leiden, 1998.* Edited by H. Bongenaar. Leiden: Netherlands Historisch-Archaeologisch Instituut te Istanbul, 2000.

———. "The Roman Economy: From Cities to Empire." Pages 28–47 in *The Transformation of Economic Life under the Roman Empire: Proceedings of the Second Workshop of the International Network, Impact of Empire (Roman Empire, c. 200 BC–AD 476).* Edited by L. de Blois and J. Rich. Amsterdam: J. C. Gieben, 2002.

Judge, E. A. "Fourth-Century Monasticism in the Papyri." Pages 613–20 in *Proceedings of the Sixteenth International Congress of Papyrology* (Chico, CA: Scholars Press, 1981).

———. "The Social Identity of the First Christians." *JRH* 11 (1980): 201–17.

Judge, E. A., and S. R. Pickering. "Papyrus Documentation of Church and Community in Egypt to the Mid-Fourth Century." *JAC* 20 (1977): 47–71.

Kaiser, W. C., Jr. "The Old Testament Promise of Material Blessings and the Contemporary Believer." *Trinity Journal* 9 (1988): 151–69.

Karayiannis, A. D., and S. Drakopolou-Dodd. "The Greek Christian Fathers." Pages 163–208 in *Ancient and Medieval Economic Ideas and Concepts of Social Justice.* Edited by S. T. Lowry and B. Gordon. Leiden: Brill, 1998.

Karris, R. J. "Poor and Rich: The Lukan Sitz in Leben." Pages 112–25 in *Perspectives on Luke-Acts.* Edited by C. H. Talbert. Danville, VA: Association of Baptist Professors of Religion, 1978.

Kearsley, R. "Women in Public Life in the Roman East: Junia Theodora, Claudia Metrodora, and Phoibe, Benefactress of Paul." *Ancient Society: Resources for Teachers* 15 (1985): 124–37.

Keck, L. E. "The Poor among the Saints in Jewish Christianity and Qumran." *ZNW* 57 (1966): 54–78.

———. "The Poor among the Saints in the New Testament." *ZNW* 56 (1965): 100–129.

Keenan, A. E. *Thasci Caecili Cypriani—De Habitu Virginum: A Commentary with an Introduction and Translation.* Catholic University of America Patristic Studies 34. Washington, DC: Catholic University of America Press, 1932.

Kidd, R. M. *Wealth and Beneficence in the Pastoral Epistles.* SBL Diss 122. Missoula: Scholars Press, 1990.

Kim, K.-J. *Stewardship and Almsgiving in Luke's Theology.* JSNTSup 155. Sheffield: Sheffield Academic Press, 1998.

Klijn, A. F. J. *The Acts of Thomas: Introduction, Text, and Commentary.* 2nd rev. ed. Leiden: Brill, 2003.

Klingshirn, W. "Charity and Power: Caesarius of Arles and the Ransoming of Captives in Sub-Roman Gaul." *JRS* 75 (1985): 183–203.

Kloosterman, N. D. "Clement of Alexandria's Ethic of Wealth as an Ethic of Grace." *Mid-AJT* 2 (1986): 138–48.

Kloppenborg, J. S. "Associations in the Ancient World." Pages 329–30 in *The Historical Jesus in Context.* Edited by A.-J. Levine, D. C. Allison, and J. D. Crossan. Princeton: Princeton University Press, 2006.

————. "The Transformation of Moral Exhortation in Didache 1–5." Pages 88–109 in *The Didache in Context: Essays on Its Text, History, and Transmission.* Edited by C. N. Jefford. Leiden: Brill, 1995.

Knipfing, J. R. "The Libelli of the Decian Persecution." *HTR* 16 (1923): 345–90.

Keresztes, P. "The Decian *Libelli* and Contemporary Literature." *Latomus* 34 (1975): 761–81.

Küng, H. "An Ethical Framework for the Global Market Economy." Pages 145–58 in *Making Globalization Good: The Moral Challenges of Global Capitalism.* Edited by J. H. Dunning. Oxford: Oxford University Press, 2003.

Kvalbein, H. "Jesus and the Poor: Two Texts and a Tentative Conclusion." *Themelios* 12 (1987): 80–87.

Lampe, P. *From Paul to Valentinus: Christians at Rome in the First Two Centuries.* Translated by M. Steinhauser. Edited by M. D. Johnson. Minneapolis: Fortress, 2003.

Landes, R. "Lest the Millennium be Fulfilled: Apocalyptic Expectations and the Pattern of Western Chronography, 100–800 CE." Pages 137–211 in *The Use and Abuse of Eschatology in the Middle Ages.* Edited by W. Verbeke, D. Verheist, and A. Welken-huysen. Leuven, Belgium: Leuven University Press, 1988.

Langan, J. P. "What Jerusalem Says to Athens." Pages 152–80 in *The Faith That Does Justice: Examing the Christian Sources for Social Change.* Edited by J. C. Haughey. New York: Paulist Press, 1977.

Layton, B. *The Gnostic Scriptures.* New York: Doubleday, 1987.

Lee, S. T. D. *Jakes: America's New Preacher.* New York: New York University Press, 2005.

Le Glay, Marcel, Jean-Louis Voisin, and Yann Le Bohec. *A History of Rome.* 3rd ed. Oxford: Blackwell, 2004.

Liaou, A. E. "The Church, Economic Thought and Economic Practice." Pages 435–64 in *The Christian East: Its Institutions & Its Thoughts: A Critical Reflection.* Edited by R. F. Taft. *Orientalia Christiana Analecta* 251. Rome: Pontificio Instituto Orientale, 1996.

Lilla, S. R. C. *Clement of Alexandria: A Study in Christian Platonism and Gnosticism.* Oxford: Oxford University Press, 1971.

Lindberg, C. *Beyond Charity: Reformation Initiatives for the Poor.* Minneapolis: Fortress, 1993.

————. "Through a Glass Darkly: A History of the Church's Vision of the Poor and Poverty." *Ecumenical Review* 33 (1981): 37–52.

Lieu, J. M. *Christian Identity in the Jewish and Graeco-Roman World.* Oxford: Oxford University Press, 2004.

————. "'Impregnable Ramparts and Wall of Iron': Boundary and Identity in Early 'Judaism' and 'Christianity.'" *NTS* 48 (2002): 297–313.

Long, A. A. *Hellenistic Philosophy: Stoics, Epicureans, Sceptics.* 2nd ed. Berkeley: University of California Press, 1986.

————. *Stoic Studies.* Cambridge: Cambridge University Press, 1996.

Longenecker, Bruce W. *Remember the Poor: Paul, Poverty, and the Greco-Roman World.* Grand Rapids: Eerdmans, 2010.

Longenecker, Bruce W., and Kelly D. Liebengood, eds. *Engaging Economics: New Testament Scenarios and Early Christian Reception.* Grand Rapids: Eerdmans, 2009.

Lüdemann, G. *Early Christianity according to the Traditions in Acts.* Minneapolis: Fortress, 1989.

Luomanen, P. *Entering the Kingdom of Heaven: A Study on the Structure of Matthew's View of Salvation.* Tübingen: Mohr Siebeck, 1998.

MacMullen, R. *Christianizing the Roman Empire (A.D. 100–400).* New Haven: Yale University Press, 1984.

———. *The Second Church: Popular Christianity A.D. 200–400.* Atlanta: SBL, 2009.

Madigan, K., and C. Osiek. *Ordained Women in the Early Church: A Documentary History.* Baltimore: Johns Hopkins University Press, 2005.

Maier, H. O. "Clement of Alexandria and the Care of the Self." *JAAR* 62, no. 3 (1994): 719–45.

———. "Purity and Danger in Polycarp's Epistle to the Philippians: The Sin of Valens in Social Perspective." *JECS* 1 (1993): 229–47.

———. *The Social Setting of the Ministry as Reflected in the Writings of Hermas, Clement, and Ignatius.* Canadian Corporation for Studies in Religion, Dissertation SR 1. Waterloo, ON: Wilfrid Laurier University Press, 1991.

Malherbe, A. J. "Paul's Self-Sufficiency (Philippians 4:11)." Pages 125–39 in *Friendship, Flattery and Frankness of Speech.* Edited by J. T. Fitzgerald. Lieden: Brill, 1996.

———. *Social Aspects of Early Christianity.* Philadelphia: Fortress, 1982.

Malina, B. "Embedded Economics: The Irrelevance of Christian Fictive Domestic Economy." *Forum for Social Economics* 26 (1997): 1–20.

———. "Wealth and Poverty in the New Testament and Its World." *Interpretation* 41 (1987): 354–67.

Maloney, R. P. "The Teaching of the Fathers on Usury." Pages 345–69 in *Christian Life: Acts of Piety in the Early Church.* Edited by E. Ferguson. Vol. 17 of *Studies in Early Christianity: A Collection of Scholarly Essays.* New York: Garland, 1993. Repr. from *VC* 27 (1973): 241–65.

Manning, C. E. "Liberalitas—The Decline and Rehabilitation of a Virtue." *Greece & Rome* 32, no. 1 (1985): 73–83.

Manning, J. G., and I. Morris. *The Ancient Economy: Evidence and Models.* Stanford: Stanford University Press, 2005.

Mara, M. G. "Rich-Riches-Property." *Encyclopedia of the Early Church* (1992): 736–37.

Martin, B. "New Mutations of the Protestant Ethic among Latin American Pentecostals." *Religion* 25 (1995): 101–17.

Martin, D. *Pentecostalism: The World Their Parish.* Oxford: Blackwell, 2002.

Marty, M. E. "Postscript: Materialism and Spirituality in American Religion." Pages 237–53 in *Rethinking Materialism: Perspectives on the Spiritual Dimension of Economic Behavior.* Edited by R. Wuthnow. Grand Rapids: Eerdmans, 1995.

Matthews, S. *The First Converts: Rich Pagan Women and the Rhetoric of Mission in Early Judaism and Christianity.* Stanford: Stanford University Press, 2001.

Mattingly, D. J. "Oil for Export: A Comparison of Spanish, African and Tripolitanian Olive Oil Production." *JRA* 1 (1988): 33–56.

Mattingly, D. J., and J. Salmon. "The Productive Past: Economics beyond Agriculture." Pages 3–14 in *Economics beyond Agriculture in the Classical World*. Edited by D. J. Mattingly and J. Salmon. London: Routledge, 2001.

Matz, B. "The Use of Patristic Socioethical Texts in Catholic Social Thought." Pages 287–93 in *Wealth and Poverty in Early Church and Society*. Edited by S. R. Holman. Grand Rapids: Baker Academic, 2008.

Maxwell, D. *African Gifts of the Spirit: Pentecostalism and the Rise of a Zimbabwean Transnational Religious Movement*. Athens: Ohio University Press, 2007.

———. *Christians and Chiefs in Zimbabwe*. Edinburgh: Edinburgh University Press, 1999.

———. "Delivered from the Spirit of Poverty." *Journal of Religion in Africa* 28, no. 3 (1998): 350–73.

Mayer, W. "Poverty and Generosity toward the Poor in the Time of John Chrysostom." Pages 140–58 in *Wealth and Poverty in Early Church and Society*. Edited by S. R. Holman. Grand Rapids: Baker Academic, 2008.

———. "Poverty and Society in the World of John Chrysostom." Pages 465–84 in *Social and Political Life in Late Antiquity*. Edited by W. Bowden, A. Gutteridge, and C. Machado. Late Antique Archaeology 3. Leiden: Brill, 2005.

Maynard-Reid, P. U. *Poverty and Wealth in James*. Maryknoll, NY: Orbis Books, 1987.

Mays, J. L. "Justice: Perspectives from the Prophetic Tradition." *Interpretation* 37 (1983): 5–17.

McCarthy, David Matzko. *The Heart of Catholic Social Teaching: Its Origins and Contemporary Significance*. Grand Rapids: Brazos, 2008.

McConnell, D. R. *A Different Gospel: A Historical and Biblical Analysis of the Modern Faith Movement*. Peabody, MA: Hendrickson, 1988.

McGinn, B. "Apocalypticism and Violence: Aspects of Their Relation in Antiquity and the Middle Ages." Pages 209–29 in *Scripture and Pluralism: Reading the Bible in the Religiously Plural Worlds of the Middle Ages and Renaissance*. Edited by T. J. Heffernan and T. E. Burman. Leiden: Brill, 2005.

———. "Turning Points in Early Christian Apocalypse Exegesis." Pages 81–105 in *Apocalyptic Thought in Early Christianity*. Edited by R. J. Daly, SJ. Holy Cross Studies in Patristic Theology and History. Grand Rapids: Baker Academic, 2009.

McGinn, T. A. J. "Widows, Orphans and Social History [Review of Krause 1994–95]." *JRA* 12 (1999): 617–32.

McGuire, M. R. "Epigraphical Evidence for Social Charity in the Roman West." *American Journal of Philology* 67 (1946): 129–50.

McKee, A. "A Rejoinder to Malina on Biblical Economics." *Forum for Social Economics* 27 (1998): 61–65.

McNanus, W. E. "Stewardship and Almsgiving in the Roman Catholic Tradition." Pages 115–33 in *Faith and Philanthropy in America: Exploring the Role of Religion in America's Voluntary Sector*. Edited by R. Wuthnow and V. A. Hodgkinson. San Francisco: Jossey-Bass, 1990.

Mealand, D. L. "Philo of Alexandria's Attitude to Riches." *ZNW* 69 (1978): 58–64.

Meeks, A. D. "Being Human in the Market Society." *QR* 21 (2003): 254–65.

Meeks, M. D. *God the Economist: The Doctrine of God and Political Economy.* Minneapolis: Fortress, 1989.

Meeks, W. A. *The First Urban Christians: The Social World of the Apostle Paul.* New Haven: Yale University Press, 1983.

————. *The Origins of Christian Morality: The First Two Centuries.* New Haven: Yale University Press, 1993.

————. "Social Functions of Apocalyptic Language in Pauline Christianity." Pages 687–706 in *Apocalypticism in the Mediterranean World and in the Near East.* Edited by D. Hellholm. Tübingen: J. C. B. Mohr, 1983.

Meggitt, J. J. *Paul, Poverty and Survival.* Edinburgh: T&T Clark, 1998.

Meilaender, G. "To Throw Oneself into the Wave: The Problem of Possessions." Pages 72–86 in *Preferential Option for the Poor.* Edited by R. J. Neuhaus. Grand Rapids: Eerdmans, 1988.

Meland, D. L. *Poverty and Expectation in the Gospels.* London: SCM, 1980.

Melitz, J., and D. Winch. *Religious Thought and Economic Society: Four Chapters of an Unfinished Work by Jacob Viner.* Durham, NC: Duke University Press, 1978.

Methuen, C. "The 'Virgin Widow': A Problematic Social Role for the Early Church?" *HTR* 90 (1997): 285–98.

Meyer, B. "Commodities and the Power of Prayer: Pentecostalist Attitudes towards Consumption in Ghana." *Development and Change* 29 (1998): 751–76.

Michaels, J. R. "Almsgiving and the Kingdom within: Tertullian on Luke 17:21." *CBQ* 60 (1998): 475–83.

Migeotte, L. *The Economy of the Greek Cities: From the Archaic Period to the Early Roman Empire.* Translated by J. Lloyd. Berkeley: University of California Press, 2009.

Millar, F. "Paul of Samosata, Zenobia and Aurellian: The Church, Local Culture and Political Allegiance in Third-Century Syria." *JRS* 61 (1971): 1–17.

Miller, D., and T. Yamamori. *Global Pentecostalism: The New Face of Christian Social Engagement.* Berkeley: University of California Press, 2007.

Miller, P. "Property and Possession in Light of the Ten Commandments." Pages 17–50 in *Having: Property and Possession in Religious and Social Life.* Edited by W. Schweiker and C. Matthews. Grand Rapids: Eerdmans, 2004.

Mitchem, S. Y. *Name It and Claim It? Prosperity Preaching in the Black Church.* Cleveland: Pilgrim, 2007.

Molinari, A. L. *The Acts of Peter and the Twelve Apostles (NHC 6.1): Allegory, Ascent, and Ministry in the Wake of the Decian Persecution.* SBL Dissertation Series 174. Atlanta: SBL, 2000.

Montgomery, H. "Pontius' *Vita S. Cypriani* and the Making of a Saint." *Symbolae Osloenses* 71 (1996): 195–215.

————. "Saint Cyprian's Secular Heritage." Pages 214–23 in *Studies in Ancient History and Numismatics Presented to Rudi Thomsen.* Edited by A. Damsgaard-Madsen, E. Christiansen, and E. Hallager. Aarhus, Denmark: Aarhus University Press, 1988.

Moore, E. "Wealth, Poverty, and the Value of the Person: Some Notes in the Hymn of the Pearl and Its Early Christian Context." Pages 56–63 in *Wealth and Poverty in Early Church and Society*. Edited by S. Holman. Grand Rapids: Baker Academic, 2008.

Morken, H. "Bishop T. D. Jakes: A Ministry for Empowerment." Pages 25–52 in *Religious Leaders and Faith-Based Politics*. Edited by J. R. Formicola and H. Morken. Lanham, MD: Rowman & Littlefield, 2001.

Mott, S. C. "The Partiality of Biblical Justice." Pages 81–99 in *Christianity and Economics in the Post-Cold War Era: The Oxford Declaration and Beyond*. Edited by H. Schlossberg, V. Samuel, and R. J. Sider. Grand Rapids: Eerdmans, 1994.

———. "The Power of Giving and Receiving: Reciprocity in Hellenistic Benevolence." Pages 60–72 in *Current Issues in Biblical and Patristic Interpretation*. Edited by G. F. Hawthorne. Grand Rapids: Eerdmans, 1975.

Mott, S. C., and R. J. Sider, "Economic Justice: A Biblical Paradigm." Pages 15–45 in *Toward a Just and Caring Society*. Edited by D. P. Gushee. Grand Rapids: Baker, 1999.

Mouw, R. J. "Toward an Evangelical Theology of Poverty." Pages 218–38 in *Christian Faith and Practice in the Modern World*. Edited by M. Noll and D. Wells. Grand Rapids: Eerdmans, 1988.

Moxnes, H. *The Economy of the Kingdom*. Philadelphia: Fortress, 1988.

———. "Of Households and Economies." Pages 140–58 in *Biblical Principles and Economics: The Foundations*. Edited by R. C. Chewning. Colorado Springs: NavPress, 1989.

Mullen, R. L. *The Expansion of Christianity: A Gazetteer of Its First Three Centuries*. VCSup 69. Leiden: Brill, 2004.

Mullin, R. *The Wealth of Christians*. Maryknoll, NY: Orbis Books, 1984.

Murphy, C. M. *Wealth in the Dead Sea Scrolls and in the Qumran Community*. Leiden: Brill, 2002.

Musurillo, H. "Early Christian Economy: A Reconsideration of P. Amherst 3(a)." *Chronique d'Egypte* 31 (1956): 124–34.

Nardoni, Enrique. *Rise Up, O Judge: A Study of Justice in the Biblical World*. Peabody, MA: Hendrickson, 2004.

Newhauser, R. G. *The Early History of Greed: The Sin of Avarice in Early Medieval Thought and Literature*. Cambridge: Cambridge University Press, 2006.

Nicholson, O. P. "The Source of the Dates in Lactantius' Divine Institutes." *JTS* 36 (1985): 291–310.

Nickelsburg, G. W. E. *1 Enoch 1: A Commentary on the Book of 1 Enoch, Chapters 1–36; 81–108*. Hermeneia. Minneapolis: Fortress, 2001.

———. "Eschatology (Early Jewish)." Pages 579–94 in vol. 2 of *ABD*. Edited by D. N. Freedman. New York: Doubleday, 1992.

———. "Revisiting the Rich and the Poor in 1 Enoch 92–105 and the Gospel according to Luke." Pages 579–605 in *Society of Biblical Literature 1998 Seminar Papers Part Two*. Atlanta: Scholars Press, 1998.

———. "Riches, the Rich, and God's Judgment in I Enoch 92–105 and the Gospel according to Luke." *NTS* 25 (1978–79): 324–44.

————. "Scripture in 1 Enoch and 1 Enoch as Scripture." Pages 333–54 in *Texts and Contexts: Biblical Texts in Their Textual and Situational Contexts: Essays in Honor of Lars Hartman*. Edited by T. Fornberg and D. Hellholm. Oslo: Scandinavian University Press, 1995.

Nickle, K. F. *The Collection: A Study of Paul's Strategy*. London: SCM, 1966.

Nicolai, V. F., F. Bisconti, and D. Mazzoleni. *The Christian Catacombs of Rome: History, Decoration, Inscriptions*. 2nd ed. Regensburg: Schnell & Steiner, 2002.

Niederwimmer, K. *The Didache: A Commentary*. Hermeneia. Translated by L. M. Maloney. Minneapolis: Fortress, 1998.

Noell, E. S. "Loving One's Neighbor in the Marketplace: Justice in Exchange and the Poor in the Old Testament." Paper presented to the Wheaton College Department of Business and Economics, 2007.

————. "A 'Marketless World'? An Examination of Wealth and Exchange in the Gospels and First-Century Palestine." *JMM* 10 (2007): 85–114.

Novak, M. *In Praise of the Free Economy*. Translated by S. Gregg. Smithfield, NSW, Australia: Center for Independent Studies, 1999.

————. *The Spirit of Democratic Capitalism*. New York: Simon & Schuster, 1982.

————. *Will It Liberate? Questions about Liberation Theology*. New York: Paulist, 1986.

Oakes, P. "Constructing Poverty Scales for Graeco-Roman Society: A Response to Steven Friesen's 'Poverty in Pauline Studies.'" *JSNT* 26 (2004): 367–71.

Oakman, D. "The Ancient Economy." Pages 126–43 in *The Social Sciences and New Testament Interpretation*. Edited by R. L. Rohrbaugh. Peabody, MA: Hendrikson, 1996.

O'Brien, D. "Rich Clients and Poor Patrons: Functions of Friendship in Clement of Alexandria's *Quis Dives Salvatur*." PhD diss., University of Oxford, 2004.

Ocker, C. "*Unius Arbitrio Mundum Regi Necesse Est*: Lactantius' Concern for the Preservation of Roman Society." *VC* 40, no. 4 (1986): 348–64.

Oden, T. "The Poor in Classical Christian Teaching." Pages 105–25 in *The Bulletin: Moravian Theological Seminary*. Bethlehem, PA: Moravian Theological Seminary, 1985.

O'Neil, E. N. "De Cupiditate Divitiarum (Moralia 523c–528B)." Pages 289–362 in *Plutarch's Ethical Writings and Early Christian Literature*. Edited by H. D. Betz. Studia ad corpus Hellenisticum Novi Testamenti 4. Leiden: Brill, 1978.

Osiek, C. "The Early Second Century through the Eyes of Hermas: Continuity and Change." *BTB* 20 (1990): 116–22.

————. "The Genre and Function of the Shepherd of Hermas." Pages 113–21 in *Early Christian Apocalypticism: Genre and Social Setting*. Edited by A. Y. Collins. Semeia 36. Decatur, GA: Scholars Press, 1986.

————. "The Patronage of Women in Early Christianity." Pages 173–92 in *A Feminist Companion to Patristic Literature*. Edited by A.-J. Levine. London: Continuum, 2008.

————. "The Ransom of Captives: Evolution of a Tradition." *HTR* (1981): 365–86.

———. *Rich and Poor in the Shepherd of Hermas: An Exegetical-Social Investigation.* CBQ Monograph Series 15. Washington, DC: Catholic Biblical Association of America, 1983.

———. "Roman and Christian Burial Practices and the Patronage of Women." Pages 243–70 in *Commemorating the Dead: Texts and Artifacts in Context: Studies of Roman, Jewish, and Christian Burials.* Edited by L. Brink and D. Green. Berlin: Walter de Gruyter, 2008.

———. *The Shepherd of Hermas: A Commentary.* Hermeneia. Minneapolis: Augsburg Fortress, 1999.

———. "Wealth and Poverty in the Shepherd of Hermas." *StPatr* 17 (1982): 725–30.

———. *What Are They Saying about the Social Setting of the New Testament?* New York: Paulist Press, 1992.

———. "The Widow as Altar: The Rise and Fall of a Symbol." *SecCent* 3, no. 3 (1983): 159–69.

Otabil, M. *Beyond the Rivers of Ethiopia.* Bakersfield, CA: Pneuma Life; Accra-North, Ghana: International Central Gospel Church, 1993.

Pappu, S. "The Preacher." *Atlantic Monthly* 297, no. 2 (2006): 92–103.

Parker, A. J. "Classical Antiquity: The Maritime Dimension." *Antiquity* 64 (1990): 335–46.

Parkin, A. R. "Poverty in the Early Roman Empire: Ancient and Modern Conceptions and Constructs." PhD diss., Cambridge University, 2001.

Paterson, J. "Salvation from the Sea: Amphorae and Trade in the Roman West." *JRS* 72 (1982): 146–57.

Patlagean, E. *Pauvreté économique et pauvreté sociale à Byzance, 4e-7e siècles.* Civilisations et sociétés 48. Paris: Mouton, 1977.

———. "The Poor." Pages 15–42 in *The Byzantines.* Edited by G. Cavallo. Translated by T. Dunlap, T. L. Fagan, and C. Lambert. Chicago: University of Chicago Press, 1997.

Peachin, M. "Introduction." Pages 1–13 in *Specvlvm Ivris: Roman Law as a Reflection of Social and Economic Life in Antiquity.* Edited by J.-J. Aubert and B. Sirks. Ann Arbor: University of Michigan Press, 2002.

Pearson, B. A. "A Coptic Homily On Riches Attributed to St. Peter of Alexandria." *StPatr* 26 (1993): 296–307.

———. "Philanthropy in the Greco-Roman World and in Early Christianity." Pages 186–213 in *The Emergence of the Christian Religion: Essays on Early Christianity.* Edited by B. A. Pearson. Harrisburg, PA: Trinity Press International, 1997.

Petersen, D. "Latin American Pentecostalism: Social Capital, Networks, and Politics." *PNEUMA: The Journal of the Society for Pentecostal Studies* 26 (2004): 293–306.

Petry, R. C. *Christian Eschatology and Social Thought: A Historical Essay on the Social Implications of Some Selected Aspects in Christian Eschatology to A.D. 1500.* New York: Abingdon, 1956.

Phillips, T. E. "Reading Recent Readings of Issues of Wealth and Poverty in Luke and Acts." *Currents in Biblical Research* 1, no. 2 (2003): 231–69.

———. "Revisiting Philo: Discussions of Wealth and Poverty in Philo's Ethical Discourse." *JSNT* 83 (2001): 111–21.

Pilgrim, W. E. *Good News to the Poor: Wealth and Poverty in Luke-Acts*. Minneapolis: Augsburg, 1981.

Pleins, J. D. "Poverty in the Social World of the Wise." *JSOT* 37 (1987): 61–78.

Polanyi, K. *Primitive, Archaic, and Modern Economies: Essays of Karl Polanyi*. Garden City, NY: Anchor Books, 1968.

Pomeroy, S. "Women in Roman Egypt: A Preliminary Study Based on Papyri." Pages 303–22 in *Reflections of Women in Antiquity*. Edited by H. Foley. New York: Gordon and Breach Science Publishers, 1981.

Purcell, N. "The Populace Rome in Late Antiquity: Problems of Classification and Historical Description." Pages 135–61 in *The Transformations of Urbs Roma in Late Antiquity*. Edited by W. V. Harris. Journal of Roman Archaeology Supplementary Series 33. Portsmouth, RI: Journal of Roman Archaeology, 1999.

———. "Tomb and Suburb." Pages 25–41 in *Römische Gräberstrassen: Selbstdarstellung, Status, Standard*. Edited by H. von Hesberg and P. Zanker. Munich: Bayerischen Akademie der Wissenschaften, 1987.

Raditsa, L. "The Appearance of Women and Contact: Tertullian's De Habitu Feminarum." *Athenaeum* 63 (1985): 297–326.

Rajak, T. "Benefactors in the Greco-Roman Diaspora." Pages 305–22 in vol. 1 of *Geschichte—Tradition—Reflexion: Festschrift für Martin Hengel zum 70*. Edited by H. Cancik, H. Lichtenberger, and P. Schäfer. Tübingen: Mohr Siebeck, 1996.

Ramsey, B. "Almsgiving in the Latin Church: The Late Fourth and Early Fifth Centuries." *TS* 43 (1982): 226–59.

———. "Christian Attitudes to Poverty and Wealth." Pages 256–65 in *Early Christianity: Origins and Evolution to AD 600*. Edited by W. H. C. Frend. Nashville: Abingdon, 1991.

Rankin, D. I. "Class Distinction as a Way of Doing Church: The Early Fathers and the Christian Plebs." *VC* 58 (2004): 298–315.

———. *From Clement to Origen: The Social and Historical Context of the Church Fathers*. Aldershot, UK: Ashgate, 2006.

Rebenack, E. V. "Thasci Caecili Cypriani: De Opere et Eleemosynis." Translated, with an introduction and commentary. PhD diss., Catholic University of America, 1962.

Regnault, L. *The Day-to-Day Life of the Desert Fathers in Fourth-Century Egypt*. Translated by E. Poirier. Petersham, MA: St. Bede's Publications, 1999.

Rhee, H. *Early Christian Literature: Christ and Culture in the Second and Third Centuries*. London: Routledge, 2005.

———. "Wealth, Poverty, and Eschatology: Pre-Constantine Jewish and Christian Social Thoughts and the Hope for the World to Come." Pages 64–84 in *Patristic Social Ethics: Issues and Challenges*. Edited by J. Leemans, B. Matz, and J. Verstraeten. Washington, DC: Catholic University of America Press, 2011.

———. "Wealth and the Wealthy in the Acts of Peter." *StPatr* 65 (2010): 343–47.

———. "Wealth and Poverty in Acts of Thomas." Pages 111–18 in *Prayer and Spirituality in the Early Church*. Vol. 5 of *Poverty and Riches*. Edited by G. D. Dunn, D. Luckensmeyer, and L. Cross. Strathfield, Australia: St. Pauls, 2009.

Richards, Jay W. *Greed, Money, and God: Why Capitalism Is the Solution Not the Problem*. San Francisco: HarperOne, 2009.

Riddle, D. W. "Early Christian Hospitality: A Factor in the Gospel Transmission." *JBL* 57 (1938): 141–54.

Rimell, V. "The Poor Man's Feast: Juvenal." Pages 81–94 in *The Cambridge Companion to Roman Satire*. Edited by K. Freudenburg. Cambridge: Cambridge University Press, 2005.

Rist, J. M. *Stoic Philosophy*. Cambridge: Cambridge University Press, 1969.

Rosenfeld, B.-Z., and J. Menirav. "The Ancient Synagogue as an Economic Center." *Joural of Near Eastern Studies* 58 (1999): 259–76.

Rostovtzeff, M. *The Social and Economic History of the Roman Empire*. 2 Vols. 2nd ed. Oxford: Clarendon, 1957.

Rowland, R. J. "The 'Very Poor' and the Grain Dole at Rome and Oxyrhynchus." *ZPE* 21 (1976): 69–72.

Royalty, R. M., Jr. *The Streets of Heaven: The Ideology of Wealth in the Apocalypse of John*. Macon, GA: Mercer University Press, 1998.

Rubenson, S. "Asceticism and Monasticism, I: Eastern." Pages 637–68 in *Constantine to c. 600*. Vol. 2 of *The Cambridge History of Christianity*. Edited by A. Casiday and F. Norris. Cambridge: Cambridge University Press, 2007.

———. "Power and Politics of Poverty in Early Monasticism." Pages 91–110 in *Poverty and Riches*. Vol. 5 of *Prayer and Spirituality in the Early Church*. Edited by G. D. Dunn, D. Luckensmeyer, and L. Cross. Strathfield, Australia: St. Pauls, 2009.

Rutgers, L. V. *Subterranean Rome: In Search of the Roots of Christianity in the Catacombs of the Eternal City*. Leuven: Peteers, 2000.

Sachs, Jeffrey. *The End of Poverty: Economic Possibilities for Our Time*. New York: Penguin, 2005.

Sage, M. M. *Cyprian*. Patristic Monograph Series 1. Cambridge, MA: Philadelphia Patristic Foundation, 1975.

Saller, R. P. "Framing the Debate over Growth in the Ancient Economy." Pages 223–38 in *The Ancient Economy: Evidence and Models*. Edited by J. G. Manning and I. Morris. Stanford: Stanford University Press, 2005.

———. *Personal Patronage under the Early Empire*. Cambridge: Cambridge University Press, 1982.

———. "Poverty, Honor and Obligation in Imperial Rome." *Criterion* 37 (1998): 12–20.

———. "Status and Patronage." Pages 817–54 in *The High Empire, AD 70–192*. Vol. 11 of *The Cambridge Ancient History*. 2nd ed. Edited by A. K. Bowman, P. Garnsey, and D. Rathbone. Cambridge: Cambridge University Press, 2000.

———. "Women, Slaves, and the Economy of the Roman Household." Pages 185–205 in *Early Christian Families in Context: An Interdisciplinary Dialogue*. Edited by D. L. Balchi and C. Osiek. Grand Rapids: Eerdmans, 2003.

Saxer, Victor. "Reflets de la culture des eveques africains dans d'oeuvre de Saint Cyprien." *Revue Benedictine* 94 (1984): 257–84.

Ste. Croix, G. E. M. de. "Early Christian Attitudes to Property and Slavery." Pages 1–38 in *Church, Society and Politics*. Edited by D. Baker. Oxford: Basil Blackwell, 1975.

———. *The Class Struggle in the Ancient Greek World: From the Archaic Age to the Arab Conquests*. Ithaca, NY: Cornell University Press, 1981.

———. "Suffragium: From Vote to Patronage." *BJS* 5 (1954): 33–48.

Scheidel, W. "Demographic and Economic Development in the Ancient Mediterranean World." *Journal of Institutional and Theoretical Economics* 160 (2004): 743–57.

———. "A Model of Demographic and Economic Change in Roman Egypt after the Antonine Plague." *JRA* 15 (2002): 97–114.

Scheidel, W., and S. J. Friesen. "The Size of the Economy and the Distribution of Income in the Roman Empire." *JRS* 99 (2009): 61–91.

Scheidel, W., I. Morris, and R. P. Saller, eds. *The Cambridge Economic History of the Greco-Roman World*. Cambridge: Cambridge University Press, 2007.

Scheidel, W., and S. Von Reden, eds. *The Ancient Economy*. New York: Routledge, 2002.

Schmidt, T. E. *Hostility to Wealth in the Synoptic Gospels*. Sheffield: JSOT Press, 1987.

Schneider, J. R. *Godly Materialism: Rethinking Money and Possessions*. Downers Grove, IL: InterVarsity, 1994.

———. *The Good of Affluence: Seeking God in a Culture of Wealth*. Grand Rapids: Eerdmans, 2002.

Schoedel, W. R. *Ignatius of Antioch: A Commentary on the Letters of Ignatius of Antioch*. Philadelphia: Fortress, 1985.

Seccombe, D. P. *Possessions and the Poor in Luke-Acts*. Linz: Peeters, 1982.

———. "Was There Organized Charity in Jerusalem before the Christians?" *JTS* 29 (1978): 140–43.

Shaw, B. D. "Loving the Poor." *New York Review of Books* 49, no. 18 (2002): 42–45.

Sheather, M. "Pronouncements of the Cappadocians on Issues of Poverty and Wealth." Pages 375–92 in *Prayer and Spirituality in the Early Church*. Edited by P. Allen, R. Canning, and L. Cross. Everton Park, Queensland, Australia: Centre for Early Christian Studies, 1998.

Sider, R. J. *Just Generosity: A New Vision for Overcoming Poverty in America*. 2nd ed. Grand Rapids: Baker Books, 2007.

———. *Rich Christians in an Age of Hunger: Moving from Affluence to Generosity*. 4th ed. Dallas: Word, 1997.

Smith, D. E. *From Symposium to Eucharist: The Banquet in the Early Christian World*. Minneapolis: Fortress, 2003.

Snyder, G. F. *Ante Pacem: Archaeological Evidence of Church Life before Constantine*. Macon, GA: Mercer University Press, 1985, 1991.

Stackhouse, M. L. "The New Moral Context of Economic Life." *QR* 21 (2003): 239–53.

Stambaugh, J. E., and D. L. Balch. *The New Testament in Its Social Environment*. Philadelphia: Westminster, 1986.

Stanley, A. P. "The Rich Young Ruler and Salvation." *Bibliotheca Sacra* 163 (2006): 46–62.

Stark, R. *The Rise of Christianity*. Princeton, NJ: Princeton University Press, 1996.

Stassen, G. H., and D. P. Gushee. *Kingdom Ethics: Following Jesus in Contemporary Context*. Downers Grove, IL: InterVarsity, 2003.

Stegemann, E. W., and W. Stegemann. *The Jesus Movement: A Social History of Its First Century*. Translated by O. C. Dean Jr. Minneapolis: Fortress, 1999.

Stegemann, W. *The Gospel and the Poor*. Translated by D. Elliott. Philadelphia: Fortress, 1984.

Stewart-Sykes, A. "Hermas the Prophet and Hippolytus the Preacher: The Roman Homily and Its Social Context." Pages 33–63 in *Preacher and Audience: Studies on Early Christian and Byzantine Homiletics*. Edited by M. B. Cunningham and P. Allen. Leiden: Brill, 1998.

———. "Ordination Rites and Patronage Systems in the Third-Century Africa." *VC* 56, no. 2 (2002): 115–30.

Stone, M. E. "Apocalyptic Literature." Pages 383–441 in *Jewish Writings of the Second Temple Period: Apocrypha, Pseudepigrapha, Qumran Sectarian Writings, Philo, Josephus*. Edited by M. E. Stone. Philadelphia: Fortress; Assen: Van Gorcum, 1984.

———. "Lists of Revealed Things in the Apocalyptic Literature." Pages 379–418 in *Selected Studies in Pseudepigrapha and Apocrypha*. Leiden: Brill, 1991.

Stoops, R. F., Jr. "Christ as Patron in the Acts of Peter." *Semeia* 56 (1992): 143–57.

———. "Patronage in the Acts of Peter." *Semeia* 38 (1986): 91–100.

Straw, C. E. "Cyprian and Matthew 5:45: The Evolution of Christian Patronage." *StPatr* 18, no. 3 (1989): 329–39.

Swift, L. J. "Lactantius and the Golden Age." *AJP* 89, no. 2 (1968): 144–56.

Tanner, K. *Theories of Culture: A New Agenda for Theology*. Minneapolis: Fortress, 1997.

Temin, P. "A Market Economy in the Early Roman Empire." *JRS* 91 (2001): 169–81.

Theissen, G. "Itinerant Radicalism: The Tradition of Jesus's Sayings from the Perspective of the Sociology of Literature." *ZTK* 70 (1973): 245–71.

———. "Social Conflicts in the Corinthian Community: Further Remarks on J. J. Meggitt, Paul, Poverty and Survival." *JSNT* 25 (2003): 371–91.

———. *The Social Setting of Pauline Christianity: Essays on Corinth*. Philadelphia: Fortress, 1982.

Thomas, C. "Placing the Dead: Funerary Practice and Social Stratification in the Early Roman Period at Corinth and Ephesos." Pages 281–304 in *Urban Religion in Roman Corinth: Interdisciplinary Approaches*. Edited by D. N. Schowalter and S. J. Friesen. Cambridge, MA: Harvard University Press, 2005.

Thurston, B. B. *The Widows: A Women's Ministry in the Early Church*. Minneapolis: Fortress, 1989.

Tiller, P. A. "The Rich and Poor in James: An Apocalyptic Proclamation." Pages 909–20 in *Society of Biblical Literature 1998 Seminar Papers Part Two*. Atlanta: Scholars Press, 1998.

Tulloch, J. H. "Women Leaders in Family Funerary Banquets." Pages 164–93, 289–96, in *A Woman's Place: House Churches in Earliest Christianity*. Edited by C. Osiek and M. Y. MacDonald with J. H. Tulloch. Minneapolis: Fortress, 2006.

Turner, E. G. "Oxyrhynchus and Rome." *HSCP* 79 (1975): 16–23.

Tvarnø, H. "Roman Social Structure: Different Approaches for Different Purposes." Pages 114–23 in *Studies in Ancient History and Numismatics Presented to Rudi Thomsen*. Edited by A. Damsgaard-Madsen, E. Christiansen, and E. Hallager. Aarhus, Denmark: Aarhus University Press, 1988.

Uro, R. *Thomas: Seeking the Historical Context and the Gospel of Thomas*. London: T&T Clark, 2003.

Valantasis, R. *The Gospel of Thomas*. New Testament Readings. London: Routledge, 1997.

Van Bremen, R. "Women and Wealth." Pages 223–42 in *Images of Women in Antiquity*. Edited by A. Cameron and A. Kuhrt. Detroit: Wayne State University Press, 1993.

Van de Sandt, H., and D. Flusser. *The Didache: Its Jewish Sources and Its Place in Early Judaism and Christianity*. Compendia Rerum Iudaicarum ad Novum Testamentum. Assen: Royal Van Corgum; Minneapolis: Fortress, 2002.

Van Drimmelen, R. "Living Faithfully in the Global Economy." *QR* 21 (2003): 227–38.

Van Nijf, O. M. "Collegia and Civic Guards: Two Chapters in the History of Sociability." Pages 305–40 in *After the Past*. Edited by W. Jongman and M. Kleijwegt. Leiden: Brill, 2002.

Van Til, K. A. *Less Than Two Dollars a Day: A Christian View of World Poverty and the Free Market*. Grand Rapids: Eerdmans, 2007.

—————. "Poverty and Morality in Christianity." Pages 62–82 in *Poverty and Morality: Religious and Secular Perspectives*. Edited by W. A. Galston and P. H. Hoffenberg. Cambridge: Cambridge University Press, 2010.

Veyne, P. *Bread and Circuses: Historical Sociology and Political Pluralism*. Translated by B. Pearce. New York: Allen Lane/Penguin, 1990.

—————, ed. *From Pagan Rome to Byzantium*. Vol. 1 of *A History of Private Life*. Translated by A. Goldhammer. Cambridge, MA: Belknap Press of Harvard University Press, 1987.

Viner, J. "The Economic Doctrines of the Christian Fathers." *HPT* 10 (1978): 9–45.

Vivian, T. *St. Peter of Alexandria: Bishop and Martyr*. Studies in Antiquity & Christianity. Philadelphia: Fortress, 1988.

Vokes, F. E. "Life and Order in an Early Church: The Didache." *ANRW* 2.27.1 (1993): 209–33.

Volf, M. "In the Cage of Vanities: Christian Faith and the Dynamics of Economic Progress." Pages 169–91 in *Rethinking Materialism: Perspectives on the Spiritual Dimension of Economic Behavior*. Edited by R. Wuthnow. Grand Rapids: Eerdmans, 1995.

Von Campenhausen, H. "Early Christian Asceticism." Pages 90–122 in *Tradition and Life in the Church*. Philadelphia: Fortress, 1968. Repr. on pages 178–210 in *Acts of Piety in the Early Church*. Edited by E. Ferguson. Vol. 17 of *Studies in Early Christianity: A Collection of Scholarly Essays*. New York: Garland, 1993.

Wagner, W. H. "Lubricating the Camel: Clement of Alexandria on Wealth and the Wealthy." Pages 64–77, 235–36 in *Festschrift: A Tribute to Dr. William Hordern*. Edited by W. Freitag. Saskatoon: University of Saskatchewan Press, 1985.

Wallace-Hadrill, A. ed. *Patronage in Ancient Society*. New York: Routledge, 1989.

—————. "Patronage in Roman Society: From Republic to Empire." Pages 63–87 in *Patronage in Ancient Society*. Edited by A. Wallace-Hadrill. New York: Routledge, 1989.

———. *Rome's Cultural Revolution*. Cambridge: Cambridge University Press, 2008.

———. "The Social Spread of Roman Luxury: Sampling Pompeii and Herculanum." *Papers of the British School at Rome* 58 (1990): 145–92.

Walsh, W. J., and J. P. Langan. "Patristic Social Consciousness—The Church and the Poor." Pages 113–51 in *The Faith That Does Justice*. Edited by J. Haughey. New York: Paulist Press, 1977.

Walton, J. L. "Empowered: The Entrepreneurial Ministry of T. D. Jakes." *Christian Century*, July 10, 2007, 25–28.

———. *Watch This! The Ethics and Aesthetics of Black Televangelism*. New York: New York University Press, 2009.

Weaver, P. R. C. "Social Mobility in the Early Roman Empire." Pages 121–40 in *Studies in Ancient Society: Past and Present Series*. Edited by M. I. Finley. London: Routledge and Kegan Paul, 1974.

Weaver, R. H. "Wealth and Poverty in the Early Church." *Interpretation* 41 (1987): 368–81.

Wesche, K. P. "Theosis in Freedom and Love: The Patristic Vision of Stewardship." Pages 118–28 in *The Consuming Passion: Christianity & the Consumer Culture*. Edited by R. Clapp. Downers Grove, IL: InterVarsity, 1998.

Wheeler, S. E. *Wealth as Peril and Obligation: The New Testament on Possessions*. Grand Rapids: Eerdmans, 1995.

Whelan, C. F. "Amica Pauli: The Role of Phoebe in the Early Church." *JSNT* 49 (1993): 67–85.

White, L. M. *Building God's Houses in the Roman World: Architectural Adaptation among Pagans, Jews, and Christians*. Vol. 1 of *The Social Origins of Christian Architecture*. Valley Forge, PA: Trinity Press International, 1990.

———. "Regulating Fellowship in the Communal Meal: Early Jewish and Christian Evidence." Pages 177–205 in *Meals in a Social Context: Aspects of the Communal Meal in the Hellenistic and Roman World*. Edited by I. Nielsen and H. S. Nielsen. Aarhus, Denmark: Aarhus University Press, 1998.

———. "Scholars and Patrons: Christianity and High Society in Alexandria." Pages 328–42 in *Christian Teaching: Studies in Honor of LeMoine G. Lewis*. Edited by E. Ferguson. Abilene, TX: Abilene Christian University Press, 1981.

———. *Texts and Monuments for the Domus Ecclesiae*. Vol. 2 of *The Social Origins of Christian Architecture*. Valley Forge, PA: Trinity Press International, 1997.

Whittaker, C. R. "The Poor." Pages 272–99 in *The Romans*. Edited by A. Giardina. Translated by L. G. Cochrane. Chicago: University of Chicago Press, 1993. Also printed as "The Poor in the City of Rome." Pages 301–33 in *Land, City, and Trade in the Roman Empire*. Edited by C. R. Whittacker. Variorum Collected Studies, CS 408. Aldershot, UK: Ashgate, 1993.

Whybray, R. N. *Wealth and Poverty in the Book of Proverbs*. JSOTSup 99. Sheffield: JSOT Press, 1990.

Wiegele, K. L. *Investing in Miracles: El Shaddai and the Transformation of Popular Catholicism in the Philippines*. Honolulu: University of Hawaii Press, 2005.

Wilhite, D. E. "Tertullian on Widows: A North African Appropriation of Pauline Household Economics." Pages 222–42 in *Engaging Economics: New Testament*

Scenarios and Early Christian Reception. Edited by B. W. Longenecker and K. D. Liebengood. Grand Rapids: Eerdmans, 2009.

Wilken, R. L. *The Christians as the Romans Saw Them.* New Haven: Yale University Press, 1984.

Williams, F. E. "Is Almsgiving the Point of the Unjust Steward?" *JBL* 83 (1964): 293–97.

Winslow, D. F. "Poverty and Riches: An Embarrassment for the Early Church." *StPatr* 18 (1989): 317–28.

Winter, B. *Seek the Welfare of the City: Christians as Benefactors and Citizens.* Grand Rapids: Eerdmans, 1994.

Wischmeyer, W. "Der Bishof im Prozess: Cyprian als episcopus, patronus, advocatus und martyr vor dem Prokonsul." Pages 363–71 in *Fructus centesimus. Melanges offerts a Gerard J. M. Bartelink á l'occasion de son soixante-cinquieme anniversaire.* Edited by A. A. R. Bastiaensen, A. Hilhorst, and C. H. Kneepkens. Turnhout: Brepols, 1989.

———. "The Sociology of Pre-Constantine Christianity: Approach from the Visible." Pages 121–52 in *The Origins of Christendom in the West.* Edited by A. Kreider. Edinburgh: T&T Clark, 2001.

Witherington, Ben, III. *Jesus and Money: A Guide for Times of Financial Crisis.* Grand Rapids: Brazos, 2010.

Witten, M. G. " 'Where Your Treasure Is': Popular Evangelical Views of Work, Money, and Materialism." Pages 117–41 in *Rethinking Materialism: Perspectives on the Spiritual Dimension of Economic Behavior.* Edited by R. Wuthnow. Grand Rapids: Eerdmans, 1995.

Wolterstorff, N. "Has the Cloak Become a Cage? Charity, Justice, and Economic Activity." Pages 145–68 in *Rethinking Materialism: Perspectives on the Spiritual Dimension of Economic Behavior.* Edited by R. Wuthnow. Grand Rapids: Eerdmans, 1995.

Woolf, G. "Food, Poverty, and Patronage: The Significance of the Epigraphy of the Roman Alimentary Schemes in Early Imperial Italy." *PBSR* 58 (1990): 197–228.

———. "Imperialism, Empire and the Integration of the Roman Economy." *World Archaeology* 23, no. 3 (1992): 283–93.

Wright, B. G., III. "The Discourse of Riches and Poverty in the Book of Ben Sira." Pages 559–78 in *Society of Biblical Literature 1998 Seminar Papers Part Two.* Atlanta: Scholars Press, 1998.

Wuthnow, R. *God and Mammon in America.* New York: Free Press, 1994.

———. "A Good Life and a Good Society: The Debate over Materialism." Pages 1–21 in *Rethinking Materialism: Perspectives on the Spiritual Dimension of Economic Behavior.* Edited by R. Wuthnow. Grand Rapids: Eerdmans, 1995.

———. "Pious Materialism: How Americans View Faith and Money." *Christian Century,* March 3, 1993, 238–42.

———, ed. *Rethinking Materialism: Perspectives on the Spiritual Dimension of Economic Behavior.* Grand Rapids: Eerdmans, 1995.

Yong, A. *In the Days of Caesar: Pentecostalism and Political Theology.* Grand Rapids: Eerdmans, 2010.

Index of Ancient Sources

253

Author Index

269

Subject Index